Dreaming the Rational City

Dreaming the Rational City

The Myth of American City Planning

M. Christine Boyer

The MIT Press
Cambridge, Massachusetts
London, England

First MIT Press paperback edition, 1986

© 1983 by
The Massachusetts Institute of Technology

This book was set in Sabon by The MIT Press Computergraphics Department and printed and bound by The Murray Printing Co. in the United States of America.

Library of Congress Cataloging in Publication Data

Boyer, M. Christine.
  Dreaming the rational city.

  Bibliography: p.
  Includes index.
  1. City planning—United States—History.
I. Title.
HT167.B655 1983   307′.12′0973   83–5402
ISBN 0-262-02186-2 (hard)
      0-262-52111-3 (paper)

Contents

Acknowledgments

Many friends and colleagues have helped me to prepare this book. I am indebted to the students at Harvard's Graduate School of Design and Columbia University's Graduate School of Architecture and Planning, as well as to the institutions themselves, which allowed me to explore the full crisis of the city planning profession. In particular, three students, now long-time friends, have in different manners and at separate times helped to keep my gaze upon this planning text in the course of successive transformations: Theresa Shelley, Robert Major, and Christina Spellman.

A number of colleagues have shared in the development of this work: Eliot Mishler, Department of Psychiatry, Harvard University, whose post-doctorate program enabled me to explore the political codes of power and control embedded within language; Lawrence Mann, who supported my first efforts at the Harvard Graduate School of Design to structure the language of city planning into a series of courses; Peter Marcuse at Columbia University, whose enthusiastic sponsorship allowed me to develop the economic, social, and political concepts of planning; and Constantine Karalis, who beyond anyone else has discussed with me over the years the transformations and shifts within planning.

When I think of the many summer months spent writing this book, I must extend my thanks to the old women on the island of Skyros, Greece, who for three different summers have been my curious and mystified companions. Without their rare sense of humor and sympathetic support, the writing of this book would not have been such a pleasurable experience.

Introduction

This is a book about city planning in America: a discussion of the discourse on planning, the point of view of the planners, their attitudes about the physical city, the public, and the rational process of decision making. It is also an inquiry that asks about the structure of planning thought at different times, following the strategies and tactics of planning through various transformations and across compelling contradictions and misconceptions. In the end this book traces the eclipse of physical planning as it abandons once and for all its traditional focus on the physical order of the American city.

Planning and the focus on urban problems burst upon the scene from multiple directions in the latter part of the nineteenth century. The fact that there had been earlier colonial town plans for the American city, or nineteenth-century industrial grid patterns, or utopian garden cities in no manner answers the basic question of why comprehensive physical planning was suddenly generalized across the proposals of such disparate groups as tenement house surveyors, industrial efficiency experts, and municipal art societies. Nor does it offer the reasons why the planning dialogue in pursuit of an order for the American city persisted over decades in spite of its obvious failures to implement its plans. This book explores this quest for an order to the American city, a quest that gave rise in the twentieth century to a body of planning knowledge and a series of institutional procedures.

In questioning how a field of knowledge is produced and separated from a sphere of conjecture, opinion, and falsehoods, Michel Foucault has written, "Here then is the hypothesis I want to advance. . . . I am supposing that in every society the production of discourse is at once controlled, selected, organized and redistributed according to a certain number of procedures, whose role is to avert its power and its dangers, to cope with chance events, to evade its ponderous, awesome materiality." (171:216) Genealogical work, Foucault claims, does not criticize a discourse for its lack of scientific grounding, its class distortions, or its self-professed insecurities. Instead its "truth" and "knowledge" are rooted in its historical context; they are the manner in which a society searches to order and to discipline itself.

> Genealogy does not resemble the evolution of a species and does not map the destiny of a people. On the contrary, to follow the complex course of descent is to maintain passing events in their proper dispersion; it is to identify the accidents, the minute deviations—or conversely, the complete reversals—the errors, the false appraisals, and the faulty calculations that gave birth to those things that continue to exist and have value for us; it is to discover that truth or being do not lie at the root of what we know and what we are but the exteriority of accidents. (174:146)

This book does not contain a functional causal argument of the evolutionary history of city planning, nor does it identify the planners. There are several books on the history of city planning of this nature; readers in search of these answers will find useful Mel Scott's *American City Planning* (479) or a collection of essays, *The American City* (103). Nor does this book provide a sociology of the profession. First, I do not stick with seminal thinkers, autonomous actors upon the stage of history who dominate the determination of the ideas of planning for the American cities. Secondly, I do not place the planning mentality in a causal framework. This means that the intervening variables are not specified, so that we do not know how the planners were influenced by their fathers, how they related to those who hired them (whether corporate directors or ladies' improvement societies), and what their internal feelings and conflicts or their disagreement and debates over particular planning procedures were. On the other hand, I do not credit institutions such as business corporations or municipal bureaucracies with causal intent or examine how these institutions in turn determined the planning mentality. For many reasons, these are not the questions I am addressing.

The origins of the discourse on planning are multiple; many lines are drawn from the park and city beautiful movement, from municipal art and architectural schemes, from housing reforms and charity reorganizations, and from municipal reform groups and elite professionals. In this form of history, which collects together a network of disparate dialogues,

> One has to dispense with the constituent subject, to get rid of the subject itself, that is to say, to attain an analysis which can account for the constitution of the subject within the historical texture . . . that is, a form of history which accounts for the constitution of knowledges (Foucault's

savoir), discourses, domains of objects, etc., without having to refer to the subject, whether it be transcendental in relations to the field of events or whether it chase in its empty identity throughout history. (176:35)

Any number of subjects from any number of institutional positions can take part in this planning dialogue. What is important, therefore, is everything that is said in a given domain, even in its minutest detail and repetitive pattern. The discourse on planning should not search for cause and effect. Instead what holds our attention is the apparatus of planning: what Foucault has defined as the relationships among a set of distinct elements such as professional discourses, governmental institutions, administrative procedures, regulatory laws, legal concepts, architectural forms and plans, scientific statements, and moral proclamations. (177:194)

These elements and their shifting relationships are clearly revealed in the written record of the American planners. Since we no longer expect to find a causal argument presented, we must search for the relationships that planning texts create between the knowledge that they inscribe and a power that this language programs. This involves us in the question of tactics and strategies, where the comprehensive plan, zoning ordinances, regional plans, and urban renewal programs can be seen as so many planning tactics employed for so many strategic purposes such as the eradication of poverty, cultural improvement, or economic growth. In the interaction between planning knowledge and its strategies, the state supports and implements some of these strategies, such as unemployment assistance, regulatory land use controls, and expanded powers of eminent domain. Once the state intervenes into the social and physical city, it does so according to a disciplinary program and a classificatory grid. This is what Foucault has referred to as the existence of power everywhere yet a power that does not exist. "In reality," Foucault writes, "power means relations, a more-or-less organized, hierarchical, co-ordinated cluster of relations." (177:199)

In this book I use a mixed archive of texts in an attempt to understand urban policy. These little works—*The Century, World's Work*, and the *Journal of the American Institute of Planners*, among others—reveal much we have forgotten about social problems, institutional creations, and strategies of response. They also reveal the contradictory and idealistic expressions of the consciousness or mentality of the times. City planners had no official journal nor were they offered a professional degree until the 1930s, so it is not so surprising that their archive is a motley collection.

Foucault has written that "genealogy is gray, meticulous, and patiently documentary. It operates on a field of entangled and confused parchments, on documents that have been scratched over and recopied many times."(174:139) Beyond the "major texts" stand "documents of little glory," a totally conscious, organized, and thought-out strategy read in a mass of unknown accounts. (431:105) Submerged texts are consequently those that have been buried or passed over by most historians in quest of functional causal explanations or structural systematizations. Instead the genealogical project pays attention to "the claims of local, discontinuous, disqualified, illegitimate knowledge against the claims of a unitary body of theory which would filter, hierarchicalize, and order them in the name of some true knowledge and some arbitrary idea of what constitutes a science, and its objects." (177:81–82) With respect to the disciplinary order of the planning mentality, we must agree that power begins in little places and in terms of little things. Thus the archive becomes a heterogeneous array of texts and authors, not read with respect to their coherence or unitary interests for there is no expectation that there will be a sole and unique author who writes a discourse on truth; instead we will discover the relativism between a knowledge which this archive defines and a power which it programs.

This book is offered in the spirit of Michel Foucault. When asked what was his conception of a book, he replied that it was a tool box, for within its depths lay the formation of rules of other texts and other books. (174:131)

I

WOULD AMERICA PRODUCE A CIVILIZATION OF CITIES? 1890–1909

1

The Rupture of a Rural Order

Near the end of the nineteenth century, an "instinct for improvement" rolled across the cities of America, a movement rooted in personal annoyance at ugly and chaotic city conditions and a belief that the urban environment was an unnatural and unhealthy location for human beings. This instinct transformed itself into a movement of benevolence to elevate, through natural and beautiful surroundings, the whole urban population, a movement that would minister "to the elemental needs of man as well as uplift intelligence and taste." (450:222) These forces of improvement were searching as well for "the material dignity of the city" in an effort that aimed to "lessen [the city's] imperfections and to make the outward form of the city a more harmonious embodiment of its indwelling spirit." (93:657–658)

Less than twenty years later John Nolen would write from a totally different perspective about an appeal for order to replace chaotic city conditions. This new appeal, he explained, was embodied in the demand for expert official planning in cities, a recognition of a new profession of city planning standing "in growing appreciation of a city's organic unity, of the interdependence of its diverse elements and of the profound manner in which the future of this whole is controlled by the actions and omissions of today." (378:1) Between the terms *instinct, upliftance, harmony* and those of *organic unity, expert, control,* a radical realignment of discourse had occurred.

In order for us to understand these two formulations, one stemming from the myth of a harmonious natural order enveloping humans and nature and the other thrusting forward into the rational organization and scientific development of cities, we have to analyze the nature of the space that divides the two dispositions. Held against the ideal standard of nature, the city's purpose, form, and growth were impossible to describe rationally. But a rationally controlled city form progressing toward perfection could become the vehicle by which the nation would develop along the path of civilization. To allow a planning mentality to rise, a total reorientation of discourse was required, a gathering together of new insights into the nature of the city that turned toward a new language of urban problems as well as a new responsibility of the state for the individual in an urban society.

As America developed industrial power in the nineteenth century, a tremendous work force from the rural fields and from other lands streamed into the manufacturing centers. Metropolitan areas expanded to extraordinary proportions and burst into public attention, demanding recognition. At that time no one had envisaged an urban ethic, a language, an ideology to orient human feelings, hopes, sense of responsibility, and legitimations toward the norms that would obtain in a civilization of cities. Americans thought of themselves as a rural-frontier people; their Jeffersonian ethic idealized agrarian virtues. How, then, could they accommodate the urban artifact as a reality of everyday experience? In 1893 Americans stood lost on the edge of their new urban wilderness in a mood of uncertainty and doubt.

Much has been written about the American frontier and how it forged the character of Americans into one of independence, resourcefulness, and strong-willed individualism; how the force of social regeneration found itself reborn anew in the pioneers who challenged and conquered their adversary, the savage and relentless wilderness. (327) What appears to be important about this frontier myth that rolled across the boundaries of American thought with uncritical acceptance was the concept of limit and the change of sympathies it entailed. When Americans reached the end of westward expansion and were finally forced to turn inward upon themselves, it was with hostility and embarrassment that they observed their disfigured and inhumane cities. Was this to be the forge upon which the future of American civilization would be cast? Could these assemblages of immigrant ways, corrupt political manners, dominating power, and material devastations preserve and extol the virtues of democracy?

The American city gave no evidence that it was equal to the task. Concentrated and industrialized conditions seemed to exacerbate social tensions into violent strife—between capital and labor, among wage earners and the unemployed, within industries and firms, among native Americans and immigrants—so that by the 1890s it was apparent that the harmonies of a free market system and an open and fair democracy were imperfectly tuned. If the frontier was closed, if Americans had lost touch with the strenuous challenge of rural life, if instead they were folded back upon themselves, what would orient the progress of their civilization along the path of democracy and economic development?

Not surprisingly, themes of nationalism began to spring forward in the 1890s, themes that were expressed in fears of labor leaders and foreigners within and in imperialistic ventures overseas. In 1893 American marines invaded Hawaii, and troops were in the Philippines by 1898. Two vital stepping-stones had thus been secured in the leap across the Pacific to Asia, a leap that would carry American markets and American civilization to the southern rim. Cuba by 1897 and Puerto Rico in 1898 had also become necessary to the "economic welfare" of the United States. (554) It was expected that economic expansion into the world's markets would restore American economic vitality and shore up democracy against incipient social unrest. With self-righteous superiority and economic militarism, capital moralists believed that America had been called upon to take up the burden of bringing a civilization of peace and prosperity to the understratum of society across the world. Economic expansion and American ideological supremacy were the overseas equivalent to civic improvements and domestic tranquility at home. Indeed it was the development of a network of world markets that brought an end to the economic depressions of the 1890s and allowed for the implementation of urban improvement schemes in the years to follow. (554:18–89)

When economic prosperity returned and domestic production responded to a rush of export demands, commercial and industrial prosperity prevailed for ten years. (392:108–183) As prosperity returned, the workers too felt the civilizing influence of capital, which Marx had described in the following manner:

The worker's participation in the higher, even cultural satisfactions, the agitation for his own interests, newspaper subscriptions, attending lectures, educating his children, developing his taste, etc., his only share of civilization which distinguishes him from the slave, is economically only possible by widening the sphere of his pleasures when business is good, where saving is to a certain degree possible. (334:287)

Thus in the long-range economic expansion of the period between 1897 and 1914 the city fabric, urban laborers, the poor and restless rabble-rousers were to be marked by a nexus of improvement schemes.[1]

Economic prosperity would be used to mask the problems of social unrest and the devastating conditions of congested cities. Some of the surplus capital could be turned aside to improve the city's facade. If investment philanthropy was given a clear headway, the improvers believed, congested city centers, overcrowded tenement dwellings, pauperization and destitution of the laboring classes, and uncouth frontier and country manners would dissolve with the overall rise in economic prosperity. Low wage standards and exploitative working conditions were seen simply as

oversights in the rapid race for capital accumulation. "There is no doubt,"
Robert Woods, a settlement house organizer from Boston, wrote,

that the holding down of the wage standard, like the artificial maintenance
of the price standard, has conduced largely to the making of some of the
great personal fortunes; but it is certain that the future historian will
find . . . to have been distinctly detrimental to the economic, quite as well
as the social and political well-being of the [urban] community. This
unthrift in the matter of the prime essential productive force and economic
value is again partly accounted for by the very pressure of opportunity
afforded by unlimited resources and the insatiable demand of the world
market. There has not even been sufficient time for consideration of many
economies in process and administration whose value to manufacturers
would be unquestioned. (566:530)

Improvement thus contained a political economy of its own; it could
mollify the urban experience by turning aside some of the surplus capital
into civilizing and socializing currents. City improvers could take hold of
the physical environment of the American city. Those select missionaries
of taste would reveal the secrets of a natural and rational order with a
degree of perfection that could discipline alike the baser instincts of common man and the exploitative impulses of the capitalist. The urban environment, the physical embodiment of a new social order, presented to
these men of taste a material form they could mold for the protection of
the social whole.

Behind every one of their improvement plans lay the belief that environmental reform was the most important disciplinary order upon which
the new civilization of cities would rise. Contact with the moral elite,
public contemplation of nature, of civic orientation, of classical architecture
were expected to result in a new disciplinary order. Far from grasping the
actual distance between the ideal form and reality, particular improvement
societies proposed narrow reforms to mask both the void between classes
and the fear that cultural assimilation was failing within the city. Searching
for ways to exercise social control, a ceremonial harmony was imposed
upon the facade of the American city.

Among the problems of unrest stood the constantly fluctuating social
framework of the city. Rapid turnover rates of labor flowing from city
to city and back to Europe had to be moderated. The political protests
emanating from segregated ethnic neighborhoods required amelioration.
So did the constant demolition of tenement neighborhoods when commercial, manufacturing, and administrative uses expanded.[2] All of these
factors culminated in a growing awareness that educational, cultural, health,
and housing conditions needed improvement. Those not provided directly
or even indirectly in the production sphere (industrial housing provided

by the capitalists or higher wages for food, clothing, health services) must be offset by municipal services and infrastructure. Thus the American city in the late nineteenth century began to provide urban parks and recreational facilities in order to sustain the physical endurance of the labor force. Regulatory controls were placed upon tenement squalor in order to improve sanitary conditions and relieve crowding. Meager aid to the destitute and downtrodden was systematized to avoid their pauperization. A comprehensive public education system linked to Americanization programs was designed to produce a labor force diversely skilled and disciplined in American civic morality. (551)

Simultaneously the built environment was utilized to stimulate economic activity. The great needs of most older and larger cities were the extension of gas, electricity, water, and sewer lines; the establishment of cheap and efficient streetcar railway systems, subways, bridges, and tunnels; and the construction of public buildings and private dwellings. During periods of prosperity most cities spent money on these infrastructure and transportation improvements. For example, New York at the end of the nineteenth century had spent $24 million for subways, bridges, pavings, and water supplies. Its projected rapid-transit tunnel would cost $20 million, the East River tunnel $6 million, and three new bridges around $60 million. Philadelphia had spent $20 million to improve its water system, and Chicago $225 million for public improvements, and so on in cities across the United States. (151) Bunched at the beginning of a period of economic growth, these investments in the built environment became the motive force for accelerated buildup in all other sectors of the economy. (181:255)

Side by side with the creation of a disciplinary order and ceremonial harmony to the American city, then, improvers gave heed to the creation of an infrastructural framework and a regulatory land order. The needs to stimulate private investment in the built environment, to organize public development, to minimize the cost of producing and circulating goods within the city, lent their own set of disciplinary forms to the creation of a planning mentality.

The discourse about cities, a language focused on the cultural and economic needs of an urban nation, arose in order to articulate and transcend the contradictions embedded in the city. Hence the appearance of the professions of improvement was part of a system of reorganized thought about the urban populace and city form. From it emerged a discourse about the boundaries and qualities of urban experience. Before city planning could arise as a discipline, however, a new role was needed for the state in the solving of economic and cultural barriers to progress. This new role required the reorganization of municipal politics, consequently bringing with it a new focus on the need for expert advisers to guide municipal affairs.

Before we turn to the rise of this planning mentality, we must examine the original dispositions about city life and urban form in which the new language took root. We must look to the time when Americans were forced to question the existence of life in an urban order, to come up against the limitations and pathologies effected by a closed and unnatural environment. It was only at this point—when they transcended this rural-urban opposition—that the development of a planning mentality became possible.[3] As long as the rural order was considered to be the source of national vitality, spiritual renewal, and democratic control, the American city would appear morbid and artificial. Because of the belief that urban society had been abruptly cut off from the harmonies of a natural order, it was held that it could be rejuvenated only by inserting the values and ethos of the rural past into the fabric of the urban order. Thus it was in order to amend the damaged harmony of the American city that the professions of improvement were first developed. But it was the necessity for a totally new orientation, a threshold beyond the natural and the ceremonial, that eventually gave rise to the planning mentality.

2

The Quest for Disciplinary Control

With the emergence of the vast American metropolis after the Civil War two problems arose: how to discipline and regulate the urban masses in order to eradicate the dangers of social unrest, physical degeneration, and congested contagion, which all cities seemed to breed, and how to control and arrange the spatial growth of these gigantic places so that they would support industrial production and the development of a civilization of cities. These questions of discipline and order forged a new relationship between the urban public and social science knowledge, as well as the architectural adornment of urban space and the rational treatment of spatial development. These new relationships called forth the process of city planning. The prologue for popular discipline and spatial order belongs to the middle years of the nineteenth century.

One way to organize the diversity of texts and discourses dealing with the social problems of the American city in the last half of the nineteenth century is to focus on disciplinary control. For these early improvers their texts operated around two poles. One considered the exploitation of the urban worker and its potential for riots and protests, and the other concerned the fears of a damaged urban environment and the conditions of overcrowding and slum congestion responsible for moral and behavioral decay in the urban population. Both poles of concern revealed a fear of the urban crowd and a belief that the city was an unnatural abode for humanity.

The Exploitation of the Worker

American cities and industrial might experienced unparalleled growth after the Civil War. (278, 554) After the opening of the transcontinental railroad in the 1860s and the communications revolution of the telegraph and telephone of the 1840s and 1870s, there was a vast influx of capital and labor into new regions. This westward sweep of the American empire created a network of manufacturing, industrial, and retail centers across the United States.

In 1860 only 141 cities had populations greater than 8,000, but within a decade there were 226, and after another two decades there were 448. (368) The larger cities experienced the most dramatic growth, for they were the products of the need of capital to reduce distance and time between the site of production and the place of consumption; they became the centers of manufacturing and assembling, of exchange and distribution. (219)

American economic growth in the nineteenth century depended upon the widespread adoption of technical innovations rather than the application of a skilled and well-trained working force. (367) H. J. Habakkuk has argued that the scarcity of labor in America during the first half of the nineteenth century was an important stimulus for the adoption of technical innovations and the development of labor-saving machinery. By 1850 America was producing highly mechanized and standardized products such as doors, boots, ploughs, and biscuits. In these areas management had already discovered that the relatively scarce labor, that of unskilled operators, was the most easily mechanized. In addition American capital investment markets were young and poorly organized; thus most U.S. manufacturers reinvested profits in their own concerns, enabling more capital-intensive machinery to be quickly adopted. Even after immigration increased, reaching its peak in 1882, American industry maintained a bias toward labor-saving, capital-intensive techniques, mechanical processes that could be operated readily by cheap and unskilled labor. (210)

In the search for greater profits and a belief in economic growth, little attention was focused on the labor force, since this seemed to be naturally augmented by waves of immigration and migration. And little concern was directed to the improvement of working conditions and hours or the reduction of industrial accidents. As long as employment opportunities held strong, labor unrest appeared to be under control. Rapid urbanization accompanied by a vast supply of cheap labor enabled the capitalist to keep wages low.

The American economy experienced business stagnation between 1873 and 1878, between 1882 and 1885, and between 1893 and 1897. Contemporary accounts compared these money crises and banking panics to natural phenomena. Depressions, they said, were like the tropical atmosphere preceding a storm after which fair weather inevitably returned; or, they explained, economic downturns were produced by a sequence of causes, such as the seed that follows the bud, the flower, and the fruit. (273) This discourse fostered a popular belief that nothing could be done about depression except to wait patiently until eventual recovery. Two of these depressions, however, were widespread enough and sufficiently deep to require some form of work relief.

Although nineteenth-century statistics of unemployment are highly unreliable, a contemporary report placed the number of employed workers in 1873 at 3 million. The New York Association for Improving the Condition of the Poor conservatively estimated that 93,750 persons, one-fourth of the city's work force, were unemployed in the first year of this depression. Labor and capital stood on opposite sides as they fought over wage rates, commodity prices, and the reduction of working hours, but capital generally won. During the 1870s depression, capital tended to lengthen the working day while simultaneously depressing wages. Workers struck across the country, and the capitalists resorted to further wage cuts until the workers went back to their jobs. In July 1877 the Baltimore and Ohio Railroad announced a second major wage reduction of 10 percent. In protest a mob turned on the company's Baltimore station, burning it to the ground; they were not quelled until federal troops, employed for the first time in labor strifes, were sent into battle. (153:39–62)

Unemployment relief measures were meager. Limited public relief consisted of road building, stone breaking, gravel moving, or street grading for unskilled labor. Charitable agencies questioned the inefficient and demoralizing aspect of public relief, which they claimed did more to encourage pauperism than relieve the poor.

In Chicago the Relief and Aid Society had a special Fire Fund collected from all over the world after its dramatic fire of 1871. In 1873 this fund, held for the future use of the fire victims, amounted to $700,000. Unemployed workers asked that this sum be used for relief, but the society refused to shift its priorities. Even the mayor requested the society to lend the city the necessary aid, but to no avail. Finally a protesting mob bringing more than 2,000 applicants to the society's doors produced the desired response. Slowly the society began to investigate each applicant, finding about 40 percent of the total to be "deserving relief." (153:39–62)

Even those charitable figures who were struggling to obtain private money for unemployment relief held little sympathy with either strikers or with religious organizations that liberally opened soup kitchens and sleeping lodges. In New York City, they pointed out, so many religious organizations had rushed to provide free lunches in the 1870s that 34 small eating houses were forced to go out of business. Relief was still considered a private affair; indeed even the legality of public relief was questioned and feared for the encouragement it offered to paupers. (153)

Between 1881 and 1892 more than 12,000 recorded strike actions took place across America pressing for reforms of the wage system, the length of the workday, the state of working conditions, the use of labor-saving machines, and cheap labor. Relief efforts were slow to come. By the 1890s trade unions began to demand an expansion of public works rather than relief and admonished their members to patronize low-cost restaurants rather than charitable soup kitchens and breadlines. Higher wages rather than public relief would remain their preferred plan. (511)

Between 1893 and 1898 the American economy underwent another period of economic depression. By the end of 1893 a quarter of the capital invested in railroads was in receivership; mills, factories, and mines had been shut down in large numbers, furnaces were slack, and capital timid, new construction was suspended, some 500 banks and 15,000 businesses had failed, and a ruinous wheat crop and a limited European demand had cut back agricultural output. Employment, especially in the northeastern cities, began to fall drastically. Estimates of unemployment during 1893 varied from 1 million to 4.5 million. One report held that there were 10,000 unemployed in Baltimore, 15,000 in Cleveland, 38,000 in Boston, 50,000 in Philadelphia, 85,000 in New York, and 100,000 in Chicago. (106)

Chicago had special problems. Its employment problems were exacerbated by the closing in the early fall of the Chicago World's Fairgrounds, which discharged an unusually expanded number of workers. During the fall of 1893 labor demonstrations were held in many of the city's parks—demonstrations that police troops were called upon to control. Recruited from all over the country, "petitioners in boots" marched on Washington in the spring of 1894. Labeled Coxey's army, these marchers demanded unemployment relief and federal appropriations for public works and road building. (153:71–94) Bloody clashes with workers protesting low wages and unemployment had rocked the country when Pinkerton men were called out in 1892 to quell strikers at the Homestead Steel Plant and when federal troops moved against railroad strikers in the Pullman strike of 1894. Because of the degree of social unrest and the length and breadth of the economic downturn, many perceived the crisis of the 1890s as a harbinger of social chaos and political revolution.

As the social and economic crises of the 1890s deepened, the fears of the propertyless masses grew, for any organization of workers, any collective demand of the unemployed upon capital, was seen as yet one more barrier to capital accumulation. Labor leaders were singled out as the ones to hold responsible for organizing laborers. They were the ones who were seen as standing against the educated people, creating a breach between the employer and the labor force, for it was they who drew the line between the vast understratum of society, which they controlled, and the higher-skilled workers in contact with the managers of capital. (482) Thus a small body of men were believed to guide the movements of the laboring class in any large city. Without these agitators, it was thought, the restless demand for perpetual reform would be naturally dampened by home responsibilities, family ties, and steady employment, which economic growth could provide. (482) For the previous 100 years labor reform had been achieved through private negotiations; now, however, labor leaders were calling for governmental action, for they had taken their cue from the tendency toward centralization rapidly advancing across society.

In the discussion of employment relief, the capitalists were thrown into contradiction. Following the social thought of the decade, they too were beginning to see a distinction between the idle undeserving poor and those who were caught by the economic conditions over which they had no control.

Before the panic of 1893 the standard of living among workingmen had reached a high point. Increased wages with reduction of working hours had led to greater consumption. In many cities workers had begun to use their savings to purchase homes, but the interest, taxes, street assessments and the payments due upon their properties were heavy burdens. Fear of losing their savings caused great distress. Communities were aroused not only by the plight of these workers, but also by that of other self-supporting families who were suffering hardships from the exactions of installment houses and the exorbitant charges of storage companies who offered to lend money upon furniture which families were forced to store. (153:87)

Until the 1890s capitalists had expected workers to save for unusually hard times. Now capitalists joined social reformers in agreement; something had to be done to meet the challenges to the American social and economic order.

There was much concern about the dangers of making the poor into permanent burdens of the state, developing unrealistic expectations of the public dole, the disintegrating and demoralizing effect of public expenditures upon individual self-reliance. But in the 1890s capital was caught by the contradiction between public relief and economic growth. If relief was to remain private, with the worker saving money during good times in order to withstand hard times, then how could this same savings be exchanged for commodities that were glutting the market? How could prosperity return in the 1890s without an upturn in consumption rates to spur on the wheels of production? Here then we find the real roots of public relief. Public relief was not designed solely to lessen the hardships and burdens thrust upon the unexpected poor; instead it was to serve as a regulator of the economy, a fundamental precondition for production and economic expansion.

In the 1890s relief measures began to expand slowly. Some labor unions were sufficiently organized to care for their own skilled workers, leaving only the unskilled labor to search for outside relief. The absolutely destitute and homeless were given useless work, such as leaf raking, which constituted a labor test for the worthy, a condition upon which relief would be offered. (153:190–215) It was held that "Money without work is a great temptation to character, and the poor are not usually too robust in their preference for independence." (11:440) Many cities thus began to devise ̇ procedures by which to test the willingness of the poor to work by offering them labor relief rather than the dole. Able-bodied men who would not work, it was proclaimed, deserved no consideration.(11)

In many cities work relief was refused to all single men and to men without families. This relief generally consisted of heavy outdoor labor, mostly employed during the winter months on such jobs as stone crushing, street grading, or sewer construction. Only a very few able-bodied workers could do such work. (153:190–215) In an experiment in Rochester, New York, during the winter of 1895, labor tickets were offered for only two days, and work was broken up on Monday and Tuesday or Friday and Saturday so that no man would be tempted to leave his regular job for the work relief of breaking, teaming and hauling stone. Earnings were paid by the piece, not by the hour. Thus "a spirit of emulation urges them on to beat each other's record . . . you see a wholesome zeal and energy which has a moral value." (11:442) Additionally, earnings were paid in goods rather than in cash, a plan designed to save "some of the weaker men from pledging their earnings to the liquor dealers. (11)

The Fear of a Damaged Urban Environment

The other pole of improvement, whose discourse also revealed the fear of social unrest, borrowed its concepts from preevolutionary biology. These improvers perceived that the environment alone determined survival; it offered some a congenial milieu in which to develop and for others threw up barriers they could never surmount.[1] The failure of many to meet the new requirements of the urban environment reflected their "disadvantage in the struggle for existence," for failure brought with it a "gradual elimination from the community through . . . natural selection such as disease and vice, or of artificial selection operating through the criminal code and the poor law." (472:300)

These early city improvers operated under two basic premises: that the physical environment itself could discipline humans to achieve a harmonious order with their urban world, and that the provision of the most conducive environment, which would ensure the stability of the social order and the progress of civilization, would require constant supervision and disciplinary correction from a centralized political authority. For effective control and endorsement, then, the improvement crusade eventually would have to become institutionalized at the state level. Let us examine these two premises, for they, like schemes for work relief, form part of the prehistory of planning.

Two themes in the improvers' discourse continually reflected the fundamental belief in the potency of the environment: the illusion that a logically ordered environment could discipline and turn to social advantage the base instincts of the individual and the idea that the process of affirmation to the preferred order occurred in the home and hence it was as near to this level as possible that society should and must intervene to achieve social control. (100)

For example, the housing question, it was argued in 1899, was fundamentally a social question relating to the environment. There existed a close relationship between humanity and the home environment, for "strong willed, intelligent people may create or modify environment" whereas "the weaker-willed, the careless and the unreflecting are dominated by environment." It could be said that "for all but the strong and virile, the home environment determines the trend of life." (201:379) Thus, "a good, clean, wholesome home ought to be within the reach of every honest, temperate, and respectable man and woman; that only from such homes can the best children and the best citizens come forth to help forward the progress of the nation." (299:433) The home was a "vital part of our Christian civilization"; upon it depended the stability of government and the patriotism of the people. "Without a home a man is prey to all evil . . . the anarchist, revolutionist, dangerous and discontented elements." (108:56)

By the end of the nineteenth century, as rapid-transit systems began to carry the well-to-do population to the suburbs, other important land-use shifts occurred within the center of the city. Leftover spaces between business districts and manufacturing areas were quickly filled in with overcrowded, unfit homes for the lower grades of the industrial population. This juxtaposition of the business district and the homes of the very poor was a familiar phenomenon in the American city. Charles Mulford Robinson tells us:

It was based on the social necessity that the least paid wage earners live within a walking distance of their work; on the willingness, and even desire, of the well-to-do to live at a distance from the noise and smoke of business sections; and on the attraction which the constant stimulus of "city" life exerts on those who have few other sources of entertainment. (456:814)

As a result of congestion and overcrowding, high land values, high rentals, and the erection of "lofty" buildings and structures that covered a large proportion of the land were common features of the American city. Congestion, the improvers noted, meant a lack of privacy, which led to moral deterioration; inadequate lighting, ventilation, and sanitation, which created disease and physical deterioration; and insufficient recreational facilities, which created an inability to study and improve one's mind and in turn caused mental deterioration and the large number of backward children. (423)

Congestion and overcrowding in city centers brought other social disorders. Great sections of the downtown district of Pittsburgh, for example, were held under a landlord system reminiscent of feudal times:

Thirty-three million dollars worth of real estate located almost wholly in the downtown district [were] held by five estates, some of the holders living abroad permanently, others traveling much of the time. . . . Much of the most objectionable tenement house property [was] held by two of these estates. Absentee landlordism thus oddly parallel[ed] absentee capitalism. To the fact that the industrial authorities [were] remote and, by controlling many plants, [could] take the fiscal rather than the close range administrative view of industry, must be largely traced that stern reprobation of any equity on the part of the workman in his work, which has on occasion made, and will again make Pittsburgh the country's chief point of social unrest and danger. (566:531)

As society advanced, as people were increasingly alienated from nature, the artificial urban environment became the cause of social sicknesses that multiplied in greater proportion, diseases that seemed to create new species and forms with every bend and turn of the political and economic structure. So, the improvers believed, the essence of every social problem was part of the fabric of the city and embodied within it; all varieties of social, physical, and spiritual disorders—crime, saloons, decline of the birthrate, physical fatigue, a steady deterioration of mind and body—developed out of the chaos and physical disarray of the urban form. This disorder was a "contaminating poison," recruiting members of the lowest grade of humanity. (219)

Since large cities were believed to produce conditions that fostered social unrest and political disorder, the uninterrupted stream of men and women flowing into American cities was looked upon with growing alarm. The fear of riots and street conflicts was constant. (128) The untrained, unorganized poor massing in the city centers appeared to the improvers to be a submerged and undisciplined class beneath the range of cooperation; they seemed suspicious and contemptuous of all constituted authority. (454) Until about 1875 America had maintained a somewhat ambivalent policy toward immigration. On the one hand, the nation needed foreign laborers to create an abundant and willing supply of labor; but their foreign ways and beliefs produced among the native born a deep suspicion and dread of foreign-born radicalism. (454) Suddenly, toward the end of the nineteenth century, a fear arose that the environment of the American city failed to raise the level of the foreign population and was itself dragged down to a lower level by the parasitic and dependent conditions that it fostered among the immigrants. (85)

Although the fear of the mob and the immigrant lay just beneath the improvers' zeal, some began to say that the answers to social unrest lay in the environmental deprivations that created the ambivalent loyalties and anomalous behaviors of the poor. (31) The improvers believed that moral example and disciplinary education would direct the minds of the immigrants and the poor into more acceptable directions. (31) These new-comers to the American city had to be taught to accept their proper role as citizens of this country; all should be made worthy of receiving the benefits that the country had to offer.

The key to upliftance lay in environmental reform. Slums had long been "the sore spots to shame society." But more than that, slumdom was "humanity sick and ignorant"; it needed to be healed and taught. (131) "We speak," said one improver, "of a city's slums as though they were a local evil . . . while . . . they form a sore which denotes disease in every part of the body politic." (572:486) The whole collection of city ills—its filth, ugliness, and disorder, its congestion, violence, and poverty—was a collective disease whose strength spread a pale across society. This, then, was the great fear: the American city had become the receptacle for multiple crimes perpetrated against the whole society. Evil vices, loose morals, bad habits, intemperance, and idleness were undesirable traits first evidenced in the condition of paupers that were found, within the congested tenements, to diffuse their degrading influence. Populous masses, crowded one upon another, remained helpless against the influences surrounding them. (233).

City neighborhoods yielded no trace of healthy village life; hence no common bond occurred among the social classes, no natural ties of friendship or moral support developed to aid the poor to withstand and to transcend their crushing misfortunes and debilitating environments. There was no control over housing conditions, water supply, or sanitary codes, and fears mounted that the slums, fermenting and festering, would turn in upon themselves and become a threat to all in their immediate vicinity. (445)

Thus the environmental chaos of the American city became linked in the minds of the improvers to the social pathologies of urban life. Long before poverty, poor housing, and slums were thought of as economic and political symptoms, improvers saw a link between environmental conditions and the social order, between physical and moral contagion. This tendency toward pauperism and crime, toward evil and degrading lives, they argued, could be disciplined by proper environmental conditions. A sanitary, well-ordered environment could confine these undesirable traits, such that the natural, socially responsible man would appear from beneath the vice of depravity. If the external milieu was tolerable, then poverty would take care of itself.

Experience has shown that people living in clean, quiet, orderly streets, in tenements well kept, both as to sanitary arrangements and cleanliness, keep, as a general thing, their own apartments neat and clean, and also that their whole bearing is one of self-respect. (357:438–439)

Improvers, then, sought not to help those condemned to seething tenement cores but to protect the rest of the society from the disorder that threatened to escape from within the city perimeter.[2] It has been assumed, and indeed was professed by these same improvers, that citizen motives and the impulse of neighborliness drew the better classes to the aid of the downtrodden and that out of this grew an understanding and need to provide a decent home and environment for every American. Action must be taken, it was argued in 1895, on "grounds of public morality and public health," for there was a "moral responsibility towards those who are in a certain way dependent on our efforts." The workingman himself never realized that "one house or one locality should be part of a large scheme; he has no leisure to read why certain cities are well-built and well-planned, why certain localities are pure and healthy, while others are subject to disease." (299:433)

A Model for a Perfectly Disciplined Society

Physical conditions in the American cities in the last half of the nineteenth century were abominable. Pigs still served as garbage scavengers. There were miles of crude paving, usually of cobble, granite, or wood. Sewers were infrequent and flush toilets rare. Wooden construction, still prevailing in the centers of most cities, made tenements a firetrap. In consequence waterworks were designed more for the needs of firefighting than from any concept of pure water or public health needs. (208)

Following upon English precedent, public health needs were beginning to be accepted as fundamental requirements of large urban complexes. As early as 1848 the newly formed American Medical Association recommended adoption of the English sewer system on the revolutionary principle that all waste should be removed before it decomposed and created disease. (413) A network of connections were drawn across the

American city relating excessive squalor and neglected sanitary conditions with rates of mortality, the prevalence of crime and moral destitution, the proclivity for labor unrest and social protests.

The model for a healthy and moral society was found within the philosophy that the United States Sanitary Commission developed during the Civil War. Never enthusiastic about this voluntary association, which was privately financed and organized, Lincoln had referred to it as "a fifth wheel to the coach." Nevertheless this improvement group was determined to utilize the latest medical and sanitary knowledge in the inspection of civil war camps and hospitals, drainage and water supplies, ventilation, and dietary methods. The commission also aimed to unite all local relief societies into a national organization that would direct the work of thousands of volunteer women's societies. (79) Local branches of the commission collected money, food, clothing, and bandages before distributing them among hospitals, battlefields, and emergency aid stations. The commission also tabulated vital statistics on military personnel and prepared and supplied thousands of medical monographs to military doctors. In the largest cities the commission provided lodging, food, and convalescent homes and nursing services, offering aid to soldiers who needed to obtain back pay, bounties, or pensions and organizing a hospital directory to help locate the wounded or missing.

This voluntary association thus enabled hundreds of civilians to participate directly in the war effort as useful citizens. The commission's first secretary-general was Frederick Law Olmsted. He believed that sanitary reform required a strong central direction ruled by a small number of commissioners trained in social scientific and medical principles. In order to avoid duplication, needless expenditure, and bad hygienic conditions, sanitary workers must display perfect subordination and accountability. Discipline, Olmsted believed, was prompt and exact obedience to authoritarian directives. Shunning any connection with governmental powers, distrustful of corrupt and incompetent politicians, the commission prided itself on its moral rectitude and honor. (336) Olmsted had criticized Washington, D.C., for being a mirror of national slovenliness and frontier indifference. Not only an offense to good taste, he claimed, this backwardness and carelessness caused America to lose prestige among foreign nations. "Nothing," he said, "was more evident during the whole war than that the members of Congress and most of the popular leaders never trod on any firm ground of conviction about the popular character." (336:16) In consequence, Olmsted believed the commission was an opportunity for men of intellect to educate the nation to the value and dignity of organized work and disciplined duty.[3]

A spontaneous outpouring of relief by private citizens took place at the beginning of the Civil War. The relief efforts of these zealous volunteers, Olmsted felt, must be controlled and moderated by experts. Thus the Sanitary Commission erected itself as a mediator between the overgenerous charity of the people and the army, for it was believed that this instinct of benevolence if left uncontrolled would wreck the army and then the state. Only professionally paid sanitary workers, not zealous volunteers, it was felt, could hold this mediatory position, for the right to dictate authoritatively depended upon professional knowledge of regulations and sanitary service. (183) Although the immediate concern of the Sanitary Commission was the delivery of nursing and medical services to the Union army, its approach to the problems of the needy was hardhearted; its claim was that it was utilizing scientific knowledge and planning expertise to distribute goods and allocate money. Frederickson, in his historical account of the role of intellectuals in the nineteenth century, says that conservative elites were unable to find a place within the prewar sanitary and philanthropic reform movements. Thus the Sanitary Commission offered them a new role and hope that a disciplined society of order and stability would take place under their tutelage.[4]

Philanthropic reformers in the last quarter of the nineteenth century would draw upon this model of a disciplined society. In their varied responses to the problems of pauperism, congestion, environmental chaos, and aesthetic disarray, they would be concerned more with the moral strength of the individual's character than the actual concerns of the needy; they would apply the latest techniques of scientific inquiry and knowledge in order to discipline and control both the benevolence of the giver and the self-sufficiency of the receiver; and they would represent a mediatory role outside of governmental authority, a moral elite free of political pressure yet trained not to meddle with the evolutionary currents that determined social and economic life. (183)

The burst of philanthropic activity following the Civil War was greatly influenced by the success and professionalism of the Sanitary Commission. The rapid expansion of charitable outpouring, however, sounded an alarm among Social Darwinists, for it was feared that feelings of benevolence and overgenerous almsgiving would interfere with the struggle for existence and undermine the evolutionary progress that could take place only at great human cost. (183) For the first time, supervisory control over local institutions of charity was offered at the state level in 1863 when Massachusetts formed the voluntary and advisory Board of State Charities. Other states in the years to come would adopt similar procedures. (511)

The economic panic of 1873 brought further awareness that the gap between the wealthy and the poor was expanding, that relief work was conducive to greater pauperization, that private charity work was wasteful and ineffective. Thriftlessness, laziness, and drunkenness, it was argued, could be eliminated only by morally transforming the depraved character through disciplinary control. Pauperism was a personal defect rather than an economic effect; hence charity work needed to be remedial and individual, not preventative and social. Mrs. Josephine Shaw Lowell, the principal founder of the New York Charity Organization Society, believed that pauperism was hereditary among certain groups and that "relief is an evil—always. . . . One reason that it is an evil is because energy, independence, industry and self-reliance are undermined by it and since these are the qualities which make self-support and self-respect possible, to weaken or undermine them is a serious injury to inflict on any man." (537:219–220, note 4)

What was needed more than economic aid or almsgiving, it was further believed, was personal kindness. "Friendly visitors" would dispense understanding and spiritual counsel and in this manner discipline the unfortunate to withstand depravity and to struggle against pauperism. These morally and materially superior friends would prevent a loss of character and permanently uplift the poor, and they would cement the missing link of understanding and cooperation between the rich and the deprived. A dialogue was proposed, a discussion that transmitted through patient explanation and moral example of enlightened men and women, a discussion that aimed to restore the poor to the natural and normal state of mankind. Therefore these friendly visitors, while offering minimal forms of material aid, distributed advice on household management, good standards of sanitation, admonitions on intemperance and idleness, and lessons on the benefits of self-help and independence. (90:3–10)

The utopian myth that the American city would soon be restored to its natural state, free from every social and physical disease, rested upon the improvers' faith in enlightened education. Because social diseases began by enveloping the child, the home, the neighborhood, and finally the city, the reformers had to begin with the earliest link to protect the last. Thus the key to reconstruction for many of the improvers lay in the disciplinary education and training of children, for it was the child whose open naiveté gave the best evidence of the natural state of mankind. A child denied a conducive environment in which to mature developed tendencies toward crime and chaotic behavior. Thus the natural feelings of children, their impulses for honesty, beauty, cleanliness, efficiency, and order, had to be cultivated and sustained at an early age. In consequence school and supervised playgrounds became essential institutions in the effort to increase the community's power over individual conduct and discipline. (219)

Small parks and playgrounds for children in crowded wards formed part of the improvers' plans, for the working-class child, it was argued, needed vigorous play, which made a wholesome moral and ethical life. Supervised play stressed cooperation and obedience to authority and taught honesty, unselfishness, and gentle manners. In the 1880s three sand gardens, and then ten, appeared in Boston under the supervision of the Massachusetts Emergency and Hygiene Association. The first real playfield opened on a vacant lot in Chicago in 1893, a project managed by Jane Addams' Settlement House. By the end of the century 13 cities had supervised playgrounds, and the number increased to 38 by 1906. (476)

As cities grew and the values of real estate spiraled in their central cores, play areas for children disappeared. This, the improvers argued, gave rise to increasing delinquency and crime. Although many cities by the last quarter of the nineteenth century had proposed grandiose plans for metropolitan park systems, none had allocated a system of playgrounds for immigrant children. In November 1891 one hundred prominent New York clergymen preached on behalf of this reform. As a combined effort of the press and the pulpit, the daily newspapers covered their organized action for two weeks. The results of the promotional efforts were slim: a small corner of Central Park would be allotted for a children's park and two or three "breathing spaces" privately donated in two of the more congested wards. (426) Nevertheless the playground movement gained in force, the purpose being "to get children off the streets, to direct their capacities through orderly and animated group activity." (552:112)

By the end of the century the private agencies, which tended to promote and supervise the work of playgrounds, turned their efforts to convincing the city to take over this responsibility. They pointed to the correlation between juvenile delinquency and inadequate play facilities, the relation of street play to failure in sound concentration habits, the prevalence of gang association with the dampening of political loyalty. (330) In Boston, the leader of the movement, ten such playgrounds were publicly supported in 1898, and enabling legislation existed for another ten in order to complete a comprehensive system of twenty equitably distributed play areas. (413) Slowly private groups in other cities followed Boston's lead—first in New York City, then Providence, Philadelphia, and Chicago.

By the beginning of the twentieth century New York City began to locate recreational spaces next to schoolhouses. These were thought of as the "natural nucleus of a Neighborhood Center" about which all the buildings having to do with the community's common life might be grouped. In addition the city began to provide gymnastic apparatus and to build tennis courts and ball fields. The second stories of eight public docks were devoted exclusively to play use, and twenty-six blocks in congested areas were closed to traffic so that children could play. (167) Boston also provided playgrounds, baths, and gymnasiums, which its mayor, Josiah Quincy, claimed were needed to promote the development of a healthy body: "It is not too much to say, as by far the larger number of persons must earn their livelihood by some form of manual labor, that a sound body is even greater practical importance to the average individual than a well-instructed mind." (430:141)

Chicago's plan was to provide neighborhood parks, which would include a center with baths, gymnasium, refectory service, club rooms, and reading rooms for the community it served. These smaller parks were to be located on proposed circuit boulevards and connected to each other by cross streets so that the city would be threaded together by these neighborhood nodes. These small parks were designed "to improve the health and morals of the people, and to stimulate local pride and patriotism." (356:44)

Many cities tried to follow the Chicago ideal. Perhaps it was nowhere so well developed as in a St. Louis plan for a neighborhood grouping of public parks and playgrounds with public schools, public branch libraries, model tenements, social settlements, churches, and police and fire stations. These models for improvement were expected to develop a neighborhood feeling and extend to

the immigrant—ignorant of customs and institutions—a personal contact with the higher functions which the government exercises towards him, developing his interests in municipal activities by substituting for a feeling of governmental antagonism towards him, as manifested in the only municipal institutions with which he is brought in contact—the police station—a feeling that the government is, after all, maintained for his individual well being as well as for that of the native born inhabitant. (101:37)

From the focus on the child, improvers turned to the next link of social disorder, for part of a sustaining environment and the revitalization of community life lay in the creation of a stable and harmonious family life: "The Charity Organization Society has discovered that poverty is a contagious disease, one family in a house applies and gets relief, another woman asks herself, 'why work so hard?' and thus applies herself. This is the beginning of the breaking down of the family's self-respect." (201:397)

The reformers believed that self-respect and morality could be nurtured and assisted within the family unit. If the children were given the opportunity for supervised play, if the mother was offered a sanitary home environment and taught how to maintain it, if overwork ceased and dangerous working conditions were eliminated, then the poor would be able to withstand the degradation of poverty.

As economic downturns continued to thwart economic prosperity throughout the late nineteenth century, it was feared that inexperienced charity workers were a threat to the standards of a moral order. What was needed was a professional and permanent organization to train relief workers and discipline their volunteer activities under a strict system of rules. The creation of charity organization societies in city after city reflected this need. By 1892, 52 cities had such societies, which controlled more than 6,000 voluntary workers. (511) Although friendly visitations remained their predominant activity, now these societies scientifically investigated each case requesting assistance to evaluate its need; a central record-keeping system insured against the duplication of relief efforts; each recipient, moreover, was required to submit to a work test in order to ferret out the worthy poor from the unworthy; thrift services were provided such as penny savings banks, coal savings funds, or provident wood yards; and workrooms were developed where women were trained to serve as nursemaids, laundresses, and seamstresses. (79)

Focus on the child and then the family, however, still left untouched other problems that thwarted the social cohesion of the crowded American city. Urbanization had destroyed a sense of community. Underneath the presence of so many unassimilated foreigners lay the threat of social unrest. When the improvers looked around the fragmented city, they could find no link between social classes, and almsgiving, moreover, seemed to enlarge the division between the wealthy and the poor. Often the improvers found that the only social center in a neighborhood was the local saloon, where its influence of debauchery and indulgence sapped the vitality of the laboring class. Since the lack of elementary sanitation and noisy, unattractive houses compelled slum dwellers to search for outside relief, it was considered that the massing of saloons in low-income neighborhoods where the worst housing conditions prevailed was more than "simple coincidence." (201) Instead neighborhood centers were needed to mold the character of people, to help discipline and control local communities. Robert Park pointed out to generations of future planners that "local interests and associations breed local sentiment. . . . [Therefore] the neighborhood becomes the basis of control . . . [and] the purpose of social settlements . . . to reconstruct city life." (402:580)

The neighborhood is the vital public arena to the majority of men, to nearly all women, and to all children. . . . It is in the gradual public self-revelation of the neighborhood . . . in its inner public values and in its harmony of interests with other neighborhoods . . . that the reverse detachments of citizenship are to be swung into the battle of good municipal administration and good administration of cultural association in the city at large. (565:16)

Thus a new fusing of neighborhood well-being and disciplinary control was being forged across the American city when neighborhood settlement houses joined the efforts of charity workers.

Settlement houses drew a special focus on the social causes of distress; they stood as protests against the conditions that forced their clients into poverty. Primarily educational institutions, they called themselves institutions of fellowship with "that class of working people of small but regular earnings who most strenuously fight for economic independence, and stand in more or less constant fear of sickness, death or unemployment." (243:76)

The origin of the settlement house movement stemmed from "the organic life of society crying out against inorganic conditions." (8:28) It was not because of a philanthropic motive or an inner desire to help the suffering but because the settlement house workers "themselves needed as much to be placed in organic relation with those others and those others needed to be placed once more in organic connection with themselves, that we are members of one another, and that we should no longer be dissociated from one another. . . . The mere fact that we dwell in a certain place carries with it certain obligations, . . . spatial nearness constitutes a chain." (8:28)

By 1902 in Chicago settlement houses and the charity organization society had worked out a new relationship. Settlement workers wanted the charity organization to order the entire charitable machine of the city to bring "the charities of any community into such harmonious association as will permit of perfect individual expression . . . no conflict, no overlapping, no waste, in the enormous charity activity of a great city." (243:79) Settlement houses also demanded that relief to the poor be swift, adequate, and beneficent and that a directive agency be created so that all the poor would know the one agency to which to apply. On their side the charities protested the "gush and sentimentality" exhibited by many untrained settlement-house workers; they pointed out that relief should be careful, considerate, administered to "uplift instead of degrade." Settlement-house workers were thus characterized as the "Don Quixote type," constantly doing, arguing, pushing forward, and sometimes tilting windmills as they went, but always with earnestness and worthwhile purpose. Charity workers, on the other hand, were "Hamlet types," pondering whether "to do or not to do." Together, however, these two agencies of relief were moving toward a new totalization surrounding the question of poverty, bringing attention to the social causes of poverty and creating an "enlightened policy in dealing with dependent and defective classes." (243:87)

Placing the children in schools and supervised playgrounds, exposing the family to friendly visitors at home, and disciplining neighborhood life through the moral example of settlement-house workers enabled the social disorders of the city to be confined within a curative environment. An improver's zeal held a perfect social order to be near at hand: poverty, tenement slums, poor health and evil morals would soon vanish from the American city. Those disciplined poor who held out against every adversity would soon be liberated within the overall order of increasing prosperity. (472)

The Politics of Voluntary Improvement

Now let us return to the second premise upon which the improvement crusade was based: the necessity to centralize and supervise its operations by an institutionalized authority. City improvers recognized that the individual and his environment must be protected from the dangers of sickness and unemployment, the liabilities of congestion and degrading surroundings. Some system of assistance needed to be offered by which the general interests of the American city would be protected from disorder.

The settlement houses, charity organizations, and tenement house, congestion, and sanitation committees were all concerned with protecting individuals without disturbing their self-reliance and individual independence. With slightly varying focus their improvement efforts recognized that urban diseases and complications of poverty had become a collective phenomenon. No longer to be cured by individual treatment and assistance, they required an overlapping of inspections and regulations. They believed poverty was a recurrent yet changing phenomenon; tied to cycles of economic growth and decline, its treatment was to be temporary and flexible. Cities created a double burden to society by both housing and maintaining the diseased and degenerate and thereby perpetuating a progressively multiple and infinite disorder. (270) Curative relief demanded in consequence a double checkpoint: not only must social intervention be circumscribed and restrained such that the philanthropic instinct of the generous not be allowed to victimize the self-respect of the poor, but poverty and degrading environments must also be investigated and analyzed so that a comprehensive and collectively controlled policy of assistance could be instituted. (90)

Voluntary philanthropy or philanthropic investment was the American style of social reform. The state could control and enforce regulatory standards and meet elementary social needs, but the experimental educational work, the provision of assistance in the American city, was to be done by volunteer organizations. Because welfare provisions, the improvers claimed, were not the result of popular pressure and public needs but the response of charitable people, an irrational outpouring of the impulse to charity had to be disciplined and controlled by developing a political consciousness and a professionalization among the improvers themselves. (323)

To reduce excessive and ill-distributed generosity, welfare relief required a coordinated and centrally directed organization. Charity workers and friendly visitors should provide assistance only where absolutely necessary. Free food, clothing, shelter, and money indiscriminately distributed with no understanding of real needs of the worthiness of assistance in response to a willingness to accept work undermined the self-reliance and determination of the energetic poor. Large amounts of money donated by the generous in response to brief spasms of unemployment and destitution needed to be systematically and professionally managed to offset the spiraling demand for perpetual sustenance. Charity organizations and state boards of charities, instituted throughout the American cities by the end of the nineteenth century, were mediatory mechanisms designed to control the system through which the poor obtained relief. Excessive duplication of aid and multiple sources of relief had meant no one unit was responsible for investigating and controlling poverty-reducing conditions. (243)

Charles Mulford Robinson was one of the first journalists to call himself a "city improver." He investigated and wrote about many improvement schemes in the American cities during the 1890s and the early decades of the 1900s. When he turned his eyes upon charity organization societies in 1899, he found that these organizations, created during the 1880s and 1890s in most major cities, were the result of that "strange evil of excessive urban generosity," a direct effort to protest against the waste and duplication of relief. In 1898 a New York City directory listed 1,323 organized forms of philanthropic effort: 106 official public charities, 438 societies for temporary relief, 95 for special services, 36 for foreigners, 158 for permanent relief, 328 for surgical and medical assistance, 50 homes and asylums for the afflicted, 103 improvement societies, and 9 provident and savings societies. (454:526) Slowly these societies were beginning to divide the city into districts and to distribute them among the various philanthropic groups, making each responsible for a particular district's moral elevation and material care. (454)

Charity, it was argued, is a means by which society acts as umpire and director for a family in need of relief. In the treatment of families in their homes, however, no such fundamental need of umpiring or bringing their problems into public view (and consequently into public responsibility) existed. "Therefore, it is that many people, having perceived human suffering, without thought of the importance of correlation, or adequate knowledge, or of umpiring, took the easy means of giving money and food and clothing without recognition of anything beyond . . . simply as distributors of material things." (323:860)

Lack of cooperation produced a confused sense of responsibility and the application of wrong remedies. At times, it was pointed out, able-bodied men with families had been aided through public charities when they should have been given the careful attention of private societies, which would have provided them with employment rather than relief. Duplication of relief without thorough investigation meant "the dowering of a family which needs something else than financial aid, or . . . the inadequate dowering which compels an otherwise decent family to beg from different quarters, thus inculcating the begging habit." (323:862)

Collective restraint and disciplinary controls were necessary to curb the spirit of charity. Also needed was a study of the living and working conditions in the American city so that a corrective order could be developed. (357) For such a study to be effective, information and material resources had to be organized under a central authority. Thus semiofficial bodies of improvers formed the charity organizations, the sanitary commissions, the tenement house committees, and the municipal research bureaus not only to discipline their own activities but to survey, report, and exhibit the sanitary and health conditions of tenements and slum neighborhoods, the needs for public relief and employment aid, and the development of reform policy according to scientific procedures.[5] An infinite chain of information began to subject the disorders of the American city to a new totalizing perspective.

The causes of tenements and slums, the improvers claimed, were multiple: the neglect of the board of health, a landlord's indifference, the carelessness and ignorance of the tenants. Since the environment deeply affects the people whom it surrounds, an association was needed to oversee the sanitary arrangement and construction of tenement houses and to arouse public interest in regulating the worst sanitation offenses.

In 1895 Buffalo's Charity Organization Society undertook a month-long survey of the sanitary conditions of housing. Thirty-one percent of the inspected houses were found to be "wretched and unsanitary." Garbage and refuse collected upon vacant lots; hallways and stairways were unkept; cellars were filled with refuse. Upon the publication of these facts, a city ordinance was adopted governing the erection and maintenance of tenement and lodging houses. In a continued effort to enforce this ordinance, the Civic Club of Buffalo, together with the Charity Organization and the Committee on Sanitary Conditions of the Homes of the Poor, gathered information on all tenements. They hired visitors to make sanitation inspections and kept a census of the tenement house population, the number of rooms, sizes, and amounts of rent, the nationality and number of occupants, and their occupations and sicknesses. (357)

Similarly in New York City the public agitation of health inspectors, medical doctors, model housing associations, and charity organizations had pushed for tenement house reforms since 1834. As a result many committees had been formed over the years. They looked into sanitary conditions, organized companies to build model tenements, encouraged legislative proposals to license and supervise the construction of tenement housing, established the Metropolitan Health Board, and mounted public exhibitions about tenement house conditions. (507:138) Focusing on the environmental problems that resulted from the reuse of old buildings not originally intended for occupation by so many people, this tenement reform effort struggled with the task of regulating the minimum standard of housing to be allowed for the poorest 10 to 25 percent of urban population. (19:1).

New York State's tenement law of 1901 served as the model for numerous American cities. Its history dates back to 1832, when the first tenement was built in New York City. (308, 537) From the beginning New York City's most prominent citizens had battled with the sanitary and fire hazards of tenements. Reformers hoped that model tenements would be produced by private capitalists. Voluntarily limiting their profits by offering higher sanitary and building standards, they would be rewarded in return by charitable service. But in the years after the Civil War, an era of speculative real estate development, massive profits were to be gained in lucrative tenement construction, and the reformers' pleas were ignored.

By the middle of the century, crudely converted single-family homes, stores, and warehouses, all being used as tenements, emphasized the need for reform. The Association for Improving the Condition of the Poor, founded in 1843, crusaded for these reforms, requesting sanitary investigations, the construction of model tenements with sufficient light, air, open space, and privacy, and the education of tenants. In 1856 the state created the first commission to survey the conditions of tenement houses in New York and Brooklyn, but no legislative activity ensued. Following the draft riots in 1863, a citizens' organization, the Council of Hygiene, conducted the first city-wide survey of housing conditions. Dividing the city into 29 districts, each under the supervisory control of a physician, every district was examined for topographical and drainage conditions, disease and mortality rates, building construction, and population characteristics.

The survey enumerated 15,000 tenement houses with a population of over a half million, with another 15,000 people living in cellar apartments.

The council deplored the location of slaughterhouses, milk-cow stables, and fat-boiling and gut-cleaning establishments which they found close to tenement districts. As well they pointed to the condition of streets, whose gutters were running with blood or overflowing with garbage and refuse. Preventative action had to be taken, they warned, if epidemics and social discord were to be averted. Their survey work was not sufficient to produce the necessary legislation. It was only the fear of a cholera epidemic in 1865 that finally pushed through the passage of a law creating the Metropolitan Health Board and in 1867 the first city-wide tenement house legislation.

This law defined a tenement as any house with three or more families, and it placed these structures under minimal regulation. It did not specify the size of the lot, calling only for a 10-foot yard between a front house and a rear dwelling. Dark bedrooms were requested to have a window cut through to another room that connected with the outside. A wooden ladder was satisfactory for fire requirements, and only one water closet or privy needed to be supplied for every twenty inhabitants.

Believing that these restrictions were sufficient, reformers shifted their attention in the 1870s to the production of model tenements. In 1878, as a result of an architectural competition sponsored by the *Plumber and the Sanitary Engineer*, the dumbbell tenement became popular. The winner, James E. Ware, had produced a design that connected through a central hall two five- or six-storied structures on a 25-by-100-foot lot. Each floor could contain seven rooms on each side of the hall, providing a four-room apartment in front and a three-room apartment behind. Each floor thus held four apartments, with two water closets located opposite the stairs in the central hallway. An airshaft at the side of each building, pinched in toward the central hall, offered an illusion of air and light.

At the end of the century a new investigation was undertaken by the New York Charity Organization Society, headed by Lawrence Veiller, into the sanitary and physical conditions and sweating system of tenement houses. After public inquiries and statistical exhibits, the tenement law of 1901 was created, taking supervisory control out of the Public Health Department and placing it within the Building Department. Subsequent legislative controls would prohibit narrow dumbbell light shafts and require toilets in every apartment. Stringent fire codes were adopted for tenements over five stories, and windowless rooms were forbidden.

Passage of this landmark legislation was not sufficient to prompt other communities to action, however. Nor would the collection and coordination of information at the state or municipal level be enough, for each citizen needed to be informed about the dangers of social disorder and the potentialities for legislative reform. The public consciousness needed to be alerted to those requirements that linked the destiny of society with a healthy and progressive order. It was hoped that exhibits amassing the negative details of the social and physical evils of tenement congestion and overcrowding of land eventually would produce public acceptance of the need to plan and supervise the organization and development of the American city.

In 1909 the Pittsburgh Survey of the Labor and Living Conditions graphically portrayed the relationship between the hazards of tenement housing and public negligence:

Evil conditions were found to exist in every section of the city. Over the omnipresent vaults, graceless privy sheds flouted one's sense of decency. Eyrie rookeries perched on the hillsides were swarming with men, women and children . . . entire families living in one room and accommodating "boarders" in a corner therefore. Cellar rooms were the abiding places of other families. In many houses water was a luxury, to be obtained only through much effort of toiling steps and straining muscles. Courts and alleys fouled by bad drainage and piles of rubbish were playgrounds for rickety, pale-faced grimy children. An enveloping cloud of smoke and dust through which light and air must filter intensified the evil of over-crowding . . . of houses upon lots, of families into houses, of people into rooms. . . . To cope with these conditions was a Bureau of Health, hampered by insufficient appropriation, an inadequate force of employees, and in the large an uneducated, indifferent, public opinion. (115:871–872)

Conclusion

Supervised play areas, friendly visitors, charity organization societies, settlement houses, and tenement regulations were tactics designed to create a disciplined urban society. A discontinuous series of discourses, professional knowledge, institutions, architectural forms, and legal regulations reached out to reorder the space of the American city. Each element of the complex struggled to combat the moral disorder and physical decay that large cities bred, problems that seemed to require some form of collective action. Their points of inquiry constantly overlapped: how to relieve pauperization yet avoid permanent state intervention and how to create a disciplinary moral order without crushing the ethic of a democratic society. Naive solutions, inadequately elaborated and costly in results, slowly emerged: the free gift of advice with regulatory controls where absolutely necessary to avert the total destruction of society. By virtue of moral examples and disciplined observation, the whole chain of social diseases was placed within a curative whole: the child, then the family, the neighborhood, next the city. (133:82–83)

Early improvers distributed advice to the downtrodden, analyzed the details of this social pathology, and subjected the environment to thorough examination in order to dictate standards of health and order that alone would produce a righteous and vigorous civilization of cities. Nothing in the center of the city escaped their gaze of improvement—not the streets or the alleys, the tenement cores or the public places. Although their work never took a generalized approach, it began to seem as if a network of inspectors was subjecting the urban populace to an ever more detailed surveillance. There were increasing demands for a record system to register relief applicants, to investigate their needs and test for worthiness, to collect and analyze the causes and cures uncovered in each investigation. Diffused in space and time and ever alert to new domains in which social disorders revealed possible curative traits, sanitary surveyors included house-by-house inspections of overcrowding and ventilation, of fire hazards and sanitary conditions, and neighborhood inspectors reviewed recreational facilities and population characteristics, of topographical analysis and sewage conditions. (172:107–123)

Thus the locus in which knowledge about the American city had been formed was pressing to expand. Information—detailed, collected, and analyzed—was used to carve up the field of urban disorders into specialized areas of concern. Subjecting the urban populace to constant surveillance, however, produced a finer grid of knowledge with its own tactical transformations. Attention would shift away from concerns about an individual's character and moral integrity and come to rest instead on new spatial categories and environmental causes. The dark side of urban spatial disorder would be brought into the light. Sewage and drainage systems, the relocation of nuisance land uses, housing standards and building codes, and the dispersal of congested slum districts were services the municipality could plan for and eventually provide.

3

In Search of a Spatial Order

Disciplinary order, Michel Foucault has suggested, begins with a fear of darkened places of the city, the shadowy spaces where light and vision are blocked. These are the areas of the city where the perpetrators of crime and disorder can hide. So these spaces should be open to the light and ventilated by fresh air. Discipline proceeds from the distribution of individuals in space; it requires an enclosed area, a space divided into intricate partitions where everything has a place, and every place its order of things. (177:146, 152)

The improvers' concerns with disciplining the urban populace merged with their desires to transform and improve its physical fabric. Already sanitary inspectors and friendly visitors had extended their control over the spatial arrangement of this pathogenic milieu. Tenement cores and working-class homes had been opened to the cleansing influence of light and air, and with this new vision had come the gaze of surveyors to monitor and police these dangerous situations. Now a new norm was sought against which the improvers could measure the material form of the fragmented metropolis. In this search for an order to the American city, their discourse unveiled around two poles. First, it was believed that nature could offer an exemplary form, as if the city could be rebuilt in the heart of this curative space. The other panacea was dressed in the allusions of classical architecture, creating a public realm for civic design and municipal art.

The Sentiments of Nature

As the American city expanded as a place of production and consumption, it simultaneously deteriorated as a place for human life and activity. In a nostalgic attempt to overcome these barriers, city improvers offered urban parks as normative institutions. These would be points of contact between the afflictions of congested dwellings and a curative natural environment, between uncouth masses and the social values of an ideal rural order. The time was at hand, the improvers argued, to secure the advantages of great park and boulevard systems for all the residents of the American city while prices were still moderate and the natural scenery comparatively unspoiled. They saw a need to revitalize and restore the balance between urban dwellers and nature, even if at government expense. It was right and just, they argued, that the state should regulate and control the boundaries beyond which man could not travel without being a detriment to himself and to civilization. (397:171–190)

This "back to nature" movement, which spread across the urban mentality of the late nineteenth century, valued woodlands and meadows for their spiritual impact; they were places of simple virtues and pleasures on the edge of urban disquietudes and troubles. Andrew Jackson Downing, Frederick Law Olmsted, and Charles Eliot Norton, Jr., were among those promoters of landscape design and urban parks who believed a civilization of cities would not survive if it was cut off from nature. Nature held the power to uplift the downtrodden and instill in man the best ideals from America's rural democratic past. Thus islands of nature had to be inserted into the artificial urban milieu; a synthesis had to be forged out of the rural landscape and the commercial and industrial disorder. (154, 247)

Frederick Law Olmsted, returning to the park movement after his experience with the Civil War Sanitary Commission, became the major force behind the movement to preserve wilderness parks. In 1864 President Lincoln signed the first bill of its kind, which would enable the state of California to become the trustee of Yosemite Valley. Olmsted became its chairman, and in this capacity, he was the first to believe that great public parks must be managed for the benefit and free use of the people. (247) Between 1879 and 1885 Olmsted and Charles Eliot Norton were deeply involved in a battle to preserve Niagara Falls from its likely devastation by water power generators. They saw this battle as a moral one, for Niagara Falls was "one of those works of nature which is fitted to elevate and refine the character and to quicken the true sense of the relations of man with that Nature of which he is part, to the beauty of which he should be sensitive and whose noble works he should feel himself to be the guardian." (247:173) The movement to save spectacular wilderness lands as national parks gained momentum as the century drew to a close.

In the cities, Andrew Jackson Downing stimulated the interest in landscape gardening, but it was Olmsted whose foresight and personality turned this interest into a movement. Public parks did not always meet with official favor, however. Only after many long years of promotion would America, between 1856 and 1863, receive its symbol of urban park planning, when New York City acquired and Frederick Law Olmsted and

Calvert Vaux designed Central Park. (449) It had been argued that Manhattan was surrounded with water and therefore required no artificial breathing space. What was to keep the plot of land in the center of the island, already occupied by squatters, bone boilers, and hog farmers, from becoming a great beer garden for the lowest denizens of the city and hence an economic liability to adjacent property values? (449)

Nevertheless, New York City had always been noted for its parks. The Battery and City Hall Park had existed almost from the beginning of the city. The 1807 gridiron plan had proposed a number of small parks, each to be about four blocks square, such as Bloomingdale Square, Manhattan Square, Observatory Place, Harlem Square, and the Market Place. But during the rapid development of New York in the nineteenth century, many of these parks had been seriously encroached upon or had disappeared completely. So between 1856 and 1863 New York made its first great steps toward acquiring 843 acres of Central Park at the cost of more than $6.5 million. As a pioneer in this venture, New York City acquired parkland not only far beyond the needs of its expected growth, but it set a new style of informal picturesque landscape design. New York continued to acquire parklands: Prospect Park in Brooklyn was purchased between 1864 and 1869; Riverside Drive and Park were acquired between 1872 and 1903; and so on until by the early twentieth century New York City had eleven parks, each one of 100 acres or more. (167)

Central Park was the beginning of a new movement. Philadelphia, Baltimore, Washington, D.C., St. Louis, Chicago, and San Francisco followed closely upon this "spectacle of organized beauty." In 1891 Boston began to plan for the first metropolitan system of parks. This would tie a cluster of surrounding towns to the city through a series of inner and outer parks and parkway links. Starting from the idea of piecemeal "breathing spaces" necessary for the public health and general well-being of a city, by the 1890s the park movement had achieved the idea of a regional system of parks, parkways, playgrounds, and waterfront promenades to be accomplished over time according to some well-considered plan.

The provision of parks became a major component of most improvement schemes for small and large towns alike: parks for walking, for boating, for picnics, for meditation and games, small ornamental spaces, local or neighborhood parks, with connecting boulevards or parkways linking all these units into a regional plan. As well, parks with natural and artificial styles of landscaping, with both picturesque and rugged scenery, were to be provided so that all the various prejudices of good taste may be gratified and the community as a whole take pleasure in the scenery publicly possessed. (460)

Perhaps the expression of the purpose and value of parks can best be captured in the following words of one improver:

The use of public parks is to promote the well-being and happiness of the people, to alleviate the hard conditions of crowded humanity, to encourage outdoor recreation and intimacy with nature, to fill the lungs of tired workers from city factories and shops with pure and wholesome air whenever they will or can afford to spend a day in shady groves, under spreading trees or on the jeweled meadows. They are havens of sweetness and rest for mothers and wives and sweethearts; above all, they are for the children, for all the people, high and low, rich and poor without distinction, with equal rights and privileges for every class. A city that does not acknowledge the necessity for public parks as a means for promoting the welfare and happiness of its people, and recognize the substantial advantages that follow the making of a city attractive and comfortable as a place of residence is not progressing but is already on the wane. (460:9)

In addition, by the beginning of the twentieth century,

the need for breathing spaces and recreation grounds [was] being forced upon the attention of practical men, who [were] learning to appreciate the fact that a city, in order to be a good labor-market, must provide for the health and pleasure of the great body of workers. Density of population beyond a certain point results in disorder, vice and disease, and thereby becomes the greatest menace of the well-being of the city itself. As a measure of precaution, therefore, the establishment of adequate park areas is a necessity. (356:48)

Charles Mulford Robinson clearly recognized the recreational needs of labor when he spoke of the improvement of Binghamton in 1911:

To an increasing degree [we are told], the better class of labor chooses its abode, and chooses the city where it secures the most for a given wage. Undoubtedly also opportunities for wholesome recreation increase the efficiency of labor and its contentment. When the offices of the National Cash Register Company a few years ago were seeking a city in which to locate anew their plant, one of the first questions asked was regarding the park acreage, its accessibility and the opportunity for recreation. (453:25)

The discourse about urban parks with which the improvers prodded the conscience of public officials and city fathers developed around several issues. In the mid-nineteenth century the appreciation of parks stemmed from the physical relief they offered against contagious diseases, the democratic forces they realized within urban disorder, the pleasure grounds they provided for the upper classes, the recreative opportunities they offered the laboring masses, and the enhanced value they gave to adjoining properties. By the end of the nineteenth century the discourse on urban parks intensified. Now the essential element of park improvement was found in the exercise of normative controls and disciplinary order. Threaded across ideal regional park systems were neighborhood parks, supervised playgrounds and gymnasiums, waterfront promenades, open country fields, and linking boulevards, all designed to impose civilized values and order onto the American city. The realities of urban life, the devastations and degradations of congested city environments were displaced through images of a rural order infused across the fabric of the city, the fears of social unrest dispelled by the calming presence of open vistas and pastoral promenades, by the pedagogical order imposed through supervised playgrounds and rigorous games.

The development of this discourse can be traced through the writings of the early city improvers. At first doctors and public health authorities commanded the field, followed by landscape architects and then social reformers, until the ideology of park improvement radiated from multiple sources calling attention to the disorders of urban life, alerting a social conscience to the dangers of congestion and crowding, and elaborating a theoretical plan for a system of parks to civilize and discipline the urban order.

Every large and populous city, the Pythian oracle had wisely expressed, should have open spaces as reservoirs of pure air serving to counteract the contaminating influences of the city, a check against epidemics and contagion. (432:5–6) When it was recognized in the mid-nineteenth century that the spreading city inhibited direct contact with nature, the first concern centered on how to prevent contagious diseases. It was believed that where the balance of nature had been destroyed and harmony upset, sickness and disease inevitably followed; only nature could maintain the health and well-being of urban residents. The miasma theory of infectious disease, generally accepted in the nineteenth century, warned that the noxious elements that floated in the atmosphere must be absorbed by trees provided within urban parks and controlled through the drainage of swamps near settled areas. Water-soaked surfaces exposed to too rapid evaporation caused the poison to become more virulent. Thus randomly placed "breathing spaces" would impede the evaporation process and absorb pernicious gases. (450)

Writing in 1869, Dr. John H. Rauch stated that most people did not understand the importance of parks. It was the duty of civilized people to recover the harmonies of nature that had been destroyed by the accumulation of such a mass of humans in cities. Such a collection of people was unnatural and must be relieved. Trees, he claimed, provided a threefold barrier against infection and diffusion of noxious emanations: first, by breaking the flow, second by absorbing these emanations, and third as eliminators of oxygen. (432:32, 38) Considered an authority on the effect of public parks upon the moral, physical, and sanitary conditions of large cities, Dr. Rauch offered evidence of pestilence and disease caused by the absence of trees and dense foliage. In the settlement of every new country, he explained, a period of sickness always followed the initial destruction of trees and the upturning of vegetable mould, which for ages had lain dormant and unexposed to the decomposing forces of heat and light. Disturbing this "balance of nature" inevitably brought sickness and death to the settlers. The health records of a Negro quarter in Alabama offered even a better example. After years of good health, there was suddenly an alarming outbreak of fever. When Dr. Rauch examined the evidence, he found that these quarters were located on low lands along a small creek that frequently overflowed. After the trees and dense foliage between the houses and the creek had been cleared, sickness prevailed. Dr. Rauch similarly explained the prevalence of sickness among Civil War encampments when, for the purpose of defense, most of the trees were destroyed. Applying these findings to congested urban centers, he proclaimed that trees and open parks were the necessary "lungs of the city," "air holes" in the pernicious density of city life. (432)

The improvers of the American city found congestion and the wearisome rectangularity of the city grid plan had produced social and moral degeneration as well. Nature was expected to teach men to be virtuous and self-reliant; by conserving the social values of the rural past, it prepared the individual to meet the conditions of the evil urban order. (432) Without some contact with nature, they held, civilization constricted to the American city would not survive: "Only through country freedom and country influences can the best of man be developed." (403:407–408)

Parks would have a healthy and purifying influence upon the city population by introducing quiet scenes of woods and water, gently rolling meadows, and vistas rearranged according to the best models of nature. This free and open character would stand as the antithesis of the unregulated and unchecked herding instinct of city man. (119)

The curative power of fresh air and natural scenery were needed as well for the psychic relaxation and physical regeneration of the people, to breathe health and hope into the poor and the downtrodden. (432) As "foul air prompts to vice, and oxygen to virtue," fresh air would keep the tenement dweller, often forced out of his home by its close atmosphere, from seeking relief in drink and saloons. (426:276) Parks would educate him away from the ways of vice and disease. (426) Rich and poor alike would come to breathe the same atmosphere of nature without any jealousy or conflict. What was needed in the twentieth century, then, was the insertion of "scraps of nature" among the tenements.

Parks as properly organized beauty were thought of as universal moral forces; they would become the "educators of taste," promoting a desire within for more complete perfection. (449) It was believed that parks would breed a desire for beauty and order, spreading a benign, tranquilizing influence over their surroundings, just as ugliness and disorder tended to contaminate their vicinity. (403)

Parks would also act as democratizing forces: this was one of the earliest arguments used in their support. In 1845 Andrew Jackson Downing feared that America was becoming socially aristocratic. He argued, "It is quite unworthy of us, as it is the meanest and most contemptible part of aristocracy and we owe ourselves and republican profession to set about establishing a larger and more fraternal spirit in our social life." This, Downing continued, could be accomplished "mainly by establishing refined public places of resort, parks and gardens, galleries full of really grand and beautiful trees, fresh grass, fountains, and in many cases rare plants, and shrubs, and flowers." (137:155)

When the preservation of Central Park was first debated, The *New York Daily Times* on June 30, 1853, doubted the value of reserving so large a site as was then proposed, professing that a truly democratic proposal would "dispense them [parks] over the island that the air, the trees, the flowers may be brought within the reach of all. This certainly would be less aristocratic, more democratic and far more conducive to public health."

Waterfront promenades for recreative needs were another element in the developing park movement. In 1904 the New York City Improvement Commission noted that although the waterfront extended for nearly 450 miles, most of the length was allocated to commercial and industrial uses rather than parks. These improvers advocated that the city, not private interests, should make or plan improvements so that a harmonious architectural effect and uniformity of construction could be secured. They also recommended that most of the North River waterfront at the upper end of Manhattan and certain portions of the Harlem River be reserved for parks. Parkways should be planned to connect these new riverfront parks with those already laid out in the Bronx and in Brooklyn. (442)

Chicago improvers too were cognizant of the recreative value of their waterfront areas. As far as possible they wanted the lakefront shore rights reserved for the people as one great unobstructed view, stretching into the horizon.

These views of a broad expanse are helpful alike to mind and body. They beget calm thoughts and feelings, and afford escape from the petty things of life. Mere breadth of view, however, is not all. The lake is living water, ever in motion, and ever changing in color and in the form of its waves. Across its surface comes the broad pathway of light made by the rising sun; it mirrors the ever-changing form of the clouds, and it is illuminated by the glow of the evening sky. Its colors vary with the shadows that play upon it. . . . It should be made so alluring that it will become the fixed habit of the people to seek its restful presence at every opportunity. (356:50)

The 1909 plan of Chicago, in its provision for parks and parkways, was meant to lace together suburban towns with the center of the city. The architects and landscape designers laid down a system of circumferential parkways, lakeshore drives, and local community parks threaded across the plains of Illinois. At the heart of this planning lay a shifting ideal: a new suburban trend, it was felt, would necessarily increase as the ground and buildings within the business area of the city became too valuable for any use other than commerce. (356:37) With the increasing use of the automobile, it projected, "the pleasures of suburban life [would be] brought within the reach of multitudes of people who formerly were condemned to pass their entire time in the city." (356:42)

The improvers warned that the rhythmic record of human societies was reaching an ebb; the familiar "law of reversion of types" was beginning to operate. So, they proclaimed, the suburb, the synthesizer of nature and civilization, was becoming the characteristic way of life. Taking many rural qualities and retaining many urban conveniences, the suburb would erase the line of demarcation along which marched the antagonisms of country and city. (95) Man, they argued, was an animal who did not thrive in captivity. Hence an age of metropolitan decentralization lay just ahead in which the call of the country would draw people to the suburbs, back to contact with the soil and communion with nature. (95, 414) The tide of ever-increasing commercial and industrial consolidation and central-ization, they said, had finally reached its ebb; now a countercurrent was diverting the extremes of congestion away from the city center. (95) To provide for this great escape, at least four great encircling highways and multiple radial parkways were planned on the outskirts of Chicago. These highways would strongly influence the social and material prosperity of each of the cities it touched, bringing the civilizing influences of the city to all of the farming communities along their route. (356)

Dispersal of population from the city center was the only solution to the urban dilemma for some nineteenth-century improvers. As early as 1869 Olmsted and Vaux had designed a beautiful garden suburb in Chicago for the Riverside Improvement Company. Located on 1,600 acres com-pletely separated from any development on the urban fringe, this suburb was an autonomous unit linked to the city center only by commuter trains.

It was often argued that the rapid rise in urban land values after the Civil War lay at the root of all urban problems and that this basic dilemma could be solved only in the development of autonomous garden cities surrounded by rings of open countryside. An ideal environment for the working man thus arose based upon a careful juxtaposition of the limits of population growth, a concept of self-sufficiency in industrial and agricultural development, the necessity of regulating land uses, and the spiritual fulfillment of contact with nature. (114)

Suburban developments thus offered Olmsted the best ground to form a synthesis of nature and civilization. In the 1871 report for the improvement of Staten Island, an effort that combined the work of architect H. H. Richardson, landscape architect Olmsted, public health administrator Elisha Harris, and J. M. Trowbridge, a professor from the School of Mines at Columbia College, it was suggested that here lay a unique opportunity to promote the new suburban movement. Most of the malarious areas of the island could be drained, and shore drives and transverse routes could be combined with a system of sylvan parks and green meadowlands in order to open the island to residential land speculators. (443)

The paramount task for the late nineteenth century, Annie Diggs, a social reformer, proclaimed, was providing for working men "a righteous share of the benefits of civilization they help to create." For her the problem of the submerged class, those below the range of cooperation and trade unionism, rested upon a combined solution of environment and employment needs. These, she argued, could be obtained only by planning garden cities in the suburbs and providing for all working and living needs at the outset. Demolishing the slum, she argued, only set adrift the unemployed contingent to create "other plague-spots and to convert once habitable houses into dens as reeking as their former haunts. . . . The demoralization and deprivation consequent upon congested centers of population have at length taught the Garden City economist the essential sin of divorcing the children of men from their Mother Earth." (131:631–632)

Frederick C. Howe, a progressive American reformer, noted that when England saw that generations of urban living had produced physical and moral decay in the fibre of the nation, it initiated the garden city movement. Now Howe believed that garden suburbs would not only urbanize the American countryside but would revitalize the city as well, for they represented a shifting of emphasis from property to people that would benefit country and city alike. A garden city, Howe claimed, offered the first escape from tenements and cramped apartment lives. Once man is reunited with the land, Howe continued, from which he had forcibly been divorced for a generation by inadequate transit and prohibitive land values, American cities would no more tolerate the slum and the tenement than they would the plagues that were prevalent a generation ago. (236)

Model garden cities in America were considered an organized attempt to apply scientific aesthetics and economic principles to the problem of housing. Although its theoretical definition was based on the collective purchase, design, and development of the land, it avoided (according to New York architect Grosvenor Atterbury) the price of paternalism or socialism. These collective principles offered model towns on a fair commercial basis through higher standards of land development and distribution, by placing some limits upon architectural anarchy and bad taste. Model towns would produce model citizens, for Atterbury believed that only the suburbs offered the pure environment needed to ease the martyrdom of tenement homes and enforce the economy of young married life. (29)

Housing reformer Carol Aronovici also stressed the hope of the garden city movement for industrial workers condemned to city slums. He saw "the suburbanizing of the wage-earner [as] a great social and economic opportunity. . . . It is for us to say whether this growth will result in a contamination of the open country by the city or whether garden communities will look upon the bleak horrors of our urbanized existence and give men, women and children a new lease on life and industry and a chance to serve men rather than to enslave them. . . . Utopia [can be] realized in the suburbs."[1]

Thus organized nature came to play a specialized role within the city: it could help to ventilate congested areas, relieve tenement squalor, offer recreation, augment land values, and offer an escape to the utopian suburban life. In many ways these sentiments were profoundly antiurban, holding fast to the ideal of a curative rural milieu. They were ahistorical as well, nostalgically looking backward to the frontier order. If the urgent need that called forth these sentiments was expressed in the desire to impose a rational order upon the fragmented metropolitan experience, then this strategy was too costly for the effects of discipline and order that it so slowly created. By randomly inserting "scraps of nature" or picturesque parklands into the urban fabric, it could do little to reorder the internal space of the American city and certainly failed to provide a means to control urban development and growth. Nature transformed into urban parks and trained to appear as authentic as possible was expected to educate and uplift the urban populace as well. Parks thus became functional sites for public contemplation, but such points of persuasion were discontinuous tactics to discipline the urban masses. These failures to produce a disciplined urban order would call forth other programs and strategies that could more effectively deal with the urban dilemma. Yet before the need for these new disciplinary approaches became apparent, there was one more attempt to create a ceremonial order for the American city.

A Lesson in Municipal Aesthetics

American cities in the 1890s were untidy and chaotic; they held more filth and displayed more squalor and general slovenliness in public places and roads than any European city. In contrast, those foreign cities so marveled at by Americans displayed unparalleled beauty and order, for they were ripe products of a highly concentrated civilization that had grown up by slow degrees. By necessity the American city was makeshift. It was more important in the nineteenth century to build one hundred miles of new roads than to grade and perfect ten miles already built, to subjugate rapidly the entire American territory with a "callous indifference to appearances." (555) Yet "thoughtful people," we are told by 1909, were "appalled at the results of progress; at the waste in time, strength, and money which congestion in city streets begets, at the toll of lives taken by diseases when sanitary precautions are neglected; and at the frequent outbreaks against law and order which result from narrow and pleasureless lives." (356:32)

The American city was marked by a void. It was blamed for having destroyed the uplifting qualities of the physical environment; everything had been sacrificed on the altar of industry and capital acquisition. No one had questioned every man's right to disfigure the city with heavy smoke from soft-coal furnaces, stenches from soap factories and leather tanneries, unsightly billboards, and aesthetic nuisances. As well it was felt that the city had generated a public acceptance of municipal slovenliness and chaos. Its rapid growth alone placed no claim upon its citizens for loyalty. Thus it was felt that the character of civic education and its ceremonial form would determine in the long run whether democracy and civilization would succeed in the American city. (551)

Ignorance alone, it was said, produced this national slovenliness. It could be corrected through example and education. The rapid subjugation of the vast American territory during the nineteenth century had required a daring spirit of innovation and inventiveness. There had been no time to develop the finer instincts, to transform the ideals of communal living into an adequate physical environment. (217) But now it was believed that a neodemocratic spirit was evidenced in the craving for harmony, beauty, and order. The expressions of municipal art, religious awakening, and social reform were used simultaneously for the same improvement crusades. (284)

It was not enough to reject city chaos, ugliness, congestion, and the negative defects implied by such disarray. Improvers begged for outright reform in the sense of returning to some ideal form of the city, an awakening to a new consciousness of common needs characterized by a longing for perfection. If park systems were to reconnect man with nature, then aesthetic reforms were to harmonize the opposition between degrading reality and perfected nature. As with park improvements, the concern rested upon the contemplation of exterior settings: the creation of civic vision and public pageantry in the ceremonial composition of buildings; the authority and dignity of classical architecture; the aesthetic unity of color, design, and texture; the collaborative effort of artists, architects, and engineers.

Since city making and citizen making were the same, these improvers directed their attention to citizen betterment through aesthetic reforms. Public art had long been a community educator, a stimulus to give pride and to commemorate patriotism. (131) Harmonizing advantages would thus enable the common masses to "enjoy a constructive and vitalizing force," they would enchance and emphasize the prestige of the nation, and promote among its people the desire to excel. (328, 284, 281) A happier people, a better citizen, democratically instructed and more artistic in mind and soul, would arise from this beautiful and ceremonial American city. (454)

The form of this civic art and architecture was neoclassical in design and grouped all public buildings around a civic plaza. This utilitarian advantage set the courthouse, city hall, post office, and other municipal buildings at one central core. Each portal to the city was to be adorned by a majestic railway station or commemorative monument. The streets emanating from the civic plaza were to offer a variety of vistas in every direction, broken here and there by plazas, fountains, and statuary. Orderliness, cleanliness, and whiteness epitomized the entire civic facade. (562)

For an urban image, these improvers turned away from the American city. Instead they tried to graft all civic ideals and ceremonial urbanities of the European city onto the fabric and form of the American city. Always behind their improvement schemes stood the image of the European city, especially the teachings of Paris, for this city "takes a high place among beautiful things in nature and holds it firmly, like a fine mountain, or river, or splendid country. The generation after generation of citizens, profoundly trained in matters artistic and filled with pride in the love for their city, have made Paris a model, to which civilization looks whenever the art of creating fine towns is in question." (437:8)

The architects to whom Louis XIV had turned in the seventeenth century had planned far beyond the walls of that old city. In the open field where

Paris would one day grow, they drew the central axis of the city. Straight, vast in breadth and length, this major boulevard was drawn through open country, with only a smattering of buildings located along its whole extent. The Madeleine, the Place de la Concorde, the Invalides, the axial avenue between the Tuileries and the Place de l'Etoile were also drawn as plans decades before they were actually realized. (356)

In later years Napoléon, realizing that plans for the future development of Paris were well in hand, turned to the dirty, crowded, ill-smelling streets. He opened the Rue de Rivoli north of the Tuileries gardens, created the Rue Napoléon on the axis of the Place Vendôme, and cleared away the structures from the medieval bridges. He added three new river crossings, lighted the streets at night, built new quays along the banks of the Seine, and carried out the great commemorative monuments—the Arc de Triomphe de l'Etoile, Arc du Carrousel, and Columne Vendome. Napoléon III, employing the help of the city builder Baron Haussmann, continued to open the city of Paris to the cleansing influence of "light by air" by cutting new streets and widening old ones, sweeping away unwholesome rookeries, and opening great ceremonial spaces that afford magnificent vistas of historic and civic interest. It had taken Paris and other European cities centuries to achieve their lessons of civic beauty, lessons that American cities wanted to learn overnight.

Beauty was to become the new American hallmark. If the American city had been glaringly vulgar and offensive, now the growing taste for the aesthetic was a "natural craving for things beautiful . . . a natural response to proper pride in oneself, of something within to the ideal. (92:1433) So it was argued that aesthetic environments would help to influence the moral and intellectual improvement of the whole social order. Art as an educator would be welcomed even among the lower half when these better impulses became hereditary. (85)

As offshoots of this search for an order to the American city, the municipal art, city beautiful, and civic improvement crusades grew as piecemeal efforts, movements that aimed to convert a city built primarily for utility into an ideal form through artistic street signs, well-designed municipal bridges, using color in architectural elements, and improving public squares and buildings. (281) In similar manner these crusades were aimed to express the fullness of the human spirit: the ordering of material objects so that they elevated from the commonplace, the embedding of social ideals in public buildings, statues, bridges, street ornaments, and objects so that the better impulses of the most elevated men would soon become common to all. (539)

These lofty attempts at city decoration sought a new conception of public life and civic loyalty, a restoration of a lost community ethic through the enhancement of public spaces, decorating them with monuments, beautiful street vistas, majestic and classical architecture for public buildings, and allegorical murals in public places. They were to cultivate a public acceptance, indeed expectation, of the municipality's responsibility for the physical wants of the American city. It was best, the improvers argued, to apply surplus capital to these "neutral services," which exercised no threat to free competition but maintained a physically strong and beautiful civilization of cities. As we shall see, their reforms led us backward toward some imaginary form of the city, to the ideals of unity, harmony, and perfection envisioned in a dream of a classical Olympian city.

These environmental improvers intended to impose order on American cities, which were characterized by chaos, ugliness, discord, and filth. The urban challenge thus was to control unruly growth, tidy the chaos, and return order to the arrangement of buildings according to uses. No visual stench escaped this general crusade; every moral and spiritual consequence, every ideal of democracy and freedom were claimed to gather support and strength from these physical reforms. (235)

The main struggle for those architects, landscape architects, and engineers was how to develop a social movement around their desire to improve the city's physical form. They needed to translate their interpretations and points of view about the natural order of the city into directives for disciplinary control. (284) The solution appeared easy: first an awakening to the chaotic crimes of the city, and then an education to desire more orderly environments through a few well-placed examples. The strategy, however, was more difficult. How could they awaken the cities from their long slumber of urban neglect and city abuse? To aid them in these attempts, they sought a symbol that would express their ideals of order and beauty. They found it in the "White City," the dream of perfection embodied in the World's Columbian Exposition in Chicago in 1893. They believed that this world's fair would stimulate a popular understanding and feeling that would urge the nation's leaders to remove from sight and forever keep from view the ugly, the unsightly, even the commonplace. (85) Officially American city planning places its date of birth from 1893, for if once it had been claimed that all roads led to Rome, now it would be said that all city plans stemmed from the dreams of that Great White City in Chicago. (317)

It was believed that the Chicago World's Fair would stand as a promise and pledge that the fullness of the human spirit could come to fruition in this new art of city making, which ensured the subordination of all fragmentary interests to those of the transcendental totality. (400) The Great White City was the expression of this spirit; symbolizing purity and light, it stood as the climactic expression of a more trustful national unity and a forecaster of the beginnings of a planned civilization of cities, of the hope of a more noble existence. The existing diversity of building styles and tumultuous incoherence along street facades, however, were discouraging urban realities to many American architects of the late nineteenth century.

Copley Square in Boston had been an enlightening beginning for a new civic vision. The erection in 1877 of the Boston Public Library brought together the work of the architect, the sculptor, and the painter, and a new fountain and layout for the plaza produced an ideal civic embellishment. But later examples were hard to find.

Many architects in the 1890s sought recognition for their profession; they wanted to secure an elevated position beyond the control of local taste and parochial builders. Although the American Institute of Architects had been established in 1857 to offer mutual protection against the builders' frequent attack upon their skills and territory, and although the Massachusetts Institute of Technology had established the first school of architecture in 1866 to secure the title of architect through educational training, still no system of licensing architects and no rules enforcing design competitions existed in the early 1890s. Banding together in these years, many trained architects sought not only to limit the effect of the self-proclaimed architect but to discipline architectural design and to banish the romantic license that was so prevalent in the formal arrangement of the American city. (567) In their search for professional discipline, architects thus were increasingly inclined to control the design and construction of monumental commercial and public structures.

The tradition of the Ecole des Beaux-Arts simply reinforced the architects' professional desires in their quest for monumentality.[2] If American architecture of the nineteenth century had displayed an anomolous development of architectural styles, then in opposition, the intellectual approach of the Ecole des Beaux-Arts to architectural design, with its rational ordering of architectural elements around a central mass and the application of this plan to large-scale urban compositions, would introduce a new discipline and rigor to American architectural training and civic design. Henry Van Brunt was one of the major architects who supported the Beaux-Arts ideal. He advised the architects who had been selected to design the World's Columbian Exposition—Hunt, Post, McKim, Mead, White, Peabody, Sterns, Van Brunt, Howe, Adler, Sullivan, Beman, Cobb, Jenney, Burling, and Whitehouse—to

adopt a uniform and ceremonious style . . . expressive of the highest civilization in history . . . and a common module of dimensions. These motives forbid the use of medieval or any other form of romantic, archaeological or picturesque art. The style should be distinctly secular and pompous, restrained from license by historical authority, and organized by academic discipline. It was not difficult to agree upon the use of Roman classic forms, correctly and loyally interpreted but permitting variations suggested not only by the Italians, but by the other masters of the Renaissance. (520:233)

Such a series of classical models

would present to the profession here an object-lesson so impressive of the practical value of architectural scholarship and of strict subordination to the formulas of the schools, that it would serve as a timely corrective to the national tendency to experiments in design. . . . There are many uneducated and untrained men practising as architects, and still maintaining, especially in the remote regions of the country, an impure and unhealthy vernacular, incapable of progress; men who have never seen a pure classic monument executed on a great scale, and who are ignorant of the emotions which it must excite in any breast accessible to the influences of art. To such it is hoped that these great models . . . will prove such a revelation that they will learn at last that true architecture cannot be based on undisciplined invention, illiterate originality, or, indeed, upon any audacity of ignorance. (520:233–234)

Montgomery Schuyler, another architectural critic, took an exception to the current fashion of Italian Renaissance style promoted so dramatically by the Court of Honor at the Chicago Fair. "In architecture alone," he complained, "men look back upon the masterpieces of the past not as points of departure, but as ultimate attainments, content, for their own part, if by recombining the elements and reproducing the forms of these monuments they can win from an esoteric circle of archaeologists the praise of reducing some reflex of their impressiveness." (263:111) "But in any case, the classical building embraces but a small part of the range of constructions that are available to the modern builder. To confine one's self to classic forms means therefore to ignore and reject, else to cloak and dissemble, the construction of which the classic builders were ignorant." (263:112)

Following upon the formulas of classic design, however, Van Brunt continued to advise the principle of symmetry, of a balanced correspondence of parts on each side of a central axis, which must govern the composition of the whole. "In fact, symmetry is the visible expression of unity . . . the moment the design begins to lose somewhat of its unity and to enter the domain of the picturesque, [is that moment] in which ceremony and state become secondary to considerations of comfort and convenience." (520:245)

Chicago would teach order and congruity in the architecture of our city streets. As well, Van Brunt continued, the fair had taught the great lesson of color. "It has been found . . . that the most effective surface treatment of the large masses, both of the exterior and interior in the greater buildings, is one of nearly pure white." (520:245) There were successes of the fair, Montgomery Schuyler could agree as well: a triumph of ensemble and pictorial plan; the impressiveness in size and number of buildings; and the success of illusion. But these buildings of the fair, Schuyler reminded us, were holiday buildings, a triumph of occasional architecture. This, he continued to argue, was

a stage setting for an unexampled spectacle. The White City is the most integral, the most extensive, the most illusive piece of scenic architecture that has ever been seen. . . . This is not of a useful and important contribution. . . . It is essential to the illusion of a fairy city that it should not be an American city of the nineteenth century. It is a seaport on the coast of Bohemia, it is the captial of No Man's Land. It is what you will, so long as you will not take it for an American city of the nineteenth century, nor its arcitecture for the actual or the possible or even the ideal architecture of such a city. (263:572–573)

Nevertheless it was only after the Chicago World's Fair that the AIA secured its desired legislation requiring that all federal buildings be constructed by licensed architects selected through design competitions. (413) In addition, states began to pass laws requiring that large buildings, such as churches, apartment houses, factories, and public structures, be designed by a licensed architect. (567) Professional training in design and a rigorous knowledge of architectural history, it was argued, were necessary to refine the American vernacular idiom and to apply the correct stylistic analysis to the new structures demanded by the modern metropolis. "Freedom of style," Van Brunt complained,

though it is the natural and healthy condition of architecture in our country, . . . is also a temptation to crude experiments, to tours de force, and to surprises in design such as form the characteristic features of an American city. . . . It is the aim of our architectural schools not to kill but to correct this abundant vitality and to direct it into channels of fruitful and rational progress. (520:246)

Montgomery Schuyler was not appeased. He warned that the American architect is more likely to imitate than to analyze why a building is pleasing:

He is more apt to reproduce them as he finds them, so far as this is mechanically possible. For this process our time affords facilities unprecedented in history. Photographs are available of everything striking or memorable that has been built in the world, and that survives in ruins. . . . The photograph enables him merely to reproduce what he admires, and increases the desireableness that he should admire rightly. . . . An architect who learns this will not be misled by the success of the buildings of the World's Fair into reproducing or imitating them, because he will know too well what are the necessary conditions of their effectiveness, and that these conditions cannot be reproduced except in another World's Fair, and not literally even there. (263:556–557)

Without hearing this warning, improvers of the American city drew their lessons from the Chicago World's Fair. The city, they proclaimed, was the home of the community; it expressed the good and evil in human nature to excess. In its form and spirit one could read the strengths and weaknesses of civilization. (92) Aesthetic reform would rehabilitate the American city and redeem it from the sordid, the selfish, and the base. (562) A belief in national and social progress through aesthetic achievements dominated the point of view of these environmental improvers. Behind this ideal of national dignity, valor, and prestige was hidden a mystical sense of purpose and national destiny.[3] No doubt these dreams covered a fear that the uncouth development to which the American city had been subjugated would not change. Nevertheless, they preached that once the spirit of civic design caught on, American cities would reach such eminence among the municipalities of the world that they would be difficult to excel. (561)

From ancient times, the classical cities of Greece have symbolized a return to communal unity and sovereign allegiance; hence they have become an ideal paradigm for disciplinary order. The classical, embodying universal ethical and aesthetic values, was believed to be the truly natural art. It was nature purified by the rational mind, an image reflecting the qualities of order, proportion, rhythm, equilibrium, and harmony. (401:101–112) The beautiful, the classical meaning of the visible world, was proposed as a base from which to reorder social and political reality by emulation and self-perfection. To beautify the American city meant to follow the classical laws of nature. But an overworked neoclassical formula deceived its intention. Providing only a nostalgic vision of the ideal, its purpose actually became the creation of a static ceremonial stylization by which to overcome the chaos of urban life.

The illusions of neoclassicism searched not to transform the contradictions between reality and perfection but for the norms that moral perfection must follow. Lightness, perspective, proportion, and rhythm were to uplift the individual from the sordidness of reality; they were to elevate him toward the fullness of life, which beauty and unity had now revealed. The city became a backdrop for reality; it posited eternal order and civic meaning in place of physical disorder, personal void, and political and economic exploitation. By neglecting to respond to the embedded motives of capital accumulation, status acquisition, social prestige, and imperialistic power, the synthetically prepared forms of the neoclassical mode offered only a formalized view. How, then, could the public gaze perceive a moral and civic message from among such alienated displays of order and purity?

Still cities in America, proclaimed Charles Mulford Robinson, one of the major spokesmen for the municipal art movement, must decide whether they will go forward without a plan, and be reduced to the commonplace among cities, or whether they will take into account their unique features, enhancing their beauty and attractiveness, and thus take their rank among the noble cities of the world. Since the economic profit of a city lies in its attractiveness, Robinson advised, every city should seek an artistic development of its focal points and a well-thought-out street plan. (459)

With respect to civic art, Robinson told American improvers, the fault of most cities is "the lack of definiteness in the impression they make as one approaches them." (459:39) As a work of art, the city has a right, he added, to be considered in an impressionistic manner.

On a road leading out of Boston into the suburbs there is a view through an arch of trees of the gilded dome of the State House on Beacon Hill; from a point on the Thames there is a loved view of St. Paul's with central London clustered about it . . . a vignette that stands for much. Upon just such little things as this is fixed the citizen's love for his city; its towers and domes pin his affections, and the more because in every case the composition has inevitably a meaning, a cleanness and accuracy of significance, that makes it more than merely a pretty picture. It is a work of art which speaks not to the eye alone, nor to the head alone but unitedly, to sense, brain and sentiment. (459:41)

When cities were walled, Robinson continued, their gates made a special and formal land entrance. But once these walls were razed, then the city simply tapered off, with no recognition of a threshold. Often the best place to view a city was from the water. Out of the neutral foreground of the waves the city rose in sharp and urban contrast, so the waterfront must become the major vestibule of the city. (459:41) Take the example of New York. This city had many miles of waterfront, which park improvers had eagerly grasped as valuable assets. Battery Park was chosen as the center for a civic composition. Here it was proposed to place a naval arch to frame the entrance of the city.

St. Louis, like many other cities of this period, developed a plan for the improvement of its riverfront as the natural gateway to the city. When increasing railroad transportation caused a decline in river traffic, prosperous businesses and residences moved up the hill, abandoning the riverfront. Neglected buildings grew shabby and dilapidated, unfit for business or dwelling. St. Louis turned its back upon its waterfront, allowing it to become the "rendezvous of the vicious and depraved." In 1907 an improvement commission pointed out that the steep grades along the levee made a "dignified treatment" of the waterfront an easy solution. A broad esplanade could be constructed by the city on these levees, extending the length of the river margin and terminating in two splendid bridges crossing the river. (101)

The land approach to every city must be given an adequate threshold as well. The arrival of the railroad, Robinson pointed out, enabled such a portal. Passengers by rail now had a single definite point of arrival and departure. Thus in the early 1900s a majestic railroad station of Romanesque, Gothic, or Roman form became the symbol of a city's industrial and commercial prosperity. Blocks around the station were transformed into appropriate parks, with approaching boulevards, off-setting vistas, fountains, and ornamentation. (337)

Outlining and emphasizing the thresholds of the American city, Robinson's plans for civic improvement also addressed the site location and future development of public and semipublic institutions. In order to avoid haphazard growth and make each new addition a worthy ornament of the city, structures that held a public function and were to be built by public means must never be considered as isolated buildings but in their ceremonial relationship to the community as a whole. Robinson advised that they be linked in structure and design to all the other buildings of their type. Hence the administrative center of a town with its city hall, courthouse, public library, railroad station, and post office should be given a distinct and definite focus. Collected together these buildings should be grouped around a civic plaza or park, not strung out randomly along an open street. So grouped, claimed Robinson, they suggested the cooperative spirit of all the governmental departments, a symbolic representation of the mightiness of a town's development and democracy. (459) Following these recommendations, ambitious plans for civic centers of striking architecture were developed in Cleveland and Chicago, while courageously optimistic cities of the Pacific Coast and Middle West, such as Los Angeles, Portland, Seattle, and St. Louis worked out monumental plans.

In 1906 Robinson prepared an improvement scheme for the city of Denver, Colorado. There the capitol, the courthouse, and the proposed public library all stood at different angles to each other and faced in different directions. Not one harmonized in position or design with its neighbor, so Robinson proposed to develop a parallelogram park from the capitol grounds to the courthouse, with an oblong basin of water along its length and with trees and fountains emphasizing the axis. In the basin, "there may be offered a vantage point whence the play of light and shadow, the reflection of the great buildings, or the frolic of wind ripples in the water, may be enjoyed." (461:5) The street plan was to be reorganized to relate to the capitol, while the proposed library, the new chamber of commerce auditorium, post office, and pioneers' monument were to be moved next to this parallelogram park. As a result, Robinson assured the Art Commission, this area would attract many high-class hotels and apartment houses so that the entire civic improvement project would quickly pay for itself.

Ceremonial locations of public buildings in New York City received the attention of a 1904 improvement commission. They focused on City Hall Park, an area that the improvers believed already held one of the few good monuments in the city and was well situated with reference to all parts of the greater city. The location of the post office, records and court houses, many newspaper buildings, and the entranceways to two great bridges had already made City Hall Park a natural civic center. (442) Thus they recommended that any new governmental and administrative buildings be situated close to this park, for each individual structure would thus lend to the other its "reflected glory."

The Municipal Art Society of New York found that the term *civic center* had come to mean the grouping of public buildings around a park or open space such that the advantages of light and air were gained, the length of vision that enhances architectural monuments was also secured, as well as the utilitarian efficiency of a center of activity devoted to civic business. (437:2) To give an approximate idea of how effectively New York could use such a civic center, the Municipal Art Society produced a map locating every public building in lower Manhattan that could potentially make use of this new civic center. When the society took up the cudgel for this civic plaza, it added the consideration of transportation problems to its improvement scheme, for until the general lines of circulation had been defined, it seemed impractical to plan the decorative features.

The location of a park, a monument, or a public building, if made without regard to the transportation system, might be rendered of little effect either by the laying out of new thoroughfares which would cut directly through it and make necessary its removal, or by leaving it stranded without adequate access or perspective. To produce the best results great care must be exercised in the location of public structures; but it is evident that until the street plan and lines of transit have been determined upon it is impossible to decide what points constitute the most advantageous locations.[4]

Next attention must be placed on the means of connection of the focal points. If they were plotted upon a checkerboard street plan, major diagonal thoroughfares should cut the monotonous grid pattern in order to accentuate these focuses. Robinson wrote,

It has been found that often there is no better way to redeem a slum district than by cutting into it a great highway that will be filled with the through travel of a city's industry. Like a stream of pure water cleansing what it touches, this tide of traffic, pulsing with the joyousness of the city's life of toil and purpose, when flowing through an idle or suffering district wakes it to larger interests and higher purposes. (459:21)

Thus diagonal thoroughfares cutting across tenement sections of the city and converging at local centers just off the major focuses could be used to open up these congested areas to light and fresh air. (459)

Another early city improver, J. F. Harder, drew the following analogy in 1898:

A city may be likened to a house; its waterways, bridges, railroads, and highways are the entrances, vestibules and exits; its public buildings are the drawing rooms, its streets the halls and corridors, the manufacturing districts the kitchens and workshops; tunnels and subways are its cellars, and its rookeries the attic; the parks and recreation places are its gardens, and its systems of communication, lighting and drainage are the furniture. The city is a house of many chambers, and the first condition in forming its ideal plan is the shortest route from each to each. (219:33)

When he turned to analyze the gridiron plan of New York City, Harder found that the commissioners of 1811 had completely omitted the diagonal system of thoroughfares even though the plan for the city of Washington, D.C., had been mapped and printed at least ten years before the New York commission was even appointed. (219)

It was not too late, however, for New York to take advantage of this tested method of baroque city planning for Union Square, the center of late-nineteenth-century development, offered a splendid design opportunity. If this square was extended north to Eighteenth Street, south to Eleventh Street, and east of Broadway to Third Avenue a new proposal could take shape. Only Fourteenth Street would pass through this enlarged park. On this splendid new site, monumental conditions were created for a new city hall and an official mayor's residence, and southward at Lafayette Place a fine site was now opened for a monumental building. In close proximity luxurious residential squares already existed to counterbalance this new civic order: to the north lay Gramercy Park, just eastward was Stuyvesant Square, and westward was the grand avenue of Broadway, rapidly undergoing massive improvement. From this enlarged Union Square, magnificent diagonal boulevards would be drawn in every direction. Already Fourth Avenue (present-day Park Avenue) led to the principal railroad station; Christopher Street could be extended on its diagonal, thus connecting the southwest corner of the square with the ferry terminal at its foot. Three new avenues were to be cut through tenement areas from the northeast, northwest, and southeast corners of the square. This new system of diagonal avenues, Harder argued, would result in conditions known as vistas. Instead of ending a perspective against a blank wall, at each of the intersections of these new diagonals with the rectangular gridiron pattern, an extended angle of sight was afforded and an important length of vision created for the sites of new and majestic structures. (219)

For many years Philadelphia improvement societies had pushed for the development of a broad and noble avenue wider than the Champs Elysees to pass from Fairmount Park to Logan Square. This avenue would create a ceremonial space in front of city hall, preserve the view from all sides of this building, and relieve the monotonous regularity of the grid street system. Not only was the section of the city across which this diagonal boulevard would cut of very poor and undesirable development, but (and not least of these considerations) the proposed improvement would augment the value of adjacent property, hence increasing city revenues. (254)

Manhattan too needed several diagonal streets above and below Fourteenth Street. As the New York Municipal Art Society advocated in 1903, diagonal streets would add variety to the grid pattern and directness of communication, and it would offer irregular block shapes at intersections suitable for architectural embellishment. Wherever possible, cul de sacs, those dens of tenement thieves, were to be eliminated. (437)

Perhaps nowhere more accentuated than in the 1909 plan of Chicago, diagonal boulevards were planned to cut through intensively developed property and a circumferential parkway laid out to provide circulation throughout the city. These boulevards and the parkway provided spectacular vistas to all the important public buildings by day and conveyed lines of illuminated light by night. On the westward arc of a great circumferential boulevard, which originated and terminated in lakeshore parks, was located a magnificent civic center outlined as a "monument to the spirit of civic unity." Watercolor drawings by the Parisian artist Jules Guerin sketched boulevards of such visionary expanse, building rooftops of exact alignment, lagoons with gondoliers, and elegant ladies in horse-drawn carriages. (356) All were bathed in swathes of yellow and orange light.

Conclusion

The utopia of both a neoclassical order and a city beautiful remained the background against which the realities of the American city and its ruptured past stood out in graphic array. These Beaux Arts illustrations detached fragments of the city from their historical tradition; a plurality of copies stood in place of a unique experience. By dispensing with an authentic historical and urban assemblage, a montage of civic structures and decorative ornaments was offered to a distracted public in search of an ideal order. This is what the critic Walter Benjamin called the "metaphysics of the present": where only trivialized works of art win exhibition value, their aura canceled out through mechanical reproduction, which draws the object closer to mass consumption. "To perceive the aura of an object," Benjamin wrote, "we look at means to invest it with the capacity to look at us in return." (57:188) The spatial form of the American city lost this communicative ability, which had been based on tradition and individual contemplation, and turned toward popular reception and the spell of mass suggestion. (57:225) Thus these neoclassical reproductions, which arose in every American city, became encoded with an ideological message expressing a system of needs well embedded within the economic and political sphere of capitalism: those of nationalist grandeur, economic imperialism, and political triumph.

Neoclassical architectural styles and decorative monuments were also asked, as natural and picturesque parklands had been, to hold a ceremonial function in the American city. A bricolage of perspective axes, spectacular civic plazas, and monumental entry points were dramatically juxtaposed to the existing urban fabric. The space of the city was reduced to a symbolic function whose alien codes destroyed a meaningful dialogue between the architectural object and the urban form. Antiurban and ahistorical gestures could ruthlessly destroy tenement districts and randomly enlarge and revitalize segments within the historical centers, but the fragmented city could not be rationalized and reordered through isolated allusions to classical antiquity. By virtue of example and means of deduction, these ceremonial sites could offer only ad hoc control over the city form and its restless populace. Once again the failures of the Beaux-Arts strategy embedded in the city beautiful, municipal art, and civic improvement movements released new pressures to restructure the programs and tactics with which the improvers confronted the modern metropolis.

II

THE DISCIPLINARY ORDER OF PLANNING, 1909–1916

4

The Rise of the Planning Mentality

To be exposed to the influence of nature, to the order of classical architecture, to the example of moral philanthropy: these were the problems to which the architecture of picturesque parks, civic centers and public buildings, and the inspections of charity organizations and tenement departments responded. The needs of industrial production, however, posed another type of metropolitan problem. How could the rules for efficient capital expansion and circulation be internalized in the fabric and form of the city—not as exemplary architectural sitings, spectacular fairs, or uprighteous individuals but by introjecting a disciplinary order within and under the surface of urban form in the most efficient and economical manner?

Michel Foucault has written that the utopia of a perfectly governed city, the most efficient and economical method to spread a disciplinary order, can be drawn from the seventeenth century's image of a plague-stricken town. When plague first appeared in a given city, an immediate hierarchical order was imposed upon the town. A strict partitioning of the infected areas closed them off from outside communication. An inspector was placed in control over every district and a guard on every street. Only those inspectors and guards were allowed to move about the town; everyone else was enclosed within his house. Inspection was continuous; at every town gate a guard, at every street a sentinel. Inspectors made their rounds of the streets every day, recording the name and state of health of every inhabitant of every house. In this way deaths were known, sickness revealed, and all requests for medicine, food, or travel were noted and transferred from the level of the street to the centralized authority. Absolute control was thus maintained over this enclosed and segmented town.

Against the plague, which is one of mixture [Foucault writes], discipline brings into play its power, which is one of analysis. A whole literary fiction of the festival grew up around the plague: suspended laws, lifted prohibitions, the frenzy of passing time, bodies mingling together without respect. . . . But there was also a political dream of the plague, which was exactly its reverse: not the collective festival, but strict divisions; not laws transgressed, but the penetration of regulation into even the smallest details of everyday life through the mediation of the complete hierarchy that assured the capillary function of power. . . . The plague as a form, at once real and imaginary, of disorder had as its medical and political correlative discipline. (173:197–198)

So too against the chaos of the city with its simultaneity of land uses, jumble of vehicles, multitudes of people, corrupt politicians, and labor unrest, there stood an ideal: the city as a perfectly disciplined spatial order.

Slowly a new guise for improvement was forming, one that would break away from a preestablished curative environment and a neoclassical formula and extend instead toward the causal mechanisms responsible for the production of urban disorder and disease. A change in orientation began to occur that eventually would bring a reevaluation of the potency of environmental reform and the beginning of an idea that the American city might be disciplined by the progressive development of human knowledge, state regulatory mechanisms, and public welfare provisions. At this point the politics of voluntary improvement and the necessity for state intervention join interests, for only with the cooperation of state power could the general provision of unemployment relief, the enforcement of tenement codes and congestion controls, and the employment of health inspectors and land-use regulations be expertly and continuously supervised.

By 1912 reflection allowed that "in America, initiative and experiment and educational propaganda belong to voluntary philanthropy, while control, and the enforcement of standards, and the meeting of large elementary recognized social needs fall to the state." (126:177) Thus bureaus of municipal research, state charity organizations, tenement house commissions, and public health associations were designed to make governmental action more effective, either directly as public agencies or indirectly through the formation of public opinion. State intervention was no longer viewed as paternalism but the "deliberate intention to use the governmental machinery for the doing of those things for which experience shows it to be more efficient and more economical than any other means yet devised." (126:179) The state, we are told, was simply the extension of our will, our conscience, our strong arm; state intervention followed an investment theory of taxation in which we spend to avoid disease, to strengthen our system of capitalism, and therefore eventually to increase our resources. (126)

In the late nineteenth and early twentieth centuries, the idealisms of environmental reform finally appeared to be too slow, too hidden to remove the barriers of economic growth and to prompt a return to prosperity. The state, it was argued, could promote the interests of the general welfare, answering the problems that laissez faire capitalism was unable to solve: the needs of public health, of decent housing, of unemployment, of circulation and transportation, of wage and hour conditions, and of the pressure of immigration. Regulatory power to control the limits and boundaries of capitalism had to reside at some level. So it was argued, it had best be in the more centralized levels of government, closer to the knowledge of general principles, more open to capital's control, and less accessible to the political demands of local protests. (279)

The nineteenth century had left a legacy of problems whose solution in terms of an environmental logic seemed remote. It was no longer sufficient to describe the city as an autonomous association of entities— parks, houses, civic centers, and transportation circuits—all harmoniously arranged by hidden laws of nature. It was apparent that cities had internal laws of functional organization and development, which referred to their own coherence, not to some superordinate environmental logic. The problem of explaining the process by which a city could develop in an orderly manner despite the increasing complexity and specialization of its structure and functions seemed to make special demands.

What forms the boundary, the limit of the old interplay between the individual and his natural environment? Why did the potency of environmental reform, which posited a harmonious envelope extending outward to include the city and the country in its curative hold, begin to weaken near the beginning of the twentieth century? If once it was feared that the American city housed and multiplied all the social and physical evils of decay, now the accepted stance was that the problems of the city were reactions of men struggling to defend themselves in a competitive era. Rather than seeking to contain the ills in a curative environmental envelope, the city builder must aid this struggle by promoting the best organization, the most rational plan by which the American city could develop. The environmental improvers had not been expected to ask or to answer questions about the structural organization of the city, about the control of urban development, of functional inefficiency, infrastructural needs, or industrial purpose.

The complexities of the metropolitan dilemma required that new explanations be made in terms of rational systemic processes that could mold development toward specified ends. It appeared that the American city should be an organized set of interacting components and functions that were to be coordinated in such a way as to satisfy the needs of the whole community: food had to be accumulated and distributed, land uses needed to be spatially arranged and coordinated with the surroundings, the labor force had to be carried between working place and resting place, waste matter must be collected and disposed of, energy generated and delivered. The elements of the American city had to be functionally integrated into a whole; what mattered most of all was how one part related to another and how they cooperated in support of the maintenance and reproduction of capital accumulation within the city.

Thus the reform effort began to shift as the state and the city builder reached out to gain control over the American city. Order in urban growth and plan had to be established without reference to classical or ceremonial harmony. Concerns of environmental reform had been dominated by the fear that damage to one of the laws of nature meant inevitable destruction to mankind. But these myths alone could not produce a rational organization to the city. An interventionist strategy was necessary, a planning mentality was essential—one that offered a conceptual scheme for rational development and regulated growth.

This planning mentality began to develop around 1907 and gained momentum after 1913. L. S. Rowe observed in 1908 that the "growth of social relations in city life meant that man was more a product of social rather than purely natural forces. . . . His mental and moral traits were determined largely by this environment, but it was an environment furnished him by the community rather than nature. This view of the subject carries with it a new element of responsibility." (471:58) Still earlier he had written that this new need for social responsibility arises "as we descend the scale of income, [for then] the degree of inter-dependence becomes greater. The city," Rowe concluded, "is no longer regarded as a necessary evil; it is recognized as the accompanying factor of all civilization." (471:59) But unregulated development brings with it serious evils; thus new relations of the individual to the community and a new need for government control have been borne out of the rising economic opportunities of the times. "The danger," Rowe noted, "to social welfare involved in an intelligent selection of food, drink or enjoyment, is increased rather than diminished by a rise in the rate of wages." (472:303) Why should the soap manufacturer be allowed to advertise his wares on the street or one person to ruin the architectural effect of an entire section of the city? Why should the speculative builder be permitted to foster congestion?

The environmental reforms of the early improvers had outlined the major problems of chaotic city growth, cultural needs, and social service requirements. They slowly brought into position some of the essential themes around which planning would evolve. In fragments and pieces the idea of improving the conditions of poverty, congestion, public health, recreation, and architectural order became connected with the practices and professions of engineering and architecture, charity and municipal reform, housing, and health and educational services. But an architectural practice, an engineering custom, or a municipal reform alone could not develop a total perspective on the American city. The substitution of order in the place of chaos, the control of the urban whole required the development of a concatenated specialization: comprehensive city planning. Thus a new set of needs came forward for which planning would be the response: to impose disciplinary order and supervisory direction over the spatial order of the American city.

"City planning," Benjamin Marsh could proclaim in 1909,

is the adaptation of a city to its proper function. . . . This involves a radical change in the attitude of citizens toward government and the functions of government, but one which the exigencies and the complexity of city life in nearly all great American cities is resistlessly impelling us. It compels a departure from the doctrine that government should not assume any functions aside from its primitive and restrictive activities and boldly demands the interest and effort of the government to preserve the health, morals, and efficiency of the citizens equal to the effort and the zeal which is now expended in the futile task of trying to make amends for the exploitations by private citizens and the wanton disregard of the rights of the many. (332:27)

Spatial Barriers to Economic Growth

The centralization of production and retailing within American cities generated industrial and manufacturing specialization and interdependency. This in turn created a demand from capitalists for infrastructure to parallel production needs, for cheap and efficient transportation and communication networks within and between cities, and for generalized, comprehensive water, sewer, gas, and electric systems across metropolitan areas. By the end of the nineteenth century capitalists searched for new ways to reduce the indirect costs of production and to speed up the circulation rate of capital in an effort to increase the amount of both available capital and time in which capital could be employed productively.

Bringing the product to market, pushing markets out into the world, and increasing the rate of exchange were requirements that capitalists demanded of spatial organization. Marx has portrayed this battle over spatial friction in this way:

Thus, while capital must on one side strive to tear down every spatial barrier to intercourse, i.e., to exchange, and conquer the whole earth for its market, it strives on the other side to annihilate this space with time, i.e., to reduce to a minimum the time spent in motion from one place to another. The more developed the capital, therefore, the more extensive the market over which it circulates, which forms the spatial orbit of its circulation, the more does it strive simultaneously for an even greater extension of the market and for greater annihilation of space by time. (334:539)

Continuing this explanation, Marx claimed that the more production rests on exchange and circulation of goods, the more important the physical conditions of exchange—that is, the means of communication and transportation—become.

Capital by its very nature drives beyond every spatial barrier. . . . Only in so far as the direct product can be realized in distant markets in mass quantities in proportion to reductions in the transport costs . . . only in so far as commercial traffic takes place in massive volume . . . only to that extent is the production of cheap means of communication and transport a condition for production based on capital, and promoted by it for that reason. (334:524–525)

In an era of imperialist ventures, when America was expanding its market to the whole world, every spatial barrier that thwarted this development had to be overcome. (555) Anything that impeded the circulation of goods—congested roadways, bridges, and tunnels or inadequate harbor provisions, warehouses, and market areas—had to be removed.

Transportation networks and building constuction thus became major areas of capital investment between 1893 and 1914. These investments became the motive force for overall accelerated capital growth and development. Walter Isard called this period of cyclical development the transport-building cycle. Positing a cycle that lasted roughly twenty years, Isard noted that investments in street and electric railway systems began around 1888, became rapid areas of capital activity after 1897, peaked in 1906, and then began to decline. Population growth in the center of seventeen primary cities of America showed roughly the same cycle: beginning to accelerate in 1898, reaching a peak in 1908, and declining to a low level in 1916. Industrial and commercial expansion followed closely upon the peak phase of this transport-building cycle. (255:149)

Even with rapid economic growth, not all of the needs of production and consumption could be met by individual capitalists, yet not all of these needs were shifted off to the state. Where there existed sufficient idle capital, where the investment in necessary infrastructure would bring rapidly accruing interest levels, where competition made improvements a necessity, where the cost of the outlay could be justified through a large volume of sales—there harbor facilities were improved by private shipping companies, bridges were built by farsighted capitalists, railroad terminals designed at lavish private expense, public utilities planned and controlled by corporations, and model tenement housing built by speculative real estate capital. (334:530) American capitalists also considered cheap water, gas, and electricity as essential for production and adequate housing for the working class as desirable, if somewhat less important. Were these to be undertaken by the American city as municipal enterprises in the general interest of economic growth, or were these provisions to be kept from public control?

In 1899, Wilcox accounts, there were 3,326 water plants, 965 gas plants, and 3,032 electric light plants in the American cities. Municipally owned plants represented 67.5 percent of the total capital investment in water plants, 0.6 percent of the gas plants, and 5.6 percent of the electricity plants. The sewage systems and roadway networks, on the other hand, were all but universally owned and operated by the city. (551) Street railways, gas, and electric plants tended to remain private utilities. Why? Although these were enterprises that utilized public roadbeds and though they demanded great outlays of investment capital, they also generated considerable income in the form of interest, if not in profits. In consequence they remained profitable areas for capitalists. The other general conditions for production—necessary but not profitable ventures such as waterworks and roadways—were pushed onto the shoulders of the American city. Regardless of whether these services and infrastructure provisions were publicly or privately owned, they needed to be spatially organized and locationally distributed if they were to meet the needs of all manufacturing and retail sites in the city center. Toward such disciplined spatial order the state began to plan and financially aid collective infrastructure and service needs.

One of the impediments the state faced was the private ownership of property. In order to provide collective infrastructure needs, the state required land in centralized locations at costs that did not overburden its source of revenue. But private appropriation of these same lands could always find more profitable and therefore costly uses for that land. In the long run private land uses stood as a major impediment to the rational allocation of collective infrastructure facilities. This opposition proved to be a regressive force, retarding the general rate of capital accumulation, throwing up roadblocks in the process of profitable urban investment, and augmenting the economic crises and disinvestment cycles that lay embedded within capitalist development. The greater the opposing forces and the higher the roadblocks were built, the more disciplinary plans and schemes appeared necessary for the physical improvement of the order of the American city.

Disciplinary procedures treat the city as both object and instrument of their control. One can answer the question "What is planning?" by exploring the content of its field, detailing the realm of objects that planning has appropriated as its domain: a synthesis of land uses, of building types and conditions, of circulatory networks, and so forth. But the barriers of capitalist development force another answer to this question. By focusing attention on the industrial requirements of urban space, the behavioral aspects of the city and how planning could maximize the utility of this spatial arrangement became a dominant theme. This is why the process of planning conceives of the city as an instrument of capitalist development. Now the nature of the city is to be a functional tool, a machine useful to the process of production. To increase the utility of each parcel of land, to fix their uses and regulate their development means to infuse the whole with a disciplinary order: constant assessment of changing land patterns, classification of these uses, and a distribution over time to obtain in the future a more rational whole.

In the latter half of the nineteenth century and the first decade of the twentieth, as both city population and municipal investments grew, so too taxes rose, public debt increased, and municipal revenues were squandered and lost. Concerned over the rising costs of municipal operations, state laws by the 1880s began to stipulate what powers cities held and did not hold, what services they must or must not provide. These statutes set the city's taxing power, fixed its indebtedness limits, determined the scope of its licensing powers, mandated the provision of certain municipal services, and forbade the provision of profit-generating enterprises. (368) Here then was a new dilemma: municipalities must provide and coordinate certain infrastructural and service needs, but they must also manage these enterprises efficiently and be restrained from competing against private capital in profitable investment areas. How would all of this be accomplished?

In the nineteenth century a variety of state statutes conferred varying powers on different municipalities. These powers included primary investments (for example, to lay out and construct streets, sewer lines, and public buildings); the provision of public services with potential profit earnings (such as lighting and street cleaning services, the maintenance of sewer systems and public buildings, the creation of public health and sanitation departments, police and fire departments, public parks, charities, and schools); and the entering into special types of revenue-earning services (among them, the provision of water supplies, public lighting, steam and electric utilities, transportation by ferry, telephone and messenger services, the transportation of goods, the development of marketplaces, and waterfront facilities). (227:458–490) Where permission had been granted a municipality to erect or build a public market house or open and improve a new street plan, the city could delegate this authority to some commission or engineer to determine its design, location, and size. A city, however, was not liable for neglecting to create ordinances or regulations to carry into action its delegated powers. Here, therefore, the local improvement society and the civic guardians of economic prosperity could aggressively campaign for action and reform. Not surprisingly of the listed powers (twenty-three of them) generally conferred upon a municipality, at least fourteen, and often all, of them became the basic components around which early planning documents were formulated. (227)

As George Ford proclaimed to the Newark City Planning Commission in 1911,

> To be more explicit, the problems of city planning divide themselves up into a number of groups, which deal with manufacturing, commerce, transportation by land and by water, traffic, transit, housing in town and in the suburbs, recreation for young and old, city administration, financing, legal matters and so forth. This means that the actual features dealt with are factories, warehouses, stores, office buildings, ports, docks, railway freight yards and terminals, streets, sidewalks, rapid transit lines, tenements, dwellings, parks, playgrounds, city administration buildings, schools, libraries, museums, hospitals, jails, asylums, water, sewerage, and lighting systems, and thousand and one decorative features of our streets and public property. (163:5)

Out of the complex of infrastructural and service needs, city planning from its inception became a many-faceted process, simultaneously speaking for contradictory capital interests (industrial, commercial, transportation, real estate, and financial capital) and divided among social and economic needs (citizen development and improvement schemes or efficiently managed street layouts and transportation plans). Planning documents and planning discourse unconsciously offered an ideological reconciliation of these contradictory forces. Within the envelope of their improvement schemes and rational plans, merchants' organizations grappled with railroad capitalists for better shipping facilities and lower transportation rates. Transportation engineers and zoning experts, who promoted schemes to decentralize population and industrial sites, worked against the unskilled laboring classes still confined within inner-city neighborhoods. Efficiency-minded municipal engineers struggled against commercial planners who were more interested in beautifying the city's facade than easing its vehicular circulation. Congestion and tenement reformers fought against speculative real estate agents whose ruthless efforts to capitalize upon the advantages of location and concentration of people brought successively more congestion and spiraling housing costs. The diverse and opposing strategies of industrial and financial capital, small businesses and trade groups, professional concerns and middle-class outrages formed a network across which the power of capital was intricately webbed. Planning documents became the mode through which these contradictions found physical expression and idealistic resolution; they represented discourses of constraint that selected and organized the material according to implicit controls. These documents privileged certain planned improvements with recognition and left others unmentioned. They linked those included with their chains of civic and economic support, yet failed to include voices in opposition. They appropriated certain reform strategies and submitted specific information for analysis, while they ignored other information they believed to be misconceived or erroneous. While the strategies and information presented may have contradicted each other, these planning documents presented the illusion that their proposals were a series of compatible statements. (97)

Planning documents were written at an abstracted level of discourse, never speaking of the motives and conflicts behind their production. They offered a normative resolution of what the American city ought to look like, while leaving aside structural limitations and practical barriers. To transform, correct, and improve society through a disciplined physical environment and to secure capital investments in land, physical improvements, or infrastructure through a rational spatial order—these were the neutral reasons for the existence of planning.[1] In this effort to normalize disciplinary order over urban development, the planners were to speak for the general interest of capital. Therefore they seldom outlined the dispute between traffic plans and architectural embellishments, between streetcar franchise holders and those who advocated cheap methods of decentralizing congested urban populations, of low-income housing needs and profitable urban redevelopment. To uphold business confidence so that capital would continue to invest in the physical improvement of the American city, to help to adjust capital itself to new needs expressed in the phases of capital accumulation, speculation, and disinvestment, to present alternative strategies that might lead to stable development: these were the functions of planning.

Thus what sustained the discourse about planning across the years is the minute details that could discipline the physical appearance of the American city. At issue was not whether the city was too exploitative or too unhealthful but rather its physical order as an effective instrument in the service of capital productivity. To become such an instrument, planning developed and intermixed two tactical programs. One employed the spatial form of the city as a material element in the production and circulation of goods. Could land and building investments themselves become the start of a new chain of consumption? Were there procedures that might separate profit-yielding locations and improvements from the threat of obsolete and blighted land areas? The exercise of disciplinary control over urban and spatial development embedded in a comprehensive plan thus reflected one form of planning. The second tactic employed a different perspective: how might planning help to diffuse these contradictions of uneven capital development? During times of prosperity could some of

the surplus capital be used to improve the urban facade? Might the dialogue
of planning be used to speak of a harmonious order as if that world had
materialized, as if the contradictory forces had been dissolved in a rational
manner? Could planners graphically depict an ideal urban form that welded
together these dissensions? Would not this harmonious facade itself secure
business optimism, hold up financial confidence, and maintain an illusion
of prosperity? To infuse this spirit of utopian rationality across the American
city was the second tactical program that planners struggled to meet.

Comprehensive city planning, Olmsted, Jr., could define in 1911,

is concerned with a single complex subject . . . the intelligent control and
guidance of the entire physical growth and alteration of cities; embracing
all the problems of transportation facilities or of recreation facilities,
congestion in respect to the means of supplying light, air, water or anything
else essential to the health and happiness of the people, but also in addition
to the problems of congestion, each one of the myriad problems involved
in making our cities year by year, in their physical arrangement and equipment, healthier, pleasanter and more economic instruments for the use
of the people who dwell within them. (394:5)

Part of the purpose of planning, then, was to conserve and restore
impaired land values, to supervise the use and occupation of land, to
regulate the city's tenements, office buildings, circulation means, distribution of public spaces and private land, and to promote the productivity
and efficiency of its market activities. (110, 215, 394) The intent behind
this process was to effect these civic improvements without interfering
with vested interests. (162) Planning was a rational procedure, which was
above the economic conflicts of the American city; it paid more attention
to the meshing of components, the adaptation of parts, and the procuring
of efficiency; it directed attention to the simplistic relations and elements
that could be regulated, such as the flow of traffic and the disorderly and
conflicting arrangements of land uses. Allowing the exploitative processes
of capitalism to occur behind their backs, city planners thus introduced
an ideal form into their theories, an abstract rationalization that made
possible the removal of some of the barriers that thwarted economic
growth yet protected capitalism. As upholder of an ideal solution, it was
the aim of planning to be purchased by a growing body of public administrators and voluntarily adopted by private property owners, to be
sold as a partial reform realized through efficiency techniques that transformed obsolete land uses into more productive values, provided new
infrastructural requirements for capital investments and accumulation, and
maintained a harmony of social consensus and legitimation. This is what
I have referred to as the planning mentality, but it is as much a utopian

disciplinary order as the medieval town under plague or the city of Olympian design.

Addressing the National Conference on City Planning in 1915, Frederick Ackerman proclaimed that

> city planning is the act of providing a more adequate physical expression for the composite ideals of the groups of people thrown together by social and economic forces in our communities. Our composite thought, our culture is expressed in our physical environment through many subtle forces and influences, both conscious and unconscious. City Planning is not a substitute for these forces; it is rather a conscious effort to transform our vague ideals of community living into forms which will accurately express such ideals. (1:108)

As Albert Kelsey would write, "A lamp post, an avenue, a building, a park, are not detached units, but each is one of a system of units, and each of these systems has its place in the civic scheme. The problem is to find the true place of each unit and of each system of units." (269) Above all the conflicts and contradictions floats this desire to implant a disciplinary order upon the city and over the economic contradictions that the American city expressed.

Disciplinary Space and the City Survey

What was this new disciplinary order that planners were to impose upon the urban form? Once again we turn to Michel Foucault for his explanation of how the human body itself came under the control of disciplinary systems in the eighteenth century. He recounts how the body was discovered as a new object of power: it could be manipulated, transformed, and improved. So trained, a docile body would become more skillful and productive. Disciplinary methods came to constitute a set of regulations that were invested in the army, the schools, the hospitals, the factories, and even in the prisons. Rather than acting upon each individual, these systems of discipline acted simultaneously upon groups of individuals. Their concern was the internal efficiency of operations and the productive organization of individuals controlled through a continuous system of supervision over space, time, and movement. In consequence the body came under the control of a disciplinary machinery, which explored it, broke it down, and rearranged it in order to make its movements more efficient and its productivity more useful. (173:170–256)

Disciplinary control proceeded by distributing bodies in space, allocating each individual to a cellular partition, creating a functional space out of this analytic spatial arrangement. In the end this spatial matrix became both real and ideal: a hierarchical organization of cellular space and a purely ideal order that was imposed upon its form. In becoming a target for disciplinary control, the body offered up new forms of knowledge: each disciplinary methodology thus came to describe an anatomy of detail. Nothing was too unimportant to come under constant surveillance and control. An ideal architectural model was conceived as well to house this disciplinary system, not simply for ceremonial functions from which the power of the sovereign could be deduced but an architecture that would allow disciplinary surveillance to operate continuously on the body it was trying to bend to its will, a construction of observatories that could survey the movement of each individual and every cellular space. (173)

Not surprisingly in light of the desires of the city improvers in the early twentieth century to create an efficiently organized and hierarchically controlled urban space, the American city was exposed to the training and ideal transformations embedded within such a disciplinary system. This machinery would also give rise to a body of detailed knowledge about the city and a set of ideal urban observatories that would constantly survey and correct its form. Disciplinary control would operate through a set of four procedures. First, it begins by classification of entities and their distribution into appropriate locations. Next it creates functional sites that support the process of production. Third, it focuses on each movement over time, especially on adding up and capitalizing time. Finally it composes these movable parts into an efficient and productive machine.

Above all else disciplinary space is cellular; its purpose is to be able to separate or break up confusing overlaps, to fix peripatetic land uses, to set up more useful communications among the parts of the city. This first operation required a survey that organized a multitude of activities and distributed them into cellular spaces. Thus the first requirement for disciplinary order and the basis for all city plans was an intersecting set of four streams of information: facts from the physical arrangement of the city, social facts concerning the people themselves and the relationships between them and their physical environment, economic and financial facts about a city's resources and the possibility of bringing these resources to bear upon public improvements, and legal and administrative facts, which influenced the implementation of disciplinary control. (393) In turn the surface of the city was carved up into a series of distinct entities: an exhasutive survey of all the visible aspects of squares, parks, buildings, sewers, conduit pipes, poles and wires, railways, streets, waterways, reservoirs—in short, every piece of land, building, and improvement, both public and private. (393) The act of city planning required a new totalization: a network of special investigations penetrating the conditions of housing; the working conditions in major industries; warehouse and factory quality and location; standards and ideals for public transportation, street use, and extensions; the social efficiency of equipment for water supply, waste disposal, flood and storm drainage, public recreation and markets for food supply. (162)

Between 1892 and 1903 London was the first city to undertake a city-wide survey of the living conditions of its laboring masses. This seventeen-volume study by Charles Booth, while deriving its data from secondary sources, nevertheless analyzed the patterns of unemployment along thirty-five trade groups and correlated these with information on the size of families, their age structure, their country of origin, the number of rooms they rented, their wages and sources of income, and so on. A new set of questions was asked of the conditions of unemployment. Rather than assuming they were natural products of economic depressions, now a causal arrangement was sought. As Booth's data began to reveal, it was not innate laziness or unwillingness to work that produced so much unemployment among the tailors, bootmakers, shipwrights, cabinetmakers, and tobacco workers. Rather these semiskilled artisan trades, London's oldest and traditional source of employment, were the hardest hit by changes that the industrial revolution had brought. The higher-skilled workers—shopmen, printers, wheelwrights, messengers and watchmen, white-collar government workers, and railroad employees—tended to be continuously employed even during severe economic depressions. (262)

Patrick Geddes had campaigned for city surveys in England since the early 1900s because he wondered,

Amid such vast and varied centers, such crowded phantasmagoria of life, how shall we agree upon any orderly methods of observation and description, such as that which is required in each and every department of science? . . . How are we to observe, describe, compare observations, generalise, reach some penetration of analysis, some general point of view, depth of insight . . . how are we even to communicate our ideas to each other in adequately scientific terms? (193:1)

If twenty-eight bills had been passed since Lord Shaftesbury's first housing bill in 1851 and all of these had been insufficient to solve the evils of town life, then, Geddes protested, it was time that the twenty-ninth bill took the geographical and social sciences into its counsel. Most planners lacked even the most basic materials, he pointed out. What was needed to start was an adequate collection of maps: maps describing town conditions before the industrial revolution, maps a generation later when industrial expansion was in full swing, and maps for current conditions. These could be used to show the expansion of two generations, the subsequent improvements, the mischief generally done, and the conditions for future development. (193)

City surveys, Geddes promoted,

> are not merely descriptive, or even statistical . . . they are also geographical; and they set down their main results upon their respective city plans, and thus attain a new clearness. In this way they place under our eyes a detailed, yet generalized view of the city, as a more or less large and complex hive of humanity, strangely differentiated, strangely crowded, here and there strangely defiled, strangely defective, decayed, diseased. How are we to improve this state of things? By vigorous demolition . . . or by mere expansions, mostly bad or indifferent, as with the building trade for the past hundred years? In the age of Town Planning of which we are now upon the threshold, we would fain renew the health and beauty of our deteriorated cities, and yet more thoroughly provide for these by new and better expansions. . . . Here, then, appears the need for enquiring, "How did all this disorder, which at length so shocks us by its mean or hideous aspect, its corresponding effect upon its inhabitants, actually come about?" (192:2)

Robert W. de Forest and Lawrence Veiller set the style for American inquiries into city conditions by their pioneering investigation of New York City's tenement houses during the early 1900s. Their charts, tables, plots, and diagrams, which became an exhibit traveling from city to city, aimed to prove that in New York the workingman had poorer housing conditions than in any other city in the world and that he paid more for it in money, health, and morality. Dramatically stated, this survey was followed by subsequent tenement house committees and surveys in other American cities. By 1912 thirty-eight cities claimed they had performed such activities. (308)

Still social research on a city-wide scale—with an in-depth exploration of all the infrastructural needs of the city, the living and sanitation concerns of its working population, the costs to the community for its failure to act preventatively, the trend of industrial accidents, the numbers of people in hospitals, insane asylums, brothels, and orphanages—had never been done. Every American city lacked data upon which to make plans for the relief of social and physical problems.

In 1907 the Russell Sage Foundation sponsored the first city-wide survey, the Pittsburgh Survey, in an attempt to set a standard. Here lay the base upon which all plans for city improvement must stand. For the first time a group of specialists focused on the health needs, industrial accidents, cost of living, social institutions, and civic improvements of one American city. All of these investigations were related in turn to the environmental conditions of the wage-earning classes, their housing facilities, the water and typhoid situation, the school systems, and working conditions. (267) These data, the surveyors believed, were too timely to be published in book form; they must be dramatically exhibited and widely distributed through newspaper and magazine articles, political pamphlets, and graphic exhibits. Paul Kellogg, editor of the Pittsburgh Survey, which was published in three monthly installments of the *Charities and the Commons*, tried to point out that Pittsburgh "is not merely a scapegoat city. It is the capital of a district representative of untrammeled industrial development, but of a district which, for richer, for poorer, in sickness and in health, for vigor, waste and optimism, is rampantly American." (267:525)

There is something further synthetic and clarifying [Kellogg noted] to be gained by a sizing up process that reckons at once with many factors in the life of a great civic area, not going deeply into all subjects, but offering a structural exhibit of the community as a going concern. This is what the examining physician demands before he accepts us as an insurance risk, what a modern farmer puts his soils and stock through before he plants his crops, what the consulting electrician performs as his first work when he is called in to overhaul a manufacturing plant. And this, in the large, has been the commission undertaken by the Pittsburgh Survey. (267:518)

All of these data that survey the life, labor, and leisure conditions of the people, a later advocate of city surveys explained, must be territorially represented through a city plan. (24:34) Far more than a means of popular civic education, the survey "reveals fundamentals upon which a comprehensive program can be outlined and the technique with which it is to be carved out is stated. It also contains data of scientific value upon which a positive science of Applied Sociology must eventually be built up in this country." (24:196)

The trouble with city planning in America, we are told by John Nolen, was that those in charge of the work had only a vague conception of what they were trying to do. Thus the first step in planning the American city should begin with a careful study of the underlying physical, business, and social conditions of the city. At a minimum a topographical map must display the physical contours and conditions of the land, the location of the streets, buildings, and other physical features such as the distribution of population, traffic congestion, the positions of sewers and gas, and water mains. Every city plan should contain a complete and graphic expression of its housing facts as far back as the record will permit. Then, as John Nolen outlined, on this topographical map, distinct colors should identify the one-family, two-family, and tenement houses, whether detached or in rows, with the number of stories and percentages of lot covered, and specifying if of wood or brick construction. Superimposed upon this map, Nolan suggested, should go the location and number of cases of typhoid, tuberculosis, and infant mortality for the last five years. (378) This vast array of information should be displayed upon a series of maps:

maps of the location and distribution of foreign quarters, residential areas, workers' neighborhoods; maps pinpointing the location of churches, saloons, schools, vice resorts, red-light districts; maps depicting the congested areas and the location of proposed new street systems; historical maps describing past growth patterns—maps, in short, that established the relationship of each parcel of land to another and then to the whole. (378)

Next, all the businesses and social services of the town must be causally related to their effects upon city development. Does the city depend primarily upon industry, commerce, education, or administration for its livelihood, and what is the proportional relationship among these processes? What are the typical house lots and house plans in the city? Where are the overbuilt areas, the distribution of businesses and factories within these areas, the location of recreational facilities, parks, and playgrounds? The answers to all of these questions, plus the series of maps, provided the planner with the information upon which to plan street systems, determine their widths, lay out basic transportation facilities, the distribution of water and sewer mains, the treatment of waterfront areas, the character of residential areas, and the location of industrial and employment centers. Economic conditions must be included in a city survey: ascertaining the wealth of the city in assessed property, a list of city-owned properties and public utilities, the bonded indebtedness, tax rates, and other sources of income. The appearance of nuisances that lessen the economic value of property, such as smoke, noise, billboards, and industrial wastes, must be made known. Finally a survey of the legal tools that affect the implementation of a city plan must be made: tools such as a building code, regulation of nuisances, the uses of police power, eminent domain, and taxation incentives. All of these together completed a survey of the American city, and all of this must be reflected in a map of the city. (24, 386)

This survey and the resultant maps enabled planners to see instantly where people lived and worked, where they played and relaxed, where housing was congested, in which districts crime was prevalent, how goods were transferred from factory to warehouse or store, what special district needs were, and where potential investment areas were. The ultimate step would be to draw comprehensive plans for the ideal development of the whole city, taking into consideration the financial and legal techniques with which the plan could be realized. (169)

Second, disciplinary space assigns a functional location to every land use in order to separate conflicting uses and increase the utility of the whole.

That the town should be laid out with reference to the purposes of its use, in itself marks a revolutionary step in city planning, in America, and yet unless this is done we cannot reasonably say that we are practicing city planning. (522:88)

Thus the physical entities of the city were separated into three general classes: the means of circulation, the distribution and treatment of public spaces, and the remaining private lands. (391) Functional dependencies among land uses were then ascertained and ranked accordingly: those that served the whole city and required a comparatively central position; those that served local areas and requested a neighborhood site; and those private lands subject to public control by the location and division of street systems, building and tenement codes, or taxation controls. (391) As well there existed oppositions among these functional uses—for example, when residential and industrial uses occurred within the same vicinity and these uses therefore must be given separate locations. There were other functions that determined the physical arrangement of the city, such as streets, parks, railways, and waterways; these must be given priority locations. The functioning of some elements was dependent upon others; hence the location of schools and police and fire stations must follow the planning of streets and the location of commercial and residential areas. (378) All of these functional land uses had to be isolated from each other, ranked, and structured one in relationship to another.

Before 1907 industrial development had occurred indiscriminately throughout the city, with no regard to the effect upon the whole. If industrial location could be "controlled or directed then development might lead to the organic whole functioning properly in all its parts. . . . [It would be] possible to plan improvements for the future for any section and be certain they were the proper ones when the time came to carry them out." (58:216) In other words a disciplined land order with a plan for its organization and development would offer something more than could be accounted for by the parts alone. The parts demanded organization. The utility of land had to be divided into classes and the relationships and dependencies among these residential, industrial, and commercial uses needed to be arranged into a purposive whole. Transportation locations determined the structure of the whole city plan. Business areas, for example, depended upon a close proximity to local transportation routes and intersection points of the strongest lines of local travel; industrial areas, on the other hand, could best be controlled or concentrated along the lines of the railways. The rest of the land remained for residential uses. The prestigious areas preempted the pleasing and naturally advantaged sections, general residential areas lay along thoroughfares and railways lines, and tenement areas were found close to industrial sites and in pockets close to the center of town. E. H. Bennett foresaw that if communities learned to structure their form such that industrial areas were concentrated so residential areas could remain intact, then they would develop to a maximum their industrial and commercial potentialities yet safeguard and order the city as a whole. (58)

Third, disciplinary space calls for a temporal ordering of land uses, a conscious forecasting to the extent the facts permitted of expected land needs for collective purposes and the intelligent outlining of methods to protect enough public land from private development. (394) The process of city planning was a matter of proceeding logically from the known to the unknown. It started with a careful analysis of present conditions, defined the standards to be fulfilled in the future, and then separated all of the projects and potential land uses into classes according to their urgency: "working in this way, one soon discovers that in almost every case there is one, and only one, logical and convincing solution of the problems involved." (162:31)

Before a new planning project could become a reality, it had to be matched against the general plan: a program of events to be followed one after another, a scheme that controlled and guided the future physical formation and alteration of the city in its entirety. (83) The city plan was a "device or piece of administrative machinery for preparing and keeping . . . up to date, a unified forecast and definition of the important changes, additions, and extensions of the physical equipment and arrangement of the city . . . so as to avoid . . . ignorantly wasteful action and ignorantly wasteful inaction in control of the city's physical growth." (394:12–13) It was not a fixed record mapped out on paper by a few selected authorities but instead was a reflection of the generation of needs to be met by a flexible reconstruction and readjustment of the plan (394:12) A city plan was thus conceived "as a live thing, as a growing and gradually changing aggregation of accepted ideas or projects for physical changes in the city, all consistent with each other and each surviving, by virtue of its own inherent merit and by virtue of its harmonizing with the rest." (393:5)

There is no particular place of beginning, and certainly no end in sight, for we are concerned with a continuous vital process of the social organism which we call a city. The same ground must be traversed again and again. But the line of movement is not a circle. It is a hopefully rising spiral. So long as you are headed in the right way and don't stand still, it doesn't make much difference where you begin to push first. (393:10)

City planning, F. L. Olmsted, Jr., claimed, dealt with

multifarious problems involved in the future physical growth and physical improvement of the city as a complex whole, toward the collating of the most promising solutions proposed for a great many of these diverse problems, and toward the welding of these pieces of a plan into a harmonious, self-consistent general scheme by a process of mutual adjustment, elimination and supplemental planning. (393:3)

But how were future needs to be adjusted to the traditional and valuable parts of the city? On the one hand "Good city planning is especially careful to preserve local traditions, old buildings of historical value and everything that accentuates the individuality of a city." (83:23) On the other hand, "Old buildings, old streets, old institutions must give way . . . to new and different generations." (394:10) Changes of use and the reconstruction and readjustment of the city plan were normal features of a healthy, vigorous, municipal life. (394) Since the major feature that city planning must attend to was "the conservation and restoration of impaired land values," a demolition mentality rapidly destroyed any preservation instincts. With the rapid shift of land uses in American cities, we are told that permanent blighting can result unless a new impulse from outside transforms and rebuilds the necessary areas. (110) This outside impulse must come from city planning.

As Frederick C. Howe explained,

City planning treats the city as a unit, as an organic whole, . . . [it] anticipates the future with the foresightedness of an army commander so as to secure the orderly, harmonious and symmetrical development of the community . . . [it] makes provision for people as well as industry . . . [it is] the first conscious recognition of the unit of society . . . [and it] involves a new vision of the city. It means a city built by experts, in architecture, landscape gardening, in engineering and in housing; by students of health, transportation, sanitation, water, gas, and electricity, by a new type of municipal officers who visualize the complex life of a million people. (238:186)

Fourth, and most important, the needs and demands of economic production must be considered. Conflicts among the uses of land, increasing demands for public services, and expanding populations all required an economics of scarcity and efficiency. A perfectly disciplined city was an efficient city; what was accidental was costly in time, effort, and resources necessary to achieve an adjusted balance of the whole. Thus the universal principle behind the preparation of each city plan was the calculation of "economy and the saving of waste in an endeavor to secure the desired results for a minimum of expense."[2] Not only must planning improve the efficiency of its circulatory network and hence enable a rapid exchange of goods, but it must maintain and secure private capital's investments in profitable areas and pay for itself as well.

The city plan was designed to encourage commerce and to facilitate the transaction of business. The money value of a good plan could be shown "not by forcing exaggerated values at some points, but by stimulating a healthy growth, through ease of access to all sections of the city, to schools, libraries, museums, parks and playgrounds, it [was] only necessary to examine the successive annual assessment roles of districts so favored." (295:151)

The economic logic of physical land-use planning for the American city was characterized by

an acceptance that efficient production and greater accumulation of capital depended upon a rational coordination of infrastructure and services to parallel production and circulation needs,

an allocation of land parcels to their most profitable use and the relegation of less profitable needs to cheap and unproductive land, and

the speculative hope that these higher land uses would produce an additional source of revenue and hence pay for the implementation costs of the initial improvements.

These were the arguments by which planners tried to convince private investors and property owners to look to planning. For example, after a week's tour of Detroit in 1905, F. L. Olmsted, Jr., and Charles M. Robinson concentrated their improvement plans on the front of the city, a special half-mile river margin that was the focal point of the city's economy, where all of the main streets and car lines converged, where the financial and office district was centered, and where the principal retail district tended to radiate in every direction. This was the area in which the steamboat concerns, the merchants and manufacturers who shipped and received freight by boat, the transportation franchises that took care of passengers and freight on the land side must cooperate and plan a coordinated traffic pattern. The general prosperity and economic growth of this city, they argued, depended upon the speed, convenience, and general satisfaction with which this traffic was organized. They recommended the best way to handle freight, passenger traffic, steamship pavilions, and elevated electric car tracks such that each function had its proper location, with passengers separated from the hurly-burly of heavy teams and rough teamsters and so that freight could rapidly circulate. At the base of their argument stood the belief that if this great public and private improvement scheme was adopted, then the adjacent property would become so valuable that rents from this land alone would be sufficient to pay the entire charges on any number of other municipal improvements. (467)

Another example can be drawn from the plans for a new public market for Newark, New Jersey, proposed in 1912. The old market, housed in a long one-story building, was too small a space for all of the farmers' wagons and wholesale markets, which were spreading out along the surrounding streets. Noisy farmers and retail wagons arrived during the early hours of the morning, disturbing the entire neighborhood. Located on its old site the market had become a nuisance: the smell, noise, clutter, and congestion of teams of horses and generally unsanitary conditions were objectionable to those who lived in that neighborhood. This admirably located site, planners noted, would be ideal for at least $1 million worth of office building improvement, which would produce yet another $20,000 in taxes. In addition after this nuisance was removed, all of the surrounding property would immediately increase in value. The planners estimated that when all of the additional revenues were added together, that instead of being a financial liability it would produce $60,000 to $70,000 per year. (169)

Planners could use legal and taxing powers in order to implement this disciplinary order. Since almost all of the infrastructure needs of the American city were contained in a city plan, to obtain them in the sequence and location desired required prudent financing. During the nineteenth century, it was commonly believed that future generations would benefit from planned investments; hence future generations should pay for their implementation costs. In consequence many cities and states financed their improvements in a reckless manner. New York State, for example, raised a fifty-year bond for highway improvements, borrowing $100 million to pay for ten years of roads. (296:361) Near New York City, for another example, two towns were authorized in 1865 to raise a few thousand dollars apiece for the improvement of a highway that passed through their boundaries. By 1868 this act was amended to allow the towns to raise "such sums as may be necessary" but still requiring that not more than one thousand dollars fall due in any one year. Altogether over the years in order to implement these improvements, there were 178 different bonds raised, the last of which would fall due in 1947. (296:361–362) Financial disaster was imminent, warned Nelson Lewis (a municipal engineer in New York), when cities pay for their improvements with money borrowed for a period longer than the life of the structure or service itself. Most towns, he advised, must rely on their taxation powers and apply special assessments to pay for their improvements because the larger the borrowed debt, the greater the interest and sinking fund charges and hence the less the ability to pay for future improvements. (296:363)

Most of the improvements that fell under the category of city planning were scarcely self-sustaining investments. Realignment of roadways, extension of sewer mains, erection of public buildings, bridges, and docks were often corrections of defects in a badly developed city pattern. Should property owners be assessed to pay for these defects? Lewis notes that invariably every improvement creates a local benefit of adjoining property, "and where there is local benefit there should be local assessment." (296:364) For example, when New York built its first rapid-transit subway, within seven years the actual land values in the upper parts of Manhattan and the Bronx increased $8.5 million above the normal increase of land values. If those properties had been assessed in proportion to the benefits they received, then not only would the costs of the subway have been met, but the property owners would still have netted a profit. (296:365) In general, then, would not the neighborhood that contained the location of a new public buiding assume such a character after its improvement that its value might be doubled or tripled? Should property in distant parts of the city, which remain unaffected by these improvements, bear the same proportion of the assessment burdens while neighboring properties are considerably enriched? Lewis proclaimed that to the degree that the special assessment plan is adopted, to the same degree will the city place itself upon a cash rather than upon a credit base, and to that degree improvement plans will be profitable in the city.[3]

There was no commercial mechanism whereby the public demand for civic buidings, traffic thoroughfares, schoolhouses, parks, and so forth would beget their supply; it required deliberate cooperative action. (394) Hence one of the basic features of intelligent city planning must be a careful scrutiny of the application of the police power and powers of eminent domain, which could affect the form, character, and location of improvements and the careful alteration of a city's development pattern.

It was proposed that American cities might be able to pay for improvements if they were allowed to exercise "the right of excess condemnation." If a city could acquire land adjacent or contiguous to a site of public improvement—to take into ownership through the power of eminent domain more land than was needed for an improvement—it could sell the surplus land after the project had been completed and increased land values had been realized. Thus the profit from this sale would pay for the initial improvements. Most state constitutions severely limited the taking of private property to the precise amount of land necessary for a specific improvement, which made the implementation of city plans extremely expensive. No private property could be taken through the power of eminent domain except for public use and then only by giving just compensation. The definition of this public use, moreover, was held to a limited meaning. As Nelson Lewis noted, most of the opposition against an increased meaning to "public use," and hence an expanded power of eminent domain that would enable excess condemnation, came from the fact that shrewd real estate operators derived their profits by speculating on the route or location of a public improvement, acquiring land in the surrounding district, and selling this land only after values increased as a result of the public improvement. (296:380)

In consequence planners held few powers to enforce their disciplinary order and no way to make the general public accept their plans. A change in the method of assessment, amendments to expand the powers of condemnation, circled back in the end to public acceptance. Would the property owners along a proposed street widening or within a neighborhood to be benefited by a new public building approve additional assessments or consider it a loss of property for which they had not been duly compensated? Would the reduction of speculative land costs constitute a new "public use" and hence expand the power of eminent domain? In 1904 the state of Ohio enabled its cities the right to resell excess land acquired for public purposes, but this land could be acquired and then resold with restricted uses in order to protect the view, appearance, light, air, and general usefulness of the grounds surrounding public improvements or to provide esplanades and parkways as approaches to public structures. Massachusetts also gave cities power to acquire the remnants of land near a public improvement that were too small for the erection of a new building yet were potentially damaging to adjacent property values if left to deteriorate in appearance. Rhode Island, Wisconsin, Virginia, and Maryland as well amended their constitutions to enable condemnation of private land within "reasonable limits." But these limits were tightly supervised. Essentially the definition of public use remained an inflexible concept, and courts instead tended to solidify against its expanded use. (49)

Thus the fundamental laws relating to the implementation and financing of a city plan set a severe boundary beyond which the American city was not allowed to trespass for the sake of disciplining private property to the general needs of the city or acquiring its ownership for an expanded public purpose. The only limit that appeared flexible was the use of the police power: regulating land for the health and general welfare of the community. These regulations, however, were far from compulsory preventions, and the courts continued for several decades to maintain a distinct separation between the powers of condemnation and the powers of regulation.

5

Functional Requirements of a City Plan

The new field of planning focused on the problem of inefficient and destructive land and traffic congestion, the need to separate nuisance land uses from more profitable areas, the desire to promote home ownership as a decentralizing force, and the concern to establish public services at minimal consumer costs. The comprehensive plan unfurled around these functional components and strategic tactics, all of which revealed the crisis of congestion produced by the system of private property. The inability of regulatory planning controls to solve any of their associated problems eventually gave rise to a transformation within planning—a splintering into zoning ordinances, regional plans, and finally a new alliance between economic programs and state welfare policies. Before exploring these transformations, we must attend to the initial strategies against congestion, which planning marked out upon the form of the American city.

Congestion meant an intolerable jumble of railway lines, and an uncoordinated street system within the hearts of most American cities. Inadequate port facilities and warehouse and freight depots thwarted economic prosperity. Intensive development and random assortments of land uses were destructive to the best real estate investments and throttled a rapid pace of building activity. Thus a disciplinary order—a set of land-use plans and zoning regulations—needed to be placed upon these effects of congestion. But population and land congestion created as well profitable investment areas in public service utilities such as rapid-transit lines and tenement housing. These were areas where a compulsory disciplinary order was out of harmony with the laws of private property and capital accumulation. Since the upward spiral of transport and building investment can be viewed as the motive force behind overall economic prosperity in this era of capital growth, planners were restrained from holding more than an apologetic or advisory role with respect to these primary investment areas.

Let us explore each of the production and circulation barriers that thwarted economic development in the center of the American city: traffic and harbor congestion, intensive land utilization, housing requirements, and rapid-transit provisions. As we do, we must keep in mind the major dilemma of planning under capitalism: to impose diciplinary order over urban spatial development in order to transcend some of the barriers that thwarted economic prosperity yet to secure profitable investment areas under the control of capital and not in the hands of municipal regulators.

By 1911 city planning had come to mean the promotion of an orderly and attractive development of a city and its environs. It no longer exclusively meant the promotion of municipal art or the architecture of public buildings. (295:147) The spectacular plans to create civic centers with striking architectural features in Cleveland and in Chicago, for example, were claimed to be admirable ideas, although they would mean the destruction of costly improvements and the entire rearrangements of street systems. Memphis, Kansas City, Los Angeles, and Seattle were all working toward the execution of monumental plans along lines that would stagger the more conservative cities of the East. To redeem some of our cities from the commonplace was by now a commonplace and laudable approach, but many planners felt these plans were extravagant beyond the hope of realization. (295:153)

A Battle with Land and Traffic Congestion

The new improvers believed that the American city must now not only respond to the problems of cultural and social reproduction but address the production and circulation needs of capital as well. In 1911 Nelson Lewis remarked upon these transformations; city planning, he said,

is simply the exercise of such foresight as will promote the orderly and sightly development of a city and its environs along rational lines, with proper regard for the health and convenience of the citizens and for the commercial and industrial advancement of the community. It does not mean or even include municipal art, nor does it in [Lewis's] opinion include the architecture of public or semi-public buildings . . . .
The object should be to reduce to a minimum the resistance to both intra- and inter-urban traffic. This applies not only to ordinary street traffic, whether by vehicles or surface railways, but to steam and electrically operated railroads for the transportation of passengers and freight. (295:147–148)

Hence city plans must provide for direct and ample thoroughfares, so vital for railroad lines and terminals, "in such a manner as to reduce as far as possible the time and expense of transportation to and from home, office, shop or factory, from and to points outside the city." "The city

plan," Lewis continued, "is the general plan of arterial streets and transportation lines by which the different sections of the existing and future
city will be connected with each other and with the centers of population
outside the city limits. . . . This is the real city plan which will control
future city development." (295:148, 150)

Discussing the Chicago plan of 1909, Walter Moody underlined the
same change of emphasis in city planning when he said, "Building cities
as they should be, means supplying the greatest possible lubricant to an
easy and successful commerce." To improve and systematize city thoroughfares is to facilitate the transferring and circulation of goods and
thus directly aid commerce. By making possible the best railway lines and
terminal facilities, commerce would be advanced. (355:41) The problem
was how to accomplish this goal. Thirty-five percent of the entire central
city of Chicago was given to railway approach and switching tracks. Twenty-
two trunk lines entered Chicago from different directions, and six passenger
terminals existed within the center city alone. The economic prosperity
of the city, so it was said, required that freight be dispatched at the lowest
cost through one common freight system, one common depositing and
reloading station located at the point most economically advantageous
for all. (356) A solution was sought in spite of the fact that many un-
cooperative and competitive capital interests were involved, and in consequence the massive plan of Chicago, which cost its sponsors more than
$300,000 to research and produce and which was in many ways the
crystallization of the city beautiful and civic betterment crusades, pledged
itself to produce a centralized and consolidated system of transportation.
It proposed a properly connected street system and a readjustment and
harmonization of the maze of railway facilities, and although its ideal fell
short of economic and political reality, these efforts show that the battle
against congestion was becoming more important as the 1900s advanced
than was the provision of public parks and civic architecture. (356:343)

The motive for this changing perspective rested upon the economically
wasteful pattern of land use in the American city. Rather than accept this
shifting composition as a normal and natural procedure of city evolution,
land was being reassessed as a valuable investment commodity. Securing
these investments required altering the regulatory rules. Thus let us first
explore the undisciplined laissez faire principle of land development before
turning to the reactions that arose against it.

When Richard Hurd, an investment adviser to the U.S. Mortgage and
Trust Company, searched in 1895 for a book on the production and
evolution of value in urban real estate, he found none. So he took upon
himself the task of describing the structure of cities and the flow of land
values attached to different utilities. His theories were typical of those

who believed economic order resulted by allowing natural laws their free play. For Hurd the message was simple: the utility of American land changes rapidly, and restrictions of any kind should be avoided if land values are to reach their optimum levels. In consequence the distribution of all land utilities was purely economic: land went to the highest bidder, the one who could make land earn the largest amount. (244)

An understanding of the natural or evolutionary structure of cities, Hurd believed, would help to underscore his advice. The highest priced land in any city, he explained, was the financial district. In cities without a major financial center, retail shopping land attained the highest value. Residential land values were determined not by economic principles but by social determinations, such as availability, prestige, the age of the neighborhood, and so on. In southern cities, for example, where the scale of business activity was slight, residential land values held the highest value due to the great social virtues identified with the owning and embellishing of residential areas. (244:144)

The first separation of land use occurred when business began to separate itself from dwellings (originally buildings had business on the first floor and residences above). Next, schools, hospitals, and theaters sought diverse and advantageous locations. Retail stores either clustered at the business centers or followed the major transport lines. Bulk wholesaling sought a location along these lines or close to their terminals, and small-item wholesaling located near to customers, the retail stores. Railroads located passenger terminals as close to the business center as possible and their freight terminals near the docks or bulk manufacturing areas. Separate sections slowly evolved for administration and for manufacturing uses. (244) Expansion of the city center occurred simply by acquiring adjoining land, by building upward, or by shifting the center. The banking and office districts solved their needs by building higher or pressing upon the retail and wholesale districts. Since retail shops required ground-floor frontage on thoroughfares, they began a slow but steady procession away from the center by gravitating toward the best residential districts. Left behind, the old retail areas were turned into new wholesale districts. (244:85)

Streetcar railways revolutionized the structure of cities by making available for residential purposes vast new areas of cheap land on the circumference of the city. As a result a greater part of the population now lived in the suburbs and commuted to the city for work, and traffic became more concentrated within the city center. By increasing the number of dangerous intersections, streetcar railways had hastened the movement of the higher-class retail shops. Meanwhile transfer stops with their concentration of people began to create strategic new subcenters for business. Thus in every American city, Hurd argued, more or less naturally in response to transportation innovations and ability to pay, urban land uses and values distributed themselves into financial, commercial, industrial, and residential districts. (244:95)

It was not long, however, before a host of voices began to rise against this unregulated, so-called natural land order. Land values vary in proportion to population density, said Benjamin Marsh. (332) The more congested the land, the higher its value. The cost that must be paid for land to be used for any public improvement "may be designated as the cost paid as tribute by the community for congestion of population." (332:15) Congestion of land and people results from land speculation that produces too intensive a use of land. Because capital interests desire the higher values created by more congestion and hence refuse to provide adequate and appropriate means of transportation, in turn the American city fails to adopt proper standards to control the distribution and production of its land uses. (332) "American city planning," Marsh continued, "in the main has been a method of rewarding speculation in land at the expense of the taxpayer. It has been a striking illustration of metonomy, has concerned itself chiefly with these outer and more interesting aspects of the city's development, such as parks, playgrounds, civic centers or groupings of public buildings." (332:39)

Other allegations were made against congestion and city planning. A 1911 study in New York City underlined faulty taxation and assessment methods, which enabled landowners to hold unimproved property with low tax rates off the market while improvements were taxed at the highest return. Thus developers required an intensive utilization of both land and buildings if they were to return a profit on even meager improvements. (423) Concentration of landownership was another factor creating congestion. For example, in greater New York by 1908, another study claimed that 23 corporations owned one-ninth of the total acreage of the Bronx, two real estate companies owned and controlled one-sixth of Brooklyn, and eight families owned one-twentieth of Manhattan. Many of these monopolies held their land in large, unimproved estates with moderate tax assessments. As a result development was squeezed onto available land, primarily in the heart of Manhattan. (441) By 1910 the assessed value for ordinary land in Manhattan was nearly 75 percent of the entire assessed value of greater New York. (441:10) Correlated closely with this uneven assessment pattern went industrial congestion. Over two-thirds of all factory workers in New York, for example, were concentrated in Lower Manhattan and one-half of these located on the West Side between Fourteenth and Twentieth streets on what amounted to one-seventh of the total area of the city. (441:11)

Thus the economics of land development contributed to congestion and the growth of an irrational spatial pattern. As the city grows, Lewis explained, land is subdivided into smaller blocks and lots; the better class of residential districts are converted over time into cheap tenements or into combined shops and flats, and these in turn are displaced by warehouses and factories. Far from being a natural evolution of city growth, Lewis recalled that most of the lot subdivisions were determined by real estate speculators who divide each block into lot sizes that are easy to sell. City authorities as well facilitate the most rapid development of an area into building lots and houses. The builders of tall skyscrapers in the heart of the city were no better. These structures, Lewis claimed, were seldom erected out of a felt need for more office space but built by corporations or developers on the faith that eventually they would become commercially profitable yet in the meantime hold sufficient advertising value to pay for and to justify their present construction. (296:126–127)

The failure to plan the development of land in the American city, to make provisions for the gradual adaptation of streets to new needs, caused massive traffic congestion in downtown sections. The cost of widening streets became prohibitive after land had reached a high value and these same streets had been improved with costly buildings. (441) A 1907 improvement plan for New York City estimated that the damage of land stagnation in Lower Manhattan and the devaluation of existing buildings due to street congestion ran close to $100 million. The improvement plan therefore advocated the creation of new roads and suggested the widening of several others to ease the flow of traffic and to benefit downtown land values. (442)

Pittsburgh too began to remove the stranglehold of traffic congestion from the heart of its office district. An 18.5-acre hump was leveled, street grades were lowered 16 feet or so, and buildings of twenty stories or more were underpinned and their facades remodeled in order to facilitate the overall flow of traffic. Smaller-scale improvements in other cities focused on overdeveloped city blocks by designing new street patterns for those blocks whose interiors had been filled in with unplanned structures. (296:35–41)

Slowly advisory plans were being developed for the relief of traffic congestion. Their implementation, however, was dependent upon the realization by businessmen that overall prosperity demanded a quickened pace of circulation within the American city. When George Ford described the Newark city plan of 1912 to its city fathers, he pointed to the businessman. Although the businessman was concerned with efficiency, Ford felt that too often he remained unaware that gains in production efficiency were all but lost through waste of time, money, and energy occasioned by the problems of getting his goods to and from his place of business. This was due to narrow, indirect, even badly paved streets over which he was obliged to do his trucking. Such transportation problems were exacerbated by improperly placed docks and freight terminals and due as well to the necessity of forcing workers to live in unhealthy quarters at distances too far from their work. (169:5–6) The great future in city planning, Ford predicted, lay in the recognition by businessmen that they must apply to the city as a whole the same principles of organization and efficiency that they used in their industrial and commercial plans. Hence the heart of every city plan must be to realign and regrade current streets, to effect easy and direct communication between day and night habitation for the working population, to relieve street congestion during working hours, and above all to increase the speed with which goods reached their markets and buyers their potential goods. (169:7)

Boston's city fathers called for the same relief of traffic congestion. Pressure was building up in that city too for transportation improvements. Downtown interests wanted a new street to parallel the major shopping street. Such a street would eliminate a fire hazard and would relieve traffic already jammed beyond its capacity. Neighborhoods to the south of the city wanted a new tunnel with a rapid-transit connection to the center of the city; other districts wanted a tunnel extension to the east and still other a western tunnel. It was believed that Boston's future role as the hub of New England was handicapped because there were no major thoroughfares or circumferential routes to facilitate the transfer of goods through the 39 surrounding towns and villages in the metropolitan whole. (191:108–110) Separate towns spent thousands of dollars to build streets that did not connect with one another, and transportation by wagon, motor truck, or electric car was not effectively linked. (485:432–434)

These city fathers warned that New England was experiencing industrial anemia. Almost all of its manufacturing had been established prior to the last great wave of improvements in machinery and methods. As a result manufacturing was being pulled toward the Far West and the South. (184:99–101) By reducing the costs in handling goods and materials, by perfecting Boston's equipment as a trading center, by enticing business to move to the hub, the city fathers formulated, only then would Boston be assured a bright economic future. (265:382–385) When the Panama Canal was finished, they warned, the world's pattern of commerce would change and that would call forth the real beginning of an industrial age for all coastal cities. (48) But Boston, they asserted, would be abandoned as a manufacturing center unless there was a constructive program to stem the tide. Because the city lay farther from the source of raw materials than its competitors in the Far West and the South, it had to learn how to perfect its transit and shipping facilities in order to reduce the cost of handling goods and materials. So, they argued, it must invest first in municipal improvements to facilitate the money earning capacity of Boston, and then it must promote as well a policy of labor conservation to increase the productivity of its manufacturing operations. (266)

At a time of intense competition among cities, new metropolitan-wide planning was seen as an imperative if Boston was to survive in the race for supremacy between the ports of Portland, New York, and Baltimore. Private planners complained they could no longer deal with an unplanned community in a businesslike manner, either for their own or for the city's advantage. The great railway and steamship companies devised plans to increase their usefulness to the port of Boston, and yet they could find no authority that advocated solutions from the city's point of view. Boston citizens disliked the yearly assessments imposed by metropolitan authorities for sewers, parks, and water systems; they therefore refused to allow more revenues to be allocated for better and more efficient transportation and shipping facilities. Meanwhile the great railway and steamship lines continued to plan; if no help came from Boston, then the city fathers feared they would turn to other, more competitive locations. (485)

Boston's handicaps must be overcome if for no other reason than to increase the money earning capacity of the city. The city plan they outlined organized all of the rapid-transit and steam railways in the metropolitan area into a coordinated passenger system; direct connections were drawn between the freight lines and with the waterfront; new docks were planned and located so that they connected with each other and with the railway lines; radial and circumferential thoroughfares were projected to ease the flow of goods and vehicles across the metropolitan whole. Only the adoption of a plan, the city fathers proposed, would enable Boston to link together all the productive elements that composed its industrial might. (485)

Zoning and Districts

By producing an uneven spatial development and an overintensive utilization of land, congestion was also considered an economic waste. Sections of Lower Manhattan were so poorly developed that planners claimed improvements in those areas were worthless. Between 1906 and 1916 nearly ten thousand property owners within New York filed for a reduction in the assessed value of their real estate holdings, alleging that values had been depreciated throughout the city by the erection on neighboring lands of too lofty a building or one that covered too large a proportion of the lot. Intensive land utilization meant that streets were congested, buildings deprived of direct access, the interior of blocks darkened, the character of the neighborhoods destroyed, and in consequence land values diminished. So too in the outer boroughs the sprawling character of building development created high rents but low property values. Thus the argument arose, "to preserve the value of land, and the value of buildings it is essential to regulate type, height, and area of land covered by buildings." (428)

It may seem paradoxical, Nelson Lewis advised in 1913,

to hold that a policy of restrictions tends to fuller utilization of land than a policy of no restriction; but such is undoubtedly the case. The reasons lie in the greater safety and security to investment secured by definite restrictions. The restrictions tend to fix the character of the neighborhood. The owner therefore feels that if he is to secure the maximum returns from his land, he must promptly improve it in conformity with the established restrictions. (296:348)

Unimproved and poorly utilized land, he believed, resulted because owners feel the character of a section is changing or that its permanent character is yet unknown and thus forgo investments. Restrictions, on the other hand, would forecast the general character of an area and promote the uniform arrangement and improvement of these holdings. If development remained uncontrolled, an uneven development pattern would result and an enormous loss would occur from building obsolescence. This obsolescence hazard, Lewis explained, is the lack of adaptation to function. It not only retards real estate improvements; it also leads to an inevitable decline in rental and property values if improvements are forgone and eventually imposes even greater costs when reconstruction begins. (296:349)

Not surprisingly by 1913 as an increase in building activity followed closely upon accelerating transportation investments, the leading real estate investors and business and manufacturing men in the American city started to reject the so-called natural evolution of land uses and began instead to look to methods by which the value of their improvements and buildings could be secured. On the East Coast this activity first gained momentum in New York City. Along most of the retail streets in the early 1900s, one could witness the common practice of encroachments of steps, porches, show windows, entrances, and columns into the streets. City efforts to remove these invasions generally met with resistance from individual property owners. By 1910, however, New York began to correct this abuse. It had been the common practice even with expensive buildings along Fifth Avenue to place entrances, steps, bay windows, fences, and sunken gardens so that they extended way beyond the street line. Now that these stately old homes had begun to give way to commercial buildings, vehicle and pedestrian traffic had increased along the avenue, and merchants in consequence began to pressure for a stricter enforcement of the city's rights to remove all these obtrusive encroachments. (296:263)

The same enforcements were applied to narrower downtown streets where intrusions were even more serious. Loading platforms were commonly erected in front of wholesale provision houses, and it was said that their removal would create an economic hardship and necessitate a change in the conduct of business. But slowly street ordinances requiring their removal began to go into effect, and as they did, other businessmen petitioned for their extensions, now convinced that the removal of these obstructions and the widening of streets enhanced their own undertakings. So generally had these ordinances been accepted by 1915 that

title insurance companies and financial institutions which loan money for building operations, and who were formerly inclined to be insistent upon the right of the abutting owners to occupy a portion of the sidewalk in front of their property, now refuse to insure titles or loan money on buildings having such encroachments. (296:264)

Fifth Avenue in 1911 was lined with public buildings, high-class retail shops, churches, valuable private dwellings, apartments, and hotels. Because city revenues from this land alone were so high, the city appointed the Fifth Avenue Commission to maintain the economic vitality of the area. This commission would prepare recommendations for the removal of encroachments and would suggest the establishment of uniform restrictions for cornice heights along the avenue, the relocation of sweatshops, manufacturing establishments, or dry goods and wearing apparel, and the placement and design of signs and windows. Conditions along Fifth Avenue had become so bad that during noon hour, between Fourteenth and Twenty-third streets, a multitude of factory operators loitered along the streets. It was feared that objectionable signs and billboards and misplaced street and shop lighting would turn the avenue into a gaudy replica of Broadway with an ensuing decline in land values. (425)

In 1912 the commission tried to suppress the further construction of "lofty" structures on the avenue and its side streets. Real estate values were too high, they felt, to permit the continued use of these tall buildings as factories. Property owners above Twenty-third Street were in almost unanimous agreement that the street must be saved from the blight that spread from these structures, and soon they were joined by other property owners of greater New York. (438)

One of the major factors of congestion in New York was the great concentration of factories and workers in Lower Manhattan. Between 1906 and 1907 the new factories located in greater New York numbered

3,060, of which the vast majority could be found in Manhattan alone. (441:11) The aim of city planning in New York City thus became the segregation of factories within their own districts and, if possible, their removal from Manhattan. Districts bordering the waterfront and other lines of transportation, it was agreed, were already dedicated to manufacturing and freight. These sections could thus be reserved for such uses while prohibiting their appearance elsewhere. (441:22) So, another congestion report continued, sufficient conducements and restrictions could eventually drive all manufacturing industry out of Manhattan: first by eliminating the most obnoxious, then gradually raising the standards of working conditions and prohibiting in certain areas the location of any new factories, and finally by giving cash bonuses for removal when large machinery and costly relocation were involved. (423)

Agitation for land-use controls eventually led the Board of Estimate and Apportionment in New York City to appoint a committee in 1913 to investigate and report upon the necessity for controlling the height, size, and arrangements of buildings and for distributing their uses throughout the entire city. In time, this report announced, they had found conclusive evidence for the need to control building development and charged that "the present almost unrestricted power to build to any height over any proportion of the lot, for any desired use and in any part of the city, has resulted in injury to real estate and business interest and to the health, safety and general welfare of the city." (544:2) They recommended that a charter amendment give the Board of Estimate the power to divide the city into land-use zones and to control the height and use of buildings in each zone. Fifth Avenue was to be treated as a special zone from which future factories would be excluded and where heights would be limited to one and a half times the width of the street. Only at the cross section with Forty-second Street would skyscrapers be allowed. (439)

By 1914 a draft charter amendment had become law, and by 1916 a zone plan for the City of New York had been adopted. Five classes of height districts were set, limiting building heights to a varying multiple of street widths. Throughout most of the city, four or five stories was the limit. No building of any kind could be built higher than fourteen stories except by setting it back from the street one foot for every one and a half feet in height. The skyline of New York was given special attention; mansards, dormer windows, terraces, and any design enabling light to reach the street were especially encouraged.

Two general-use restrictions were adopted for New York: no business or industry could locate in residential districts, and manufacturing, public stables, and garages were forbidden in business districts. As a result two-fifths of Manhattan and two-thirds of the entire city were reserved for strictly residential purpose. The main thoroughfares, the transit streets, and other areas thought to be appropriate for stores and showrooms were set aside as business streets. Thus the central core of Manhattan above Twenty-third Street was declared a business district, requiring the eventual removal of hundreds of factories employing thousands of workers already located in the area. (165:2)

In other American cities too land was being classified into districts and distributed according to use specifications and height regulations. Tenement houses, office structures, and rear lot buildings were regulated in Chicago, Philadelphia, Boston, and Rochester. Chicago restricted residential building heights, Boston regulated heights in its business section, and Washington imposed limits upon buildings along Pennsylvania Avenue. But none of these cities had gone as far as Los Angeles in the restriction of uses. For there an ordinance of 1909 set aside 25 widely scattered industrial districts, reserving the remainder of its land for residential purposes. Within these strictly residential districts, only 58 areas were designated to be exceptions where business could be allowed. Small laundries, backyard kilns, and machine shops were evicted from strictly residential districts. Seattle, Baltimore, Minneapolis, St. Paul, and Duluth were also among the pioneers that began to separate residential areas from industrial districts. (296:282)

A zone plan, its real estate supporters claimed, would relieve undue congestion, improve business districts by outlawing factories, protect residential areas, relieve inconveniences that thwarted rapid-transit systems, and above all else preserve and enhance real estate values. (165:5) It was noted that only "a few years ago any plan for such regulations would have had little chance of popular approval, but owners of real estate and building operations appear to realize the danger of unrestricted buildings, and to be ready and anxious to favor action which will prevent further congestion, conserve real estate values, and stabilize the character of districts where that character is desirable and improve it where it is otherwise." (296:353)

Securing real estate investments had become so important that it was not enough for the Fifth Avenue Commission to develop its own report for the avenue and then wait for the legal apparatus of the city to take effect. They wanted the factory operators out of their district. Thus between 1913 and 1915, before the zone plan had passed into law, the commission began a serious factory campaign to ensure a strict enforcement of a new occupancy law. Their tactics combined investigating garment factory conditions, obtaining enforcement promises from the State Department of Labor, and campaigning for even tighter limits on the allowable number of employees in any one factory. Slowly they began to drive the factories out of Manhattan. In 1914 the commission investigated 120 of the 700 in the Fifth Avenue district. Only twenty-three of these they found to be in full compliance with the law, but their constant surveillance forced many of the others either to let their workers go or to abandon their present location. (440) Another investigatory campaign in 1915 showed that their efforts had removed 20,000 workers, while they sought the relocation of at least another 33,000. Within that year, 200 factories employing 30,000 workers were removed. Only the cream of the trade was allowed to remain: those whose season lasted longer and could pay the higher rents, and those who could keep a small number of cutters and operators on the premises and afford to send the bulk of their goods to be made up into garments on the Lower East Side or even as far as Brownsville. (439)

Promotion lay at the heart of every successful zoning campaign. Without an aroused public interest, the law would seldom be implemented. Once again the leading merchants, real estate interests, and bankers of Fifth Avenue continued their battle to rid New York of manufacturing establishments. "Shall we save New York?" they advertised in a New York newspaper. "Shall we save it from unnatural and unnecessary crowding, from high rents, from excessive and illy distributed taxation? We can save it from all of these, so far at least as they are caused by one special evil . . . the erection of factories in the residential and famous retail section." This time instead of factory inspections, however, they promised to give preference in their purchases to every firm whose manufacturing plants were located outside the Fifth Avenue district. (296:354)

Slowly the American city was learning how to secure real estate from destructive congestion and to discipline nuisance land uses that reduced its land values. Yet two other problems still generated congestion within the center of the American city: unimproved tenement housing and inadequate rapid-transit facilities. If zoning was to begin the long push of factories toward the metropolitan rim, then how would the workers follow their path? Congestion, it had been pointed out time and again, would be remedied only when improved transit facilities with low rates were coupled with prohibitions on the building of tenements and the substitution of workers' housing in the suburbs.

Building Better Homes for the Working Class

By the early 1900s congestion of land and people had created an abnormal demand for housing, which naturally raised rents and forced the tenement population to live in progressively more congested conditions and even to take in lodgers in order to pay the exorbitant rents. Increasing rents also inflated land values, producing more congestion and lowering still further the standard of living in tenement districts. (441)

Some would argue that municipal and state provision of streets and sewers, the dedication of parks and open space, and the building of public structures and civic plazas contributed to the enrichment of society and that all of these were reflected back into the value of the land. These increases in land values and the aggregating wealth of public utility corporations and building enterprises did not generate a general increase in the wealth of the people but rather expanded the cost of living and reduced overall well-being. It was these spiraling costs and diminishing living standards, or so it was argued, that in the end minimized the amount of wealth that could be consumed and hence placed a limit upon capital's productivity. (237:137) Since land values were socially created, advocates of land reform began to argue that these social advantages embedded in land should not be privately recaptured. A single tax, they argued, would eliminate this unearned social increment without imposing other penalties based on the type of improvement, architectural attractiveness, or quality of structure. If land alone were taxed, then it was believed better buildings and better architecture would result. A single tax would force the immediate improvement of vacant land, creating a surplus, not a shortage, of dwellings, with a reduction in rents naturally following. (296:379)

"Above and beyond the value of franchise privilege, which in the final analysis is itself a land value," Boston reformer Charles Fillebrown observed,

there is one thing, viz., the private appropriation of the net rent of land [total ground rent less taxes], which constitutes the bulk of all privilege and which is of gigantic proportions. . . . The people of the city of Boston pay for the use of Boston land more than fifty millions in taxation, leaving about forty millions net rent to be privately appropriated, every dollar of which represents labor value. (159:95)

Agitation for reform of this land privilege had been underway for years, Fillebrown noted;

it has penetrated or innoculated almost every business field, up to the dead line at which every reform halts, viz., the land, which seems to be the sacred stopping place in the advance upon every social enemy. . . . When people outgrow the pagan fetish that the rent of land should go to the few, instead of to all, when they realize that, taking Boston for example, the worship of this fetish costs its people annually not less than three or four hundred dollars per family . . . then monopoly's line of battle will vanish like the morning dew. (159:96–97)

If the financial profits resulting from land congestion were secured by the community rather than property owners, then, Benjamin Marsh argued, there would be no advantage of massing so many humans on so few acres, as is the common experience in the center of American cities. (331:58)

In spite of these single-tax and social improvement advocates, to whom city planners were beginning to listen, a steady increase in land values and improvements following closely upon the development of street-railway systems kept these areas of land and building investment exclusively for capital exploitation. Between 1899 and 1913 in New York and its five boroughs, for example, the assessed value of real estate increased 207 percent. (296:402) Rough estimates were that out of a total annual investment of $150 million for the entire building construction activity in the city, $100 million of this amount went into the construction of tenements and small houses. (28:94)

We are usually led to think that a rapid rate of urbanization caused overcrowding and unsanitary conditions in the great American city of the nineteenth century, and these conditions led eventually to regulatory reforms and working-class housing legislation. This reform movement is often spoken about in terms of an evolutionary development of thought and practice: first with respect to concerns for public health and over-crowding, then a public attack on the immorality of the slum, and then finally a policy for state subsidies and state-regulated housing. (308) Earlier chapters argued that tenement house surveillance and a desire for more stringent sanitary controls and building codes that organized the spatial arrangement of tenement house life were first and foremost a necessary element for disciplinary control over an unknown and increasingly numerous poor. But this desire for disciplinary control had its own dynamic. Evolving state interest over the life and conditions of tenement dwellers was amplified or depressed by economic conditions, which at times made the profitability of tenement house construction more important than control over the morals and habits of the poor. At still other points the moral uplifting and surveillance of the idle and criminal were seen as mechanisms that themselves would make tenement construction more profitable. In the rising economic prosperity of the earlier twentieth century, these latter motives of profitability affected the discourse of the housing reformer.

Although it was said that the main reasons for a municipal land policy were to control the price of land, to prevent land speculation, and hence to reduce the level of rents for workingmen's housing, in the United States the policy would stop far short of municipal housing. The city was not to be an owner of real estate except where it was needed for nonprofitable public purposes such as road improvements and public buildings. Investment in land with a view to resale or in order to control its price was not an acceptable public purpose. (296)

It seems hardly to be doubted [we are warned] that, were the city to go into the provision of housing for its citizens on a large scale, it would serve to check private investment of the same character, and then tend to create a worse rather than a better condition. There seems to be no lack of capital to provide adequate housing in any city, provided site values have not reached a prohibitive figure. When the city enters into competition for sites within its own area, it tends to enhance their values rather than otherwise, and in this way also tends to defeat its own object. (370:103)

Instead of municipally owned and built housing, claimed Lawrence Veiller, Americans perfected a system of slum control and the removal of bad housing conditions through regulatory laws and their enforcement. The housing problem, he continued, is not just the problem of rapid transit or the provision of cheap housing, as many planners advocated. The problem is enabling the mass of people who want to live in decent surroundings to have such opportunities and to prevent other people from maintaining conditions that are a menace to the general community: "We may as well frankly admit that there is a considerable portion of our population who will live in any kind of abode that they can get irrespective of how unhygienic it may be." (526:71)

How could American cities rid themselves of unsanitary infractions caused by privy vaults if not by legislation? Would new rapid-transit lines or suburban development get rid of these vaults? What if tenement houses were vacated for garden suburbs? What would force the abandoned tenements to be demolished and their land converted to other uses? How could cities get rid of cellar dwellings except to forbid them by law? This, then, is where Lawrence Veiller placed his emphasis on housing reform, the removal of the great mass of housing evils through remedial legislation: "We must get rid of our slums before we establish garden cities. We must stop people living in cellars before we concern ourselves with changes in methods of taxation. We must make it impossible for builders to build dark rooms in new houses before we use the government to subsidize the building of houses, we must abolish privy vaults before we build model tenements." (526:77) Veiller stated in 1911 that although city planning could prevent the growth of many evils in the American city, it was no panacea. The housing problem, he claimed, was essentially the "sanitary control of diverse foreign peoples seeking to adjust themselves to urban conditions of living with which they are unfamiliar. . . . It is the problem of regulating their habits of life; of protecting them from themselves and of protecting the community from the results of their ignorance and carelessness." This sanitation problem, Veiller claimed, was chiefly an issue of good municipal housekeeping based on the prompt removal of garbage and other waste materials, the maintenance of clean streets and alleys, and the provision of proper sanitary conveniences. (522:80–81)

Not everyone agreed that this was the way to relieve housing congestion, for this type of regulatory housing legislation, by failing to make a distinction between citizen building and fortune building, had forgotten to promote the development of home ownership. By neglecting to regulate the building monopolist and land speculators, Edward Hartman felt, improved and regulated housing on new lots had to pay the increased assessments that ought to have been paid by the monopolies and hence foreclosed any opportunity to build low-cost housing: "Monopoly has this advantage over homes reached by housing laws and it also has the power to increase the other costs of living so that people have to move into poorer homes and homeownership becomes more difficult, family life is held back, good instincts are perverted and bad instincts gain a foothold." Restrictive housing laws, he charged, do nothing for wage earners who still had to pay higher rents. He could agree that perhaps better housing conditions improved the worker's efficiency, but this was to the employer's not the employee's benefit. (220:79–80)

Restrictive tenement laws tended to have another effect as well: they produced, said the commissioner of the Tenement House Department in New York, a defiant attitude in the minds of the capitalist and the builder who assumed that housing built under the new laws would not be profitable ventures. For a period of time after a tenement law was enacted, new building activity always stopped while the value of the old buildings continued to increase. Tenement owners took the position that these older buildings were in compliance with former regulations, and if the city wanted to change the standards then the city must pay for these improvements. Thus the Tenement House Department was always tender about enforcing new legislation, so tenement owners continued to rent their unsanitary and unsafe dwellings at exorbitant prices. If they began to suffer a loss in rents, which an improved building would have brought, these handicaps were quickly recouped by a subsequent reduction in taxes as their buildings continued to deteriorate. (370:99) In one form or another, regardless of restrictive legislation, tenement houses remained profitable ventures.

In cities with 150,000 population or less, John Ihlder claimed in 1912, even near the center of town, there usually was not enough demand for offices to use all the stories above the stores on the ground floor. The upper stories of these buildings, which were primarily designed for the accommodation of small retail concerns, must be rented for dwellings or they will stand vacant. "In nearly all of our cities now, such buildings are from three to four stories high and the upper floors are used as dwellings. They are tenement houses, they will continue to be tenement houses and so must be recognized." (253:90) Sections of the city, Ihlder pointed out, were suitable only for tenement house districts, for in these areas land values had risen to such a point that only the income derived from multiple dwellings could yield a fair return on building investment. In addition lots located on noisy business streets or traffic arteries were logical areas for tenement housing. "It is out of the question," said Ihlder, "to consider the detached or even semi-detached house for any but the wealthy." (253:90)

Benjamin Marsh was one of the major challengers of this opinion, wondering what advantages were to be gained by "warehousing people" on overloaded land; he believed "it is a novel statistical incursion . . . into the realm of psychology, to claim that sociability increases in proportion to the number of people living on the acre. It is doubtless a smoothing sentiment to the beneficiaries of capitalized congestion land values." The tendency today in progressive nations, he claimed, was toward small buildings and detached homes, or at least small multiple homes with a garden for each family. This was the fundamental purpose behind the passage of the English Town Planning Act of 1909, the German system of districting or zoning, and the European garden cities movement. (331:54–55) Couldn't American cities provide these opportunities as well?

The best type of workingman's dwelling, housing reformer Lawrence Veiller could agree, was the row or group house, such as the houses provided by Schnidlapp in Cincinnati, Octavia Hill in Philadelphia, and the Improved Housing Association in Philadelpia. But it was not at all desirable, he felt, that the great mass of unskilled workers own their own homes: "The man of low earning capacity has not sufficient financial reserves, nor can he accumulate them, to make it desirable or advantageous for him to become a property owner." Remembering Henry Ford's trouble, Veiller recounted that he had to learn this experience the hard way. When Ford first established his automobile plant in Detroit, he paid all of his workers five dollars a day, believing that men lived in slums because their wages were inadequate. But he soon discovered that even with five dollars a day men tended to live in squalor and filth, preferring to save their money or spend it on personal indulgences. Thus Ford learned that in order to keep control over his unskilled laborers, he had to rent rather than sell them their housing and fire those who still insisted on living in squalid conditions. (527:45, 47)

For the ordinary laborer—that is, the foreign population that predominated in American cities—the detached house, Veiller continued, was a beautiful ideal but not desirable. Unskilled workers could not afford to pay for the vacant land to the front and to the rear of a single-family dwelling. He believed that a flower garden for this class was utopian, not only because of its cost but because these workers had little time to cultivate any garden. Instead the land became unsightly, and bare patches of ground without grass turned into a gathering place for all the waste material of family existence. If planning was intended to control the order of the American city, surely it should not unwittingly support the creation of still further disorder. (522:87–88)

Considerable effort had gone into the planning, construction, and financing of tenements, but there was little thought to the creation of orderly working-class neighborhoods. Yet it was generally recognized that an important aspect of city building was the creation of residential neighborhoods for the better class of homes, in such projects as Brookline, Massachusetts, Roland Park in Baltimore, and Forest Hills Gardens in New York City. In these neighborhoods substantial property values had been secured and land restrictions imposed upon the type of allowable development in order to protect them against future economic failure, a problem commonly suffered by the rapid abandonment of other good residential areas. Insurance companies, banks, and other loan resources easily turned to invest in these carefully planned and safeguarded neighborhoods. (377:133)

Because they felt the building of small homes might be a good capital investment, the Metropolitan Life Insurance Company began to invest in 1911 in the construction and mortgaging of 200 small homes in the borough of Brooklyn. But land values in most parts of Brooklyn were so high that the company was prohibited from building at a low enough cost to come within the range of a worker's allowance. Nor could the company subsidize construction and thus reduce the selling price, for state laws limited the nature of investments that insurance companies could make. New York State, for example, required that these funds be invested to obtain the largest possible return:

It is evident [the company claimed] that the cost for examination, appraisal, supervision of the architects, and the other incidental expenses in lending one million dollars on several hundreds of small mortgages would be considerably larger than to place one such mortgage on a large office building in the heart of New York City, or any other large city, whose present value and whose future value during the period of the mortgage can be definitely determined. (180:104)

Still one of the greatest civic assets would be harmoniously planned and carefully safeguarded workingmen's neighborhoods similar to those developed for better homes. In this era when man is not judged by the number of hours he works but rather by how much he produces, can anyone deny that his efficiency is dramatically affected by his home environment? So Charles Puff claimed, results of company housing provided over the last 25 years in the northeastern section of Philadelphia spoke for themselves: "Evenness of distribution of population produces a higher moral plane, greater sense of responsibility and appreciation of various benefits provided and will tend to produce a natural protection for these [small homes and new communities]. With this cooperation greater projects can be planned and supported and in time no man will be so ignorant as not to appreciate the greatest work of art that man has ever produced— the modern city." (427:153)

Other reformers, while not suggesting the creation of model working-class neighborhoods, did advocate the destruction and redevelopment of slum and tenement districts. Olmsted, Jr., however, complained in 1911 that those who still discussed city planning from the spectacular standpoint created an impression that designing grand new streets through decaying quarters and generally reconstructing and modernizing the defective parts of the American city were regular activities. Instead, he noted, these measures are seldom taken, and "the hope of demolishing slum districts wholesale or arbitrarily converting a district of one kind into a district of a wholly different kind by any process of city planning may be dismissed as futile." (391:37)

The city plan could improve the evil of the deep lot. Since the street plan determined the size of blocks, and these in turn determined the lots, all of these elements Veiller believed could come under the control of the city plan. Thus for tenement districts, shallow lot depths could be required, and in this way housing of not more than two rooms in depth would result. (522:82–86) This is the point where the housing and city planning movements overlapped because the concern with better housing conditions meant a concern with the development of the transportation system as a whole and because the street system determined the depth of blocks and lots, the widths of streets, and the permissible heights and lot coverage for buildings. Future city planning, Olmsted advised, must differentiate between the control of major arteries, which determine the pattern and size of the blocks, and the local minor streets, which set the lot size. These later elements should always be adjusted to local needs. "There is no doubt," he argued, "that better results would often be secured, especially in tenement districts, if nearly all of these fragmentary spaces, both public and private, were aggregated into a series of connecting open spaces. . . . All or most of these open spaces could profitably be traversed by footways open to public inspection and policing and subject to public maintenance." (392:34)

One of the major difficulties in securing good residential neighborhoods for any class, a Boston reformer stressed, was failure to enact building regulations. Thus property owners have no idea what the future will bring. Forbes recounted how

a citizen built a beautiful house with an area of 50,000 square feet of land . . . and presently found himself confronted by a garage. A gentleman expended $17,000 on his place . . . and by and by a fellow citizen built a row of seven one-story shacks on the opposite side of the street. A third citizen, whose property cost him $50,000 awakened one morning to discover a Chinese laundry in the basement adjoining his own, and . . . by the master stroke of fate and an unscrupulous neighbor [his selling price plummeted] to $13,000. (161:126)

From the sociological point of view, it was wondered whether "the moral influence of the outcome of the average investment in a home by a laboring man [was not] one of the most discouraging phases of our municipal life? Are not his loyalty to the government and his sympathy with his community severely tested when his earnings are not only frequently dissipated by an unfair investment, but frequently lost by the lack of proper safeguards having been provided from the beginning?" (377:139)

In New York prior to the 1916 zoning law, few restrictions covered the utilization of land. Dwelling houses accommodating fewer than three families could cover 90 percent of the lot. Office buildings and hotels could cover 90 percent and nearly 100 percent of corner lots, with setbacks required only after the fifth story. In Chicago tenement houses had to be built at least 10 feet from the rear lot line unless the lot abutted a rear alley. Rear buildings were allowed, however, provided 10 feet existed between these back structures and the front house. In Philadelphia minimal restrictions stated that no residential building could have a frontage less than 14 feet, and at least 144 square feet of its lot had to be left unoccupied. (296) Since most American cities had only minimal building restrictions in the early twentieth century, it is not surprising that the advocates for residential neighborhoods joined the central city real estate interests in their support and promotion of zoning controls and the constitutional acceptance of ordinances providing for strictly residential districts.

While tax and housing reformers, physical planners and architects of company housing argued over the possibilities for model working-class neighborhoods, the building industry had become by 1916 a multibillion dollar a year operation. Sixty percent of this, John Nolen claimed, was spent on dwellings poorly conceived, 80 percent of them constructed out of wood and so ill planned that they were fire hazards and economic threats to the neighborhood. An example is the wooden triple-decker flat so popular in New England and New York City. Flimsy fire hazards that fell outside the control of tenement restrictions, this type of dwelling, New Englander Forbes claimed, was an ingenious effort of the land shark, the jerry builders, and shysters. (161:126) President Eliot of Harvard University also commented upon the threat of these triple deckers, for they "house a class of nomads, families that are here today and gone tomorrow, that have no stable footing in the town and no interest in its affairs. . . . Apart from the occupants of the three-decker, the building itself has a depressing effect on property values, and wherever it appears it sends down the price of real estate." (161:72) It was suggested that the triple decker be regulated as if it were a class of slum dwelling.

Even on the outskirts of villages or on back streets and alleys of small towns and in the open country, Forbes noted, were conditions exhibiting the characteristics of the worst city slums. Towns and villages may not contain slums, but they surely have "slum spots" where "moral pest houses" abound in dilapidated shacks. Next in line for improvement, he argued, are the typical tenement houses and three-family flat. (161)

If the tenement house and the triple decker were to be forbidden as the solution for the housing problem, then in congested city centers the only choice lay between the two-family and single-family house in solid rows. "It is homes," Ihlder promoted, "that we must give our people, not merely shelters, if we are to pretend to solve the housing problem." (253:92) Nevertheless the economic realities were clear: the simplest single-family house of four or five rooms with a small yard could not be provided before World War I for less than $1,200 to $2,000. The profitable rent of that house could not be less than $15 per month. Yet less than half of all workingmen in America had salaries sufficient to cover these rents. (384:3–24) How then could the housing movement provide these men with suitable dwellings to rent?

George Ford was surprised to note in 1909 that those who promoted low-cost housing seemed not to know about the architect or else avoided his attention to save the fee. But the architect as well generally seemed not to care, for only a few low-cost detached housing design appeared in any of the architectural journals. With a few notable exceptions such as the Phipps Houses in New York City, Ford claimed, almost no city or suburban tenement within reach of the poor had been the product of architectural designs. The various moral, social, and religious phases of the housing question that dominated the reform ethic, Ford said, held no relevance for the architect. Only when the questions of materials, construction, and design were raised did the housing question come near the interests of the average architect. Still he foresaw that with the rapid accumulation of capital, new capital expenditures would be used to relieve the conditions of tenement living, and with this investment would come the professional interest of architects. Already he could note European examples: the great Rothschild housing movement, which had appropriated

$100 million for the creation of "Habitations a Bon Marche"; the municipal housing programs in Stuttgart, Berlin, Hanover, and Munich; the millions of dollars expended in England, Belgium, Italy, and Austria for improved low-cost housing. (164:26–29)

More recently Gwendolyn Wright has claimed that the American architect of the nineteenth century was seldom interested in housing. Crusading against the domestic designs provided by pattern book writers, architectural critics of the 1870s called these designs commonplace and vulgar, noting they were festooned with decorations. Ridicule of low-cost domestic architecture appeared to be the basic response of the trained architect. In the 1880s, however, an interest in moderate-cost housing brought a new development. Occasionally after this point architectural journals held competitions for small houses or reviewed pattern book designs for country cottages. (567) With the opening of the first streetcar suburbs in the 1880s and 1890s, the architect began to attend to the production of model middle-class housing on new suburban tracts as a retreat for men and a refuge for women. In response the ideal Queene Anne cottage began to adorn its development. (515) But seldom did the architects design working-class homes.

Thus the construction of tenements and small homes remained a disorganized and individualized effort. Why, Grosvenor Atterbury pondered, hasn't the housing problem availed itself of the modern methods of combination, cooperation, concentration, and standardization? "You may say that the little house does not involve enough capital to make it worthwhile, but you must not forget that it is the cheapest type of watch that has 'made the dollar famous' and that you can buy about ten perfectly good 'stream-line Fords' for the cost of a single workingman's home." Nevertheles, he noted, we still try to house our poor in custom made tenements and are surprised when model housing falls far outside the range that workingmen can afford. By 1916 there were other requirements that had to be met if low-cost housing was to be brought within the reach of the working class. Atterbury claimed that scientific building regulations based on standard engineering coefficients and government tests were essential. What else could it be called but absolute confusion when two different ordinances, one in Manhattan and the other in Queens, enabled the same mixture of cement to gain some 30 percent in strength by simply crossing the East River? (28:92, 94)

Not long before World War I another housing issue became apparent. Carol Aronovici observed that Americans of that era were opportunity-seeking nomads, an awkward amalgamation of races and nationalities who were not interested in home building or in community life. Changes within industries were occurring too rapidly and employment opportunities were in flux, making residential stability impossible and home building risky. (18) John Ihlder underlined the same state of flux. Moving, he found, tended to be one of the principal diversions of tenement-house families.

A tenement-house dweller moves from one section of the city to another and neither his old nor his new neighbors know or care. The whipping of a four-year-old gangster by an exasperated storekeeper, the meeting in a police station of two fathers who never before heard of each other and there learned that their runaway daughters were chums, the greater amount of stealing among employees of the New York branch of a great business as contrasted with that among employees of the Phildelphia branch . . . are all illustrations of the social effects of tenement house life. (253:92)

The census began to reveal another dimension about mobility: home owning was decreasing in every section of the country. (108) Under the dry dust of statistics lay the disquieting reality of a shifting population. Thus, it was believed, the 1890 census showed that not only manufacturing, transportation, commerce, and financial organizations had passed into syndicate control or ownership but landholdings had too. The extinction of rural proprietorship was augmenting the rate at which men were free to drift toward the cities, becoming propertyless wage laborers subjected to the whims and powers of capital.[1]

Home ownership, the census of 1900 proclaimed, was declining. A law of urban concentration appeared to be at work such that the more congested the population, the lower the ratio of home owners. Baltimore in 1900 had a ratio of 27.9 percent of home owners to tenants, Chicago had 25 percent, Boston 20 percent, New York City 12 percent, and the Bronx and Manhattan, the most congested of all, only 6 percent. (368) Of 160 cities with a population over 25,000, at least three-quarters of the families were tenants. (551) These ratios were viewed as socially and politically unsettling since it was commonly believed "that a widespread ownership of property makes for conservatism and soberness in popular thought, whereas the propertyless element is liable to be radical in its political, social and economic views." (368:48) Perhaps the home environment could quiet this unrest, for the home was the "character unit of American society," securing the stability of government and instilling patriotism to the rule of law. A man robbed of this stabilizing environment was cast out upon troubled waters and was "therefore prey to any evil . . . the anarchist, the revolutionist, the dangerous and discontented elements." (108:56)

Aronovici claimed that the housing movement had failed to focus on the effect of housing as a factor in the social, moral, and economic progress of the nation. Reformers for 25 years had focused on the one task of setting minimum standards and as a result had lost sight of the broader question of a national housing policy. (19:1, 3) The promotion of home ownership, home building, and even tenement construction before World War I remained beyond the realm of public action.

Was a new land and housing movement about to begin? Were factories and their nuisance uses being pushed out of the American city by higher-priced land uses, by vigilante real estate interests and zoning restrictions, by excessive transport costs and high rates of taxation, by labor unrest within the center of the city? Hemmed in by rigid and inflexible street systems in the center of the city, several departments of the Baldwin Locomotive Works had already moved to the suburbs of Philadelphia. Automobile factories had grown up in Flint, Michigan, more than two hours away from congested Detroit. The Corn Products Refining Company had left Chicago for the nearby prairies of Illinois, and by now Pullman, Indiana, Duluth, Minnesota, and Gary, Indiana were already famous industrial towns.[2] Employment figures for thirteen industrial districts showed that between 1899 and 1913, the number of workers in the central cities increased by 40.8 percent while the surrounding suburbs grew by 97.7 percent. (296:195)

It was generally assumed "that the factories themselves have been or are about to be favorably located in the city outskirts, and further that the factories under consideration are arranged in an orderly, sightly manner and are not distinctly objectionable on account of smoke and other nuisances." Here lay a new opportunity for workingmen's housing, for on the outskirts of cities it would be possible for a workingman's yearly income of from $750 to $1,200 to obtain a tenth or an eighth of an acre, thus enabling the construction of a detached or semidetached single-family home with a small garden space. In the central tenement core this same sum invested in land could not command more than an eightieth of an acre.[3]

In discussing the relocation of industry and workers to the suburbs, Edward Bennett warned not to ignore the fact that families must reside within reach of work. Not all members of a household worked in the same plant, so to propose the removal of these working-class families to the country outskirts without adequate transportation would

reduce all its members to one dead level of uniformity, or instead would break up its unity. It is useless, therefore, for us even to discuss the probability of opening up new areas for housing workers, unless we can provide them varied employment or many transportation facilities to other sections. This is one of the reasons for keeping intact existing residential areas and for concentrating industrial occupations of land. (58:220)

German cities had a long tradition of industrial districting. Because they desired to eliminate the cost of transit and the expense of carfare in production, factories and workers' housing were allocated to the same districts. Within these factory districts only the workers from districted factories could reside. (441:22) Otherwise the provision of low-cost working-class housing was interlocked with the development of cheap transportation. If the American city could provide the solution for one, then the other would naturally follow.

By the second decade of the twentieth century it was clear that the American city was losing one industry after another: pushing them out with their zeal for commercial and office improvement, fearing the threat of labor unrest in the center of the city, or induced by suburban towns offering manufacturers free land sites and tax abatements for several years. (296:95) This shift in the location of factories provided a new incentive in the 1920s for the promotion of home ownership in the suburbs. For the early decades of the 1900s, however, the battle would continue to rage over the best housing policy for working-class districts, a discourse that displayed both the boundaries and contradictions a system of private property and the lucrative investment field of housing could impose upon the planning mentality. As we shall see, an interdependent transportation system would fare as poorly as working-class housing.

Public Service Franchises

An account of the provision of rapid-transit and other public service networks in the American city must explain not only the interests of the monopoly combines providing the services but the nature and form of the opposition raised sporadically against them. It is simplistic to say that in the early 1900s municipalities awakened to the economic costs incurred by their wasteful systems of public utilities and the spoils of the franchise system and began to develop a strategy for municipal control. One must look deeper, for in reality the city gained merely an advisory voice in the provision of these services, while capital secured protection for their monopoly profits. One national syndicate, Widener, Elkins, Ryan and Whitney, had not only consolidated all the surface railway lines in New York City but by the end of the century had built most of the street railway systems in New York, Chicago, Philadelphia, Pittsburgh, and one hundred other cities. With capital assets worth billions of dollars, municipal control over these profitable enterprises had to be kept to a minimum. (405)

One must also review the transport-building cycle: investments in street and electric railway systems begin around 1888, rapidly accelerate after 1897, peak around 1906, and then begin to decline. (255) In 1880 Philadelphia had 39 horse-drawn trolley car companies, New York City had

19, Pittsburgh 24, St. Louis 19, and San Francisco 16. Then in the mid-1880s the first electric railroads were introduced, bringing a burst of investment activity. Stimulated by cheap electricity and successful franchise deals, railway building boomed in the 1890s. There were only 9 electric street railways operating in the American cities in 1885 but 789 by 1890, 982 by 1902, and 1,260 by 1912. (246) Ernest Griffith calculates that the total street railroad mileage in the 1880s increased from 8,123 to 29,830. Elevated railroads brought more capital investment when they began to appear in 1892, first in New York, Chicago, and San Francisco and followed shortly by the first subway in Boston and then New York in the early 1900s. (208, 273)

The nadir of government corruption in the American city, Ernest Griffith writes, was reached between 1880 and 1893. Waves of economic growth generated by railroad and manufacturing investments and real estate and banking ventures carried the American city to unprecedented economic and population levels. In spite of massive economic growth no business ethic had been worked out for the nation as a whole. Monopolies in utilities or railroads were obtained by fair or foul play, profits acquired by watering stocks, special privileges won from state and local governments. No one thought to make a distinction between natural monopolies such as railways and utilities and the ruthless practices of laissez faire business competition. As the cities grew, so public contracts multiplied for water, gas, electricity, street railroads, and telephones, and as they expanded city franchises determined who should profit and who should fail. With no reform philosophy developed and only fitful citizen agitation, with tangled charter powers and election fraud common, businessmen could easily subvert most city governments to their own needs. If exploitative opportunities were thwarted at the municipal level, state governments would readily step forward to help circumvent local municipal powers. (208)

Griffith dates a continuous and eventually successful municipal reform movement from 1894. By then an active and organized citizenry had become outraged over frauds, extravagant costs, and lawless business exploits, and they began to battle for morally honest and economically efficient city governments. For the most part, however, these reforms still left unresolved the problems of contract and franchise graft, state government interference, corrupt city machines, and boss politics. Fundamental municipal reform would take years to be achieved, for in this era of massive economic growth, which saw the net national income expanded from $10 billion to $22 billion in the 1890s alone, municipal services were lucrative. Whatever the methods utilized, municipal control would be kept to a minimum. (208)

In 1897 private capital saw in public service investments an immense area for speculative profits. It saw no need for any government to construct or operate any of these public services. The best solution was complete monopoly: private ownership, operation, and perpetual franchises combined with a system of profit sharing with municipalities if profits became sufficient. (227)

In the beginnings of municipal service the economic advantage was always on the company's side. Cities accepted the presence of these utilities as a benefit while the companies argued that such ventures were financially risky. Hence the companies obtained favorable franchise contracts easily. But arithmetic service growth soon produced geometric profit expansion, while consumer rates became extortionate in comparison with service costs and debt structures. In fact construction costs and bonded indebtedness in these years of corruption bore no relationship to each other. Griffith accounts that in New York City the probable construction costs of the street railways between 1886 and 1896 was $5 million, while their debt increased $41 million. (208) The cities, on the other hand, received virtually nothing in revenue from these lucrative franchises. In Chicago the net earnings for one street railroad company was estimated at $44 million for which the city annually received an average of $48,000. (273) Or take the example of the New York Elevated Railroad Company chartered in 1875. Operating under monopoly control, it paid the city 5 percent annually for its concessions until 1890, refusing after that to make further payments. When it entered Brooklyn in 1888, it was able to obtain the franchise for no charge at all. (405)

By the 1890s citizens began to realize that public service franchises were a major channel of corruption within the American city, and bribes for these lucrative concessions tended to plant the seeds of graft in every corner of the municipal household. Extravagant estimates of future profits brought extravagant ideas for capitalization. Private businessmen, on the other hand, had interests in efficiently run city services, which they used in large quantities. Hence even the staunchest advocates of free enterprise began to move against the power of those utility combines. Inevitably the reaction of the combines was to curb the interference of these municipal regulators by moving toward state supervision. (325)

Already in 1875 the state of New York had passed legislation placing control over street railway franchises, rates, and power of assessment at the state, not the municipal, level. The cities, in turn, began to struggle against this interference of the state, which protected corporate interests. Franchises, they noted, were being distributed by state orders without a thought to the needs or the rights of the city. The underassessment on fixed capital involved in these public utilities kept municipal revenues at a minimum. (405) Municipalities felt they must increase competition by creating more franchises, which they thought would discipline and improve overall utility service. But competition in the gas business had already brought in its own corporate abuses, overinvestment in infrastructure, and subsequent rate wars. As a consequence investments in the provision of this utility had begun to decline. Usually the promise of a low rate for public lighting was the only condition the municipality requested before it admitted a new electric company to the city. It was not long before these utilities began to request state interference in order to protect their investments, to curb cutthroat rivalry, and to establish an arbitrator between their need to make profits and the needs of the public. In Massachusetts as early as 1885 the state Gas and Electric Commission had been formed whose purpose was to supervise all the companies in the state and to investigate the quality and price of their services. (203)

The same dilemma existed with respect to street railway competition. In Massachusetts in the 1860s mayors and aldermen decided what streets should get a new street railway, what speed the cars could travel, what gauge of tracks must be used, and so forth. In return street railway corporations constructed, operated, and maintained their tracks under fifty-year franchises. Only upon full reimbursement of expenses and after a period of ten years could the city terminate these contracts. With the transport cycle in its accelerated phase by 1897, it was easy to obtain capital investment for any interurban street railway, so municipalities began to increase their demands for improvements in return for franchise rights. Railway companies, eager to complete their roads, sell their stock, and open new roads, agreed to many of these requirements. At first rapid competition bringing eager new investors meant that streetcar rates were reasonable and the public well satisfied. But this was also a period when governments were at their high-water mark with respect to corruption. Franchise acquisition began to cost the companies more and more, and competition began to eat away at their profits, so these utilities turned to favor state over municipal regulation. (491) Realizing that without state control their profits were inadequately protected, they advocated in 1897 that intercity street railways be regulated by a commission appointed by the governor. This regulatory commission was to secure franchise contracts, investigate complaints of arbitrary rate setting, supervise the mileage basis of fares, and seek to relieve any unnecessary burdens that municipalities might impose upon their operations. (10)

No matter how great a blunder was made when the municipality first located its street railways and established franchises, no matter what the needs were for extension and coordination of railway lines, the cities complained that just at the point where coordinated planning was needed, control over these public service utilities was passing out of the hands of the city and into a state-appointed public service commission. By 1904 state legislatures were exercising increasing control over all public service corporations. (359) Commissions had been established in New York, Maine, Michigan, Connecticut, Massachusetts, and South Dakota. Settling the issue in 1913, the Supreme Court claimed that franchise control was a power delegated by the state to the city if it so desired; the power could not be brought under the direct control of the people. (491) So, for example, even those cities that owned and operated their own municipal utilities, such as Seattle and Tacoma, were being regulated by these new state public service commissions. Metropolitan areas, political scientist William Munro warned, cannot be efficiently managed under popular control. These areas need the state to interfere with local freedoms or else public services will be uncoordinated. Within a fifteen-mile radius of Boston, for example, were thirty-nine cities and towns. If each municipality was allowed to make its own arrangements with respect to public utilities, it would bring franchise chaos. Similar situations existed in every other large metropolitan area. Hence, it was increasingly argued, state legislatures must reserve for themselves final control over public service franchises. (368:66–67)

In 1904 the Municipal Arts Society of New York City proclaimed that the practice of distributing long-term passenger transport franchises to private traction companies, with inadequate controls over service, had produced increasing congestion and unsatisfactory service. Street railways find their highest profit in congested traffic; why then should they offer to provide comprehensive metropolitan-wide service if this would remove the source of their profit? The city, claimed the Municipal Arts Society, should retain control over these street railways and foster competition by enforcing short-term leases including an option to terminate the lease at any moment.[4]

Monopolistic combination of public utility concessions, they continued, is desirable only if the city maintains control over the monopoly. The same syndicate that built most of the subways also controlled the gas and electric supply of the city. This was a natural occurrence since the necessary pipelines must be constructed within the transit subways, but the city, they argued, must control these concessions.

In addition, the Society advised, the city should plan and begin to build a comprehensive transit system in order to relieve population congestion and to connect the outer boroughs with the central city. Rapid-transit lines, river tunnels and bridges, cross-town arteries, and north-south routes must be coordinated into an overall development plan. Indeed the Society felt it better that urgently needed facilities should suffer a delay rather than go forward as piecemeal provisions.

In the era of rapid-transit exploitation when the Manhattan and Brooklyn elevated systems were being developed, a number of acts and amendments from 1875 until 1906 had sought, to no avail, to empower the city with regulatory control over these transit franchises. Finally in 1906 an amendment provided the Board of Estimate and Apportionment control over the city's transit lines. At the point when overall railway investments in the American cities had peaked and were beginning to decline, the city of New York was finally allowed permission to equip and operate its own lines, as well as to limit franchises to twenty-year leases.[5] But these concessions were short-lived, replaced in 1909 by the Public Service Commission.

Thus by 1913 the only powers left to the city were advisory planning powers. A comprehensive municipal transit system, said a body of New York planners, must join all the boroughs together. This is the chief function of such a system from the planning point of view. Up to this point the rapid-transit system of New York had been designed to serve only Manhattan and the Bronx, and the Brooklyn elevated lines were intended to serve only that borough. This caused congestion and untold economic waste, for ten lines from Brooklyn throttled through two tunnels into Manhattan, but even these lines failed to service the destinations in Lower Manhattan sought by most of the passengers.

The only hope was to resort to advisory plans. Thus a dual system contract, signed in 1913, was expected to enable the city to develop its transit lines in accordance with other features of a city plan. "Transit," the planners claimed,

can now be built out into entirely undeveloped sections, thus creating new lines of travel, not adhering to old ones; preceding the population, not following the population; providing new territories for the constantly increasing population, not confining it to the existing population centers and along old lines of travel; and thereby constantly promoting the growth of the entire City as a unit, not retarding it . . . .

The City's future growth must be built on its transit skeleton. Its transportation system must be the real foundation for the city plan of the future.[6]

But stripped of regulatory and franchise control over its transit system, the American city had gained only an advisory planning voice. Capital profitability and security of investments that had already been sunk into transit fixtures remained the controlling motives.

6

The Barriers of Municipal Government and the Need For Urban Observatories

One more barrier thwarted the rapid development of urban capital: corrupt and inefficient methods of governing the American city. Since cities were political creations of the states, it was difficult to discern by the last quarter of the nineteenth century which powers had been delegated to cities and which remained state prerogatives; where the municipalities failed to direct their own self-governance and where state legislatures had become meddlesome. In order to achieve a disciplinary order within city administrations and to clarify the lines of authority between the states and the cities, hundreds of local municipal improvement societies sprang forth to wage a battle for betterment. Municipal reform, in consequence, was multidimensional: to eliminate municipal extravagance and franchise corruption, to restructure a better framework for city-state relationships, to eliminate partisan politics from the business of city management, to utilize experts and civil servants within reorganized municipal bureaucracies, to arouse an enlightened public opinion and civic spirit. (275, 368, 405)

State legislatures had reached deeply into municipal affairs during the nineteenth century. The Pennsylvania State legislature in 1870 decided Philadelphia needed new city buildings and so set about to create, through legislative action, a permanent building commission, investing it with debt-creating and tax-levying powers. As a result buildings were projected on a scale suitable for an imperial empire, not a debt-ridden city. (275) The New York State legislature between 1867 and 1880 passed more municipal laws than the entire number of laws enacted in England for the fifty years between 1835 and 1885. The Massachusetts legislature from 1885 to 1905 created at least 400 special laws concerning Boston, many said to be ill considered, unnecessary, and primarily partisan. (368)

The unparalleled growth of American cities had developed in its wake startling increases in municipal indebtedness for public works and regulated services. The history of public expenditures for the city of New York may be used as an exaggerated case of what was happening in every city across the United States. In 1812 New York City was authorized to raise through bonds $90,000 in order to erect buildings and wharves and to help lay out the city into streets, avenues, and public squares. This loan was followed in 1820 by another loan of $400,000 and another in 1825 of $700,000. By 1840 when the Croton water system was being introduced, the municipal debt exceeded $10 million. It climbed into the hundreds of millions of dollars by the end of the 1880s. Thus it was remarked that the rudder of government had become the spigot of taxation, a spigot that politicians cunningly turned and wastefully exploited. (367) These aggregated municipal expenditures and exaggerated state interventions laid the groundwork for the municipal reform movement, which strove to remove one more barrier to the efficient accumulation of capital in the American city.

Many of the municipal loans of this time were contracted under conditions that failed to provide for adequate repayment or spread repayment beyond the duration of the life of these public works. William B. Munro, a prudent student of municipal management, wrote that "much of that heavy burden which today [1913] puts some larger cities in rather straitened circumstances by reason of the vast amounts that must annually go to pay interest on bonded debt, is directly traceable to the lavish and often ill-advised exercise of municipal borrowing powers which characterized the policy of city authorities during the seventies and eighties." (368:19) Capitalist and workingman alike were affected by these municipal inefficiencies and corruption, for the worker's car fare, tax rate, cost of shelter and food, as well as investments in infrastructure and services depended upon stable public management. (540)

The 1890s began with an enlightened municipal conscience. Reforms aimed to restructure the spoils system into efficient and accountable bureaucracies and to reorganize electoral and legislative procedures. Municipal improvements, once allocated without regard to the location of earlier or future provisions, were becoming objects of conscious city building. As the size of cities continued to increase, municipal services and public infrastructures tried valiantly to match their pace. Between 1900 and 1910 twenty cities increased in population at levels between 100 percent and 250 percent, and as they grew, thousands of betterment organizations crusaded for reform. (368) Paternalistic clubs, avowedly commercial groups, associations of city officials, citizen improvement associations, and professional organizations pushed forward with special pleas for municipal betterment and public efficiency.

At the turn of the century, Wiebe has noted, middle-class interest groups began to demand that municipal governments maintain a moral order and disciplinary control over the city. Progressive reform in these years embodied both the vision of a scientifically administered city government and the hope of a rational, comprehensive city plan. (548) Historians have referred to these reformers between 1890 and 1914 as the progressives. (549) Yet some of these reformers looked back to preserve the rural order and the system of laissez faire competition, while others were advocates of the new scientific age involving governmental responsibility for the general welfare and the expectation of cooperation among individuals. Still further there were divisions between big city reformers and small town representatives, among national corporate interests and enterpreneurial enterprises, between competing economic functions such as railroad men, shipping concerns, real estate speculators, and rapid-transit interests. Whatever their position, each reform group was trying to adjust the American city to the new economic rhythm of monopoly capital and the urban tempo of metropolitan growth, and each turned to embed their ideals in the production of and belief in a comprehensive plan. (294, 309)

Around 1894, Kenneth Fox has claimed, a national coalition of elite reformers, experts in municipal law, political scientists, census and survey experts, and progressive city officials began to consider the form and organization municipal governments might take in order to respond to the problems created by metropolitan development. Progressive reformers believed that cities required a special governmental form that could perform essential functions for the entire metropolitan area. (179) One of their major goals was to obtain strong powers of self-government for cities. Objecting to the excessive interference of states, they argued that legislatures controlled by rural members failed to investigate and provide for municipal needs. They saw municipal control slipping away as state commissions began to regulate and supervise street railways, sewers, water, and electric utilities. State commissioners were appointees of the governor and thus were more accountable to the utilities' interests than to local businesses or average city taxpayers. In city after city the battle lines began to be drawn: was the city or the state to control the provision of health or education, the regulation of traffic upon a public street, the power to set utility rates? Since it was often believed that economic progress and social advancement in the American city were dependent upon the freedom of local self-government, a home-rule movement fought to exclude arbitrary state interference at the local level. It stood against the right of states to limit the level of revenues the municipality could collect, the debt it was allowed to accrue, or the appointment of special-purpose authorities and commissions that bypassed the control of locally elected representatives. (368)

Within the American city the problem was how to short-circuit corrupt machine polticians who operated under the patronage system, how to sever the links these bosses maintained with fragmented ethnic wards. Charter amendments clarifying administrative authority within the cities, a simplified city-wide election and ballot, and reorganized bureaucratic structures were some of the reforms proposed. (223) Questions of public service and municipal infrastructure, the reformers claimed, were bread-winning, not government-making, issues. Political controversies and partisan interests lay beyond the provision of these services and should have little influence on municipal policy and administration. (320) The reformers believed that politics need not enter into the exercise of municipal business and that city affairs should be separated from state and national politics and conducted on nonpartisan economic principles. (564)

John Stuart Mill had written in 1861 that "the principal business of the central authority should be to give instruction, of the local authority to apply it. Power may be localized, but knowledge, to be most useful, must be centralized." (547:21) Thus municipal government as an agent of the state must ensure efficient and practical administration of central principles and programs. Municipal reform meant improving the quality of civil servants and promoting the most efficient techniques of public administration. The urban environment, we are told, exerts a tremendous influence upon the character of men and consequently needs the appropriate form of municipal administration. (200) Reorganized and strengthened local governments, with efficient, well-trained civil servants and responsible and well-informed civic groups and city clubs, would enable municipal governments to find the point of balance among private interests vying for gain in the municipal arena.

Municipal dependence upon state legislatures produced neither genuine local spirit nor public responsibility. Reformers proclaimed that city government had to be strengthened by an enlightened public opinion and active civic spirit by correcting the failure of well-intentioned men to take control of community affairs. The trend of modern life in the pressure of competition was clearly away from mutuality of contact and interest. The social life of a city produced a common indifference to what concerned a position not one's own, a life that divided itself more and more into separate callings and separate concerns. So it was that in the large American cities there developed an "entire ignorance of more than a few who surround us, the intense competition that numbers produce, the need to struggle and the absorbing interest as well as necessity to struggle, lure men back into themselves and lead them to concentrate on home and business." (92:1429–1430)

Corruption and inefficiency in political life were laid at the doorstep of this public indifference, for "the prosperity or failure of governments . . . [was a function of] the character of the people and their interest in local affairs." (373:1506) The American city therefore needed an intelligent and wisely directed public opinion to redeem it from corrupt and incompetent government. The ultimate cure for public disorder thus remained with the people, for the philosophy behind the municipal improvement crusade was that a city must be reconstructed by its citizens working in a spirit of cooperation and mutual concession (100, 514)

Municipal reform had its own economy, just as capital, Marx explained, creates a mode of production corresponding to itself: "It posits concentration of the workers in production . . . under overseers, regimentation, greater discipline, regularity and the posited dependence in production itself on capital." (334:587) As technology and machinery develop, labor steps to the side and increasingly takes on the role of watching, regulating, and superintending the production process. The combination of workers, the division of labor, their disciplinary order, and supervised roles are not the creation of labor, however, but of capital. (337:705) By the turn of the twentieth century capital came to impose not only a disciplinary hierarchy upon labor but upon the management and organization of the American city as well.

Faulty transportation networks and the collusive effect of competitive land development, social unrest, and cultural deficiencies were already felt and thought of in the late nineteenth-century American city as barriers to the development of capital. Now the coordination and discipline of this urban land order and its physical form presupposed a watchdog and regulating force. Municipal government and its civic support structures were to become this disciplinary apparatus. (173:195–228) By the end of the nineteenth century disciplinary procedures began to be projected onto the physical order of the American city and integrated into its governmental structures. In short municipal reform was to have a twofold effect: rearranging municipal government into an efficient and disciplined machinery and clarifying its dependence upon capital itself. Not an exclusive state function this disciplinary apparatus was a double-entry system—open above to the directives of the state but responsive below to the influence of capital—an apparatus that became institutionalized in the gap between economic interest groups and the general public.

The General Interest of Capital

Technical improvements and wide-scale mechanization enabled the American economy by 1907 to produce an increasing supply of goods without simultaneously increasing the application of human labor. (490) Thus the center of gravity within the political economy began to shift; the economy needed to be coordinated and rationalized so that the level of consumption and circulation of goods matched the output of production. The order of the American city did not escape this need. The physical environment itself was subordinated to rationalized planning and development and the process of municipal administration had to internalize these disciplinary techniques and supervisory controls.

Another movement within the political economy hastened the need for a rational municipal order. The American economy after 1870 brought a new order in its wake: giant industry with dramatic rates of productivity and financial capital with its dominating and directive control. James W. Hurst has noted that it was the distribution of capital, rather than its overall rate of accumulation, that reshaped society. This distribution concentrated decision-making power in the private hands first of railroad magnates, then industrial manufacturers, next investment bankers, and then life insurance executives. (246) For the first time America was becoming cost conscious. Businessmen favored consolidation because they found capital utilization more efficient in proportion to its consolidation. Between 1897 and 1904 an amazing growth of monopoly corporations occurred. (278) Small business, unable to survive this trend, brought about a moralistic antitrust movement, arguing that centralization of capital in the hands of large trusts was immoral because it lent a hand to the strong and enabled the destruction of weaker rivals. They nostalgically claimed as well that it was far better for man to be his own master than a hireling of a large, impersonal firm. But even this effort was moderated when the Supreme Court relegated the Sherman Anti-Trust Act of 1891 to the concerns of commerce among states and foreign countries. Monopoly corporations were left to the side to continue their exploitative procedures.[1]

Marx has suggested that the wealth created each year tends to be less and less of the total capital accumulated—hence the larger and more organized the capital unit, the more likely it is to survive in the competition for restricted profits. The tighter the organization and the more rationally planned, the more centralized and consolidated are the powers of disciplinary control. Therefore we must ask if the rise of the planning mentality, the securing of watchdog observatories that would discipline urban development, was anything more than one part of a total perspective that sought to consolidate and centralize capital control over economic development. (223)

We have already examined the increasing intervention of the state into the management and administration of economic affairs. But we have yet to ask what the motives were behind this intervention and how they became part of the municipal reform movement. Under the concepts of laissez-faire economics the interests and activities of myriad capitalist units were said to operate harmoniously for the common good. Yet competition meant that there could be no long-range planning, no environment stable enough in which to predict profitable outcomes, to secure the necessary investments in increasingly capital-intensive areas. Competitive chaos among capitalist units itself imposed a barrier to economic productivity. To plan or to rationalize the influence of independent capital units meant that some parallel yet counterposed institution must weld together and reflect a general interest from among the competing and independent units. Increasingly it was the function of the state to extract and organize a whole out of these isolated units, to ensure that the dominant capital interests prevailed over political decision making even when these interests did not or could not represent themselves as a united front. With respect to comprehensive city planning and municipal reforms in the early twentieth century, these new disciplinary orders not only enabled the organization of a general interest from among the middle-class professional and commercial elites but facilitated the establishment of a businessman's point of view with respect to governmental affairs in the city. (12)

The power of capitalists had to be limited to moderate exploitation and greed: this was the crucial role of disciplinary legislation that developed throughout the late nineteenth century. (419:135–150) No one capitalist, however, would have willingly allowed his field of operation to be curtailed and bounded. (279:1–10) To focus on social unrest and unemployment needs of the working masses, to hide the contradictions of uneven capitalist development and exploitation, some mechanism, supposedly neutral, had to be developed. Increasingly the state and resulting bureaucratic commissions and special-purpose authorities came to play this role. Slowly the interventionary state came to perform functions that individual capital units could not affect—for example, the expansion of total capital through the provision of infrastructural needs such as roads, bridges, and harbors, the production and reproduction of the labor force through sanitation works and public education, and the provision of services consumed by society as a whole, such as refuse collection and water and sewer supplies. State intervention became a necessity when no one capitalist could provide certain services and projects that urban society required. Individual capital units failed to perform these functions either because they were not profitable enough areas, such as quality housing for the working class; or the time span between initial investment and final profits was too long, as was the case with educational services; or they required too large an initial capital investment, as did harbors and port facilities; or the projects could not be treated as private property but must be for everyone's free and

open use, in the sense of public roads, parks, and bridges. (390) Whatever
the reasons for failure, increasingly it fell to the municipal governments
and states to provide these necessary services.

As the center of political gravity within municipal structures was shifting
in city after city, the leading business and commercial elites, the ministers
and highest-paid professionals such as engineers, doctors, architects, and
educators meeting in their city clubs, merchant associations, and regulatory
commissions promoted the movement for municipal reform. (223) It has
been argued that the reform movement was a natural response by those
men who felt their training and ideals were prototypical of the necessary
training and ideals of city fathers; for them it was a clear identification
of civic and public interest. (325) It may be easier to explain their appearance, however, as part of the move toward consolidated and centralized
municipal structures. The imposition of a disciplinary order, an increasing
rationalization spreading across society within economic and political
structures, meant simultaneously the growth of middle-level control
groups—those that spoke directly for business interests and those that
mediated public concerns. (213)

The Businessman's Voice

Alan Anderson points out that in the years of Progressive reform, the
term *urban crisis* referred to any series of events that might halt the economic and demographic growth of the American city. As long as the
transportation system remained relatively inefficient, the economic viability
of a given city depended upon the range and quality of other urban services.
By the late nineteenth century the overall decay and chaos of the average
physical form of the city and the failure of any market or governmental
mechanism to arrest this decay led to urban crisis. Anderson argues further
that the managers of modern commercial and industrial firms during the
Progressive era were well aware of the crises facing the average city. Since
the advantages of urban locations for their firms were rapidly eroding,
they knew that only if they combined to reverse environmental and governmental decay would they continue to remain in the cities' central core.
(14) By the 1890s, then, the public services offered by an American city
were used to attract and hold both labor and business corporations, provisions deemed crucial to the economic well-being of the American city.
Boosterism, the parallel advancement of urban prosperity and civic pride
in one's city, became common characteristics of economic groups. Businessmen's clubs thus began to scrub and polish, beautify, and rationally
reorganize the material and governmental order of the American city.[2]

Even though they spearheaded the reform effort and the move toward professional city administrations, local businessmen felt they were being excluded from public decision making. The more civil service reform brought in the paid expert, the more altruistic and volunteer methods of self-government were being restricted. (325) City improvers, it was argued, needed a definite business point of view; the business needs of the American city required constant direction to yield the largest profits. Since commercial progress was tied to a city's prosperity, businessmen should be responsible for regulating and directing municipal affairs. Parks, street signs, gas, water, and railway rates, sanitation codes, public libraries, and civic buildings all were connected with the general ability of a city to attract commerce and to hold a working force. (446)

Chambers of commerce, merchants' committees, and commercial clubs were established during this period as unofficial advisers to the mayor and municipal administrations. Their control, they argued, was no less democratic than any other group of experts who assisted government administration. (265) Businessmen, they noted, were not proportionately represented on city councils, for the most successful tended to live outside the city limits and were prohibited from voting for municipal candidates. Some mechanism, they allowed, must be created to permit their voice in municipal decision making. (82)

If once business had been characterized by a selfish exploitative nature, now social responsibility and civic service were behind the "city club motive," the effort of business groups to offer their directives in honest and intelligent service in return for the just reward of commercial prosperity. (53, 446, 552) Business organizations recognized that cities would become prosperous and profitable only if expenditures for municipal improvements were wisely invested and coordinated to facilitate commercial growth; if they were so planned and coordinated, they promised prosperity in return for the acceptance of capitalist organization. Contradictions of production were translated into questions of the efficiency of a city's organization and plan, of cojoling labor unions into social, not class, orientation, of incentives to workers to join in the rewards of production rather than political protest. The well-being of the economic sphere thus became an ideological end for business organizations, and both the control of municipal structures and the promotion of planning became part of their political platform.

Businessmen's reform was an elite action using the modern business corporation as its model for centralized authority. (310) The rhetoric that called for enlightened public opinion and civic awareness was essentially equivalent to a business commmunity's acceptance that it must control municipal policy making. Thus while legislative authority would negatively regulate land uses, housing, and public services in the general interest of capital, the positive directing force, the center from which a disciplinary order would be imposed upon the functional needs and physical disarray of the American city, could be found within voluntary business institutions. Such a collection of negative regulations and positive directives would remain for the most part voluntaristic and ineffectual.[3]

City planning, these municipal fathers argued, promoted trade and commerce by systematizing a city's productive and distributive infrastructure, aiding in the efficiency of labor by increasing public health through the creation of parks and pleasure grounds, and protecting property values by controlling haphazard buildings and land uses. City planning could make trade and commerce easier to conduct in the American city and thus indirectly promote capital accumulation and profitability. So expressed by Charles Norton to the Commercial Club of Chicago, the sponsor of a comprehensive plan for the public improvement of that city:

The city plan is a business proposition and it should be developed under the direction and control of business men. Our political administrations, whether city, county, or state, are subject to frequent changes of personnel and of policy. In Cook County today there are nine independent taxing bodies besides the federal government, making plans, issuing bonds and spending money independently of one another. Occasionally they are antagonists to one another, but every one of these taxing bodies must and does bow before the central and final authority . . . the public itself. A permanent body representative of the entire city like this club must continue to further this work . . . [we] have considered every proposition that has been before us with an open mind. Absolutely nobody has had an axe to grind . . . the idea has been that in making a Plan of Chicago, any one man's real estate proposition or railroad proposition or some other individual proposition should give way to the interests of the town and to the future development of the town. . . . Such a plan for the commercial and physical development of Chicago should be so logical as a business proposition and so attractive in appearance as to appeal both to the business judgment and to the civic pride of this community. (355:327)

The effort in Boston can be held as exemplary of the many solutions that business circles advanced for the American city. (195, 369) In 1909 the most qualified members of civic advancement created an organization called Boston 1915 in order to promote that city's prosperity as the commercial capital of New England, its social regeneration, and its civic development. These businessmen bound together industrial relations and the well-being of the working people with the businesslike management of the municipal government. Reflecting upon Chicago's Haymarket Riot in 1866, they noted that Chicago had presented no vision of the city as a compelling climax, no spiritual order with which to win loyalty for a man's working years. (265:395)

Boston 1915 was a wildly utopian reform movement organized by a few prominent businessmen and professionals. It had many objectives: a public fair in 1915 to dazzle the world with Boston's exemplary achievements, the progressive reform of every one of the city's private and municipal services, the publication of a city plan for the physical improvement of metropolitan Boston, the creation of a metropolitan council of governments. By gaining the support and involvement of every civic and business group in the city, Boston 1915 was to be the locus of a metropolitan-wide survey of needs, the coalescent point for a mosaic of plans from every organization working for the greater prosperity of the metropolitan area, the center for evoking by civic example and education the cooperative spirit of every Bostonian. From all of this promotional and education effort, a city "properly planned, decently ordered and economically administered" would be born. (34, 379, 380, 487)

Boston 1915 was not to be an ordinary fair; it was to be a graphic display of Boston as a living and working city. Sightseeing tours would visit the parks, transportation facilities, manufacturing and commercial establishments, social welfare agencies, the housing of the people and their neighborhood gardens. (150) Its deeper intent, however, was to establish two metropolitan authorities from which planning, with its informational networks and disciplined rationality, would take hold. When the bills advancing a metropolitan planning commission and a separate metropolitan council of governments failed to pass the state legislature in 1912, the promotional efforts of Boston 1915 dissolved. And yet in spite of this failure, Boston 1915 established a new city planning dialogue between the economic concerns of the business elite, their position as scrupulous managers of public affairs, and their conception and description of municipal problems.

Claiming that corrupt and inefficient city government came by the default of its citizens, these improvers said that municipal infrastructural needs, labor problems and ethnic tensions, and industrial and economic productivity had to be recognized as municipal affairs and that the disciplinary powers of control had to be exercised by local citizens, not federal or state legislators. Thus Boston 1915 offered two opportunities: it was a new kind of civic club that could be a common fraternizing place for those citizens concerned with civic advancement and second, a political attempt to replace corrupt Mayor Fitzgerald with a more substantial benefactor such as Mr. Storrow. Clearly the advancement of civic prosperity required democratic discussion and civic participation, but artificial city boundary lines arbitrarily excluded the middle class from directing the affairs of the city and necessitated an alternative arrangement. (265) Reflecting this tactic, the board of directors of Boston 1915 drew representatives from more than eighty organizations across the metropolitan region. This overriding civic nerve center enabled Boston 1915 not only to keep a careful vigilance over the operations of Mayor Fitzgerald, the city council, and administrative departments but also created a public sentiment behind the tone of every legislative and administrative proposal. (104) Conflicting with no other organization and duplicating no other work, this center alone offered the "compelling power of the mere conception of the city's needs as a whole." (265)

Intelligent labor, these promoters claimed, was one of the natural resources that New England had above all other regions. As part of the policy for Boston 1915 they promised incentive programs of industrial education and business management: first to persuade labor into a cooperative spirit and second to explain to business leaders and lawmakers where the boundaries of regulation and social obligation met. (266)

Although Boston was relatively free from labor strife, these civic leaders sought still closer agreements between labor and capital. Laborers were promised that they would become highly trained workers whose skills and art would protect them from nonunion competition. There would be in consequence no need to fight for a closed shop, an effort said to be both fruitless and doomed to failure. (158) Labor unions were desired inside Boston 1915, not outside. Their leaders had struggled for better social conditions for themselves; they were now expected to turn to aid the betterment of city conditions, joining in cooperation with other socially motivated groups. (158, 509)

Cooperative labor was not sufficient for civic advancement. At a time of intense competition among the American cities, new metropolitan-wide planning was imperative if Boston was to survive in the race for capital supremacy. (485) Because of problems with the city's infrastructure and transportation facilities, which thwarted the economic prosperity of the city, Boston 1915 advocated planning: the acceptance and promotion of the city as a functionally efficient and productively effective machine and the adoption of a permanent planning commission to develop a comprehensive proposal for its industrial, social, and moral improvements. Without such a plan, they claimed, Boston could not maintain its status among the world's cities. It would not attract or hold a skilled labor force without planning for decent and reasonably priced housing, adequate transportation, and protection from disease and fire. (191) But to secure a well-planned physical order, Boston must operate as a single federated metropolitan agency that could coordinate the scattered and unrelated activities of thirty-nine separate towns and cities across the metropolitan whole. It was felt that only a metropolitan government and an advisory council consisting of the mayors and chairmen of boards of selectmen could provide such a metropolitan perspective.

Boston already held experience with metropolitan state-imposed authorities, having established in 1889 a metropolitan commission for sewers, parks, and water. But the executive heads of the thirty-nine cities had nothing to say about these improvements unless they volunteered their opinions to the governor-appointed commissioners or to their rural-dominated legislative representatives. In consequence no one authority spoke from the metropolitan point of view. Local executives were forced to act independently and to develop infrastructural improvements piecemeal. (60, 61) If the provision of public works and services was to facilitate the overall accumulation of capital, then they had to be planned and coordinated with the development of other investments. This in turn required that a new disciplinary order pervade governmental authority, replacing the ethic of self-serving politics with a commitment to expert administration.

The Rise of the Advisory Planning Commission

Since the 1890s the American city had learned to distinguish between politics and administration by excluding political partisanship from administrative services. A city's investments in infrastructure and public facilities could not be rationally promoted through policies determined by the outcome of political controversies. City government had to become a purely business affair. (122) Changes in political climate, upon which public service or administrative jobs depended, had meant that expertise in municipal administration never developed. As Charles Beard proclaimed, since the age of Jackson Americans had assumed that any intelligent man could qualify for public office, but

in an epoch when the government regulates railway rates, fixes hours of labor, controls the capitalization of public service corporations, undertakes social insurance, builds Panama Canals, operates great waterworks, establishes municipal railway plants, to talk about the duties of public offices being so simple that any man of intelligence can readily qualify for them is not merely absurd, it is criminal folly. In an epoch when the government, in fact, employs expert accountants, architects, bacteriologists, chemists, engineers of all varieties, foresters, oculists, pathologists, to say nothing of the other classes of civil servant, it is obviously impossible for any man of intelligence to prepare for any public office in a few months. (52:335)

As a result the movement for responsible government called for new city charters, thus beginning to transform the style of city administration into more consolidated and centralized structures that were more conducive to expert opinion and rational decision making. Three new city governmental forms began to appear: a commission government, where all department heads were elected and the legislative power divided among them; a city manager elected by the city council, who in turn selected his administrative heads; and a strong mayor with increased executive powers. (178)

Expanding the role of the technical expert within municipal administrations meant concomitantly producing a depoliticized public, shut off from understanding the technical and organizational necessities of an urban society. (213) The public's critical awareness and ability to challenge municipal ethics were increasingly inhibited. Jürgen Habermas has pointed out a historical connection between the development of capitalism and the dissolution of the liberal public. The consequent reduction of an active public sphere recognizes yet masks the conflict between the imperatives that governed a functional economic organization and the formulation of an active and challenging public discourse. (213) In the early twentieth century priorities of economic growth and productivity were becoming too important for popular accountability. Critical public discourse and reflection on the suitability or desirability of those governmental actions might have challenged the whole disciplinary hierarchy.

Most of the motivation for city improvement had come from the "better element," some general-purpose group who without expert knowledge of social, economic, industrial, or political problems in the American city became dissatisfied with material conditions and began to agitate for change. American reform since the middle of the nineteenth century had operated in a set sequence. First came recognition by a body of prominent citizens that an economic and social pathology existed and was infecting society. Second, improvers sought to amass data concerning the problem. Third was the publication of a plan, communications in popular journals, the exhibition and interpretation of survey results, publicity on the recorded event, a translation of professional ideals into popular form, and the molding of public opinion. And fourth was the expectation of voluntary cooperative conformance to planned remedies, freed from governmental enforcement but strengthened by the assumption of an enlightened opinion. (107, 350, 472)

If increasing administrative expertise meant decreasing public opinion, then the centralization and consolidation of decision-making power in the expert hands of a few aligned itself in direct opposition to the American expectation of popular control and direction. The public hearing that American democracy had depended upon for effective citizen redress was a useful institution "but to rely upon them to control experts [was] relying on pop-guns to destroy battleships." (52:341) Effective government meant to control the experts, counterbalancing their domination by active public boards and public criticism. (305) Thus closely parallel to the rise of public expertise grew the intelligence of citizen's groups with their own private experts, their own publications and studies, to criticize and judge the competence of government. These groups became advisers to the public in areas they considered too complicated and too technical for the average citizen to understand. (368).

Municipal research bureaus, city planning commissions, civic clubs, and chambers of commerce used detailed studies, surveys, and enlightened discussion to aid both administrative strategists and the public. They thus bridged the gap between technical expertise and practical advice. Behind these fact-finding formulations stood the belief that democracy demanded publicity and promotion if it was to avoid bureaucratic totalitarianism. These groups were responsible for taking their knowledge of municipal negligence and misdirection to the responsible officals for remedy. "If those responsible are unwilling to accept such cooperation, then the bright sunlight of publicity must be turned on the situation in order that it may be cleansed and purified." (563:66)

Thus city planning commissions evolved as an organization distinct from administrative departments, acting as a check against governmental abuses, in a position to give both expert endorsement where warranted to city authorities and promotional support behind recommended petitions. City planning was therefore to be as much a matter of public opinion and propaganda as it was technical skill and empirical observation. It lay between city authorities on the one hand and the public on the other, between expert and normative service and the capitalist logic of productivity and profitability. "Every efficient architect and engineer realizes that highly skilled technical assistance will never subordinate itself to the rule of city politics or civil service. . . . The efficient man . . . the man with the initiative, the specialist on city planning . . . always works best where he has a free hand." (355:69)

So it is that economic progress and urbanization went hand in hand in America and how it is that the state in the late nineteenth century came to play the supposedly neutral role of maintaining the conditions for capital expansion, of ameliorating the worst offenses of exploitation, and of pacifying the overt contradictions between capital and labor. The state apparatus, responsible in capitalist society for creating a cohesion out of conflicting groups and classes, intervened to overcome the economic and cultural barriers of capitalist urban development that inhibited the reproduction of capital invested in the city, curtailed the efficiency by which this capital could circulate, and failed to create a docile and efficient working force. (422:11–33)

From within this process of state intervention emerged the profession of city planning. In the search for short-term improvements that would remove these barriers to economic growth, city planning became linked to state intervention in a twofold manner: first in urban regulatory functions (such as the establishment of land-use codes, housing ordinances, utility rates, and public health requirements) and second in the locational requirements and spatial orchestration of public infrastructure and services (for example, directly through publicly owned and operated facilities or indirectly through locational tax incentives or betterment subsidies). Now regulatory legislation, urban spatial organization, infrastructural, and social service items function in the process of capital accumulation and circulation. The whole development of city planning knowledge and regulations has been to facilitate this process. Thus has developed the core ideology of planning: to provide for, maintain, regulate, and renew public and private investment and consumption in the cities, to hold up business confidence and dampen social opposition in order to augment the overall rate of capital accumulation.

Planners have detailed and discussed the problems of urbanization, but not to remove the structural deficiencies of the capitalist economic system, which creates the disintegration of cities and the irrationality of urban life. Rather, planning is a mechanism by which to remove the barriers to capital accumulation and to discipline the economic, social, and physical order of cities to new demands and new conditions of capital accumulation resulting from economic growth, speculation, and crisis. There are always limits to capital expansion, and planning is attentive to the corrections made necessary: the social costs of constant economic growth and development, such as smoke abatement or irrational land-use patterns; the surfeit of commodities and services that saturate demand or fall below the purchasing level of much of the urban population (for example, single-family housing or private modes of transportation); the irrationalities of capital relations of production, which produces periods of unemployment or relocates employment opportunities outside of working-class residential areas. Thus the full meaning of the urban crisis, at any historical moment, is the surmounting of whatever economic and political barriers exist for the continuation of capital accumulation within American cities. When we look at the history of the process of city planning, its implementation and resultant failures, we must keep clearly in mind that it is this ideological role of planning that becomes so important: the history of its rationalization processes, the evolution of its legitimating facade, a professionalized discourse on the city that both orients the public and prods the capitalist toward the awareness of transformations occurring within the economic system.

Before the term *city planning* had even been phrased, however, civic reform was being carried forward by thousands of local improvement organizations agitating for better conditions in local government and municipal provision. Most of these organizations had insufficient resources or energy to produce a thorough or reliable investigation of urban problems, much less concrete studies and plans. Only when these reform efforts were taken up by capital associations such as chambers of commerce, local commercial clubs, industrial societies, trade associations, or governmental commissions was there financial support to hire a consultant or a small group of architects to develop a city plan for municipal development. Then the art of city building or planning began to take shape. For example, the Commercial Club of Chicago hired Daniel Burham to develop a plan for the Chicago World's Fair in 1893 and in 1907 the Chicago plan; various boards of trade, park commissions, and city councils hired improvement consultant Charles Mulford Robinson or John Nolen to visit their city and develop advisory plans. As well, improvement organizations were sometimes coordinated by paternalistic city clubs such as the Boston 1915 effort, or the St. Louis plan of 1912, in an effort to secure better living conditions throughout a metropolitan area.

The Carpetbagger Planner

Once again we draw close to the dilemma posed by capitalist development: the necessity for state intervention to overcome the barriers of capital production yet the boundaries that capital itself places upon this intervention. From the beginning of the movement, planning in the American city was vexed with the problem of whether it belonged to the municipal authority as an administrative department or whether it stemmed from the community as volunteer counselors to elected officials and business elites; as an additional executive department or a persuasive unofficial advocate. (393) Initially advisory city planning commissions seemed to be the most promising route for persuasion and the most flexible institution for planning consultants.

Thus the area that was left for the extension of planning and its disciplinary order was to the side of the governmental apparatus and the compulsion of legal controls. To centralize streams of knowledge flowing upward from minute parcels of land; to observe the shifting uses of this land from neighborhood to neighborhood, district to district; to discipline this movement toward a more regulated order was the reality of the practice of planning. If there was no rigorous "correlation of particular improvements with a comprehensive plan," then it was felt that planning would remain capricious; it would fail to provide sustained and continuous direction. Only through constant observation of all urban activities, adjusting, eliminating, and supplementing where necessary, would a self-consistent general scheme be ascertained. (545) The perfected ideal of an urban order could be used to prod capitalist investors and property owners toward the acceptance of new needs within the American city; it could warn of impending fiscal crisis; it could devise new land controls and spatial designs that ought to be normalized practice. But in a period of rapid capital acceleration when urban spatial development followed closely upon the rise of transport investments, the role for these urban observatories was to uphold confidence in the commercial prosperity of the American city and to advise with respect to wise and necessary investments but to step to the side of compulsory measures. The level of its application, then, fell far below its ideal. A planning mechanism that is both dependent upon the extended power of municipal government yet independent of it: this is the space the planners accepted for themselves from the beginning.

Magali Sarfatti Larson has recently proposed that the major occupation for a newly forming profession is to attain and control a market for their special technical knowledge and skills. A profession thus maintains a strict monopoly over the production of such knowledge and skills in order to secure a market for its distinctive service, to guarantee the quality of its technical skills, and to protect the educational investment of its new recruits. The kind of knowledge upon which each profession is distinctly based becomes a crucial element to be controlled through extensive and rigorous training, licensing, and qualifying examinations. (288)

For the developing profession of city planning, however, the basic control mechanism was ideological: to sell a widespread awareness that through the voluntary acceptance of at least a few elements of an ideal comprehensive plan, some of the barriers that thwarted capitalist production and distribution in the American city could be disciplined and controlled. This was a kind of disciplinary power that was to be inserted into the fabric of the American city independent of the presence of professional exercises of this power. In fact the conception of a disciplinary order was to develop a means to achieve it through ceremonial architectural forms or utopian comprehensive plans that relied upon collective social consciousness rather than the imposition of an effective power. The body politic must be trained in disciplinary procedures and be responsible for this technology of power. In other words a disciplinary order was to be built into the design and manipulations of the new city form.

Thus the knowledge that planning appropriates for its own is not because it desires to secure a specific market for its expertise but in order to be consumed by the collectivity of diverging urban interests and to condition other discourses, strategies, and effects whose aim was to discipline the

American city. Hence when I refer to the origins of the planning mentality, it is not the professional needs that give rise to it that is our concern but the practical field where it was employed. The planning mentality represents a diversity of interrelated discourses, architectural forms, regulatory laws, and institutional locations that collectively describe and promote the same disciplinary order. Not emerging at one time planning weaves together an array of discursive events, some of which it adopts and others which it bends to its own needs. This discourse thus continually reproduces an ideological screen positing an imaginary urban order, whether nostalgic or progressive, an emotive discourse that embodies a will for utopian reform, and an exaltation of bourgeoise progress within the American city.

Comprehensive city planning was to be a free profession, without prohibitions against contributing disciplines or privileges of qualifications. Since there was no organized form of planning theory or practice, the transference of a unified code of knowledge depended not upon formal education but upon practical experience and social consciousness. The education of a planner was left as a matter of "private initiative," for only one school offered a course in city planning, and it would be twenty years before a department of planning was structured for the unified development of planning theory and the practice and training of new planners.[4] The pragmatic experience of the planners counted most; thoroughly familiar with planning endeavors in city after city, often enlightened by a European tour in which this planning mentality was fortified by exemplary forms, the planners' varied experience trained them to recognize disorder and a need for structural improvements, to think comprehensively and to relate the fragmented elements into a harmonious whole, and to achieve a comprehensive plan out of an array of perspectives dependent upon technical, administrative, legal, aesthetic, and social advice. (83)

Planning would depend upon the service of experts: the landscape architect, the architect, the civil engineer, the lawyer, and the social worker. But the profession of city planning, or city building and improvement, was a concatenated endeavor of multiple contour lines and interests. Charles Mulford Robinson perhaps exemplifies this new kind of expert. Basically self-taught in aesthetic principles and architectural criticism, well known as a journalist and propagandist for civic improvement, he was invited by city after city to advise them where and at what points their opportunities for improvement lay.

Robinson's interest in the improvement of city life first appeared publicly in three articles published in the *Atlantic Monthly* in 1899 covering the topics of philanthropic, education, and aesthetic progress. The following year he reported in *Harper's Magazine* on a trip abroad to survey European municipal development. In 1903 he published *Modern Civic Art or The City Made Beautiful*, which set down the principles of civic improvement that only an awakening public sentiment could create. By this date Robinson had also become the acting secretary of the National Association of American Park and Outdoor Art. Under his tutelage this organization in 1904 held a joint conference in St. Louis with the federated organizations of local midwestern improvement societies. Together these groups formed the American Civic Association.

After these early years of Robinson's promotional work, a series of city invitations followed and entry into the new field of city planning appeared to lay open. The first city to call upon Robinson's expert advice was Buffalo in 1902. In 1904 the Detroit Board of Commerce requested that Robinson and Olmsted, Jr., report on the improvement of that city. (467) Next came invitations from Colorado Springs to improve its street plan, from Columbus, Ohio, to tell its citizens where their opportunities lay, and from Syracuse, New York, for ten articles on that city's opportunities and especially for the need of a park commission. (351) In 1906 Denver, Honolulu, and Oakland requested his advice. (451, 460, 461) The next year he reported to Watertown, New York, Ogdensburg, New York, and Dubuque, Ohio, and in 1907 there were reports for the betterment of Cedar Rapids, Iowa, Ridgeway, New Jersey, and Pittsburgh, Pennsylvania. (351, 458, 465, 466) More reports followed these: for Santa Barbara, San Jose, Sacramento, Fort Wayne, Indiana, and Fayettesville, New York. (452, 457, 464)

Meanwhile Robinson continued with his promotional work. Another book, *The Call of the City*, appeared in 1908; it was a poetic appreciation of the many caprices and moods of the city. In 1911 *The Width and Arrangement of Streets*, later revised and retitled *City Planning*, was published.

Not only exemplary as an early promoter of the planning mentality, Robinson also gives witness to the multiple lines forming the interests of this professional ideal. By the time of his death in 1919 Robinson had been recording secretary for the American League for Civic Improvement; he sat on the City Improvement Committee for the Architectural League of America; he was the first secretary for the National Alliance of Civic Organizations; he belonged to the Advisory Council to the National Municipal League and the New York State Committee on Congestion of Population; he was an active member of the American Scenic and Historic Preservation Society, the National Housing Association, the National Conference on City Planning, the American City Planning Institute, and the American Society of Landscape Architecture. (351) Thus Robinson would look back upon the scene in 1916 and comment, "One can view the town planning movement as a battle. The troops have long been gathered, stores of ammunition are at hand, the artillery has been brought into action, and at last the order to charge has come. Every new law is like the capture of a trench or a hill." (455:230)

When the American City Planning Institute was formed in 1917, among the most active planners since the early 1900s were fourteen landscape architects, thirteen engineers, six attorneys, five architects, and four real estate investors. (479:164) Since the restrictions upon membership were simply two years of planning practice, it was therefore not a set of qualifications that defined who was equipped to speak with competence about the physical needs of the American city. These restrictions we find instead in the social location of a cross-checking and cross-referencing network of men. Grosvenor Atterbury, Harland Bartholomew, Edward Bassett, Edward Bennett, Andrew Crawford, George B. Ford, E. P. Goodrich, George Hooker, John Ihlder, George Kessler, Nelson Lewis, Horace McFarland, John Nolen, F. L. Olmsted, Jr., Flavel Shurtleff, Lawrence Veiller, and Robert Whitten, the men from whom we have taken this planning dialogue, were all charter members of the 1917 institute. These were the same men who since the 1890s had been copartners of planning firms, collaborators on planning projects, coauthors of books and articles, and coparticipants on improvement committees and in the annual housing and planning conferences.[5] Thus all of these men collectively defined a location for planning across the American city, an integrated structure of professional defenders for planning.

Planning was not simply a disciplined technique of city building; above all else it was a social consciousness. Theirs was a reform movement as spontaneous as the multitude of public-spirited citizens and morally minded societies and city clubs that pressed for municipal reform and planning improvements in city after city. When these improvement clubs took the initiative and aroused sufficient interest from among their members or city officials, they turned quickly to hire one of these planning consultants. When surveys and investigations were requested by philanthropic organizations and city planning commissions, it was to these same planning experts whom they turned for direction. Most often their planning advice was announced from the position of a visiting consultant, proclaimed out loud for the purpose of gaining acceptance for planning, of persuading business groups to finance and municipal officials to adopt a planning style of thought. Thus their dialogue, their conferences, documents, and collaborative and philanthropic efforts overlapped in innumerable ways for the sake of publicizing and propagandizing the intent and purpose of comprehensive planning.

Slowly the idea of comprehensive planning was being outlined for the American cities, and as it was a new need arose for a correlating agency to be responsible for the custody, interpretation, and amendment of the comprehensive plan, to investigate and report on physical alterations not in conformance to this ideal, to recognize the march of unforeseen events, and "to compare the hard facts and obvious tendencies of the times with the forecasts and suppositions forming the basis of every feature of the plan." (393:7)

The best way to secure a city plan was to put the work in the hands of experts—an engineer, an architect, and perhaps a social expert. (162) These experts would then report to an official planning commission, a body of volunteer members whose task was to publish an official plan: a document to be used as an educational device promoting a broader public understanding of the merits of planning and pointing out to city officials the value of farsighted disciplined planning, and as well a planning archive to stand as a continuous aggregation of all proposed or probable projects and schemes that influenced the physical form of the American city.[6]

Not absorbed as an administrative agency in the routine management of daily affairs but directed toward the future, the commission was expected to offer a unique advantage of vision. Among the territorial division of municipal power, city planning was not to abstract from or encroach upon the prerogatives of already established authorities. The planning commission was to be the "grand clearing house of effort," the supplier of a vision of time, spatial proportion, and enlightened enthusiasm among daily routines, ignorant mistakes, and passive indifference. (326)

The central idea of city planning must be comprehensiveness of design and coordination in execution; therefore, "let it not specialize, except where it must; let it not investigate so much as stimulate others to investigate; let it not criticize so much as sympathize." (326:79)

The earliest formulations of the planning mentality warned that planners must bear in mind that their plans might be interfered with by political or local prejudice and that compromise in their work was inevitable. (162) Embarrassed by a territorial division of power, planners were told to keep to their own jurisdiction and not trespass on the authority of public bureaucracies. (326) Instead the task of the planner from his urban observatory was "to become enthusiastically devoted to an ideal, to hold that ideal constantly before us and to strive constantly to spread among men and women a belief in it." (529:225)

In consequence of this ideal, we must ask, was the American city ever meant to be planned, or instead was this planning mentality simply used to reinforce a type of disciplinary power to the ends of capital development?

If this is so, then planning should shift its attentions as the economy changes from a period of rapid economic growth between 1893 and 1914 to superspeculation in the 1920s and overproduction and crisis of the 1930s.

Conclusion

From architectural ceremony to urban redevelopment the tactics of physical planning were constantly shifting. In the beginning it was proposed that the physical environment itself could civilize, moralize, and improve the new residents of the American city. To teach concepts of private property, the needs of taxation and thrift, and the morality of the single-family home were social agendas that utilized the process of city planning. When capital needs shifted away from center city cultural and infrastructure provisions in the 1920s, planning stretched its domain to discipline a regional field in order to rationalize disinvestment in the center city and superspeculation on the fringe of the metropolitan whole. As the state apparatus took on a new interventionary stance in the economic crisis of the 1930s, planning was exercised in an effort to normalize a uniform order of national resource and regional development before it was recycled to hold disciplinary control over the pattern of disinvestment and abandonment in the heart of the American city.

Even the capital interests that the planning mentality reflected shifted with changes in these phases of capital development. At first planning represented the interests of transportation and commercial and industrial capital, although plans to beautify the city's commercial facade conflicted with industrialists' needs for improved workers' housing and cheap transportation. By the 1920s real estate and commercial capital were dominant. Zoning schemes unrealistically overspecified commercial and business development, and real estate investors sought the security of homogeneous residential suburbs. The spreading highway system as well brought superspeculation to the suburbs and an evacuation of people and manufacturing from the center of the city. Then in the 1930s when real estate capital and financial capital held sway, new redevelopment plans struggled to engage large-scale reinvestment in the heart of the city. The provision of low-income housing annd the development of metropolitan regions were lost in the sole concern to find new functional uses for the heart of the decaying city. It is to these subsequent stories of planning, in quest of an order for the American city, to which we now turn.

III

SUPERSPECULATION IN THE AMERICAN CITY, 1916–1929

7

Zoning and the Single-Family Home

When World War I broke out, American financial and industrial capital was semiparalyzed. Excess selling on the stock exchange had temporarily closed the market in July 1914. European hostilities at first disastrously affected American foreign trade, but then during the summer of 1915, war orders began to give a new kick to the slumping economy. By the following winter a period of war prosperity had been successfully launched. (153:219) After the war in 1919 most of the basic infrastructure and public services in the American city had already been developed, and capital investment in the built environment was close to a standstill. If labor, raw materials, and capital had been diverted away from the war effort and into construction after 1914, this had occurred only within the major shipbuilding and armament centers. Hence a search began for ways to stimulate postwar investment in the built environment in order to keep aloft an economy that had begun to show signs of weakness.

Since the expansion of the productive forces increases the supply of commodities and goods, new consumption needs must simultaneously be created. Marx claimed this is done by quantitatively expanding to meet existing consumption needs, then by creating new needs when the circle of consumption itself is expanded, and finally by producing new needs and new commodities. (334:408) The American city during the 1920s fell under this necessity for expanding consumption. The penetration of capital into the automobile industry and the spread of suburban development revolutionized the surface of the built environment. They were simultaneously the start of a chain of new consumption that led from the single-family home to labor-saving home appliances.

The automobile was the transportation innovation that sparked a new building cycle during the 1920s. The number of registered automobiles began to rise around 1918, reaching a peak in 1923 and a trough in 1932. Urban population increments also rose, from a low in 1916 to a 1920 peak, and then fell to a low in 1932. (255:149) Building and real estate ventures followed closely upon the rise and fall of these figures. Although we would expect to find that these transportation and building investments would produce a rise in overall capital accumulation, troubles lay underneath the surface of economic prosperity. The rapid expansion of the automobile industry in the 1920s, with its linkages to the metal, machinery, paint, rubber, glass, highway, gasoline, and housing enterprises, soon ran into trouble. By 1924 new car buyers were no longer the major focus of the industry's future expansion. Now deliberate advertising campaigns, consumer financing, and planned obsolescence were needed to step up the pace of automobile consumption. (149) So too with superspeculative housing and real estate investments; they reached their limit by 1926. Thus the expansion of new and untested industries continued to pull against economic prosperity across the 1920s.

The Roaring Twenties gave witness to the discontent and disquietudes of transition and superspeculation. In spite of the prolonged economic boom, real questions of survival lay underneath the superficiality of the era, and cracks appeared in the economic facade of prosperity. During the 1920s prosperity lay dependent upon the growth of unknown industries; the automobile, electrical appliance, real estate, and chemical industries were the fastest-growing sectors of the economy, but they were also the newest industries, and their economic impacts to a great extent were uncharted and uncertain. (136:87–96) Growth in some sectors of the economy did not erase the problems within troubled industries such as coal, textiles, railroads, and agriculture, or the problem of mounting unemployment in the midst of prosperity. Further, the necessity yet emptiness of channeling discretionary income into false consumer needs, the development of an apathetic, apolitical public as socially disposable labor time was drawn off into consumer and recreational interests, privatized and depoliticized still further a critical public realm. (127)

Parallel to this transformation from infrastructure investments to consumption expenditures lay the development of a new consumer ethic, which saw increasing productivity and increasing supplies of consumer items as the route to economic prosperity. But the powers of production alone cannot secure an adequate demand; there must be an external force, for a tendency to overproduce quickly creates a greater supply of goods than market demand and continually threatens economic collapse. Consequently the economy of the 1920s had to expand not only its foreign markets but its domestic markets as well. New ways of creating commodity needs and consumer wants, new salesmanship and distributory management, as well as planned obsolescence and consumer credit strategies, became accepted practices within the evolving domestic commodity logic. As the federal government and the economic structure joined to coordinate and plan for this market expansion, a way was opened toward a new form of state intervention, a route toward federal public policy formation that would develop in full during the 1930s. To secure a balance between the rate of production and consumption, the federal government began to manipulate the individual's propensity to save through various investment and consumption incentives. Simultanously it sought to facilitate the standardization and planning of certain sectors of the economy, to stabilize market conditions and industrial coordination through business and government cooperation and information sharing. (335:1–19) Thus it was not simply the devastating impact of the 1929 depression that catapulted the federal government into the role of the major urban policy maker and economic equilibrator but a slow movement and preparation for such intervention that occurred within the fabric of economic conditions and the planning mentality of the 1920s.

The usual interpretation of the 1920s portrays a Republican era that accomplished a rollback of all the progressive reforms that had aimed to extend state power in the general interest of capital and returned instead to the vision of a laissez-faire individualism with a minimum of governmental supervision over private business activity. (554:425–438) From another perspective, however, the Twenties are better understood as the continuation of a public policy that moved toward a greater rationalization of both political and administrative affairs, a period that continued the collusion between government and capital established in the previous era but this time removed to the federal level; an era that saw the growth of state intervention to hold off economic collapse by enabling the government to organize and discipline as much of the economy as possible. It is necessary therefore to reassess this era of state intervention and to visualize Herbert Hoover in his role of secretary of commerce from 1921 and president from 1928 until 1932 as a major promoter of policy making in areas once deemed the sole territory of private entrepreneurial behavior. (17, 221)

Underneath the image of the gay flapper and the era of normalcy, there were cracks in the economic facade. These underlying troubles gave rise to political and economic questions that focused on the problems of stability within the economy, prompting a standardization and rationalization within industries and subcomponents of the economy, under an assumption that making each part work as efficiently as possible and tying the whole hierarchical structure together in one informational network would produce a rational mechanization of the totality. These cracks in the facade simultaneously created a small space in which a form of social criticism would take root, the beginnings of an attack on the mechanistic upheavals of the city and the alienating effects of consumption, but a criticism that in the end left no other alternative but to conform to the increasing rationalization of society and everyday life.

The Political Economy of Housing

As a new land and construction cycle began after 1919, a speculative mood developed. Perhaps it was encouraged by savings pent up during the war; more likely it was due to political stability as labor unrest was curtailed and wages held stable. Sustained by technical and managerial innovations in the process of production and a secure and steady expansion of world markets, a superspeculative boom was produced. This activity in turn triggered what turned out to be an unstable chain of consumption. Once labor unrest was successfully dampened through various policies such as Americanization programs, the curtailment of immigration, and the stabilizing ideology of home ownership, wages throughout the 1920s remained stable. As the rate of unemployment began to accelerate, however, purchasing ability fell far below the production of commodities. (135) A similar gap between production and consumption levels was produced by superspeculation in land and building construction. Hence the disciplinary order of planning, which at first had been called upon to create this new land and housing market, was requested in the end to rationalize and regulate destructive competition and overproduction.

If the availability of $2 billion of idle capital in savings and loans associations was the precondition for the eruption of the single-family housing sector during the 1920s, so the creation of consumers out of the labor force was a complementary aspect of this new form of capital accumulation. (259) Workers who had rented housing before the war had now become home owners. Modest consumer credit and debt financing, and especially zoning and planning regulations to guarantee investment security in construction and real estate, were indirect contributors to the accumulation of capital. Not only were zoning and planning necessary to lure consumers and mortgage lenders into the purchase or financing of a single-family home, but the commodity itself had to be modified in order to reach the level of the consumer's expenditure. This could be obtained by reducing the costs of housing through efficient production methods, cutting labor and land costs, even changing the size and design of the workingman's dwelling.

Better housing, it had been argued early in the twentieth century, would produce a more efficient and loyal labor force, one more interested in the products of their labor, with greater skills and continuity of service, fewer labor days lost through illness and intemperance, a contented community with fewer strikes and labor troubles. (527) Preparation for America's entry into the war in 1917 brought a new opportunity: the revitalization of the home ownership ethic and the realization that in the need for efficient and speedy production of ships and guns, industrial output would be greatly reduced by inadequate housing facilities and that congestion and inhuman living conditions would dramatically lower the vitality of these war laborers. "Think of men laboring and using up every bit of energy, working at great speed and under high tension, having to live the life of a sodden beast without family or home or comfortable living and with absolutely nothing to amuse themselves. Of course, that is unspeakable," warned Veiller, "and its natural result is the I.W.W." (523:23)

Only after it became apparent that private enterprise could secure neither materials nor labor to relieve the housing shortage created during World War I the federal government reluctantly took action. It was more than a year after the United States had entered the war before the Shipping Board was authorized to spend money for housing construction. (259) Finally by the spring of 1918 Congress apportioned $50 million to the emergency fleet and $60 million to the Bureau of Industrial Housing in order for them to plan, design, and subcontract the construction of housing and transportation needed in shipbuilding and armament centers. (307) "What will increase the efficiency of labor, what will produce contentment, what will avoid the extremes of socialism, what will set up a sound social structure on democratic foundations, [these] are the very things that Congress had in view in making this appropriation for war purposes." (3:7)

In the fall of 1918 with shipbuilding at its peak of activity, the Emergency Fleet Corporation and the War Industries Board served notice on several cities that unless they could provide adequate worker housing, war contracts with those cities would be cancelled and given to other areas. Labor turnover had run as high as 100 percent in many of these cities—one new worker every month for every job in the yard. The causes that produced such unrest and shifting about required analysis and remedy. Again the housing reformers proclaimed that "a decent home" must be provided for every married man and a "comfortable place" for single men. Both labor contentment and increasing productivity in the labor force were dependent upon the municipal regulation and protection of home environments.

F. L. Olmsted, Jr., claimed that planning war cantonments for training soldiers had brought responsible executives in Washington in touch with the point of view of "practical city planning." There for the first time they learned about all of the special technical fields that were involved in making complete new cities. (395) Other planners agreed: the war experience had enabled American city planners to demonstrate the practical value of their profession. (483) One of the most important contributions that planners felt they made to these wartime communities was their special ability to adapt the general requirements of diagrammatic plans to the specific topography of each site. In order to facilitate each design, these community planners experimented with curved streets, stressed the importance of parks and recreation spaces, and aimed to create attractive and self-sufficient neighborhood units. (307) The architects, engineers, landscape architects, planners, contractors, physicians, housing experts, social workers, and realtors who worked for the government during the war under the direction of F. L. Olmsted, Jr., drew up a set of recommendations for permanent postwar industrial housing developments. Three of their outstanding proposals proclaimed that row or group housing should never be more than two rooms deep; that side yards between buildings should never be less than 16 feet and preferably not less than 20 feet; and that tenements and apartment houses were generally undesirable and should be acceptable only in cities where the price of land prohibited the development of single- or two-family homes. (382)

The war, John Nolen exclaimed, had brought about a new order and had shown the real value of the home and the home environment, including the city streets, its stores, schools, and parks. Never before had there been an opportunity to witness the effect that housing had on the efficiency, intellectual alertness, physical vigor, and patriotic enthusiasm of the overseas army. Nolen believed that the war showed we must no longer hold the policy of the greatest amount of housing at the least possible cost but instead the largest amount of satisfactory housing for the greatest number of people. (382) The solution of the war emergency housing problem, Charles H. Whitaker claimed, should revitalize the belief that a house and home environment are the most desirable physical attributes of life for which men can be encouraged to struggle. Thus government housing embodying the best designs and construction techniques with provision for maximum air, light, and open space could be sold after the war at reasonable costs and lead to the reestablishment of the principles of home ownership as opposed to landlordism. (543) We should avoid the palliative character of our past housing reforms, Whitaker warned, and return to the fundamental doctrine of home ownership as the greatest asset a nation can have.

Thomas Adams claimed that the war pointed to the necessity of razing slums, for no amount of rebuilding would ameliorate them; the standards of housing codes for both new and existing structures must be raised; and government funds must be used to raise the banner of home ownership. (3) The war had taught that housing was a public utility and deserved the attention and direct involvement of the federal government in order that good housing be brought within the reach of the largest number of Americans. Most housing reformers, however, argued the opposite: government subsidies for housing cannot be the solution for American cities. Instead the government should research, experiment, and distribute the best information in order to promote home ownership, but it should stay away from the process of production in the lucrative housing market.

Drawing upon all the housing surveys that various cities had undertaken in the early years of reform, Carol Aronovici could finally hope that the American cities would put behind them their undue concentration on the pathological aspects of tenement housing and move forward toward a broader housing program involving and promoting new standards for home ownership. Beginning with the New York Tenement House Law of 1867 and culminating with the Tenement House Act of 1901, the tenement had been the dominant object of legislative control not only for New York City but for many other American cities as well. Its very success seemed to have thwarted more general housing improvements. Although housing reformers had always held the single-family home to be the American ideal, Aronovici noted that most communities still left this housing type with inadequate protection, beyond minimal fire and nuisance restrictions, and no community had done anything to facilitate and increase the numbers of citizens who owned their own homes. For him the absence of scientific data had been the most potent force standing in the way of a more comprehensive housing policy. Housing codes, he said, were based on loose measurements about spatial, ventilation, and light requirements, but these were formed upon the least amount of scientific evidence. As new methods of housing construction, ownership, and maintenance were formulated, however, these flimsy standards of control and promotion were bound to change. A new order of home ownership and suburban living, he concluded, was about to begin. (20)

Better Homes in America: The State's Responsibility

During World War I the tradition of reform already established was brought into the service of the federal government in a coordinated struggle over the problems of wartime shipping needs, the procurement of supplies and housing, labor shortages, food distribution, and issues of public health. (264) It was the first time that the functional operations of the nation as a whole came under organized scrutiny, an experience that left many experts substantially disturbed as they discovered a shocking void in national information structures, surveys, and accounts of stocks and supplies. Many of these professionals moved away from this war experience determined to find a way to discipline, efficiently and scientifically, the industrial system, to plan the achievement of nationally established economic goals. (554)

The combination of American wartime experience and the popularity of scientific management gave the engineering profession a unique advantage as the principal builder of this disciplinary order.[1] Basing his actions on the values of efficiency and functionalism, Herbert Hoover exemplified and extolled this engineering mentality. Engineers, he said, through the nature of their training, were used to precise and efficient thought. Professionally skilled in planning, organizing, and coordinating, they stood midway between the demands of labor and capital. In their collective endeavors they were constrained from representing any economic or political interest and in consequence formed a unique force capable of visualizing the nation as a single organizational unity. Engineers, Hoover maintained, had been among the oldest reform groups in America, focusing on the inefficiency and mechanical failures of a city's or state's sanitation facilities or public health or conservation measures. Promoted by Herbert Hoover, therefore, engineers and later social scientists were thus to become the national efficiency experts and disciplinary organizers who shifted planning from the local to the national level. (290)

Generalizing the steps of planning meant creating a network of national observers and collecting and propagating bodies of adequate information, which in turn had to be welded into a disciplinary order designed to increase the efficiency and functionality of each component within the industrial whole. Herbert Hoover, head of the Department of Commerce from 1921 until 1928, was instrumental in creating this new area of federal responsibility, reorganizing the state apparatus into a central clearinghouse for social and economic reforms. We shall call this reform methodology, which established a set of cooperative committees at the state level and linked them back to a system of promotional conferences and expert inquiries at the local level, the *cooperative state*.[2]

Inspired by the waste and industrial study undertaken by the Federated American Engineering Society in 1920 and 1921 and as exemplified by the President's Unemployment Conference in 1921, a style of social planning and public policy making began to take form. Between 1920 and 1922 a deadlocked and stagnated postwar economy troubled the nation. (153) Blaming the economic downturn on a business conspiracy that had created an arbitrary and greedily inflated price structure, plus a buyer hesitation that waited for the returning cycle of postwar inflation, the federal government seemed unable to readjust the economy to stabilized peacetime prosperity. Prompted by Hoover but carried out by engineering societies, a group of engineers and businessmen conducted a study of waste in selected industries. Their conclusions argued that unemployment could be counteracted if productivity was enhanced. Unemployment was seen as the direct result of poor business management: interrupted production schedules caused by seasonal employment patterns, inefficient use of machines and labor, low productivity rates intentionally caused by management and labor and indirectly affected by industrial accidents and health conditions. (290)

Unemployment was, however, in 1921, an unstudied phenomenon. No statistics or data structures existed within governments or private corporations from which could be gleaned fluctuations among the rates of employment, income, and productivity. This then could be the role of the state: through a promotional Presidential Conference on Unemployment, expert information could be collected and shared through the voluntary participation of local governments, businesses, relief associations, and employment bureaus. The state could intervene into the economy not directly through the creation of jobs or the provision of federal funds but by energizing local groups to establish work-sharing programs, by convincing local governments to delay their public work programs in years of stabilized economy so that they created a reserve of work to be used as a sponge absorbing the unemployed in slack economic periods, and by educating industrial managers to adopt modern and efficient procedures. (16, 36) Through these cooperative volunteer measures the problem of unemployment and industrial stagnation could be disciplined.

Simultaneously Hoover sought an integration of industrial units in trade associations linking these groups to the cooperative state by a series of conferences and a centralized information service. Through these structures knowledge about market conditions, investment opportunities, technical innovations, and efficiency prodedures could be effectively shared. Slowly the national economic structure was being transformed, and an acceptance was taking hold that economic stability could be obtained only with the aid of the state.[3]

This transformation had an effect on the special problems, especially housing shortages, confronting the cities. In 1912 the *American City Magazine* asked the Commerce Department for a list of services it offered to cities. The answer was: census statistics. Repeating the same request in 1927, the answer this time was: in addition to census statistics, the Department of Commerce offered the development and standardization of performance requirements of local business and professional groups, standards for local public utility services, vital and financial statistics, and a variety of advisory commissions on building codes, city planning, zoning, airport location, and street and highway safety. (493) Here we find the cooperative state in operation: the sharing of disciplinary procedures and codes among federal and local governments and industrial and professional groups, as well as an inclusion in the process of governmental decision making of voluntary groups committed to the promotion of efficiency and functional organization.

In order to explore fully the effects of this cooperative state on planning, we must return to the problems that evolved from the collapse of the building industry in 1919, a crisis that combined an extreme housing shortage with a vacuum in governmental machinery to deal with the problem. Government war bonds had obstructed the flow of capital into all building activity. An embargo on many articles used in the construction process and the end of a transport-building cycle, combined with increasing postwar labor struggles, placed the building industry in a stagnating hold. To meet the unemployment crisis, to loosen the flow of money, and to establish new consumer markets in housing, the construction blockade had to be broken. Hoover's solution was to infuse a disciplinary order within the operations of the building industry.

There existed, planners argued, an untapped supply of potential home owners in the American cities. Before the war a majority of urban residents had preferred to be tenants; consequently there had been no attempt to get wage earners to own their own homes, to transfer their savings into new investment areas through easy monthly credit payments. (80) "If only one half of the two billion dollars of the people's money deposited in savings departments of national banks were released into housing through mortgages up to sixty percent of the value, nearly half a million new houses could be financed from this one source alone." (259: 433) But to draw this money into such investment areas and to guarantee the establishment of mortgage credit would require an insurance policy that the single-family home owner's investment would be protected in stable neighborhood communities through zoning, economy of land uses, and the intelligent planning of improvements. "Many . . . men although willing to acquire homes, were afraid to do so lest they later ruined their investment if an apartment, stable, laundry or public garage were built next door . . . Big industries and businessmen therefore have good reason to work for the establishment of protected residential zones, as a definite encouragement to home ownership and to more stable labor conditions. (99:32) So long as undesirable properties could encroach upon an area in which good residences and good income-bearing properties were already established, there would be no stability or trust in real estate as an investment. (99:31–43)

What then would be the state's role in restoring the basis for profitable production in the building industry? First, no standardization of industrial parts existed before 1921; there were instead more than twenty-two thousand items of house hardware listed in catalogs, many of which changed style and form from year to year. "If electric supplies, hardware and mill parts were sufficiently standardized to make it possible to buy a house, like a Ford car, manufactured by the thousands, costs would be greatly reduced, without the least necessity of making the houses all look alike. Savings could be effected through standardization of parts." (259:340) Adopting scientifically based building codes and efficient construction procedures would reduce unnecessary and unwieldy expenses, as would uniform fire insurance rates and building regulations updated to consider modern materials and processes. (259)

If before the war the price of a $1,800 to $2,000 house lay beyond the reach of the unskilled $15-a-week man, then either the cost of the house, the size of the lot, and the standards of health had to be reduced or the wages of the workers sufficiently raised to bring housing within their reach. During the war the federal government had commandeered labor, materials, and capital out of the construction industry and into munition production. An ordinary mechanic's home that could be built in 1918 for $3,000 by 1920 cost between $6,000 and $8,000, with a rent of $65 per month; in consequence it lay far beyond the purchasing power of the ordinary workman. (525) Although the housing shortage in 1920 was not accurately monitored, it was believed to lie somewhere between 1 millon and 3 million homes. Some blamed the failure to build more housing on the cost of materials. Methods of construction and the high cost of labor as well took part of the blame. As a result housing in American cities doubled and tripled in rent, and increasing numbers of people crowded into fewer rooms, on more congested and expensive land.

Labor pointed its finger at the housing profiteer; speculators in land titles, in the borrowing of money, inflated the high cost of materials and contractors' fees. Five years of housing needs were to be met in one year; no wonder a shortage of labor, materials, and capital resulted as preference was given to those consumers willing to pay the highest prices. Since larger loans and larger profits were made on luxury types of construction, "preference [was] given to the construction of hotels and high class apartment houses, large office buildings and other types, and the discrimination against the erection of homes and schools [played] a most prominent part in making conditions what they [were]." (182:7)

In New York City during 1923 steady and rapid growth of commercial land uses caused land values to spiral. Land that a few years before had been available for residential use had become too expensive. Thus entire neighborhoods in formerly residential sections of the city were demolished to make way for speculative office structures and luxury shops. Residential properties were not being built at a rate sufficient to keep pace with their demolition, thus adding to the problem of obsolescence and overcrowding. (517)

If the housing problem was the result of an increase in the cost of materials, labor, and land profiteering, how could an effective market be organized around the construction of the single-family home? One approach was to attack the inefficiency with which buildings were constructed and materials were produced in order to reduce the cost of production. In the early 1920s houses were largely handmade; more than twenty different types of labor were needed to construct even simple cottages. The industry had not availed itself of modern methods of industrial combination, co-operation, construction, and standardization. Even model tenement dwellings were custom-made, thus failing to bring their rent levels down within the means of the poor. (504)

One of the greatest expenses in construction was wood, and lumber production was notoriously wasteful. For the lumberer to keep to a profitable production pace, an average day's run produced at least 10 percent waste and from 15 to 20 percent low-grade stock, which was too short to fit regular standards. Perhaps house builders could send their orders directly to the lumberer, who could organize and ship these parts, even utilizing the wasted wood where possible, and securing a savings of at least 25 percent. Transportation also added to the cost of materials. A congressional committee in 1920 discovered that the excessive cost of coal and of railroad transportation were basic factors producing the high costs of building materials. (504, 525) Thus the solution, which the federal government would promote, was the standardization of not only the plan and the design of different types of workingmen's houses but all the materials and structural elements and even transportation costs as well, in order to produce a standard dwelling that could be manufactured and fabricated wholesale. (28, 76)

Second, the state as general policy coordinator could efficiently spread the best information about zoning, mortgages, and real estate developments among builders, architects, city planners, and potential home owners on the assumption that if all the facts were known, then individuals would be intelligent enough to put them to good use. The federal government sought not to enter the field of competition with private enterprise but instead to promote research, experimentation, and the distribution of information.[4] Congress in 1921 enabled the Department of Commerce to do just that: to establish a Division of Building and Housing with an advisory structure of committees and study groups to approve methods in building, planning, and construction standardization; to establish efficient methods in the manufacturing, distribution, and utilization of building materials; to spread data on prices and volume of construction, on fuel, and labor costs, on available stocks of building materials, rental values, and credit rates; and to remove unnecessary and costly state and municipal building regulations. (259, 272)

Third, the state could secure appropriate financial guarantees to back up investments in single-family homes. In 1920 the only nonemergency houses built in the United States with government funds were the twelve houses constructed by the Homestead Commission in Lowell, Massachusetts. Even the Emergency Fleet Corporation's and the U.S. Housing Corporation's wartime operations had simply been to advance money to local housing companies for the purchase of land and to provide the balance of funds needed for the construction of houses. Immediately at the end of the war, these operations stopped, and whatever housing efforts were left unfinished were abandoned. In 1919 the state of Wisconsin passed an act enabling its cities to make loans for housing operations, but only Milwaukee had so acted when its council decided to subscribe to the stock of a corporation organized for the purpose of building workingmen's homes. Nothing resulted from an effort in New York State to pass such a bill. In Massachusetts during 1920 an act was passed empowering municipalities to provide shelter for their inhabitants only in case of "devastation by flood, conflagration, cyclone or other convulsions of nature." (525:324) In other words state sponsorship of municipal housing operations was all but nonexistent.

Some blamed the deadlock in housing on governmental interference with the established channels of investment. At the point where government bonds had been exempted from taxation and federal income tax shelters on mortgages were set at a wartime low, it was said, the flow of investment capital into the building industry essentially stopped. Since the government had taken capital out of the housing industry and into the war effort, it was indirectly responsible for creating conditions under which labor, materials, and investment capital were hard to find. Thus the state had a national responsibility for creating a new housing policy. (3)

For the majority of Americans, the building and loan associations propounded, there was no way to solve the housing shortage in the American city except through the formula of "hard work and savings." In New York City, residential areas were being driven farther away from the city center into Queens, up into the Bronx, and into the small towns throughout the region. Over 60 percent of all the money that had been taken in by the Bowery Savings Bank had gone into mortgage loans, a large porportion of which were for homes in those new suburban regions. The Bowery's policy stated "that it [was] very good business to go out into the outlying districts and lend $3000, $4000, or $5000 on a little home that a man occupies himself, or on a little two-family house of which the owner occupies part. [They thought] that this [was] a better proposition in the long run than to lend hundreds of thousands of dollars on big apartment buildings." (276:114)

Financial institutions such as the Metropolitan Life Insurance Company had adopted a new policy as well and forsaken their former role of offering only large loans on high-priced real estate in the center of the city. Instead they began to focus almost all of their loans on providing workingmen's living accommodations. By 1920 they had promised to loan between $8 million and $10 million for single-family homes in fifty to sixty cities across the United States. (525)

Even the Americanization problem was being overcome, for it was discovered after the war that every second person in New York City had a savings bank account in spite of the fact that a large proportion of this population was foreign born. "That means that those foreigners who were being accused of being unAmerican [from the Bowery Bank's point of view, were] American enough to save money. . . . A savings bank account [they said] and a Communist don't live well together. They are incompatible." (276:115)

By 1923 it was suggested that there was enough money in savings banks to build all the housing required and at prices far below the current levels if these savings could be placed in a revolving fund. Those who loaned money to the fund would receive around 4 percent interest, and those who borrowed for home building would pay 5 percent. With this profit plans could be developed to purchase and subdivide large parcels of land and to order building materials in quantity and directly from the manufacturers—in short, to eliminate as much of the middleman profit as possible. (182)

Tax incentives might also draw investment money into the production and consumption of housing. In 1921 after only four months of operation in New York, a tax exemption on new housing investments had meant that 20,897 plans for "little-honest-to-goodness-homes" had been filed for the outlying sections of the city and new apartment house construction had taken out a healthy new lease on life. (116)

The fourth area in which the state could intervene was to secure a better public understanding and wider acceptance of the necessity for zoning and comprehensive land-use planning. Thus the state mounted a proselytizing effort to publicize through popular journals, newspapers, local exhibits, and parades the social virtues and community ethic tied to the spirit of home ownership. This effort culminated in the development of a network of professional and private interest groups called Better Homes in America, of which Hoover was the president.[5] The American Institute of Architects and various real estate associations backed up by expert committees and volunteer groups designed model building codes and zoning and planning laws. Then through 5,648 local committees and over 30,000 campaigners, Better Homes in America carried pamphlets from door to door, set up exhibits on model homes, and lectured on household management until a swelling and constant demand for homes took flight. (179, 221) This movement as well was designed to encourage thrift for home ownership and to spread knowledge as to the financing and purchasing or construction of homes, to teach techniques that would eliminate the drudgery and waste of effort in housekeeping, and to encourage the improvement of gardens and backyard playgrounds. Local committees sponsored the National Better Homes in America Week, set up home-improvement and architectural drawing contests, and awarded prizes for those who produced houses of the best design and the soundest financing measures. (170) When this promotional effort was coupled with both the optimistic boomer spirit of many real estate entrepreneurs and the opening routes to the suburbs promised by the automobile and the developing highway programs, a superspeculative spreading of uncontrollable fringe developments took hold and produced a new metropolitan order.

The Selling of the Discipline of Zoning

Zoning, the division of the American city into a structure of cells, hierarchically controlled and rearranged, was a technical solution meant to secure an orderly and stable development of the urban land market. Promoting a disciplinary order, with its values of efficiency and functionality already etched out in the planning mentality by 1914, the core purpose of zoning was to remove and separate conflicting land uses and dysfunctional districts that might impede or destroy solid investments in land. Never meant to tamper with the ethic of private property, American zoning was intended instead to secure the interest of property owners by enhancing the economic stability of home ownership and promoting the speculative development of real estate in the center of the American cities.

As Thomas Adams formulated in 1922, there were three main purposes for city planning: the stabilization of economic conditions and the control of land uses, the provision of adequate and proper facilities for industrial development, and the securing of wholesome housing conditions and the encouragement of home ownership.[6] Zoning was to have been only one factor among many under a concept of proper city planning, but it soon came to dominate planning and to provide the only solution in the 1920s to the vexing problems of the metropolis. Since business and real estate interests dominated the movement, zoning soon became divorced from comprehensive planning. The cudgel of a promotional and selling campaign cohesively organized by the state apparatus and implemented across the American cities, zoning quickly lost its pretensions of scientific and engineering exactness. Based upon little information and widely optimistic estimates of future commercial and industrial land needs, it simply reflected the realities of market exchange. In the end the practice of zoning required little specialized knowledge. A suppression rather than an exercise of imagination, it fell the victim of reified application: the splitting of quality into quantitiy and the rapid facilitation of capital exchange. (160, 512)

Thus as the commodity structure developed in the 1920s to include an expanded participation of workers in the holding of a single-family home and all the commodities needed to support this adventure, there occurred the consequent isolation and abstraction of the uses of land from the qualitative needs of the American city. The categories and characteristics of urban land policies now became dominated by the economic need to create exchangeable parcels of land, marked and coordinated by the universal application of a zoning law. Uncontrolled urban growth and congestion, development of community services, unequal access to jobs and transportation, homogeneous yet fragmented residential districts were results of the economic, racial, and cultural equations of zoning. Nothing was left of the spatial quality and uses of land in the American city except that which could be defined as common and characteristic to each circulating and marketable parcel.

After 1920 planners became preoccupied with the physical layout and mechanical arrangement of the American city. For the most part the conditions of unemployment, the fears of social unrest, and the problems of housing and feeding the destitute were lost within an overall faith in prosperity and economic growth. The older aesthetics of the city beautiful and civic center monumentality were soon discredited as well, while planning adjusted itself to practical problems. In the business world of the 1920s these earlier urges to ornament the American city were the skeleton in the closet of city planning; they were seen as fancy excuses for authorizing raids on the public pocketbook. Thus the era of practicality would annihilate the last remnants of a ceremonial aura to the city; a new realism would invade the metropolitan whole intent on the goal of constant consumption and rapid mobility.

George B. Ford warned that we were making a fetish of the efficient; more and more we were reducing the world to a soul-killing machine. (166) And John Nolen, another seasoned planner, worried over the same tendency, for he said the utilitarian needs of the modern city wrongly assumed that the beautiful was opposed to the practical or was at best an extravagant expense. Hence the business interests and men who controlled city governments no longer supported city planning. It was the city plan, Nolen said, that made the city beautiful by providing for the location and arrangement of buildings, the elevation and gradient of streets, the foreground and background context, the vistas and street scenes, the sense of scale and balance, and the opportunity to assemble and compose spatial groups. (387)

Few were willing to listen to the nostalgic memories of these early planners for it was believed that no one person, let alone a visionary city planner, could comprehensively foresee the constructive needs of the modern metropolis. It was the unguided and misguided private citizen who really molded the American urban form, and it was his activities that the practical planner must discipline toward an orderly growth. (573)

By the end of the 1920s it was evident that the American architect and planner had failed. City streets still were clogged with traffic, living and working conditions remained congested, city dwellers and workers existed without sunlight, and the tragedy of unemployment had scarcely been questioned. (250) Paul Fechter claimed that these failures were embodied in the architect's desire to experience the quality of American space through sheer size. As a result massive architectural structures bore no relationship to the space that formed their immediate context, and fragmented suburban areas held no relationship to the metropolitan whole. Because of this grotesque discord American buildings were doomed to be perpetually destroyed, and the urban fabric would constantly unravel. Americans had built a transformable city; they had developed a business community without ever envisioning a unifying form to embody their fundamental ideal of success. Hence the skyscraper became the true icon of the prosperous American city of the 1920s: an inert juxtaposition of one person upon another with no relation to the earth, to space, or to true collectivity. (152:274) The order was only exacerbated by the formless suburban subdivisions on the edge of the metropolitan rim.

In the search for a new order to the American city, the division of land uses and regulations restricting building heights and bulk became tactical rearrangements. The city would no longer contain monumental forms to discipline either the urban populace or the physical order through exemplary norms. Now an abstract order was imposed upon the American city to make it as practical as possible. The documentation of land-use types and building forms, this new empirical realism became evidence to be used as a means of control and a method of disciplining urban development and growth. A new metropolitan form would take shape, or so it was hoped, to the degree that boundary maintenance was perfected. If beforehand land had been distributed into cellular districts, these zoning schemes had been upheld as a kind of preventative nuisance control, designed to exclude such uses as laundries, livery stables, brick kilns, or stone-crushing operations that were an annoyance to residential areas. The New York Zoning ordinance of 1916, on the other hand, was the first use of zoning to be based upon the ideal of planning and controlling metropolitan development.

Zoning, it was claimed, embodied and exemplified the idea of orderliness in city development; it encouraged the erection of the right building, in the right form, in the right place. "What would we think of a housewife who insisted on keeping her gas range in the parlor and her piano in the kitchen?" Yet these were commonplace anomalies in the American city of the 1920s: gas tanks next to parks, garages next to schools, boiler shops next to hospitals, stables next to churches, and funeral parlors next to dwelling houses. (498) These dramatic events of destructive land uses, supercongestion of central city land, and exploitative real estate practices culminated in an effort to force all of this development energy into the disciplinary framework of the nation's first city-wide zoning law. Restricting the height and bulk of buildings, the uses of land, and the density of population was believed to be the only way to obtain a rational land-use pattern of the metropolitan whole. Use districts were necessary to prohibit the intrusion of inappropriate and destructive uses into good residential areas. Once a block of homes had been invaded by an apartment house, for example, no further investment in homes ever occurred for that block became marked as "on the toboggan." The hope of all adjacent property owners was that their land would soon become as commercially remunerative as the neighboring apartment house, a belief that was destructive to the security of the residential order. Height districts and bulk restrictions were also needed to secure the rational order of the American city: to guarantee that the proper amount of light and air would surround tall buildings and that traffic congestion on the streets below was held to a minimum. (99)

To Secure Investments in Land

Crowding too many activities upon limited amounts of land checked movement and growth, shut out light and air, and destroyed both the value and best use of property. To overcome these problems was one of the main purposes of zoning. Taking the American city by storm, within seven years after the passage of the pioneer New York City zoning ordinance of 1916 at least 40 percent of the urban population, or 182 towns, cities, and villages, had passed some type of zoning ordinance, and by 1929 60 percent of the urban population—750 towns—had secured a zoning plan. (241)

The economic functions of zoning were to open up new real estate markets, especially in singe-family homes, and to maintain the urban economic base and ensure that capital already invested in land within the city center would enhance future urban development and growth. (573) Zoning was thus to compartmentalize different categories of land use by providing proper districts for industry, commerce, trade, and residences and to find the boundary point between profitable and nonprofitable uses.

In order to develop a new market for the single-family home, the American city required an equitable land policy. It was argued that higher standards of living created a vicious circle by pushing up center city land values and rents and thus driving families to the suburbs where land was cheaper. In the escape to the cities, a new spiral of land prices in the outlying areas was realized, which in turn drove up the central core prices even further. There was nothing wrong about rising land prices; indeed it was felt to be both the result of successful manipulations within the real estate market and the real source of rapid accumulation of wealth that occurred during the 1920s. But superspeculation and uncontrolled land development could lead to overproduction. (196:197)

In a contradictory and antagonistic manner, then, superspeculation in privately owned land, whether an indication of rapid economic growth, the reflection of a so-called spontaneous population movement, or the result of a state-organized publicity campaign, drove land prices to such heights that unintentional, unplanned land uses exhausted their rational base. Agricultural land in close proximity to cities was pressed into more economical uses. Exorbitant suburban land costs meant that new owners were unable to afford quality housing even if they obtained additional mortgages. Spiraling housing costs produced cheap designs and poor construction methods on overbuilt and congested plots. (196) Ruthless subdividers, pursuing the easy sell and speculating on quick profits, left the American cities with a criss-crossing network of strangled streets, inadequate public improvements, and a patchwork of insolvent areas. (499:437) An alternative method was needed to produce a rational pattern for urban development and to curtail the unraveling of randomly allocated residential suburbs.

As it was initially proposed, zoning would stabilize the economic base of the American city as well by increasing the functional interrelations of land uses, separating conflicting functions that occurred within the same environment, and maintaining boundaries that could stabilize growth. The application of these zoning operations to urban land was a necessary corollary of private property, a system that guaranteed the clear delimitation of boundaries and ownership rights for specific parcels of land. A zoning ordinance, then, became the mechanism by which property values within bounded districts would reach competitive heights. Not only would a clear-cut division of land uses offer a greater security for mortgage loans and thus stimulate home ownership, but a disciplined land order would prohibit undesirable uses from encroaching upon good residential, apartment, and income-bearing property and still guarantee a separate and definite place for industrial development.

After the 1916 New York zoning plan was put into place, land values throughout Manhattan began to increase. The only district zoned for very high buildings was in the office and financial district of Lower Manhattan and a small portion of the waterfront of Brooklyn. Here land values had regained their highest assessments by 1923 and increased 38.9 percent over their 1916 base, while assessed values of buildings increased 65.7 percent. From the financial district northward in a broad belt through the center of Manhattan to Fifty-ninth Street, tall structures were restricted to two commercial sections. In these districts zoning prohibited the location of any manufacturing uses, public stables, or garages. Here too land values had stabilized by 1923 and in the finest shopping district of Fifth Avenue, assessed values doubled and land values had increased by 24 percent. (429)

Before 1916 Fifth Avenue had been overrun with tens of thousands of garment workers, profitable office building space had been turned into manufacturing lofts, and real estate values had plummeted to the lowest level of manufacturing uses. A high-class business district had nearly been ruined by allowing manufacturing uses to locate in the wrong area. It was adjustments of this kind that the disciplinary order of zoning was designed to alleviate. (498)

Unless mutually interdependent industries located in similar areas, with factories and warehouses placed next to freight terminals and transportation lines, such a congestion of downtown streets occurred that business suffered financial loss and inefficiency.

If a safe area for industry could not be provided within the city limits, then not only would their infringement upon residential districts and other profitable areas continue, but the increasing congestion and competition among these other uses would ultimately drive profitable industries out of the city altogether. To hold on to businesses and their welcome tax revenues, industrial zones excluding residential and higher-class uses were needed. As factories, warehouses, stables, and laundries were the first elements to be excluded by a zoning ordinance, industries progressively found themselves without a safe official location in which they could expand. Residential owners surrounding industrial areas often refused to be taxed for heavy hauling pavements, extra-large sewers, or high-pressure mains, all essential for the development of an efficient and productive industrial base. (498) Preyed upon by the protest of home owners and by uncertainties over the future use of adjacent property that was allowed to deteriorate into slums and low-rental uses, central city industrial property thus lost its own competitive advantage and started to evacuate the American city.

An Environment for Children

The intent of the 1916 pioneering zoning ordinance in New York City had been not only to protect commercial real estate investments but to protect residential districts on the city fringe. As this scheme was adopted throughout American cities, the effects were somewhat identical. In New York zoning during the 1920s created stable "villa districts" outside the high-priced land of Manhattan, strewn along the rapid-transit lines extending into Queens, the Bronx, and Brooklyn, and seeded in the open country along the routes of the spreading highway system.

In residential neighborhoods in New York, side streets were zoned for strictly residential use wherever possible. Along the ends of the block and down the main thoroughfares, business districts were designated. In order to secure a larger and more self-contained residential area in less-developed sections, every second or third avenue had been allocated to business uses. So, the theorists of zoning advocated, economic conditions in a given area determined the amount of space needed for retail business, for the smaller the income of the local residents, the greater portion of it was spent in local stores. Well-to-do families, on the other hand, spent a greater proportion of their income outside their local residential areas. Thus in less well-to-do areas, the neighborhood store became a common feature of zoning schemes, and in tenement sections an even greater allowance was made for retail space. (544:9)

The exclusion of businesses from single-family residential areas and the creation of villa districts on the suburban fringe would become the crucial test for the constitutionality of the zoning concept. Here the struggle would rest upon the argument that the "preservation of detached house districts in large cities is desirable where children can play on the earth without going to public playgrounds, where there can be some vegetation and where there can be an abundance of light and air." (49:10) This is where the innovation would take place with respect to the extension of the police power. Already before the 1920s courts had agreed that the American city could protect its citizens from annoying and injurious nuisances, but these protections had yet to be applied to the need for "peaceable enjoyment of property rights" as embodied in the concept of the single-family home. In 1922 came the test case. The Village of Euclid, near Cleveland, Ohio, passed a general comprehensive zoning ordinance districting the village into residential land uses, with most of it allocated for single-family homes. In spite of the fact that the village lay in the direct path of industrial growth, these uses were henceforth forbidden. In 1926 a Supreme Court decision firmly established the right of the Village of Euclid to exclude certain uses from its residential areas even if these uses did not of themselves constitute nuisances. (420) This decision gave American cities the legal right to establish and maintain areas for exclusively residential purposes.

A battle against this concept of restrictive zoning was embedded in the arguments held against the Village of Euclid. In fact the lower court had determined against residential zoning, claiming that the intent of the zoning ordinance was "to place all the property in an undeveloped area of 16 square miles in a strait-jacket. The purpose to be accomplished is really to regulate the mode of living of persons who may hereafter inhabit it. In the last analysis, the result to be accomplished is to classify the population according to their income or situation of life."[7]

The U.S. Supreme Court heard some of the objections raised against exclusionary residential zoning. Newton D. Baker, the counsel for the realty company, wrote in his brief:

The territory south of Euclid Avenue, which is wooded hillside, and the territory north of Lake Shore Boulevard . . . are obviously the most health-ful and desirable residence portions of the Village, yet from both of these all are excluded except those who are able to maintain the more costly establishments of the single-family residences. . . . No apartment house or two-family house can be erected in either, and yet the men, women and children who . . . live in apartment houses or in the more restricted surroundings of two-family residences are of all others most in need of the refreshing access to the lake or the better air of the wooded upland. (346:38)

More important the real complaints of the realty company were eco-nomic. As Baker pointed out, "In effect [the village] erects a dam to hold back the flood of industrial development and thus to preserve a rural character in portions of the Village which, under the operation of natural economic laws, would be devoted most profitably to industrial under-takings. This, the evidence shows, destroys values without compensation to the owners of lands who have acquired and are holding them for industrial uses." (346)

The Supreme Court's opinion detoured around the issues of an unjust taking without compensation and upheld the right of the village to zone:

The matter of zoning has received much attention at the hands of com-missions and experts, and the results of their investigations have been set forth in comprehensive reports. These reports, which bear every evidence of painstaking consideration, concur in the view that segregation of residential, business, and industrial buildings will make it easier to provide fire apparatus suitable for the character and intensity of the development in each section; that it will increase the safety and security of home life; greatly tend to prevent street accidents, especially to children, by reducing the traffic and resulting confusion in residential sections; decrease noise and other conditions which produce or intensify nervous disorders; preserve a more favorable environment in which to rear children. (346:454)

The Aesthetics of Zoning

Zoning would define its own architectural form and envision a new kind of city. New York was the exemplary American city revealing its fascination with the possibilities of a mechanical order to be embodied in both the majestic skyscraper and the metropolitan order to come. Although New York's zoning ordinance had been passed in 1916, still the effect of this modern and novel idea remained a matter of speculation during the early 1920s as the building industry stood still. (148)

Aymar Embury II, a New York architect, predicted that two unexpected but beneficial effects of the ordinance would be to increase the possibilities of interesting treatment of the upper stories of high buildings and to unify cornice lines along street facades. The tendency would be to create architecturally uniform districts, Embury noted, for each class of activity requires buildings more or less of the same type and form; individuality in design resolutions would keep these buildings from being standardized. In similar fashion height limitations that lay dependent upon street widths would lend themselves to variety and not establish one uniform cornice height within a given district. Since the limit was set not upon the total height of a given building but on the vertical height at the building line, all types of projections and designs could ornament the upper reaches of the skyscraper as long as they remained within the zoning envelope or diagonal line drawn through the center of the street and the limiting height of the building lines. (148)

Another architectural critic hoped that the zoning ordinance would bring about a complete readjustment of optical standards produced in skyscraper designs. Solon felt that for years the typical skyscraper had been based upon a fraudulent artistic argument. It was assumed that the structural mass should be articulated by a base, the main shaft of the building, and an ornamental terminal. In various guises, Solon lamented, the orders were the emblems for its architectural ornamentation. But the fundamental element of an adequate solution must be recognition of the steel frame and an end to the optical fraud of covering the frame with traditional solutions. (492) So, Irving Pond claimed, zoning had been called upon to direct architecture into proper channels of expression. Architectural schools and licensing boards in 1921 were not supplying the public with artistic means to interpret the basic ideals of their life. The classic formula entailed a wide, overhanging proportion at the cornice line, which grew in scale as the building did in height. But the 1916 zoning ordinance, Pond felt, would bring the architect to his senses and would produce new "tower buildings" rather than structures that were merely accompanied by a tower. (421)

Nevertheless modification in architectural appearances came slowly, and still it could be wondered in 1924 what influence zoning would hold for the skyline of the American city. Harvey Corbett, another New York architect, surmised that since property values were the dominant force behind city development, they alone would force every developer to build to the limit allowed by the zoning law, this producing not only a uniform cornice line along the streets but creating many very high structures. This, he deduced, would tend to equalize and distribute the volume of pedestrian and vehicular traffic and produce a city with greater density per square mile but lower congestion. "The origins of the American city slum," Corbett argued, "lie in the inequalities of city planning. Skyscrapers next to mean business blocks, palaces next to hovels, will be unknown under more rational city building." (112:149–150)

Of the 377 American skyscrapers standing in 1929, 188 of these were in New York City. It was easy to project the trend for the metropolis of tomorrow: closely juxtaposed towers must somehow accommodate the street congestion they created. Ferris envisioned the city of tomorrow where skyscraper setbacks at the twentieth floor or so became automobile highways. Pedestrians would use arcaded and elevated walkways bridging traffic intersections and tunneling through structures. A matrix network of highways radiating at star points and located a half mile apart would be the new city's grid. At intersections the new supertowers would arise: one center for business, another for art, a third for science. (157)

The legal discipline of zoning had thus created an image of a new architectural order. Now building lots were being assembled so that massive structures arching over the streets would soon cover more than two city blocks. Credit has been given to George Ford for first visualizing the potentials of the zoning envelope within which the architectural form of tall buildings would have to lie, but it was Harvey Corbett, with the aid of designer Hugh Ferriss, who imagined its full potential. (111) Corbett explained that in order to allow light to permeate the conical form of the envelope, courts had to be cut from the outside into the building bulk. For structural and economic reasons, the tower, which was allowed to rise to infinite heights on at least 25 percent of the lot, had to be moderated and the setbacks balanced at distances offering reasonable floor areas. The whole design process had been inverted with the passing of this zoning decree: Instead of proceeding from plan to section and then elevation, now the architect designed the facade and then moved inward toward the plan.

The Universal Application of the Zoning Discipline

In the early 1920s zoning was called a new science whose principles were being worked out by the cities, the architects, and the courts. The process was slow and fraught with perils and disappointments, for often a city would create zones that were unreasonable. Many American cities tried to use zoning to surround themselves with the best uses of land in protected areas and dumped into low-class districts or neighboring towns every necessary but disagreeable service.[8] In drafting zoning ordinances many cities also set down generous areas that were not restricted from intensive use. Property owners soon took this to mean that land values automatically reflected this maximum intensity. Zoning thus encouraged the neglect of these city properties and the establishment of miscellaneous temporary uses while their owners waited until the town was ripe for permanent and intensive development. This generosity in the most intensive-use areas of the city reflected a basic flaw in the technique of zoning, which the administrative appeal and zoning exception only exacerbated. If zoning was to be constitutional, then cities had to guarantee a universal application and reasonable extension of their power to zone.[9] This is the crossoads where the discipline of zoning and the tactics of the corporate state would meet and then travel forward together.

Another movement stood just behind the concept of zoning, lending its influence and prestige of technical and empirical pretension. Scientific management of labor productivity and corporate administration, adopted in the early twentieth century, was a basic aspect of America's prodigious economic achievements in the 1920s. Rejecting traditional lines of hierarchy or military control, Frederick W. Taylor's system substituted functional management. Each manager became responsible for one unit or function of the whole, and these separate functions were then grouped into the most efficient hierarchy. The planning department became the nerve center for the system of scientific management. Now the general structure of a business corporation was planned in accordance with its primary goal; the whole work process was reconstructed on the principle that there was one best way to build up elementary operations, each one of which had been scientifically studied and efficiently rationalized. With the publication of *The Principles of Scientific Management* in 1911, Taylor's system was shifted from the business to the social sphere: engineers would now discover and apply scientific laws to the solution of social problems. (290)

Zoning, the practice of boundary management, depended upon the separation of conflicting functional uses that took place in the same environment. Its main procedures were based upon defining land-use districts in a manner analogous to the steps of scientific management, steps that separated a job into elementary movements before synthesizing these operations into the correct sequence of timing and motion for performing the task. The basic value was one of economic utility: achievement of a perfectly efficient and functional machine. The quality of the product, the end purpose of the American city, was lost in the details of technical efficiency as the battle of zoning in the 1920s was fought over the allocation of height scales and the segregation and boundaries of nuisance and semi-nuisance uses. (4) Permission to enforce such a code would depend upon a universal application and reasonable extension of police powers. (289)

Initial court decisions refused to support the extension of this police power. A Minnesota court in 1920 rejected the right of its cities to exclude multiple dwellings from single-family residential districts. Only after an outpouring of sentiment in the newspapers, an action that revealed a real estate lobby in support of these ordinances, would the court reverse its position. (525) Considerable confusion surrounded the question of what was within or without the power to zone. Brookline, with the support of the commonwealth of Massachusetts, declared that single-family residential districts could prohibit multifamily dwellings. New Jersey and California courts said they could not. Milton, Massachusetts, prohibited stores from residential districts claiming that if residences at will could become stores, the benefit of zoning would be obliterated. Missouri and New Jersey courts failed to understand or accept this reasoning.[10]

The system of private property reflected the complex interconnection of ownership protection and investment incentives; zoning was an integral part of this theory of land economics. But without the intervention of the state, it was feared that a stabilized and uniform pattern of zoning could not be secured. So in 1921 Hoover appointed the Advisory Committee on Zoning within the Division of Building and Housing of the Commerce Department. Its three members, Edward Bassett, Lawrence Veiller, and Nelson Lewis, who had helped to establish the New York City Zoning Plan of 1916, brought a combined focus on the interests of law, housing, and municipal engineering. By 1922 this committee had drafted and the federal government had published "A Standard State Zoning Enabling Act," providing state legislatures with a procedure, based upon an accepted concept of property rights and careful legal precedent, for each community to follow.

The concept of zoning rested upon the right of the state to impose a restriction upon the economic return a property owner could rightfully expect from the use of his land. The concept required a search for a new equilibrium between the costs incurred by the general public if questionable land uses continued and the costs to the landowners and to the state if restriction upon such uses was enforced. The question depended upon how far a community could or should go to correct the harmful effects of uncontrolled and wasteful patterns of urban growth. But there existed no exact and helpful definition of the police power—what Ernest Freund in 1904 called "the most comprehensive and therefore necessarily the vaguest of legal concepts." (185:2)

Carefully framed zoning districts were preconditions for the application of this police power. The structure recommended in the Standard Enabling Act contained five essential elements: first, a transfer of power from the state to local communities to regulate height, bulk, use, yards, courts, and population density; second, a contextual requirement that the preliminary needs of each district be ascertained in a public hearing before a zoning code could legally generate an impartial application of restrictive regulations; third, a legislative procedure enabling district and boundary revisions after written protests by property owners and after a majority consent of the city council; fourth, a structural provision for a board of appeals through which the zoning map and strict application of the ordinance could vary in cases of undue hardship and impractical considerations; and finally, a provision for legal enforcement and penalties.[11]

The operations and procedures of the zoning mechanism and the definition of boundaries and uses depended upon a cooperative discourse between the zoning commission and at least some of the property owners within each district of the city. (99) Technical facts compiled by the commission staff provided the exact allocation of zones. These were then summarized on a map, the easiest procedure being to mark out the industrial and business sectors and to let the residential uses fill in the leftover spaces. In conjunction with representative property owners, the zoning commissioners moved neighborhood by neighborhood, establishing boundaries where business, residential, and industrial zones would be placed. After a neighborhood meeting ratified its cellular zone, the commissioners compiled these neighborhood cells, printed the overall zoning map, and drafted its ordinance. One more public meeting, this time on a city-wide basis, tested the facts before the public, and then the map and the ordinance were sent to the city's legislative body to be ratified into law.[12]

Even a strict adherence to this model, however, could generate an infinite variety of use districts. Thus the legal test for the classification and districting of specific uses would rest upon the universality of the generating structure rather than the specific applications and contextual problems of zoning. If the ordinances reflected ambiguous language or the structure was developed without a comprehensive plan for city development, then the application of zoning might not be subordinated to the reasonable use of the police power. (59:69) Based upon a state enabling act that guaranteed a standard form and structure, it was believed that zoning might be upheld. Even so the language of zoning required restraint, for a town that classified itself as a single-family residential zone, excluding all two-family and multifamily houses along with all churches, hospitals, stores, laundries, and factories, was clearly a town where the power to zone had run wild.[13] By stretching the concept of zoning, a town could destroy the confidence a community might place in this exclusionary power.

In conjunction with comprehensive planning, it was thus argued, zoning would promote the stable and intelligent development of cities, reserving in advance adequate land uses necessary for a city's future growth and development. When the legality of the zoning concept was challenged, its defense would be stronger if it could say that all the zoning regulations were mutually interdependent and part of a common comprehensive plan.[14] Then zoning would operate as a science and not as a political or popular expedient. But zoning as a panacea for the building depression, as an active promoter of real estate investments, even as a generator of new architectural forms, was quickly divorced from the planning idea. The ultimate end would split the practice of zoning from the concept of planning: a procedure that argued, in reverse, that until zoning was completed, no city could prove its case with regard to the necessary layout and demand for streets, sewers, parks, or public buildings.[15]

The Social Order of Zoning

A balanced development of land uses in the American city grew to be an exception as economic stability became the result of zoning. Dividing the city into use districts meant that each partial system tended to become more independent from the others in organization and structure. Each unit, thought of as a unique function to be mechanically and hierarchically ordered, forgot to relate to the functioning of the totality. Social ethics were left out of these operations; segregation of uses implied economic, social, and racial segregation as well. Indeed racial hatred played no small part in bringing into existence the earliest zoning ordinances. In San Francisco and other northern California towns during the 1870s to 1890s, in what has been referred to as a period of "violent anti-Chinese disturbances," Chinese laundries were found to be objectionable uses when located adjacent to home districts and certain businesses. (99) Most of these laundries were of frame structures, and so it was argued when combined with the presence of irons, boiling water, and wood stoves, presented a fire hazard. The use of large quantities of water and soap, which they liberally poured into open gutters and drains, and the stringing of drying lines on top of their roofs annoyed adjacent property owners, who complained that their land values depreciated. Hence these cities began to pass ordinances forbidding the location of laundries in certain sections of the city. (99)

Bruno Lasker formulated that increased specialization within American cities brought about greater geographical separation of population by tastes, habits, and opportunities. The tendency developed for the wealthier to live apart from the problems of the social totality, while the working classes were placed in industrial towns or central city slums far removed from the amenities of the better classes. By the 1920s the middle class disappeared behind walls marked off by zoning restrictions in areas of monotonous character. The districts that accepted the most stringent zoning codes were those occupied by the more expensive residential uses. The special requirements of each section of town were translated in zoning practice to mean that class distinctions became disciplinary legalized regulations. Why, asked Lasker, do so many zoning commissions divide the city into use districts that distinguish between residential needs of different classes, that aim for the greater prosperity of those who own central city land, office buildings, and stores? Zoning ordinances and city plans, he noted, should be a formulation of the changing needs and desires of the common people; they should be studied by all classes and reinforced by strong political action. (289)

Since zoning was supported by financial and banking interests as a guarantor of property values, it necessarily meant economic and racial segregation. For some this was a natural expectation, an obvious trend toward the segregation of economic classes strengthened by zoning devices. Robert Whitten was among the supporters who claimed that bankers and leading businessmen should live in the same residential districts, storekeepers, clerks, and technicians in another district, and working people in yet another. Nothing was to be gained from mutual association. Neighborhoods of similar economic status provided the most intelligent interests in public affairs, the independence of thought and action so necessary for a healthy civic life. In homogeneous neighborhoods the potential for racial and class conflict dissolved, and the lower classes, given the opportunity for self-development, became more intelligent and responsible. (289)

The zoning plan in Atlanta, Georgia, Whitten submitted, was the first to embody overtly the principles of segregation in its composition. Residential areas were divided into three racial districts: all white, all black, and undetermined. No black families were permitted to live in the white districts and no whites in the black. (289) Prior to zoning, Whitten continued in praise of the Atlanta plan, race segregation and hatred had destroyed the savings of poor families when hundreds of acres were left undeveloped because of the uncertainty of whether their future development would be for whites or for blacks. (546) Many real estate investors, however, were opposed to the Atlanta zone. It interfered with the land market and tampered with the sale of lots. Hence they denounced the ordinance as invalid and an inappropriate exercise of the police power as early as 1917. (289)

On the other hand using the police power to create restricted nuisance districts, MacLaurin warned, established the subtle corollary that the legal rights of home owners were nowhere protected from industrial wastes and pollution. (321, 322) Setting residential against industrial uses simply based on the degree of nuisance created by the latter did nothing to aid the health or general welfare of a community. Zoning, he continued, should not allow industries immunity from applying the best-known means in pollution abatement. No one, MacLaurin felt, had raised the issue of abating the social cost of industrial pollution altogether. Dust, fumes, odors, and noxious gases were not scientifically managed through segregated-use districts but polluted the atmosphere for miles around. Overlooked was the problem that one polluting industry could cause infinite injury to another if combined with unrestricted nuisance areas. Abatement of all nuisances, he insisted, should be regarded as a paying proposition, for it frequently resulted in the improvement of chemical and mechanical procedures and led as well toward better working conditions. "The accepted view of zoning is an 'architectural plan' of dealing with municipal problems which offend the sight of the fastidious. But pirates of the air disfigure the beauty of public buildings and parks. Trade waste nuisances must be dealt with more comprehensively than by mere exclusion." (321:504) MacLaurin pointed out that the elimination of every form of waste was one of the objectives of scientific managment and the idea that it was an advantage for one industry to be maintained as a public nuisance had no scientific basis in fact: "Progressive business firms no longer tolerate nuisance as it is regarded as a stigma on the conduct of business." (322:259)

Nevertheless in the 1920s economic growth was the common assumption behind zoning, a disciplinary movement designed to facilitate the development of domestic consumption patterns and to stabilize center city property values. In consequence zoning was scarcely the target of a critical or questioning discourse. The legal advocates of zoning, not the disciplinary planner, felt that zoning must be applied and tested as many times as possible before the constitutionality of its regulatory power was questioned. They argued that only if zoning was based upon a universal application of the same procedure and backed up by a dossier of lower court trials would the rationality and reasonableness of this extended use of the police power survive its inevitable Supreme Court challenge. Thus the mechanical procedures of zoning, while guaranteeing its universal application, liquidated two of the major reasons for which the disciplinary order of planning and then zoning had been created: both the control of metropolitan growth and the development of quality environments.

The Roots of Fiscal Crisis

Zoning experts viewed the American city as a gigantic machine; therefore both the division of land uses into functional zones and the reduction of architectural design to regulatory controls were permissible. As the tempo of change in the machine city accelerated, zoning was expected to answer all the city's malfunctions. Zoning represented the promise of scientific progress; technical efficiency experts would manipulate and manage the order of this new city. Yet facilitating the mobility of population and accelerating the pace of land changes meant that zoning produced a gap between the techniques of regulatory control and the aesthetic and social form of the American city. Caught up within an immense real estate boom, by the late 1920s skyscrapers dominated the American city's skyline, and suburban tract towns sprawled along major highway and railroad lines. If zoning was to have created a new rational urban order in the 1920s, by the 1930s the realities of jammed traffic lanes along canyon streets surrounded with multistoried monstrosities and a formless metropolitan sprawl no longer seemed so heroic. Escape by automobile into the hinterlands appeared to be the only solution.

Thus behind the selling of zoning and the rise of the residential suburbs stood yet another disquieting story. By 1930 the urban trend that had witnessed thousands of people pushed off the farms and out of rural counties had stopped. Now the flow of people into the city center had become a regional trend, an outward movement of people and employment from the central city into the smaller villages, towns, and suburbs on the metropolitan rim. This outward movement following the major transportation routes reproduced another vicious circle. Dumping more people onto residential land with insufficient infrastructure provisions, allowing this land to be developed to the maximum limit that the transit facilities provided, meant that within time these areas too would have streets that were overcongested, a wasteful distribution of land uses, incomplete systems of public utilites, and expensive outlays for duplicated municipal services. In New York City by 1925, for example, a population almost seven times that of the whole United States boarded rapid-transit trains in the business district of Manhattan. This figure was four times that which boarded such trains in 1904 and twice the number even in 1913. New York had developed parallel lines of transportation, which continued to saturate the outlying boroughs with as much population as they could hold. (516)

Between 1920 and 1930 Manhattan Island was deserted by nearly half a million people, or 18.2 percent of its population. Over the same period the Bronx gained 72.8 percent, Queens 130.1 percent, Richmond 35.9 percent, and Brooklyn 26.9 percent. In the heart of the city abandoned and boarded tenements stood witness. This exodus annually cost the city an estimated $40 million or $50 million in rent alone, besides an uncalculated loss of trade, taxes, and labor. (468) Similar results occurred within other large cities, where suburban regions were growing at a faster rate than their inner-city cores. (21)

The automobile and the rapid commuter railroads, the process of zoning and the security of the single-family home, had created an exodus from the city. The groundwork for the fiscal crisis of the city had been laid well in advance of the 1930s economic depression.

Traversing a Regional Domain

Zoning focused on the efficient use and distribution of land for the purpose of increasing the productivity of space but not its organization from the point of view of social needs and uses. It offered no blueprint for society, no comprehensive plan for development and urban growth. The necessary security of the single-family home, all the economic values linked to the efficiency of industrial areas, and the social ethic of racial and economic segregation determined the lines and boundaries of zoning. While pointing out what ought to be done, zoning then allowed the major real estate interests to do the actual planning and be in control of the allocation and regulatory system. (4)

Within the discourse of city planning, a conflict occurred between two methods of land control to which the future development and growth of the city was to be entrusted—one through a legal apparatus and the other by preventative planned forethought. Since the force by which the urban land market gained momentum was more readily facilitated by a legal apparatus than by deliberate and gradual planning, it was not until March 1927 that the Commerce Department gave a legal status to the master plan. (In the 1920s the term *master plan* replaced *comprehensive planning* or *general* planning.) By this time, however, the damage had been done: separating zoning from planning entrusted the disciplinary code of land use controls to lawyers and realtors rather than planners.

A matrix of social and economic factors marked the practical process of planning in the 1920s; these had to be brought into its purview. But city planning above all accepted the view that a metropolitan area should have a structural and internally consistent organization, which only planning could achieve.

Harland Bartholomew in 1922 described city planning as the phase of municipal activity that analyzed the character and probably the extent of city growth and suggested certain readjustments and coordinations for future improvements. As he defined it, however, city planning was concerned solely with the physical development of American cities and had virtually nothing to do with political or administrative policies. (44)

In the early 1920s the sequence of operations in city planning work related to the four groups of problems already outlined by 1914: the broadest set of architectural problems stemming from proper design standards and arrangements of public and private buildings and land uses, the social problems related to the relief of congestion and the provision of sanitary and wholesome environments, the engineering problems centered on the street plan and the general structure of the city, and the economic questions concerned with the effective provision of municipal services and the financial devices and effects of implementation. (297) City planning was concerned with the physical and economic development of the center of the American city. By the end of the 1920s, however, planning had extended its narrow horizons. Now a regional motif dominated efforts as state and regional planning commissions had joined the procession, as had the wide-scale enactment of zoning legislation in regional towns and suburbs, the planning considerations for subregional shopping centers, the conception and building of distinctive new towns and suburban subdivisions, and the regionwide distribution of highways and airports. (102:89)

This transitional era of the 1920s was important for in it lay the roots of future modifications within planning. In the search for a new physical order for the machine city of the 1920s, planning would begin to abandon the center of the city in an expectation that a new future and new beginnings could be found outside the city in metropolitan regions. Here we can witness the evolving concept of interest groups and pluralist politics. So too we find a split between social and physical planning and a critical awareness of unmet human needs despite economic advancement and social development. These are the paths that led forward to the destructive procedures that formed the modern American city characterized by a wrenching urban renewal tearing away at its center and the unraveling and puckering of urban fabric where suburbs stretched across a regional frame.

Lewis Mumford wrote in 1924 of the hope that America's cities could be planned anew. The convenience of the checkerboard plan, wrote Mumford, served only the hasty and the avaricious, and it was by means of this plan that the American city had received its characteristic imprint. (361) The tyranny of engineers laid out each city without any knowledge of its topographical situation and with little understanding of the processes of city growth. These grid plans have nothing to do with the real problems of city planning, those of coordination in industry and housing, the elimination of wasteful methods of rapid transit, and the rehabilitation of center city neighborhoods. "Yesterday our American city expressed the haste and dead-sureness of the pioneer; today [Mumford complained] the morbid, relentless inertia of the machine process." (361) Still a new modern future for the American city was about to begin, for he continued, "America is the land of the reformer, the land of the clean start." (361)

The new beginning would come in an unexpected manner, for once again in the 1920s a transportation innovation delivered its impact upon the American city. The automobile and the paved highway spread the urban population over the surrounding countryside, absorbing old satellite communities, forming congeries of business centers, open fields, suburban villas, and factory towns yet still retaining densely populated tenements and scraping skyscrapers in the city center. This sudden growth of the automobile started a continent-wide redistribution of population and industry. (500) In consequence it became dramatically clear that country and city were one functional unit, that the allocation of highways, the determination of national trunk lines for public utilities and transport facilities had little or no relationship to political boundaries. (54)

The city [had] never been a thoroughly satisfactory unit for planning. The opportunity for really effective work [had] been limited by arbitrary boundaries . . . [while] meantime urban development [had] extended beyond the city boundaries with little or no intelligent planning or control . . . [where] the same costly problem of reorganization and reconstruction [was] being reproduced. (216:119)

Regional planning, after all, was only "city planning carried to its logical conclusions, under modern economic and social conditions." (130:5) Since the metropolitan area bore little relation to its corporate limits, it was "the logical step in city and town planning to find a way of controlling and directing the development of the whole contributory region. . . ." (168:1)

Thus city planning extended its boundaries to traverse a regional domain—a new apparatus by which it was hoped that a gap between the center city, the suburbs, and the open country might be reevaluated and closed, by which the restrictive segregations of local zoning and property controls might be surpassed through a voluntary cooperative yet supragovernmental regional unit. This then was the planning strategy of the 1920s: to form a new synthesis of discourse on the regional level with new standards of regulatory control and disciplinary order.

In the largest cities the signs of agglomeration had already appeared. Land overcrowding checked the free flow of population; overgrown buildings shut out light and air; a spatial gap now existed between the place of work and the location of homes, a friction that dissipated workers' energy on long and tiresome journeys to work and whose remedy simply set off a circle when transportation networks designed to overcome this gap increased congestion and compounded tensions. No doubt, it was argued, the first consideration in planning the American city should be the economic need of business; indeed this was the precondition for the official existence of the planning profession. Left alone, however, businesses formed larger and larger corporations and acquired a momentum, which reached far beyond the size of efficiency, a waste of both energy and time. Hence by instinct and in an effort to overcome this problem of agglomeration, planners remarked, various businesses instinctively segregated themselves into specialized subcenters of the regional city. (168)

Thomas Adams first presented the idea of regional planning to the National Planning Conference in 1919, noting that modern urban growth made it essential to regulate this expansion on elastic principles, over wider areas, and at greater expense of time and money than had been necessary. A regional plan, while tentative and elastic, must establish a skeleton plan for the entire region before developing a series of practical and workable city and town plans. (5) A new breed of regional planners sounded the alarm: with no control over municipal congestion, the whole social machinery worked more slowly and less efficiently. Thus these metropolitan agglomerations must be reorganized by planning standards that set limits to their growth into surrounding regions and forced them to decentralize their industrial and commercial activities and population into autonomous functional subunits. (250)

In 1924 William Bailey looked across the American cities and proclaimed that the twentieth-century city was the "suburbanized city" and with this new tendency had come a shift in attention from the center to the circumference. Regional planning must look to the tributary towns, villages, and rural areas to solve modern urban problems. (35) Because of Henry Ford, the center of the American city was doomed. The future would be a chain of small towns traversing the countryside clustered around factories and inhabited by a new type of man dividing his time between the factory and the farm. It was believed that the era of the great American city was passing; the new way of life would have less crime, less poverty, less wealth, less unrest, and less of the fierce nervous strain under which all city dwellers lived. (224)

Two regional motifs, one in tune with the pace of the automobile and the rhythm of suburban life and the other in search of a route to pass beyond these obstructions and to establish a new rural-industrial balance, were intertwined at first within the discourse on regional planning. But as the city became increasingly more oppressive to the utopian regionalists, those practical planners who supported the suburb and stressed its dependency on the automobile and the highway came under attack and rejection. At this juncture the utopian quest set off on its own to envision a revolutionary new order of cities.[1]

The Technically Tenuous City

During the 1920s the antiurban regional motif reflected the reality that the machine and its automatic processes had invaded the city; it dominated and captured the city dweller in its vice. The American city had been subjected to revolutionary mechanization factors: the building of skyscrapers, a bewildering increase in the manufacture and use of motor vehicles, and the distribution of household electricity, which brought with it an array of mechanical gadgets. Tools and machinery divided the city with elevated railroads, with the displacement of work and home locations, with automobiles dominating the pathways and demanding new city forms, with mechanical procedures invading everyday life and even the home. In consequence the imagery of the city branched out from references about the fears of a chaotic and disorderly environment, immigrant hordes and the threat of the mob, to fears of mechanization and standardization. (362) Being caught in a new revolution, the concept of the city as a tool, as a mechanism, to thrust civilization forward in unknown directions had to be recognized and absorbed. (298)

As Georg Lukács explained in 1923, the structure of the capitalist mentality of the 1920s was concentrated in one repetitive image of the automatic machine. (311:88–89) Production had evolved over the years from a relationship between the worker and the objects he fashioned with the aid of his tools to a rationalized machine process that eliminated the qualitative and human attributes of workers and broke the work process into specialized, objectively calculable operations. As the production process became the product of a collection of arbitrarily connected operations, the worker lost touch with the creation of the whole product, no longer the master of his work but a part of the autonomous mechanical system to which he passively conformed. The worker's stance toward the world was transformed into silent acceptance of a presupposed set of ends impervious to his intervention. The principle of rational mechanization came to embrace every aspect of life, and every individual was subjected to the dominating imperatives of the machine cycle offered and accepted as a given totality.

The changing nature of advanced capitalism in the 1920s with its commodity logic broke out into the open. The creation of needs where no needs existed, the growing discrepancies between uneven sectors and regions of the economy, the dedication to economic before social needs, resulted in a revolt against the poverty of existence in the American city, at least a revolt among those cultural critics who struggled to find their location within a transforming society. This commodity crack brought in focus the social and cultural deficiencies of urban life. (490) Doom was apparent in the voices of many of these urban critics; voicing the antithesis of the boomer spirit, they spoke instead of the inevitability of disintegration and technical collapse of the mechanical American city in tones that portrayed disillusionment and despair. (113, 250) Their concern centered on the problems of machine technology and its implications for social relations. Interested in the quality of urban life and the quest for conditions that they said would create the good life, they searched to humanize the city machine, to establish new conceptions of man's relationship to the environment in an opposing reaction to the alienation and superorganization of the mechanical logic that seemed to pervade all urban life. If the machine could produce the material satisfactions of life, who would be concerned with the quality of such a life? When the only relevant question seemed to be the technical requisite of "does it work?" or "does it threaten to break down?" they felt this pragmatic criterion of workability alone fell far beneath the cultural and social needs of urbanized life. (98)

To understand the development of this critical antagonism to the large metropolitan city, we have to understand the historical context that motivated it. On one side stood the process of mechanization, what has been described as the point where increased production no longer required an increase in living labor, and labor in turn was released to apply its skill to other areas. Mechanization was thus accompanied by the accelerated development of intellectuals and other mental workers; teachers, artists, freelance writers, and professional critics formed part of this liberated force. Many of these intellectual workers sought to become the guiding national conscience for those who stood against the conforming herd, trying to forge a life-style apart from the market system where work and social relations might once again fulfill human needs. (490) For this reason some of these intellectual critics placed themselves against the trend of metropolitan life, as fugitives on the outside of consumer society looking beyond the immediate logic of capitalist society.

On the other side of the critic's struggle stood the realities of capitalist development. By 1920 the urban population, having been drawn to employment centers and having been pushed off the land by the mechanization of agricultural production, surpassed the census numbers categorized as rural. America had become a nation of cities. The trouble with American cities, the critics complained, was that they had been planned too rigorously. (360:143) Those who could escaped to the suburbs, but they escaped the doom of mechanical encroachment only briefly as the maw of the great city moved out to catch them. As Lewis Mumford criticized, almost all American cities accepted the motive of metropolitan expansion. Promoted by the desire for increasing land values, they based their future expectations on unlimited population growth. Guided by this premise of expansion and subsequent congestion, the only beneficiaries of this regional motif were the landlords, mortgage holders, and real estate speculators. (363)

These regional planners, Mumford lamented, were not offering a rational plan but a religion, a deep-seated mystical impulse in which traffic, commerce, property regulations, and zoned heights were the presiding deities. Their city ideal reflected the hard quality of the current mechanical culture; humans perceived as units designed to run or use these elaborate mechanical devices were consequently sacrificed to the steely jungles of commerce. (366:270) Routine and habit kept industry fettered to sites where high land values could be easily transformed into consumer prices, where vast fortunes kept amassing through the continued congestion of expanding populations. (362)

Another critic, Stuart Chase, pointed out that megalopolis would become increasingly congested, its vast transportation systems pumping us back and forth from "places where we would rather not live to places where we would rather not work" until a sudden and disastrous technical breakdown or a less dramatic surfeit of citizens would produce a steady emigration and an ultimate collapse of land values within the center cities. If the water mains burst within the city, they could create more havoc than dynamite exploded in the center; one punctured gas main meant wholesale death; any stoppage or failure of telephones, electricity, subways, sewers, ambulances, elevators, and so forth would cause untold disaster. So interconnected had this city machine become that "if one prime nerve [was] cut for any length of time, the urban environment [would] start rapidly to disintegrate . . . the failing of one nerve [was] almost certain to result in the rupture of others." We had a choice, claimed Stuart Chase: to await the inevitable collapse of cities or to abandon the real estate complex and plan the city for its proper functions, protecting it with open spaces and balanced loads and ensuring its order by adequate disciplinary control and constant supervision. A ruthless civic will, he said, must operate until a totally new orientation of work areas, recreational places, and home regions became established and permanently protected. (98)

So the regional planners, both practical and utopian, began to search for a new order to the metropolitan whole, a regional form to be based upon a continually shifting and contingent field. The collective action of the cooperative state of the 1920s would draw a brand-new American city. Implicit in this desire was a distaste for the mechanical and decomposed order of the old American city and the relentless temper and technical theories of zoning advocates. Yet not one of the proposals offered for new regional centers got rid of this alliance with a technical world. One type of practical regional planning would see the future as lying along the routes of the spreading highways and the promise of the automobile and in this sense planned a globally mechanized city; another regional proposal visualized a new order based upon giant power and industrial relocation policies and thus formed their utopia out of old garden city ideals. Neither valued the center city: for one it was set up to battle with the suburban ideal; for another it was a negative threat to the new order, which was to be destroyed and plundered. Let us turn to explore the discourse of these regional planners, one seeking a new metropolitan machine and the other seeing brand new towns on open fields of green.

A Practical Order for Regional Needs

As metropolitan areas emerged during the Progressive era, a number of interest groups such as the gas, electricity, and transit utilities sought to draw power from the state at the expense of local control. In response wealthy businessmen, improvement societies, commercial clubs, and chambers of commerce formed a coalition to promote a metropolitan-wide organization guiding public opinion on regional planning issues. But there was little hope for carrying out a regional plan without the aid of a governmental unit to correspond to this regional domain. The problem that obstructed the solution of practical regional planning assumed a special character when it was noted that in the metropolitan Boston area, for example, there were more than 49 independent cities and towns. Metropolitan New York contained parts of three states and 22 counties and more than 400 towns. So too with other American cities. (434:349–360) Regional planners could no longer rely upon annexation to solve the metropolitan problem. Indeed the larger and older the communities in the regional whole, the stronger they resisted merging with the central city. How then could the discipline of planning be ordered across these fragmented regions?

There were other pressing regional problems to solve, the most urgent being the metropolitan provision of adequate sewerage systems and water supplies. Arbitrary governmental boundaries often stood in the way. For example, the most efficient drainage system from populated St. Louis County lay toward the Mississippi River across the political boundaries of the city of St. Louis. Although the city and the county drew their water from the same point on the Missouri River, their water supply was provided by two different companies. Thus both systems represented an unnecessary duplication of works, filtration beds, and pipelines at untold expense to the users. Since sizable capital outlays for water and sewer infrastructure were necessary, outlying units frequently were unable to provide themselves with adequate provisions for either. All in all when the American city was assessed, the high property values, which could be taxed for revenues to pay for these necessary metropolitan services, still lay in the heart of the city, in high-class suburbs, or in large industrial towns. Most of the ordinary suburbs with only a small-scale industrial base found it difficult to pay for such capital-intensive developments. (434:353–354)

An improved and coordinated highway system was essential to the prosperity of the city, yet no matter how the planners drew coordinated transportation lines, the poorer towns and suburbs had no means to construct them. State highway aid continued to be allocated to rural areas and avoided incorporated towns. (434:356) Not surprisingly, then, transportation, traffic, and highway solutions formed the heart of most regional planning strategies in the 1920s.[2]

Estimates claimed that in 1913 fewer than 150 motor cars had crossed the continent. By 1923 it was believed more than 25,000 cars had carried more than 100,000 people across the Lincoln Highway alone. In those ten years interest in developing a system of national highways revived. By 1922 the Highway Green Book listed 24 transcontinental and 22 interstate highway organizations, all pressuring for the development of a national highway system. In support of highway development the Federal Aid Act of 1916 created the Bureau of Public Roads in the Department of Agriculture, and a 1921 law promoted the organization of state highway commissions to help implement a ten-year plan for the improvement of national highways, already outlined on a map of the United States. (258) Still this plan, which was more concerned with main routes, farm-to-market roads, and even scenic and recreational highways, ignored essential roadways into, through, and around the central core of the city. (15)

Traffic regulations were another problem. No uniform standards existed when each town and county held to its own regulatory form. In a suburb of St. Louis, for example, the middle of the street was also the boundary line between two municipalities; hence speed limits differed on either side of the street, and at intersections some traffic lights were hung above and others at the side of the road. (434:358) This was an area where the cooperative state could help. Thus national conferences were organized in the 1920s to stimulate local governments, without state compulsion, to act responsibly and to coordinate standards for traffic control and highway safety among all the levels involved. (86:336)

Streetcar railroad and subway systems were no longer profitable investments. (255:149) When city-street interurbans had been constructed, the automobile and paved highway were still in their infancy. But as new automobile registrations reached their peak near 1923 and populations rapidly spread out across the region, streetcar transport with its fixed rails and high investment costs started to decline. Motor buses automatically presented a competitive solution, for their flexible route patterns could easily capitalize on reduced or shifting commuter patterns. At the exact point where many streetcar franchise holders were faced with great expenditures for rail and paving renewal on unimportant extensions or crosstown lines, individually owned jitney buses began to crowd out the electric railways. By 1922, however, control over the operation of these jitneys and motor buses began to pass into the hands of the streetcar franchises, not necessarily to make them operate more profitably but to reduce the franchise's losses incident to serving scarce metropolitan populations. Under franchise control lightly traveled railways needing renewal or extension could be abandoned and replaced by the company's own motor buses. (256) Rapid streetcar transit had had its heyday; now the automobile held sway and would come to dominate every practical planner's regional transportation solutions.

The same fragmented governmental jurisdictions that thwarted a rational and regional distribution of transportation infrastructure, water resources, and sanitation services retarded a rapid accumulation of capital in the larger, more consolidated corporations. In the 1920s these capital units began not only to create nationwide consumer markets but started to spread interdependent stages of production across different regions. (135) Were these corporations to bargain with each fragmented governmental unit for adequate highway systems and sufficient land, water, and electricity to parallel production needs? Were they to pay a disproportionate share of taxes for services that some towns within a region were unable to afford? As many of these manufacturing and industrial enterprises were being pushed or pulled out of the center of the American cities toward the metropolitan rim, how else could they provide for essential production supports or coordinate the flow of investments across the metropolis except through regional planning? In response large-scale corporations, the fastest-growing monopoly units of production, became early and eager sponsors of regional governments and regional planning. (388) Not so surprisingly regional or metropolitan planning bodies often organized around the provision of a public utility near large industrial areas. The Lucas County Planning Commission (near Toledo, Ohio) prompted the orderly development of highways and parks; the Miami Conservancy District of Ohio organized in 1915 for the purpose of constructing and maintaining dams and channels for flood controls; and the East Bay Municipal Utility District of 1921 provided public services to the metropolitan region of Oakland, California. (258)

In the 1920s regional planning commissions sprang up from coast to coast. (479:212–221) The Boston Metropolitan Planning Commission, established in 1923, was an advisory apparatus that combined the voices of three volunteer commissioners with representatives from the Commission of Public Works, the Department of Public Utilities, and the Transit Department. This commission was expected to voice opinions on the need for metropolitan-wide transportation services and public utilities. The Los Angeles County Regional Planning Commission was another advisory authority, also established in 1923, and intended to comment upon regional needs for highways, water conservation, sanitation, zoning, and parks. (258) In New York State five regional planning bodies took shape: the Niagara Frontier Planning Board, the Onondaga County Regional Planning Board, the Capitol District Regional Planning Association, the Central Hudson Valley Regional Planning Association, and the Regional Plan of New York and Its Environs. (436)

Each advisory regional apparatus reproduced a set of economic and disciplinary functions that responded to the needs of a metropolitan society rapidly learning to consume automobiles, suburban homes, and household appliances. Although these planners' desire was to establish rational growth controls for the metropolitan city, it was really the rapid pace of suburbanization, a shattering infusion of freeways and automobiles, and an upheaval in manufacturing locations that gave rise to this particular ethic. Nevertheless seizing upon agglomeration, these regional planners searched for new classifications, new data, new methods of deduction that would describe the threshold of industrial saturation, the limits of population density and size, beyond which a city should not grow. The basic instrument of analysis was a survey, which carved up regional space into social and economic categories and analyzed distributory flows of industry, population, and land. (5) Then hypothetical laws of growth made it possible to deduce from the survey of facts how fast and to what extent a city should grow. (385) Of them all, one advisory regional planning effort stands out as representative of this process: the Regional Plan of New York and Its Environs.

As early as 1915 Charles Norton had commented that

no plan of New York will command recognition unless it includes all the area in which all New Yorkers earn their livelihood and make their homes. From the City Hall a circle must be swung which will include the Atlantic Highlands and Princeton; the lovely Jersey hills back of Morristown and Tuxedo; the incomparable Hudson as far as Newburgh; the Westchester lakes and ridges, to Bridgeport and beyond, and all of Long Island. (416)

New York City had experimented with the formation of a regional planning body in the early decades of the twentieth century. With the opening of the Panama Canal in 1914, major Manhattan business interests tried to improve the transit and harbor facilities of the port of New York. At this time all but two of the major intercontinental railroads had their terminals on the Jersey waterfront, so all of their freight had to be transported across the harbor by boat to distribution terminals in Manhattan. This chaos of multiple transportation lines and transshipment delays became more evident during World War I. In consequence a New York-New Jersey Port and Harbor Development Commission was established in 1917, and in 1921 the Port of New York Authority was given a legislative mandate to create a plan for the physical development of the port. New York was beginning to learn how to plan on a regional scale, but there existed no regional authority to implement the improvement proposals. (261:53–85)

Since no one governmental unit had jurisdiction over this region, no public treasury could create such a plan. Not surprisingly the Russell Sage Foundation sponsored the creation of a committee to work toward such a regional plan. By 1922 this committee, soon to be known as the Regional Plan of New York and Its Environs, had outlined the necessary survey work: an economic and industrial survey that would analyze the fundamental reasons for the existence of New York; a survey mapping the physical conditions of the region and giving special attention to the railway and water transportation network; a legal survey outlining the process of zoning, excess condemnation, shore rights, and land under water; and a survey of social and living conditions stressing the factors that produce healthy and satisfying housing and home environments. (416)

Transportation and public utility needs, zoning, and the single-family home underscored the intent of each survey. Already in 1920 the New York-New Jersy Port and Harbor Development Commission had outlined the basic problem for the port of New York. It recommended the creation of a Port Authority, producing a comprehensive plan for the rationalization of railroad chaos and outlining circumferential highways, underground tunnels, and an automatic electric goods delivery system within Manhattan. When this Port Authority was created, however, the large waterfront cities in the region opposed it and each railroad company, wanting to maintain monopoly control over its own lines and terminal, forced the port Authority into an impasse. A new organization was needed to develop a regional plan, and that would be the role for the Regional Plan of New York and Its Environs. (261:53–85)

In commenting upon the timeliness of this new conception of regional city building, Herbert Hoover drew attention to yet another need:

The great growth of industry since New York was originally planned presents a host of new problems. The cost of distribution of necessities within the boundaries of the city increases each year until today the congestion, the inadequate system of terminals of transportation and commodity distribution generally tax New York with ten or fifteen percent upon the cost of living above more adequately served centers.

Many of our industries are seasonal. If we are to secure high living standards and to gain in national productivity, these industries must be so interlocked as to give more continuous employment. The fact that New York has at all times the largest proportion of unemployment of any of our cities is due partially to this ill adjustment. . . .

One part of such a plan must be a realization of each economic group in the community as to its function to the whole great community of which it is a part. With this in mind, residential districts whose interests center largely around low cost living and educational and recreation facilities would see their interests in better means of distribution and the development of public utilities. The manufacturing districts must find not only better aligned transportation but coordination to residential areas which can be developed upon human lines. (416)

Thus industrial location patterns brought a new import to the New York Regional Plan. A study of the metal industry, the largest employer in the New York region, disclosed that since 1900 metal manufacturing in New York and its environs had shifted from heavy industry to predominantly light industry. Only small plants that depended upon market accessibility remained within the city. So too with the food industry: only two types of manufacturing plants were likely to remain in Manhattan: those requiring a large and fluctuating number of workers such as cracker, biscuit, and candy plants and those that gained advantages in distribution such as bread, bakeries, and ice cream plants. (258) Even the great department stores were moving to suburban shopping centers. Thus innovative surveys, sponsored by the Regional Plan, began to ask new questions about the economic base of the region. By surveying the basic industries in the New York region, consultants advised, it could be determined which industries were leaving the city and which were staying; upon these figures broad regional population trends could be projected and the regional whole adjusted to shifting industrial trends. (261:229–293)

Another basic problem for the Regional Plan to solve was automobile traffic. By 1920 the metropolitan area surrounding New York City had 540,000 registered motor vehicles and by 1926 over 1.3 million, producing massive traffic jams on inadequate downtown streets during the day and on colonial highway routes during weekends. Since the railroads, even under the gentle prodding of the Regional Plan, would not consolidate or cooperate, the only solution for distribution of population was along established rail lines or in coordination with the spreading highway system. Thus the planners distributed cheap single-family homes along the rapid-transit lines and motor roadways and replanned the deteriorated central areas by opening up new traffic ways and creating new open spaces carefully allocated to enhance existing property values. "Scatter the skyscraper!" became a byword, in order to prevent clusters of high buildings in one area from forming undue traffic congestion on the ground and blocking the light and air of neighboring buildings. Searching back through all the old improvement plans for the New York region, the Regional Plan graphically redrew Nelson Lewis's express highways around the Manhattan waterfront, Olmsted's old boulevards across Brooklyn and Queens, Burnham's old plans for Long Island Parkways, with additional circumferential highways and radial routes in the hinterland, double- and triple-decker traffic flows within the center, and new bridges linking Manhattan, Queens, and the Bronx. (261:26–52, 229–389)

By and large dismissing the decaying and deserted central core, the Regional Plan thought its impact should be on the unbuilt sections in the suburbs. High-grade residential areas that depended upon access to the center city must be protected from intrusion by industries and working classes, which no longer needed any linkage to the central city. These luxury residential areas should be located along select radial lines of transportation, and more intensive development could be directed into separate subsectors, some of which might approximate industrial satellite towns. Even Jersey City and Hoboken were viewed as too congested and disorganized to provide suitable residential districts. Thus a linear city in New Jersey was proposed to straddle the Lehigh Valley railway, and special financial incentives were suggested to enable speculative developers to build low-priced, low-rental housing for one- or two-family residences. (261:142–228)

As early as 1922 the English planner Raymond Unwin had advised the Regional Committee to base its planning surveys on provisional hypotheses: first, that increased transportation facilities could not cure congestion unless they were accompanied by regulatory restrictions upon the concentration of high buildings; second, that fewer streets should be allowed to traverse residential areas while main streets carrying traffic between important places should be located on viaducts bridging over cross-street traffic; third, that private automobile traffic should be regulated, with specific routes allocated to its exclusive use; and finally, that all of this unnecessary movement and mobility of goods, people, and vehicles could be eliminated if certain industries were decentralized from Manhattan and if lives were "localized" by improving local industrial functions, developing new suburbs and garden cities, and controlling haphazard urban development. (261:142–228)

As the New York Regional Plan developed under the leadership of Thomas Adams, however, regional planning came to look more like a map of proposals for future metropolitan land use and infrastructure development and less like a set of proposals to improve economic and social conditions of the metropolitan whole. Now the predominant theme was how to accommodate, not to limit, future population growth in order to reap the benefits of agglomeration without suffering the losses of congestion. (261:265–266) By the mid-1920s a grave split occurred between the two different regional motifs: those that promoted metropolitan growth and became apologists for and rationalizers of the suburban trend and those that advocated a utopian order by controlling population growth and industrial centralization through autonomous garden cities in the regional hinterland.

Was regional planning to attend to political control when city boundaries always lagged far behind the spread of population? Annexation, the process by which the center city acquired control over its neighbors, no longer seemed feasible as suburbanites increasingly forsook the central city and deliberately declared their preference for smaller, autonomous communities. Yet financial interdependence of contiguous rural and urban regions demanded an equitable readjustment and the creation of regional governments with limited functions. Not to be seen as a method to aggrandize the power of any one unit, political scientists suggested the region could be the colocation of a financial and a governmental apparatus providing for the equitable planning and preservation of rural and urban relationships. (168) To secure the order of regional control meant to reverse the hold of vested political interests yet simultaneously to recognize that a regional plan enormously affected active property interests.

The Regional Corollary

Thus it fell to those outside the discourse describing the disciplinary details of regional planning to suggest a new governmental apparatus that might implement public utility and transportation needs. Beyond regional planning, with its hierarchy of functional subunits linked by highway systems to the business core, a new metropolitan theory took form that stressed not the control of urban growth but the logic of political power and the forces of economic self-interest. Political scientists argued that a regional plan should not only secure a uniform public service and transportation policy applied to the metropolitan whole but also achieve an equitable adjustment of financial burdens among the various portions of the community. (5) If it was to obtain both requirements, infrastructure policy and equitable revenues, then planning must close the gap between theory and practice by systematically grouping communities within a new governmental apparatus. Such a reordering would depend upon a (regional) corollary . . . of analyzing and exposing to public gaze, on one hand, the various economic interests that [were] likely to gain more money by keeping things as they [were] or by forcing anti-social development, and, on the other hand, the economic groups that [might] be enlisted [behind the regional plan] in virtue of their practical interests on the side of a comprehensive community scheme. (54:278)

Charles Beard carefully argued and presented to the planners the pluralist theory of interest group conflicts:

Applying this doctrine to the city, I would say that in every city there grow up of necessity a real estate interest, public utility interests, various manufacturing interests, commercial interests, shipping and carrying interests, banking interests, an organized labor interest and office-holding interest, with many lesser interests, dividing the citizens into different groups actuated by different sentiments and views with respect to any concrete readjustment of tangible values by a city plan. While it may be true that the rank and file in these groups only understand vaguely the nature of their interest, I believe that each of the groups or sub-groups has powerful and effective leaders who have very definite ideas as to the probable effect which any readjustment would have upon their balance sheets. Occasionally, they may be wrong in their guesses . . . indeed often . . . but they must be right most of the time or they would all disappear in bankruptcy and failure. (51:67)

Beard's argument proposed elaboration of the planner's dialogue to include a regional corollary, enabling them to interpret all the economic and political factors that formerly lay outside the scope of planning but were determinant forces behind regional growth and development. (54:278) In spite of this well-intentioned advice, the threadbare regional dream, not the political economy of the regional corollary, became the practical planners' strategy. Never clearly worked out with the underlying political and economic antagonisms, regional planning was carried along on the waves that sent voluntary cooperation rolling across the institutional base of 1920s America. Regional planning, it was said, must be done through cooperation: decentralized local government in harmony with planning advice. (5) As Bassett recommended to the Committee of the New York Regional Plan, "Let the cooperating public official take all the credit they could for any plan. The purpose of the Committee ought to be to secure results, not to win public praise and recognition for itself." (261:131) Regional planning should proceed with the same promotional campaign that was winning the battle for zoning: proselytize, provide information, stress citizen involvement and control by local officials, recruit influential citizens to advise the staff, and then send them back to their communities to implement the Regional Plan's goals. (261:229–293) This regional motif thus remained but a suggestion as to how local authorities and property owners might conform to the imperatives of regional development.

In the gap between technical knowledge and the capacity to achieve based upon this knowledge, city and regional planners had assumed that any rational scheme would force the allegiance of enlightened self-interests (54) To ensure that a regional city be built according to design, not only must the area adopt and carry out an official plan but it must obtain the conformity of all private and public uses of land. The first requirement presented little difficulty, but how to gain the promise of public and private support? This gap between theory and practice, a space in which the tensions between technical advice and state implementation were drawn, was filled by the category of public opinion, a concept dependent upon a discourse with citizen groups, conveying to the general public the body of practical rules and technical objectives embodied within a regional strategy.

The environment of an industrial society, mediated many times over by the automobile, the elevator, the radio, and the telephone, was envisioned as a complex of multidimensional elements. Nothing seemed to link the mass of individuals to the collective whole, while meantime the multiplication of units and the growing complexities of everyday life fragmented the ragged ensemble into expanding disorder. Communities, it was claimed, had "disintegrated into a kind of futile automicity. . . . Neighbors . . . are simply human integers in spatial juxtaposition. . . . We are going [thus] to think more and more of citizens as group citizens, not as atomic citizens." (399:130) The problem in the 1920s was how to revitalize community life: encouraging group membership and enlisting their support behind vital community projects, focusing upon those growing edges where political relationships depended more upon goodwill and agreement than upon authority and coercive force. (475) If planners were to realize their regional strategies, then they must find the disciplinary ethic to compel their victory; they must possess an organizational force that presupposed public acceptance and continuity of support. The degree to which they could control the pattern of regional development depended upon the greater power and practice of group interests.

In order to prevent a monopoly of control within a progressively more centralized government bureaucracy, to avoid the objectification of class contradictions as more areas of the economy were brought under state purview, and to legitimate these interventions, Hoover espoused the ideal of a cooperative state. (399) By balancing political power among the three functional groups of labor, capital, and the state, by encouraging the idea of cooperative voluntary association and mutual restraint, the reality of economic inequities and the specifics of institutionalized power were effectively occluded. The subsequent role of the city and regional planner was not only to publicize the ideology of association but to coordinate

and integrate multiple decision centers, to diffuse political power throughout the regional ensemble, and yet to relink that participation back to a
central administrative and planning apparatus.

Paralleling and defusing the pluralist ideology, the city federation thus
became an imaginary structure of multiple urban groups. "Civic organization," it was explained, was "based on definite group life. . . . [They]
organize around some definite center . . . they or their chosen representative . . . meet to promote a still larger group life . . . a federation of these
[becomes] the city . . . [a] council of control for all the matters which
concern the whole community." (518:85) Power for the planners, Overstreet declared, was achieved through the combination of individuals:

> If we wish to do things, we should seek first of all to get them in their
> social groups. Then the doing is not only more powerful, but it is so
> profoundly liked that it becomes the joyous part of the life of those that
> do. (City planners) should . . . get across to these voluntary groups in a
> community. When the interest of a voluntary group is enlisted . . . one
> has the whole power of that group back of the idea. The pride of the
> group is involved and the pride of the group pushes the project into
> success. (399:128–129)

Planning thus presented could become the rallying point for all of the
constructive forces in a given region, but its implementary power—that
is, the local vote and persuasion of public officials—could be obtained
only if local interest groups agreed to these planning proposals. This in
turn depended upon successfully influencing these citizen groups. The
weakest link in the planning chain was stated to be the public's general
lack of understanding of city and regional planning—its purpose, its methods, its advantages, its costs, its legitimations. (383) Citizen committees
aligned with planning commissions were therefore essential to fill the gap
between the ignorant public and the technical planner. They could initiate
city and regional planning work long before it was generally appreciated
by the public at large, they could guide city planning once a program had
been made, and by keeping the proposals before the public they could
help city government put across projects approved by city officials. (381:29)
Volunteer mediative groups were superior to public administrative groups;
they could initiate and experiment where public officials could not; they
could represent minority opinions and limit their monetary gifts to special
interests while public authorities must not. (381)

Effective public administration demanded control over the public mind.
Thus planners advised each other to reveal to the public only simple facts
with obvious implications and appeal. Public officials who later had to
accept or reject the plan should be given something to interest them lest
their indifference work against the plan's successful implementation. (297)

If the greater public was to be educated, then planners must present to them a tentative but fairly complete plan and ask for their opinions and constructive suggestions. If the plan was well constructed, there would be no further suggestions because each new idea would entail so many changes that the task would appear beyond the abilities of the ordinary citizen. Nevertheless the asking would arouse friendliness and support behind the plan not otherwise achieved. (399)

Citizen participation in the city and regional planning discourse of the 1920s was confined to a neutral accepting stance. Planning possessed no legal authority over the development of private property. It had to rely upon public acceptance. But a depoliticized public sphere, still accepting of elite authority and more distracted by its developing interests in consumer and leisure-time activities, failed to produce powerful participatory involvement. Thus it was left for the planners to create widespread citizen acceptance for planning. (297) In consequence the emphasis fell upon the need to create a public opinion that recognized and promoted the legitimacy of the regional planning authority.

As planning gathered together the streams of technical information that flowed from political science, social economics, engineering, architecture, and public health, it acquired knowledge that it organized into distinct categories, standards, and codes. Out of this disciplinary synthesis grew the idea that a planner, although a man of practical common sense, was in truth a transprofessional expert. (399) Not only must he draw together from practical experience the regularities of a variety of technical professions, but he must also diffuse these ideas in both the technical language of scientific discourse and a popular form of public relations. So far the profession of planning had advanced without an institutionalized federal authority. Although city planners had failed continuously since Benjamin March's efforts in 1909 to gain a federal national city planning commission, now once more in 1929 they pressured for a national clearinghouse of planning information. (479) They argued that not only should the discourse of planning be delimited by a recognized professional education when the first city planning school opened at Harvard University in 1929, but its disciplinary order and practical regularities might be voluntarily enforced by organizing its information, research, and promotional programs at the national level. (221, 264) In this fashion city and regional planning in the 1920s reflected the economic and political functions of the cooperative state: a state that served as a national clearinghouse for surveying, compiling, interpreting, publicizing, and exchanging information that it subsequently revealed as a body of acceptable public policies. (264) The political and economic realities of implementary control, the possibility of enforcing the disciplinary order of city and regional planning, remained beyond the grasp of the regional planner. No matter how realistic or practical they tried to draw their proposals, they remained idealistic dreams scarcely deterring the rapid growth and destruction of the metropolitan city.

A Regional Utopia

Our sacred American cities, Lewis Mumford complained in 1926, are based on the hard quality of our present mechanical culture; they treat human beings as units, designed to run or to use elaborate mechanical appliances; instead the city should have a humane base. (366) Mumford claimed that the only hope for the American city lay outside itself: to think of the region as a whole and the city as part of it. Metropolitan sprawl and center city congestion, he noted, were simply the crude application of the mechanical and mathematical sciences to urban development. In the garden city ideal, however, a counterrevolution was offered based upon the humane arts and sciences: those of biology, medicine, psychology, education, and architecture. (365)

The new American city, Mumford claimed, must have a human base; it must be adapted to the needs of human life. Thus the main focus for planning should be the creation of a shell favorable to the best life: a policy to limit population growth within urban areas and to seed stabilized communities in the rural hinterlands. (363) Both social relations and physical environments condition each other; they must therefore be transformed together. So it was that these regional utopian planners represented a form of social criticism, a critical act that aimed at a principled reform of the profession itself, as well as a process of planning that could generate more humane environments. This regional motif of the 1920s stood as a witness to the mounting alienation of modern man whose work no longer appeared self-gratifying, whose professional ethic was not expressible within the increasing commodification of American society.

The process of mechanization with its liberated intellectual worker and the realities of capitalist consumption, which placed the real estate complex in charge of urban spatial development, converged to create this special regional motif, a nostalgic escape that opposed the growth of mechanization, dehumanization, and urban reification and stressed in return a continuous environmental balance borne of a new community ethic. This regional ethic would contain a critical awareness of the values of cultural regionalism, ecological harmony, and a balanced and controlled urban development.

At first this effort revolved around the issue of how to promote good housing and sound community planning at minimal costs. These planners and architects formed their initial ideal of community planning in the design and building of World War I cantonments. (306) Since it was no longer economically feasible to produce low-cost housing under postwar conditions of inflation and scarcity of materials, they advocated state subsidies, regulatory controls over speculative land practices, and community supervision of industrial location policies, transportation decisions, and housing allocations. Initially after the war this group of planners continued their discourse within the Committee of Community Planning of the American Institute of Architects, but as they began to lean toward a regional motif and garden city ideal, they openly criticized and then broke with the practical planners' bias promoting metropolitan growth and suburban diffusion. At this point, in 1923, twenty planners and architects, among them Lewis Mumford, Henry Wright, Clarence Stein, Frederick Ackerman, Benton MacKay, Clarence Perry, and Stuart Chase, formed the Regional Planning Association of America hoping that together they could develop and understand the principles and motives behind the "community man" so that they would be able to design residential environments satisfying every biological and social need.[3] These men simultaneously searched for an alternative professional role. Declaring that the instinct of workmanship and capitalism were incompatible as long as the profit motive remained primary, they sought a community association by which social planners, architects, and laymen could collectively plan and manage a community's development. (365)

Searching for a theory of metropolitan control to answer the new infrastructure problems of the 1920s and breathing in the air of Hoover's cooperative state with its voluntary spirit, these regional planners fell back upon selling and promoting the garden city ideal first elaborated by Ebenezer Howard in the 1890s. (168) If population was concentrated in subcenters of the region, not allowed to fall like an avalanche across the metropolitan rim, then public utilities and transportation needs could be more economically administered. Instead of a concentrated mass at the center, the metropolitan region could be envisioned as a hierarchical summation of economically related but autonomous units: a central core with its financial and administrative functions and a series of contiguous regional subcenters in which businesses and industries were naturally segregating themselves. Placing a boundary of open space in rings around each local unit and threading a service structure and highway network across the whole, this regional motif etched out a skeleton for the metropolitan area while allowing the specifics of local municipal zoning, site planning, and housing regulations to fill in the details.

In the beginning Raymond Unwin, a designer and theorist of English garden cities, held a major directive role over this new community ethic. Unwin lamented that the American city of the early 1920s was filled with a disorganized rabble, all too intent on individual struggles to give thought to their city. This rabble furthermore was too confused to organize themselves and too numerous to be easily controlled. They presented no city community nor offered the good life of our ideals. In consequence this overelaborate urbanized civilization must break down, for without any organization of this unwieldy mass of men, American cities were helpless in any emergency and at the mercy of any panic-stricken group. (518)

The first requisite of our new concept of planning, Unwin continued, must be the provision of room for every person to live, work, and play for health, efficiency, pleasure, and beauty. Thus communities must be organized around primary group life, and these units must then focus on a definite center. Grouped into boroughs, suburbs, or satellites, a federation of these will form a council of control for all the greater matters concerning the whole American city. This meant a complete break with the usual American method of drafting-board city planning, which had produced a maze of monotonous and repetitious city blocks whose ordered regularity was its only dignifying feature. Instead this new concept of planning was based on recognition of the right of a growing city community to see that the land around it and over which it must expand shall be used and reserved for those purposes that the whole city determines are best. (518)

This regional motif was not an implementable mode of planning, or a disciplinary code, or a planning diagram but a style of thought and a visionary program. (26) A balanced control of the environment, population, and technical functions of the city required or necessitated a regional framework, a revolutionary outlook that could both reverse the trend of population and centralization and rejuvenate the decline of rural agricultural areas. Placing its accent on the conservation of humane with natural values, this regional ethic spoke of the "reinvigoration and rehabilitation of whole regions so that the products of culture and civilization [would] . . . be available to everyone at every point in a region." (365:152) Seeking an alternative to metropolitan centralization and suburban diffusions, the motif explained that deliberately planned regional subcenters—a collocation of administrative, economic, cultural, and judicial life—would be the basis for a reinvigoration and realignment of population, housing, agricultural, and industrial development. (365:152)

Finally, Mumford proclaimed, we may begin to plan cities on new ideals not based upon the conditions of the past. For the last several decades, a group had grown up slowly, first centered about Ebenezer Howard and his garden city group and now by a group of planners in America who considered that "the congested metropolis is not primarily bad or miserable: it is merely wasteful, inefficient, technologically obsolete. That is to say it arose out of industrial and commercial conditions which have ceased to operate in full force today, and may not operate at all tomorrow." (362:290) Giant power and industrial planning were capable of reconstructing the American city ideal on a completely new basis:

> Giant power . . . carries with it the notion of distributing electricity in districts where a balanced day and night load may be carried along the same mains: this requires a community devoted to both domesticity and industry, not a community in which these things are separated, as they are in the big city and its suburbs. . . . (362:290)
>
> Whereas for a century we have lived where industrial and commercial opportunities seemed greatest, we can now reverse the process, and deliberately plant our industries and our communities in regions where the human opportunities for living are best. In the light of this, our ingenious plans for super-cities, with super-congestion, super-subways, super-tenements, and super-skyscrapers are . . . a little superficial. (362:291)

The future of the American city, Mumford proclaimed, will thus involve limited growth and the deliberate planning and development of new communities in the hinterland. These new communities will differ dramatically from the suburban ideal. First, they will be located in relationship to water and power resources and in the open country where land values are still low. A permanent belt of open agricultural land will surround each community, providing it with a local food supply and preserving open spaces. Second, these communities will start with all the institutions necessary for a population of 10,000 to 50,000. Land needed for schools, churches, hospitals, libraries, theaters, municipal buildings, playgrounds, and parks will be planned in advance, and so will the land needed for shops, offices, and factories. Residential areas will be designed for quiet, safety, and beauty. Here Mumford offered the American city a choice: growth by the explicit foundation of new communities fully designed for working, learning, and living or growth by "mechanical extension" of the existing center where the remedies simply added to the disease. (362)

The 1926 Report of the Commission on Housing and Regional Planning in the State of New York typified this regional motif. (436) Between 1880 and 1920, this report complained, the independent farms and communal units that composed the state of New York had been destroyed. The city became the dominant center, offset only be specialized dairy and fruit-raising farms. During these years more than 5.7 million acres of farmland were abandoned, and more than a half of the counties declined in population. Local industries such as the sawmills, tanneries, gristmills, and woolen factories found their markets supplanted by national manufacturing establishments located predominantly in urban centers. By 1921, however, electricity had surpassed steam in importance as a motive power, and the flexible automobile had replaced the rigid lines of the railroad. These technological innovations would produce a new pattern of spatial development. They made decentralization of population and industry possible. Now the power requirements of the factory, being supplied by long-distance electric transmission plants at low costs, placed no barriers upon industrial and manufacturing locations. Factories that used to locate near congested urban centers in order to obtain supplies of labor and raw materials could now draw workers and materials by automobile, bus, or motor trucks within regional districts. Certain forces that for years had driven farmers to the cities would be removed. "With the passing of rural and small town life have gone natural facilities for recreation. . . . The home has suffered; the shadows of pyramiding land prices steal across one window after another until in the characteristic tenements in New York City two out of three rooms are sealed in perpetual darkness and twilight." (436:51) This congestion had compelled the artisan to escape to the suburbs, bred economic resistance to further growth, and raised physical problems that defied solution.

"Manifestly, the suburb," Mumford noted, "is a public acknowledgement of the fact that congestion and bad housing and blank vistas and lack of recreational opportunity and endless subway rides are not humanly endurable. The suburbanite is merely an intelligent heretic who has discovered that the mass of New York or Chicago or Zenith is a mean environment." (362:287) But the suburb was not the answer either, because very soon the

forces that created the suburb moved out, inexorably, with icy relentlessness, and began to destroy this idyllic environment, which had the neighborliness of a small community and the beauty of gardens and parks and easy access to nature. Inevitably the suburb grew and, growing, it became more like the city it had only apparently broken away from: the market street lengthened into a garish main street, ungainly offices and lunchrooms sprang up, an apartment house was built near the railroad tracks. Land values boomed; but taxes, alas, rose too. . . . All the costs of sewers, paving, unnecessarily wide residential streets, street lighting, gas, electricity, and police went up so rapidly that presently the newcomers could no longer afford a roomy, comfortable house. (362:287)

In opposition, regional planning, Lewis Mumford argued in the 1926 report, asked not how wide an area could be brought under the influence of the metropolis but how population and cultural facilities could be distributed in order to stimulate an active life throughout whole regions, a region being any geographic area that possessed a certain unity of climate, soil, vegetation, industry, and culture.

Determined by its earlier industrial and commercial constraints, the present megalopolis was inefficient, wasteful, and technologically obsolete.

When railroads dominated transportation corridors, urban growth took place along linear lines at points where these networks coalesced or crossed. Modern airplane and automobile transportation, however, favored a more even distribution of population, a more flexible network of roads culminating in regionally decentralized centers, not metropolitan-wide congested development. Energy, space, and time referred back one upon the other. Giant power, the consolidation of the electrical industry into a few holding companies, carried with it the vision of a better alignment between urban and rural areas, opening up the backward rural areas through deliberate reallocation of industry and people. (204) New communities would be located in rural areas, in ecological balance to water and power sources, in districts where land values were low. Surrounded by belts of agricultural land, these regional centers would soon become agriculturally self-sustained, fully planned with living, working, and learning in mind. They would establish a symbiotic relationship between the country and the city. The substitution of superpower combines for isolated steam power would check the flow of population to congested centers. Dirt, smoke, noise, and slums would be replaced with decentralized suburban and rural living environments.

Homes close to work, removal of congested and dangerous roadways from neighborhood groups, open spaces, good public schools, and adequate low-cost housing were among the essential ingredients of the good life envisioned for these regional communities. With this social orientation, new concepts were introduced into the planner's discourse—such concepts as livability, amenities of life, humanized environments, all conceptual orientations designed to supply the missing relationships between the everyday practical sphere and the technical mechanical domain. Bringing the needs of everyday life to the attention of the planners, a preoccupation with the ends of human activities and the aims of human institutions, presented an important reorientation, for some planning would henceforth be grounded in the life base and needs of metropolitan dwellers and from this point on the social planner would have to "get beneath the skin-of-the citizens of his community. He must, in short, forget his own point of view and find theirs." (399:132)

For the most part, however, regional planning in the 1920s was in the hands of practical commissioners who represented commercial and industrial interests. Not surprisingly master plans and regional plans etched out the configuration of economics, transportation, zoning, and land-use needs but neglected issues of rural abandonment, unemployment, and illiteracy. While many cultural and social issues had captured the fears of earlier city improvers, now that social unrest and the threat of the immigrant had subsided, physical planning in the American city was reduced to functional metropolitan planning.

The utopian regionalists placed their discourse of criticism outside consumer society, looking in as defenders of humane qualities of life containing nostalgic memories of a preindustrial past. Perhaps this regional motif was nowhere better summarized than in a University of Virginia meeting, "Problems of Municipal Administration," which brought together in 1931 those who had mobilized these ideals across the 1920s. Reporting upon the conference, Charles Ascher commented that when he arrived the captains and the kings were departing, replaced during the following week by an array of poets, agricultural chemists, sociologists, city planners, philosophers, architects, and lawyers who met to discuss what they called regionalism. The challenge for these critics was whether there were other values beyond the waste of shifting land uses, population mobility, difficulties in planning highways, transit, and water supplies to which regional planning in the new South should direct itself; whether, in spite of its efficiency in circulation and transportation, the metropolitan centers of America had been able to provide a high quality of life. (26)

Southerners at the conference expressed their fears that the new metropolitan industrialism would turn them into communities based on the old pattern of the industrial city. Stringfellow Barr, editor of the *Virginia Quarterly Review*, pleaded that the death of the plantation as an economic organization need not mean the end of the social-cultural values that had flowered under it. John Gould Fletcher, a poet in the neo-Confederate style, extolled the genius of the region—those forces of place, work, and folk—in contrast with "false cosmopolitanism." (26)

This regional utopia, formed out of the human sciences for the first time, placed man, his social formations, his needs, and the society against which these needs were measured as the central focus of planning. When these measures were translated to the spatial dimension, however, the mathemetical order of the grid plan, the mechanization of everyday life, and the technical prerequisites of the automobile and the skyscraper presented to these regionalists such obstacles that the only solution was to flee. The old metropolitan form under the control of real estate speculators and the randomly organized building trades could never offer a humane existence. There was no other choice but to build a new urban order in the country. But the more these regionalists focused on the norms of community life and the new forms of group housing that encapsulated their ideals, the more they left intact the contradictory realities of the metropolis. They offered nothing with which to cover over or to solve the decay eating away at the central core of the American city or the suburban disarray tormenting its metropolitan fringe.

The weakness of this regional motif was to attempt a cultural critique in a sphere where exchange values dominated, so that these theories became one more spatial utopia separated from economic realities. Central to the critique lay a concern that drew attention to the imbalances and disharmonies of material reality. The discourse, however, constructed a utopian regional order and a revolutionary realignment of industrial forces which it supposed would be voluntarily adopted and developed.

Stepping to the side of the capitalist system, this social critique of the 1920s accepted as natural the assumptions of private property, the increasing concentration of wealth, and the enlightened administrative directives and organizational functions of the cooperative state. In short these critics aided in the transition to state administrative controls by proclaiming that modern society had become so complex that only the engineers could understand and operate it. The layman, a fugitive at best, could neither intervene against nor change much of the life that he faced. Because of the mounting fragmentation and specialization of work, an individual could no longer grasp the total process of production, much less his everyday life. An increasing hierarchy of mediators, administrative and managerial planners intervening between capital and labor, business and government, public groups and the state bureaucracies, orchestrated the order of the whole. This meant that only at the lowest subsystem levels of the community and the home could the regional planner's influence be visible.

Abandoned City Centers

Superspeculation in land and real estate and the overproduction and underconsumption of consumer goods in the 1920s ended in the economic catastrophe of 1929. Not a segment of the American economy remained unscarred. Yet at the beginning planning had little to offer, either in theory or practice. The regional critics of the 1920s with their old set of antagonisms to the American cities continued to attack the failures of the metropolitan complexity. Standing in the orientation of the 1920s but facing a crisis of enormous proportion, they still saw economic depression as a disease imposed upon the city by speculative, overmaterialistic businessmen and the American faith in competition by mere size.

Urban expansion and congestion, depression and unemployment, criminal behavior and racketeering were best expressed in medical terms as the diseased products of unfortuitous and unregulated economic and political forces. American cities, these critics complained, had passed through their period of growth and development and were now facing the problems of mature civilizations: their main arteries, through which flowed the stream of goods and people in support of a healthy economy, had begun to harden. "Arrested circulation," "auto-intoxication" followed by "local congestion" and "community scurvy" were the danger signs of this "national arteriosclerosis." (291) Without a national authority to shape and mold an integrated and functional system and with but meager and insufficient funds, the self-healing spontaneous powers of capital expansion would be insufficient for recovery. The more complex and mature an organization, the less its adaptive abilities and the more danger there was that it would succumb to crisis manifestations. (510)

In the depression of the 1930s urban real estate would become a burden to its owners and a menace to municipalities. The building industry would collapse, all municipal improvements would halt, agricultural productivity would drastically decline, and more than 5 million people would live at less than subsistence level. These calamities brought a quarter of a century of regional community planning to a standstill. Carol Aronovici claimed that "scientific city planning will begin only when our confidence in the city of today will have come to an end."[4] By 1936, he commented, planning in terms of the layout of highways, the provision of parks and recreation areas, the design of civic centers, and the establishment of zoning controls no longer made any sense. (23)

Planners of the 1920s, he lamented, obsessed with the movement of freight and human beings, had piled up huge debts for public highways and public transit systems. Their emphasis had simply sped up the obsolescence of houses, apartments, offices, and manufacturing plants in the city center. The radio, the telephone, television, highways, and the impending promise of air travel made the city largely a tradition devoid of the conveniences of modern efficient living. We need, Aronovici continued, a complete reevaluation of the central city: a junking of what is obsolescent and a replacement of the economic and individual functionalism of the past. Cities must reach out into the regional areas from which they take their raw materials, collect their water, and harvest their food. They must learn to plan anew on the basis of soil conditions, climatic ranges, diversity of resources, and the distribution of waterways. (22)

Henry Wright would also hold up the regional dream as the 1930s solution to the orgy of land speculation that had left every metropolitan region with both a surplus and a slack in its land development. Comparing city building to the art of weaving, he claimed, we had planned the warp, our important lines of transportation, too far in advance of the weft, thus making the urban pattern sag and pucker; stitches had been dropped and the important binding process neglected. Left behind, the blighted areas of the city were a mass of misshapen, puckered, raveling, and worthless fabric. We must reconstruct a new urban order based on a new principle of group housing and suburban subdivision controls. (569, 571)

Cumulatively during the 1930s planners would turn their backs upon the disorder of the American metropolis. The quest for an order to the city would once more be abandoned, first by the regional planners as they reached out to look at natural resource allocations and regional redevelopment and then by the housing experts who claimed there was nothing left to preserve in the American city. No longer interested in the historic centers of the city or even the metropolitan physical form, the city and regional planners would move to Washington to join hands with public administrators within New Deal bureaucracies. The lawyers, the real estate developers, and local politicians would be left behind to put together the last pieces of what would be known as the urban renewal game. A city of fragmented voids and textual insertions, new oases representing cultural and civic centers, or housing and office tower projects would be the inadvertent result.

IV
CITIES AND REGIONS IN ECONOMIC CRISIS, 1929–1945

9

Must American Cities Decay?

The task of economic recovery in the depression of the 1930s brought a new set of demands to planners, who abandoned their quest for an order to the American city. Mechanisms designed to stabilize the economy and to offer some unemployment relief were hastily assembled from the older apparatuses of the cooperative state: Hoover's volunteer committee structures and presidential conference reports. But as the depression extended, these methods underwent dramatic changes. When they did, planning was lifted from the realm of a struggling profession, from the field of abstract scientific discourse, and made a matter of national policy. (30) There new transformations and interweavings of separate discourses took place, producing new political alliances, new methodological procedures, and new collective tactics.

Across the 1930s planning reverberated under the influence of quite diverse problems and strategies forged together in crisis. The disciplinary order of physical planning was stretched to cover not only the control of urban and metropolitan land uses but rural and agricultural land allocations, as well as whole river basins and natural resource areas. Under these new stresses the boundaries of the planning dialogue were nebulous. Social planning soon came to challenge the prerogatives of physical planning. Now the concerns of unemployment relief, the need for a comprehensive social welfare system to withstand recurring cycles of depression, and all the evil effects on the health, morals, and welfare that bad housing conditions still imposed upon many Americans stood beside the physical order of cities. Economic planning added its own set of concerns: In order to return to prosperity, it was argued, not only must general price levels be controlled, but wage and hours as well as the condition of services must be placed under disciplined supervision. A rationally planned and allocated system of public works must absorb unemployed workers in order to put money back in their pockets and consequently unleash a stymied consumption and production cycle. (205) As the federal government began to develop strategies to fill some of these needs, a political process of planning began to take form. In America, it was claimed, even with planned governmental intervention, democratic planning was to advance the common good and reflect the interests of the bulk of the community. (343)

Threading across all of these discourses and strategies, planning struggled to carve out its own place in relation to these new social, economic, and political sectors. Up until 1932, Charles W. Eliot II told an audience of planners, city planning had been concerned with physical matters—the moving of dirt and the building of structures. Planning had been taught to think big and to have imagination, but plans are also the record of the public will as to the use of the physical areas over which it has control. It is not a revolutionary process but an evolving set of possibilities. Planning emphasizes prevention rather than cure; it avoids waste by preventing mistakes. Therefore in the end planning is concerned first with the determination of a stated goal and then with the timing and coordination of activities designed to meet this goal. (146:121)

When Charles Merriam asked in 1940, What is planning? he replied that it is an

organized effort to utilize social intelligence in the determination of national policies. Planning is based upon fundamental facts regarding resources, carefully assembled and thoroughly analysed; upon a look around at the various factors which must be grouped together in order to avoid clashing of policies or lack of unity in general direction; upon a look forward as well as a look around, and backward. Considering our resources and trends as carefully as possible and focusing on the emerging problems, planners look forward to the determination of longtime policies. (343:173)

The statements of Eliot and Merriam, both instrumental in securing a new role for planning within national economic recovery policies, reveal different strains within the disciplinary order of planning. At first planning, a preventative process, could lend its efficiency and achievement criteria to the process of economic recovery. But national recovery would not be without its own dilemmas for it was located at the intersection of different domains. Would economic recovery arise from rural stabilization and natural resource conservation or from urban rehabilitation and redevelopment? Was the public sector to invade the private sphere, dictating industrial location patterns, destroying profits within the housing industry, and regulating wage and hours across different industries, or would the cities organize themselves to demand recognition of a new urban point of view and would private enterprises retain competitive control and decision-making power over industrial and municipal redevelopment processes? How would political relationships between the federal government, the states, and local municipal governments be recorded under the new relief allocations? The more the disciplinary control of planning intervened into the economy and the political order, the more it met with resistance from private and local minicipal spheres. The more it was beaten back, the more it turned inwards toward abstract policy formation, research, and information collection. Comprehensive control over the physical fabric of the American city, economic disciplinary order within the national economy, would stand as ideals severely curtailed by the end of the depression. Badly fragmented, planning would reach out to join hands with the administrative process of policy making and abandon finally its physical intention: to order the American city.

Passing through a period of strain and reorganization in which planning gained a theoretical and political insight, by the end of the depression the definition of economic crisis had been transformed, in the planners' discourse, into a systems equilibrium concept. Expressing this new viewpoint, Lewis Mumford explained in 1940 that the era of physical urban growth had come to an end. Now the culturally important problem was how to maintain a dynamic equilibrium in a field constantly in flux. (364) The reshuffling of population drawn from economically starved farmlands and driven toward fiscally burdened metropolitan areas, drained from central cities by the surge of costly and wasteful suburban development, buffeted by the tensions of uneven regional development, made instability and change the background for city and regional planning. (156) Only national policy planning, he argued, could direct the forces and energy that made a city into a constantly changing and living entity. Systems stability meant balance, not expansion; renewal, not exploitation; cultivation, not conquest. A new phase of redevelopment was about to begin, Mumford continued, in which eroded central cities, overexpanded metropolises, the flux of population, would be resettled and rebuilt by cultivating resources and putting them to the task of more intensive use and purposeful plan, demonstrating a wider and richer cooperation. (481:25)

The concept of systems stability emerged out of the growing awareness during the 1930s that steering control over capital resources demanded national planning and a complex array of intergovernmental responsibilities and powers. This in turn required recognizing the role of the American cities as the fundamental building blocks in the national economy and moving toward a tighter collusion between the economy and state such that recurring cycles of prosperity, superspeculation, and depression might end. These tactics were developed slowly only after experience within four different stages of depression planning. Even then it was within severe boundaries imposed by the system of private enterprise and local municipal control.

First, between 1929 and 1932 the general pattern of federal, state, and local responsibility for unemployment and urban fiscal crisis in the American city began to develop, though still within the voluntaristic spirit of the 1920s cooperative state. (222) Then with a change of governments, between 1932 and 1935 followed a time in which planning gained a national scope. The planning of public works and industrial and natural resources for the whole nation was seen as the solution to economic crisis. This endeavor did little to alleviate unemployment or return the American cities and farms to economic prosperity; nevertheless motivated by the spirit and style of national planning, there occurred an intersection of planning discourses among the ideals of cultural, administrative, economic, natural resource, and physical planning.

Next came the third stage, between 1935 and 1940, in which state intervention was seen as the only path by which to achieve economic stability. At first the appropriate response was to use the state as an organizational factor: that is, to recognize an urban crisis and to call for governmental study of the role of cities in the national economy, a national inventory of urban needs, theorems, and causal demonstrations. But planning measures without interventionary control could do little against impending crisis. Consequently the state turned at last to take an explicitly interventionist stance using a series of economic and fiscal policies to increase government spending, such as minimum allowances for housing, unemployment insurance, health benefits, and old age pensions, in an effort to move toward economic stability and growth. As the state and economy moved closer together and more areas became the jurisdiction of planned administrative steering control, these actions required new forms of public legitimation. Theories of citizen participation and administrative responsibility in a democratic government began to appear slowly.

When preparation for and entry into World War II finally answered the crisis of depression, national planners between 1940 and 1945 began to look ahead to the final stage of reconstruction. Fearing that depression would return when the war ended, corporate and national planners searched for a method by which to secure the reorganization of metropolitan governments. Once again concerns centered around the metropolitan whole. Louis Wirth admonished the planning conference in 1942 that cities and regions still continued to grow with no design. The lines of mutual influence between the center city and its smallest hamlet are so complex that they defy orderly statements; so enmeshed with a hinterland of varying scope has the center city become that "it is for the planners to recognize the actuality of the new leviathan that has been created by the economic, social and political forces of our time. . . . The area of control must be the area of interdependence . . . the invention of a new unit for planning which will make local autonomy in the enlarged regional sense possible." (557:151)

Our gaze is thus led across the 1930s to the destitute farmlands and agricultural regions, then back again to the blight in the centers of the city, before escaping once more to the metropolitan rim. The great pioneering areas for planning work in the 1930s, the rural and metropolitan regions, kept drawing planners away from their focus on cities. There was nothing left of value in the historical centers to hold their attention. A collage of textural insertions ignorant of the preexisting fabric would be the result: skyscrapers on spatial platforms floating above the tangled streets and strangled by city highways, isolated blocks of public housing and civic or cultural centers cordoned off within their own sectors. These insertions would add their own impact to the decomposed urban order. The territorial layout of the American city, the overlaying of historical and modern architectural elements, were lost concerns against a changing urban field.

As the cooperative state of the 1920s was transformed into the interventionary state of the 1930s, planning for a nation of cities took place on two different levels. First, at the national level, the economic well-being of rural areas and then cities as basic units in the national economy became new areas for public policy. Second, within the American city itself planning was called upon to maintain and preserve sound capital investments already committed to infrastructure and real estate from areas experiencing blight, abandonment, and disinvestment. Piecemeal planning efforts at neighborhood conservation and block redevelopment were successful procedures that began to secure private investments behind barricaded neighborhood strongholds. Expanded powers of eminent domain, new forms of federal subsidization, and large-scale housing development plans were new experiments designed to entice private capital to reinvest in the center city. We turn to explore the effects of these two transformations upon the planning methods: one that recognized a new urban policy for economic stability at the national level and the other that developed a new strategy for urban renewal.

The Disciplinary Order of Municipal Relief

In spite of the mounting number of unemployed, it was not clear in the early years of the depression what city authorities should do. At first unemployment relief remained under the control of Hoover's cooperative state. It stressed temporary volunteer relief, disciplined so that it would not be destructive of self-reliance or an individual's natural resistance to the dole. Depression was understood as a temporary crisis, an inevitable spasmodic symptom of the cyclical fluctuations of business activity. Knowledge of the causes of these cycles was pitifully meager; consequently these swings of business eluded immediate control, and a remedy remained inaccessible. (245)

Slowly it began to be noted that economic depression was a chronic ailment of industrial society. Since 1870 there had been more than twenty years of depression accompanying the rapid commercial and industrial expansion of the American cities and metropolitan regions. Despite these repetitive experiences the cities remained without any advance preparation for relief to aid their unemployed and with inadequate sources of municipal aid. (245) With the new expectation that returning prosperity would be followed eventually by new depression, however, two series of remedies began to evolve. At first municipal unemployment organizations were designed to function continuously but were held within a structure of temporary relief and cooperative information sharing. Then with the increasing severity of economic crisis, the last confrontation with the necessity for federally imposed intervention occurred. Planning for unemployment relief and national economic recovery were henceforth locked together.

Let us examine the first series of unemployment remedies. Held within this cooperative approach, unemployment, no matter what its cause, was always to meet the same generalized form of voluntary support: an inventory of unemployment needs rationally collected and cooperatively coordinated. Since unemployment in any one industry or business was taken as a measure of inefficiency, better management would automatically expand employment opportunities. (484) It was argued that inefficiencies meant unstable wages as well. These in turn produced consumption maladjustments and the inevitable cycle of booms and panics. The preventative tactic was to stabilize and equalize employment and to give every family a living wage. The main responsibility for such programs was given to local businesses and industries. Any public monies essential for relief must be structured in a temporary manner in no way competitive with regular jobs, in no way conducive to permanent acceptance, yet designed to aid the habit of industry. (75)

The obligation of every American city was to forgo the dole and create instead a "permanent committee on stabilizing employment," a neutral coordinating and cooperative structure from which a method of unemployment relief could be applied. (145) Reliable data and a census of employment needs were the crucial but unknown factors needed to stabilize unemployment. To gather facts about trends of business, to study the occurrences of unemployment, its types of phases and industrial locations, and the kind of aid required from locality to locality was the beginning of a preventative program. Knowledge of unemployment needs could be ascertained only by local inspection of both homes and industries. Yet even local inspections were not without some friction. In New York City, for example, employing the police force to produce an unemployment census created anxiety and unreliable accounts. A lack of coordination and cooperation among relief agencies led to conspicuous waste and duplication of effort. (484)

Early in 1929 the city of Cincinnati developed an exemplary method for relief. A house-to-house survey first established the forms of unemployment and sorted them into categories. The next stage tried to secure the voluntary acceptance by industries of the principle of continuous employment by either reducing the number of hours in a work week or by staggering employment to avoid unnecessary layoffs. Then after convincing public agencies to extend their improvement programs whenever possible and urging private citizens to provide temporary jobs in any manner, whatever minimal unemployment remained was handled through relief work on projects useful to the community at large. By 1930 many American cities had adopted some modified form of this so-called Cincinnati plan, but most cities were unable to apply a method that required both permanent preventative action prior to unemployment crisis as well as cooperation among local industries and relief agencies. (245) Emergency relief needs and carefully planned prevention were incompatible efforts.

Cities could no longer come to the aid of the expanding numbers of unemployed and destitute with municipal organizations formed at the bottom of each wave of depression and disbanded at the first signs of renewed prosperity. The need for some system of permanent unemployment relief could no longer be denied. Yet when relief measures were formulated early in the depression, it was argued that the fight against unemployment must be a local battle because business conditions, the characteristics of unemployment, the nature of its industries and the type of aid required varied among cities. Federal or state unemployment agencies would be costly and cumbersome, resulting in red tape, a constant shifting of personnel, loss of efficiency, and other problems arising from overcentralization. There was no channel through which federal aid could flow swiftly and effectively to the cities in times of economic stress. The state apparatus must act only as a clearinghouse for municipal organizations. (245)

Instead it was argued that every city should prepare itself to meet depression crisis in a permanent fashion. A municipal employment exchange should provide information to employers in times of prosperity and of depression. A bureau of unemployment statistics must collect, interpret, and record consistent data on employment patterns, forecasts on the economic future, municipal building programs, and existing unemployment facilities. Finally a permanent relief agency must coordinate the activity of all private and public agencies and be the channel through which aid could flow. (245) This volunteer disciplinary order was designed not to remove the causes of economic depression but to police inefficient factories and the vagrant unemployed.

As the depression continued, many American cities were confronted with serious problems in delinquent and unpaid taxes. Not only were revenues reduced below expectations but still further devaluations in assessment rates were necessary yet hazardous gestures taken by cities in order to persuade owners to hold on to their property. Curtailment of physical improvement programs, municipal purchasing cut back to a minimum, and reductions in governmental personnel and municipal services enabled some American cities to bring their expenditures near to their declining revenue base. But when they took such measures, they could not offer expanded programs for unemployment relief. (67) As the burden on the cities continued to pyramid, agitation for some type of federal action began to increase.

Bounded and limited by local revenue drawn from property taxes and charity funds, the source of municipal unemployment aid began to evaporate. By the end of 1931 cities, counties, and states as the sole bearers of the burden of relief realized that their unemployment needs far exceeded their taxpayers' willing support or bankers' ability to loan. Fiscal crisis approaching bankruptcy produced the inevitable response: an effort to adjust expenditures to declining revenues, to eliminate waste and mismanagement in unemployment services, to improve the organization and planning of relief, and finally a catapulting leap into the lap of federal responsibility. (38)

When angry crowds of unemployed workers began to march on city halls in 1930 and 1931, the frightened mayors and city officials rushed to their state legislatures to demand additional relief, but rural-dominated state legislatures were deaf to their cries. And cities held no uniform voice, no organized leadership with which to pressure Washington for help. Just one city mayor, Frank Murphy of Detroit, having struggled for municipal relief since 1927 when automobile production began to slide, started in 1931 to organize big city mayors and to concentrate his focus on obtaining federal aid. (194:27–35)

By the spring of 1932 New York and Chicago as well as Detroit knew that nothing short of federal aid would help them feed and clothe their destitute, maintain basic municipal services, and offset bankruptcy. It was apparent by now that without plans, without strong leadership, with meager and uncertain funds, the fallacy that private and municipal funds could cope with the expanding unemployment situation was exposed. (234) Gelfand writes that a national conference of mayors from twenty-nine cities meeting in June 1932 marks a turning point in American urban history. For the first time the federal government became a focus for the lobbying efforts of cities. This conference requested from the federal government not only $5 billion in public works expenditures but a system of municipal loans to enable cities to refinance their maturing obligations. (194:37–38) Hoover, committed to local responsibility and volunteer cooperation, remained unsympathetic to their cries. Instead the Emergency Relief and Construction Act of 1932 authorized $1.5 billion for self-liquidating relief projects, ignored the municipal debt problem, and set aside a meager $300 million for emergency relief needs. Relief loans were disastrously tied to state highway programs, and city requests for aid had to be filtered through and approved by the state. Hence any suggestion to use these funds to pacify urban ills met strong resistance. (194:40)

Even Hoover's legislation for federal unemployment relief was not obtained without controversy. The first bill suggested would have allocated emergency funds to states for two years in proportion to their population and on the basis of demonstrated need. Further specifications requested that each state outline its administrative policies, plans, and personnel for relief measures—time-consuming specifications that would have strangled the urgent need for unemployment relief. Testimony counter to federal intervention was offered by those who believed it would discourage, not stimulate, state and local curative efforts. Those who feared duplicating the European experience submitted that federal aid once offered would never be withdrawn. They argued as well that no evidence existed by which to claim that local resources were insufficient to prevent actual starvation. (285) But as a majority of states and cities could no longer maintain even minimum levels of subsistence aid under prolonged depression conditions and as the 1932 election year neared in which the Democrats began promising expansive federal aid, a new system of relief was nearly at hand.[1] As the fear that state intervention would destroy local independence slowly disappeared in the greater fear over economic and social disintegration, the space lay open for a planned national recovery.[2]

National Planning from an Urban Point of View

From the beginning of the New Deal an uncertainty over recovery procedures and the rapid succession of one program and procedural event after another gave rise to a complex of conflicts. Was recovery to be guided primarily by a social or an economic purpose? Which would control the mediation of this crisis of capitalism: a planning or financial superstructure? Where would the location of control be: in federal, state, or local authorities? Rules of private property and the constitutionality of federal regulation of business, norms that stressed minimum standards for health, housing, and working conditions, principles of economic regulation that set production and price controls—these confronted each other within the discourse of recovery planning, affecting one another in their accounts of economic disintegration, testing the feasible limits of their proffered solutions. Crisis, therefore, meant that the relationships between the American cities and the national economy, courts, labor, capitalists, and government were being shifted about in search of renewal and reform.

When the discourse on the process of planning and the crisis of depression first intermingled at the federal level of government, they contained the same way of characterizing the problems of the American city, deriving analogies from the series of issues that had surrounded metropolitan growth in the 1920s. Planning, after all, had carefully carved out its own abstract way of perceiving the urban system: a set of relationships among functional elements harmoniously coordinated and projected into the future by means of a disciplinary plan. The federal recognition of this stance was taken as further evidence that this style of abstract and coordinative planning would prevail. (30, 69, 124, 375)

The most dramatic event that had occurred during the 1920s, Ladislas Segoe told the joint conference on City, Regional, State and National Planning in 1935, was the growth of the satellite communities and suburban areas rather than the centers of the cities. Thus suburban areas within the district of Detroit increased twice as fast as in the city itself, and the same could be said of the San Francisco-Oakland district. The increase was three times as fast in the Chicago, Pittsburgh, and New York regions, six times as fast in Philadelphia, more than ten times in St. Louis, and eleven times in Cleveland. (480:4)

Looking ahead to determine the physical form of the American city in the next twenty-five years, Charles Merriam declared in 1931 that he could not tell whether there would be skyscrapers scraping still higher or garden pancake cities. But it did seem clear to him that the city would include the metropolitan area more than it currently did, either because cities would be able to annex their satellite cities or by federation or some other functional reorganization. He said that rural dominance over the cities through state legislatures was a thing of the past and that there would be some form of experimentation in the creation of city-states. Finally the cities of the future would be organized; they would have learned to cooperate with each other and to present in combination more effective political demands. Merriam reminded his audience that more than one-half of the nation now lived in cities, and in another twenty-five years this would probably reach the level of two-thirds of the population: "Urban standards, urban practices, urban leaders, and urban ideals will determine the position and policy of the United States. . . . The smoke and stench still hang heavily over the battlefield but some of us think we see victory turning to the side of the urban community." (339:12)

Uneven development within metropolitan regions was considered initially to be the reason for their economic collapse. Repetitious pronouncements still claimed that the American city was among the most wasteful creations of mankind. Increased debt, mounting taxes, and unsatisfactory living conditions were surface expressions of its deep-seated economic ills and unsound social standards. The expansive period of the 1920s had produced a drastic loss of population in almost every large American city. A demanding flow of infrastructure overhead and public service costs to the newer outlying areas had caused an enormous economic shock in each center city. It was an erroneous assumption to expect a rapid growth of population to compensate for these losses. (434:13)

Totally new functions had to be found for the central cities within the metropolitan context. The right balance had to be struck to prevent their economic disintegration and abandonment. Urbanization was a slow and costly process, which demanded an economically planned and stabilized land base. A careful projection of population growth over the next twenty to thirty years and a scientific determination of the total area necessary for urban purposes must set the base for a new form of land economics. Then the familiar dependence of planning upon what one had learned about the location of population at appropriate densities and the distribution of industrial, residential, and commercial land uses would set the rules for urban expansion. (45) Was this significantly different from what planning had proposed in the 1920s? The mutations are subtle. Growth controls, balanced land uses, and a projection of planned forethought to determine the metropolitan unity presupposed the same series of statements defining the metropolitan-regional system as they had in the 1920s. But particular observations began to change the composition of the whole. To conserve the central cities, and rehabilitate and reverse their financial quagmire was a new component in the quest for order in the American city.

Another shift was that this new planning dialogue demanded an urban rather than a rural point of view. But President Roosevelt maintained a staunch antiurban opinion, claiming in a campaign speech in 1932 that people were moving away from the cities and back to the land, where during the depression they could be sure of food and shelter. We can, he stated, plan an even better distribution of our population between large cities and small-town country communities and thus be better prepared to withstand future economic depressions. (469) Regionalist Benton

MacKaye sided with Roosevelt, stating that the push of population from the center of the city toward the suburb and beyond had begun. The environment of the pseudocity, the metropolis, had been recognized as an intrusion; a massing, not a unit; a collection, not a community. (319:441) Regional planning, rural land-use development, and natural resource conservation dominated national planning in the New Deal, utilizing planners who cared little for the old order of urban development. (109)

Let the cities perish, proclaimed Aronovici in 1932. The hydra-like reach of the metropolis's tentacles into the suburban areas of growth have kept them as vassals to the great city, a form of organized parasitism. He claimed that a new concept of community building must be formulated, for the old definition of city planning—where the physical structure of the city is adjusted in harmony to a set of established conventions, practices, and objects—is no longer valid. These elements must come under scrutiny and challenge. The economic structure of cities was fast giving way; blighted areas were draining the city's resources, community equipment was obsolete, and cultural advantages were migrating to the periphery. This urban vacuum and obsolescence needed reconstruction along lines of new social trends in work, leisure, civic, and cultural advances. (22)

Understanding Roosevelt's regional bias and his planners' support, the initial New Deal programs returned greater dividends to the rural areas, and relief expenditures favored counties and states over cities. What began as an attempt to save American cities from bankruptcy was politically subverted by a rurally dominated Congress and a strong presidential advocacy. (194) Thus it fell back upon another set of city planners to promote and popularize the series of urban dilemmas that depression conditions produced, although this would be within a professional discourse already badly divided between a regional motif and an urban inquiry, one that experienced increasing abstractions and realignment across the years of recovery planning.

In 1931 the question raised at the National Planning Conference was whether city planning had been able to influence the full growth of American cities, or whether it was simply playing around the edges of forces that could never be controlled. By now the first stages of a new and untried movement had passed, and city planning was recognized as a sound activity to aid the development of every city, town, and region. But those prophets of decentralization, Harland Bartholomew criticized, turned their back on the center city instead of attending to its maintenance. Too much of planning had dealt with the two extremities of the American city— those of the suburbs and the business district—while overlooking the blighted intermediate districts. The rehabilitation of these areas was the greatest future planning problem; planners' reputations as masters of comprehensiveness in scale and balance depended on their solutions. Collectively as a people, Bartholomew continued, "we have not truly accepted urban life. The automobile has contributed to this delusion of individual escape. We can each live out on the edge of things. If we accepted urban life and united in planning for it, we could bring most of the advantages of city and country to the great majority of our people." (42:16)

At the 1932 planning conference Bartholomew continued the same line of thought. Decentralization meant that as much population as possible had been moved from the centers of the city to the outskirts, and stores and shops were distributed indiscriminately throughout the whole city. Regionalism had become a new religion before it was understood. Based upon a form of economic geography, it assumed that large amounts of population and industry could be transferred to so-called economic regions closer to natural resources and more widely and evenly distributed across the land than were metropolitan areas. The crash of 1929, however, had forced a reexamination of the city center that seemed to be based upon sounder economics and more logical social science. The problems of the American city, Bartholomew argued, were hardly ones of form. They were rather the result of our urban abuse. Now in face of economic disaster we have to stop asking whether we can transform our urban population into a rural or agricultural people, whether we are at the end of an industrial era. Instead we have to ask ourselves, What are the economic consequences of abandonment of our present American city structures? What are the economic disadvantages inherent in a new mode of regional planning or decentralization? Must American cities inevitably decay? (45)

We have been told for so many years that the modern American city is obsolete, complained Thomas Adams, and that we need not to mend industrialism but to do away with the city and replace it with "communistic garden cities." There is nothing wrong with cities that proper disciplinary control and planning cannot remedy. Now that population growth will be less rapid, there will be less injurious speculation; hence fewer blighted districts and fewer slums will result because we will no longer tolerate the production of either. "The skyscrapers and the motor cars will have become the servants of the community instead of the masters. Public taxation—will descend to a reasonable level. . . . There will be more space—because it will be discovered that there is sufficient land in America to provide for light, room, air, recreation and traffic." (2:63)

Henry Wright claimed that the problem with planning was its crusading spirit, spending its energy on the mechanics and publicity of the method of planning rather than changing industrial and business procedures. Instead of preparing plans, planners should have been determining what the cities' problems were and whether they could be changed or eradicated. Policy must become more important to planners than depiction. (571)

Economic reality brought new reasons for focusing on the center of American cities, for something had to be done to keep them from bankruptcy. By the end of 1932 American cities desperately needed relief. For two years private philanthropy and municipal governments had struggled with unemployment problems that were now national in scope. Cities of varying sizes in different parts of America were experiencing serious unemployment. In July 1932 conditions were so serious in Chicago that $3 million of federal aid was allocated to the state of Illinois. The sum was soon exhausted, and another $6 million was given in order to carry the state over through the fall, when still another $5 million was necessary. Forty percent of the total working population was unemployed. In Philadelphia close to 250,000 persons faced starvation. Food allowances had dropped to practically nothing and no allowances existed for rents, while relief rolls steadily climbed. A national calamity was occurring: cities across the country suffered from expanding relief needs along with diminishing revenues and the exhaustion of private funds. (38)

With the passage of the Federal Emergency Relief Act of 1933, the federal government joined planners in a new alliance. But at this juncture two incompatible architectures were built side by side: new structures for the decaying metropolitan centers became divorced from the economic framework of relief and recovery. Both themes fought against each other. The authorities that guided federal action held to other principles of intervention and control than the city planners' dreams of urban improvement. With agriculture, manufacturing, and business at a standstill, the production of public works in slum-clearance projects, building programs such as public schools and hospitals, and even leaf raking and park planting were necessary relief measures. (277)

The soundness of attacking unemployment through public works, planner Russell Black noted in 1933, could not be questioned for it would take 25 million labor years of 300 days each to fill the needs of the nation with respect to housing, street, and road improvements and reforestation. There was enough work just to bring these needs up to a reasonable standard, or so he projected, to consume the total maximum level of unemployment for two and a half years. (70) Since the building industry was the least mechanized of all the major trades, public work projects in this field offered the largest volume of work. (252) At least one-third of all the unemployed came from the prostrate building trades and related industries; hence it was essential that the federal government try to mobilize capital back into the housing and building trades.

A Plan for a Plan

What path would lead from federal recovery policies to urban redevelopment and stabilization, and how would it reorganize intergovernmental relationships and deal with the rural bias? Although informal volunteer ties had been forged during Hoover's cooperative state, especially in zoning, planning, and transportation, still the United States in 1932 was the only nation with no direct link between the central and local municipal governments. (435:452) After 1933 not a piece of national recovery legislation would be passed that would not affect cities in some way. One of the most powerful interventions in the early New Deal was the National Industrial Recovery Act of 1933 with its subsidiary Public Works Administration. This piece of legislation argued that economic recovery through the stimulation of purchasing power would result only if prices were held down, wages were raised, and employment was spread uniformly across each industry. (91) Urban and natural resource planning must be reformulated in order to surmount the current limits of capital growth, and new buying power must be stimulated by relief employment on public works located in economically strategic positions. (222)

The discovery of these strategic locations would reveal a decidedly rural and regional bias, for public works needed to be coordinated with regional land utilization plans and with schemes for withdrawing land from particular uses. Now after the experience of dust storms and crop failures, it was apparent that withdrawals of land must be correlated with policies of reclamation that aimed to place more land under cultivation or to turn it back into forests. (105:14) The new National Land Use Planning Committee in the Department of Agriculture found that the problem of rural land classification and rural land planning involved the same principles and approaches and similar techniques and objectives as did city and regional planning. (63:15) There was to be no division between regional and rural land planners, and cooperative efforts between the two groups were considered essential to recovery. Regional planning was given its greatest recognition in the Muscle Shoals bill of 1934, which authorized the president to make a regional plan for the Tennessee River Valley region. Other watershed areas were studied and their development replanned: the Mississippi River Valley, Missouri River Valley Committee, the Red River Valley Committee, and the Arkansas River Valley Committee. (248)

Planning, it was hoped, might also be an effective antidote to some of the waste that came about from the system of pork-barrel politics, which distributed public works to those areas with the most successful lobbyists and politicians. F. L. Olmsted, Jr., worked out the principle of curves of urgency for public works, which established the most opportune time for carrying out any given project. If a coherent plan was developed, then the relative value or urgency of a single element of the whole could be determined more truly by those who had to decide what was to be done. A well-coordinated plan that covered an entire state, moreover, might avoid wasteful choices that threw into the same set of scales basically different classes of projects. (105:12–17)

Thus work relief, the timing of public works, and regional planning were harmonious items to be strategically developed together. If public works were to act as a damper on economic fluctuations, then they must be accompanied by some program such as a regional plan. Without such a plan the delivery of requested projects was slow. Yet if the public works expenditures were allocated too swiftly, then many of these projects would be ill considered and incoherent. Programs for alleviating depression were beset by doubts and conflicting interests, and they retained only spasmodic interest, while those of regional planning were steadier and more likely to be sustained during prosperity. (105:18–19)

A new planning structure was needed, one that could coordinate relief work, public improvements, data collection, and research. The old cooperative apparatus—that of the advisory committees on zoning and planning that had helped to coordinate federal planning policies in the 1920s and to promote city and regional planning commissions—had almost all fallen prey to the depression sharpshooters who called them unnecessary frills at public expense. (234:71) Thus planning, whose sole intent had been the perfection of a disciplinary order for public improvements and land development, had suffered in the flurry of financial retrenchment. Why should the American cities and regions pay for elaborate studies and expensive consultants to produce advisory plans for municipal and regional infrastructure when their most pressing problems were how to finance unemployment relief? Thus when planning was pushed to the national level, a gap existed between the gathering and dissemination of planning data on public works or infrastructure improvement needs and the creation of overall relief policies and coordinated directives. Even if planning was no longer desirable at the local level, it would be adopted enthusiastically by a new breed of federal planners. By executive order the National Planning Board was established in 1933 under the authority of the Public Works Administration. Frederick Delano, Charles Merriam, Wesley Mitchell, and Charles Eliot, all experienced advocates of planning, were selected to insert this dialogue into federal recovery policies. (248) This advisory body was to promote the idea of planning in the coordination, selection, and sequencing of public works priorities and needs and in the stimulation and preparation of comprehensive regional plans through the active cooperation of state, regional, and city planning commissions. (63, 530)

American cities were finding that they had to systematize their capital expenditures, but not more than a hundred cities and regions in 1933 had plans to guide their yearly investments in public works. It was apparent that planning must include a capital budget showing what improvements should take place and how much they would cost. If this was necessary at the city level, so much more must it be translated to the national planning of public works and capital improvements. (338) The possibility of using public works construction as a stabilizer during economic downturns had been discussed for years. In order to put federal money to work on useful projects, however, each city, state, and county government needed systematic advance planning. Attention must be given to the development of long-range public works programs, creating a national inventory of such projects matched against their potential employment figures. (344)

More important for planning, this National Planning Board brought a new constellation of discourses, centralized at the level of federal policy making but spreading over the domains of physical landscape and urban planning, which belonged to Eliot and Delano, economic planning, which was Mitchell's domain, and administrative-governmental organization, the province of Merriam. Paradoxically these advocates of national planning believed that the period of depression withdrawal lent itself to the nurture and application of planning and developed the desire to create a new whole out of parts so fractionalized through the failures of collective control that they had lost their functional relevancy. (301) Primarily concerned with the timing and coordination of activities with respect to the national goal of economic stability, planning would establish standards of accomplishment in every field and use these standards as elements to regulate the organized administration of forces toward the selected objective. (209)

National planning brought economic and administrative policies to focus on the problems of rural land use and natural resource development. Forging a new style of thought, they applied the general disciplinary principles of city and regional planning to the national level. Thus the location and extent of major physical developments with national impact were to be linked together by a national master plan. Into this scheme the pieces of every city, county, and regional plan were to be fitted. There were as well other requirements that gathered support around planning. Eligibility for public money was determined in reference to state and local plans, and all proposals were to be accompanied by the comments and suggestions of state and local planning boards. The question of watersheds and regional development, the relationship of transportation and cost of electricity to community growth, the necessity and practicality of reclamation projects, harbor improvements, and correction of soil erosion were all to be studied and planned by the National Planning Board. (248)

Meanwhile the allocation of expenditures for public works projects was stalled in long-term planning. The Civil Works Administration was created to speed employment during the disastrous winter economy of 1934. Although it existed for only four months, it played an important role in stimulating the planning effort. Through the creation of emergency relief it put some 4 million men and women to work. Among these efforts it produced hundreds of planning studies and provided employment on understaffed planning commissions for thousands of unemployed workers. Undertaking a real property inventory, these relief workers enumerated residential properties in 64 cities to be offered as a factual base upon which planning for economic revival in the construction and building industries could proceed. Notorious for its lack of statistical information, the building industry could not even agree if the nation had been overbuilt or underbuilt, no information existed with regard to the supply and demand of housing, and data pertaining to the uses, occupancy, rates, and conditions of housing were nowhere to be found. Moreover no coordination had been established between the number and kinds of existing facilities, construction and renovation studies, and financial and economic factors affecting property values. Only scant information could be discovered that reflected the existing debt limit, the tax arrears, and the financing practices in particular housing areas, information that the federal government needed in order to develop insurance programs designed to curb the slippage of private capital away from the housing market. No wonder, then, the planners noted, relief procedures were experiencing difficulty in achieving economic recovery. (129, 530)

Relief employment, especially on long-range planning studies, brought a new series of difficulties and delays. It was above all a costly endeavor; not only had jobs to be generated and workers trained, but they must be secured in areas not competitive with private employment and at wages well below the prevailing standards in order to avoid creating the habit of public assistance. Since there was no direct path between federal stimulation and local action, more delays resulted. At most the federal administration could create plans and policies for public works, but states and local governments had to do the essential work of requesting the funds and setting administrative criteria and standards of planning. A crisis outlook, however, thwarted the Planning Board's intention; economically sound and socially desirable works required advanced, rational forethought and careful planning. But emergency action and purposive planning conflicted; carefully thought-out procedures and tools of planning were lost against the pressure brought on by crisis for recovery and economic stimulation. Cities, counties, and regions that already had master plans could mobilize action for public works construction in a short time, but where such planning provisions were scant, hastily conceived, and ill adjusted, improvements resulted in wasteful liabilities to the pattern of national and urban development. (345)

Planning had emerged out of two streams of thought in the 1920s. One recognized the wastes of unplanned and uncoordinated efforts among the different administrative endeavors and public improvements in the American city and its metropolitan region. The other was the zoning movement: a disciplinary classification placed upon the use and development potential of private land. Meanwhile studies of economic land practices and rural land classification schemes had developed during the 1920s, completely separated from the planning profession yet embodying the same mode of thought. The depression itself forged these streams together. Thus national planning embodied principles borrowed from efficiency management that recognized the waste produced when planning efforts among different levels of government were uncoordinated. It also began to blend together the grids of urban land uses with the independent classification of rural lands. (94:613, 120) If efficiency management had dominated the early efforts of the National Planning Board, in 1934 resource specification would become increasingly important as the NPB was transformed into the National Resources Board (NRB). This shift of focus underscored the awareness that the national assets underlying economic wealth were the extensive base of land, waterpower, and minerals, to which could be added mechanical inventiveness and organizing abilities. (249) A new inventory of national urban and rural resources was about to begin, for the task of the NRB was to study both housing and natural resources, to report on land use and river use, and to plan for public works. (120)

Planning grew out of architecture and engineering, social reforms, and civic improvements; now the federal government was forcing the planners to develop new fields of thought. Before the federal government planned more deeply, it needed to know if it was desirable to build larger cities. Did it want to sponsor satellite or greenbelt towns? Might it want to follow a policy of industrial decentralization? Wherever the government began a new type of urban or rural service, the same facts confronted them. The fundamental question that planners had raised in their initial dialogue about economic recovery, What was the place of the urban community in the national economy? was now juxtaposed in dialogue with the opposite questions, What were the inner connections between a rural way of life and an urban style of living, and what was the role of the country in a nation of cities? On this inverse problem planners had not thought clearly or sharply enough. No urban development policy could be evolved before it was known what forces bound metropolitan centers to subsistence homesteads, what barriers of growth forced the uneven development of urban and rural communities. Planners had failed to define what kinds of values ought to be developed in cities and what should be preserved from contact with nature in isolation and solitude. (344)

Economic recovery had started with the problems of fiscal crisis and decay within the central cities. Economic disintegration was said to be caused by uneven metropolitan development patterns and balkanized governmental fiefdoms, which had often made physical planning fruitless and fundamentally impractical. It was found that we needed to examine our social and economic institutions and governmental procedures and regulations that set the limits and boundaries to the influence of plans we had accepted up to now as theoretically and practically desirable. Now we had to include in our planning analyses the influences of commerce, transportation, power and natural resources, government, art, recreation, inventions, and geniuses, all the vertical forces that caused the horizontal order of the American city to grow or decline. We had to analyze not only the negative elements on city development—zoning, the limitation of a city's borrowing capacity, tax boundaries—but the positive elements as well—the influence of transportation rates and structure, the reservation of land uses in advance of growth, the taxation system as a motive behind urban dispersal. Finally we had to draw a synthesis at the level of governmental organization, recognizing the necessary coordination among federal, state, and local planning authorities, encouraging their growth and giving them new direction and guidance. To make such a plan for a plan, an approach to an approach, was the obligation of the National Resources Board. (147)

Policy Planning

Too much effort, the national planners said, had been placed on the preparation and efficacy of the plan itself. Now urban formulations must focus on the definition of problems and the depiction of policy actions. These were to be the new areas for planning intervention. (571:468) If there were planners who began to study the process of urbanization from a national and comparative viewpoint, if the planner now had executive advisory authority, it was because economic growth and stability had become the regulatory property of the state apparatus, bringing into view the role of cities in the national economy and the relationships of urban to rural development. Thus national planning emerged as a synthesis but one that awkwardly coordinated many disparate themes: the restoration of agricultural prosperity, the redevelopment of river basins, the regulation of wages and hours, prices and quantity of consumer commodities, social programs for public health, education relief, crime detection, locational and land-use planning, and the integration and regulation of major systems of transportation. (205)

In an effort to coordinate the national economy, planning, it was warned, had come "to mean so much of anything and everything that there was the danger that it would mean nothing in particular," that by becoming at once "logically all-inclusive" maybe it would grow increasingly harder to implement. (63:17) Planning needed a new terminology; this would stimulate and preserve its uniqueness. A separate classification differentiating national economic planning from comprehensive master planning, the specification of location theory and land-use planning from the planning of social services and needs, the planning involved in administrative coordination from the planning of action and implementation of projects. This classification would mark off the unique distinctions of each style of planning. (225) Federal intervention in recovery planning had already outlined the boundary between physical land-use planning and economic and administrative planning. Now it was left to the planners in their organizations and conferences to reflect on these changes.

Such was the type of comparison that Charles Eliot II began to rearrange into a new configuration. Stemming from the older logic of city improvement, physical planning had traditionally embraced the purposive assignment of a fixed design upon the land, thus reflecting the functional components of a systemic whole. Eliot placed in comparison the articulation of economic planning around the activity of charting, that is, directing and arranging the course of industrial production. The Commerce Department, the National Industrial Recovery Board, and the NRB had been charting agencies. In between these two distinctions lay the vast field of administrative or governmental planning, dependent upon both physical and economic planning for its content. But it identified in its operations a new series of actions—programming, budgeting, organizing, and projecting—which it brought within the planning perspective. To choose among alternative projects and courses of action meant to program events. Locating the level of expenditures and degree of financial control was budgeting. Organizing must be the stimulation of planning and policy making through the appropriate governmental forms. And projecting combined all of these with the delivery of services. These new and tentative delineations began to outline the grid of administrative planning. (292:490)

Planning in the American city was losing its physical basis as it began to blend with governmental policy making. Henceforth planning would

increasingly focus on the problems of administrative planning: the articulation of rational procedures of choice among alternative ends, principles
of municipal financing and revenue sharing, methods securing the best
organizational unit to enforce its supervisory opinions. (533) City officials
and real estate interests would begin to slacken their control over the
process, if not the content, of planning as those techniques became more
abstract and the base increasingly elaborate. Now they would struggle
against the forces of state directives and national planning proposals, warning against overly conscientious detailing of national planning that inhibited
local initiatives in recovery efforts. In fact no sooner had banks begun to
recover and federal emergency measures had put a little money back into
people's pockets than a strain of municipal and state protests arose against
the privileged position of national planning. By the end of 1934 these
protests pushed for the elimination of industrial and production codes
that were embedded in the actions of the 1933 National Industrial Recovery
Act and for a return to free market options.[3] Political aversion to state
and industry collusion began to dismantle the early New Deal reforms.
Local control and national planning had collided. Now a rezoning of
governmental powers would take place in their stead.

Although this retreat was evidence that the federal government had
already entered into a new role as banker, financer, and friend to the
American cities, a rebalance of national planning occurred that questioned
where the locus of planning authority should lie. Could the federal government best serve the cities by controlling every detail and specification
of its allocated services, or should this power be decentralized so that
local initiative could function under reasonable federal principles and
standards? (89) Federal planning control had played a negative recovery
role. Augmented by its desire to safeguard a proper disciplinary order,
honest financing, and sound construction, it had failed to provide the
nation with a definite recovery strategy. Now it was argued that a careful
rezoning of governmental powers would be the new basis for recovery
action. Rather than a comprehensive national control of everything, certain
strategic points in a working arrangement—those that held the system in
balance—must be equally shared. (340)

If a major part of the financial burden for public works and community
infrastructure had become a permanent task of the federal government,
nevertheless local officials and redevelopment interests had to participate
in apportioning these funds, controlling their expenditures, and preventing
their diversion into private benefits or profits. Historically the American
land racket had been the most pernicious method by which private speculators absorbed and destroyed the allocation of public improvements.
To prevent such action was a worthy federal concern, but of more im-

portance was the declaration among federal authorities of certain broad principles and the retention by the American cities of the largest degree of initiative and responsibility. Let Congress place strings upon the allocation of improvement funds, as they had done with the aid for highway construction, but let the cities and states take notice. To avoid centralized federal domination, they were told to control their own selfish real estate interests and shortsighted taxpayer groups, which destroyed the value of public improvements and inhibited a better contribution of community effort. (89)

No matter how much Roosevelt proffered agricultural and natural resource policies, in spite of regional development plans and farm resettlement programs, economic recovery demanded a new urban consciousness. As the United States Conference of Mayors pressured for both municipal control over federal relief programs and for the acceptance of an urban consciousness at the national level and as local real estate interests and construction lobbies gathered in opposition to federal invasions into the building industry, attention was redrawn to focus upon the role of cities in the national economy. (194:65–70)

Lessons Drawn from the Urbanism Committee

In consequence a new urban lobby—the United States Conference of Mayors, the American Municipal Association, and the newly organized American Society of Planning Officials—began to pressure the national government to turn central planning focus on the plight of the American city and to aid destitute real estate capital left with obsolete inner-city properties. This new lobby group questioned whether the national government had ever paid sufficient attention to the problem of urban dwellers. By 1935 one-fifth of the people on relief lived in cities, although the government had yet to concern itself with the living and working conditions of these urban places. Unprecedented trends, producing unplanned and unexpected changes, had captured this urban nation unprepared. A nation of cities had arisen, industries and commercial enterprises had been concentrated within metropolitan districts, and a sudden rise of public employees and governmental expenditures had become established norms. (211)

Although counties that contained the 155 largest industrial cities embraced 75 percent of all industrial wage earners and 65 percent of all industrial establishments, the cities and their urban regions had remained the forgotten items on the nation's agenda. (72) No reliable information existed on urbanism and unemployment, and no unit at any governmental level had studied the daily problems facing every American city. No policy

or program considered cities on a national scale. (144) America as symbolized by the city had never entered the public consciousness. Still the
vulnerability of urban life, the drastic inequalities of income and cyclical
unemployment, and the rapid obsolescence of the city's inner neighborhoods and infrastructure had to be faced. Only a national urban policy
could help cities meet their problems of insecurity and unemployment.
(143) Their precarious fiscal insecurity, their third-generation infrastructural
and housing provisions, and their archaic taxing systems had to be brought
to federal awareness. New urban policies and urban programs had to be
proposed. (144)

American cities demonstrated widespread poverty and cyclical unemployment, which threatened consumption and hence menaced the country's
powers of production. As well the physical plan and infrastructure base
of these cities, for the most part developed before 1919, were rapidly
disintegrating. Uncontrolled subdivisions and speculative land practices
had robbed these cities of any rational spatial order. Substandard housing,
blighted areas, dirt, smoke, grime, and water pollution plagued the city.
Failure to recognize the fundamental relationship between urbanization
and industrial prosperity, to preserve the city as the keystone of a dynamic
and strong nation, this neglect had made it impossible to adjust the country
to social and economic transformations. (521)

In response to these pressures, the Urbanism Committee was created
under the NRB with the mandate to explore the facts, processes, problems,
and prospects of urban America, to compare the relative advantages and
disadvantages of various types and sizes of cities, and to improve the
instruments by which future development of urban land could be more
rationally controlled and developed. (72) In the same manner in which
the dynamics of capitalism had fostered an uneven development between
town and country, so it now created the same antagonisms between the
center and periphery of metropolitan areas. Once again attention was
brought back to focus on the problems of the central cities as the Urbanism
Committee unveiled its recommendations in 1937.

The automobile, cheap power, unscrupulous land profiteering, and federal highway allocations during the 1920s had produced the rapid development of metropolitan complexities on a regional scale. Therein lay
the problems of the central cores. As people had tended to move to the
suburbs, expanding industries had pushed to the fringe areas, and new
commercial locations followed into suburban subcenters. (72) The center
of the American cities now began to display unusual characteristics: while
they became increasingly more important as financial and administrative
centers, they simultaneously experienced widespread poverty and cyclical
unemployment among the working-class populations confined to their

residential cores. (444) Moreover since the 1900s increasing suburban populations had been accompanied by a burgeoning multiplicity of governmental authorities and administrative districts, a complication undermining the economic and social base of the central cities. Sprawling metropolitan regions required a reorganization of this medley of independent governments in order to make their political and administrative structures conform to the whole, to make their conflicting fiscal policies uniform and equitable. (72) The rapid obsolescence of the physical plan and plant of the American city, the persistent public health problems within poor and blighted neighborhoods, and the separatist and sectional ethnic group were still disrupting the metropolitan whole. (444)

The decline of population, especially in the city center, presaged a number of important changes: a lessened need for expansion, a renewed opportunity for improving public utilities and welfare services, and more gradual changes in land values. In the future, however, new urban populations would be drawn from economically and culturally backward rural areas; hence the center cities would have to bear additional social and personal costs needed to help these new migrants adjust to city life. The Urbanism Committee therefore recommended that a more equitable distribution of public revenues might be made so that rural improvements could prepare these migrants for life in cities and even lessen this urban drift. While manufacturing and merchandising had been pushed or pulled out of the center of cities, they had also shifted toward larger units. Now the locational mobility of these larger monopoly units no longer evidenced the same rationale. With the costs of relocation so high, probably these monopoly units would stay where they were. (72)

The Urbanism Committee set about to redefine the structure of the urban center within the metropolitan whole. It recommended a better articulation of industrial and land-use controls; better knowledge about the conditions of cities by means of a nationally organized system of urban reporting and research; better transportation power and fiscal policies; a federal credit agency authorized to make loans and grants to local governments for public works and public utility construction; and cooperation between the federal government and private enterprise on a national policy for rehousing the poor and rehabilitating blighted areas. (532:341–356) Above all would stand a permanent National Planning Board in an attempt to raise the standard of national and urban preparedness and to foresee, and consequently to meet, the insecurity and unemployment needs of recycling depressions. (444) Through careful analysis and thoughtful recommendations, the Urbanism Committee stressed, there was a central need for national planning in order to rationalize the structure and differentiation of metropolitan space and capital infrastructure investments. (532:341–356)

To function more effectively within these realigned governmental powers, the Urbanism Committee suggested that a new political location be created for planning by placing it closer to the local legislative body, the chief executive, and the administrative departments. (444) From this impetus came the movement to reconstitute the field of planning into a permanent administrative activity. Planning was an administrative process, nothing more, as it was claimed, "than an incidental phase in the accomplishment of work or the attainment of an objective" prescribed within every administrative policy and directive. (494:80) Administrative planning was an outgrowth of the futility of static plans, of an overemphasis on the value and usefulness of paper plans and printed reports. (71) For another, it was the dissolution of the nonpartisan volunteer planning board consisting of citizens who held no knowledge of planning specialization, who inconsistently paid attention to their official duties, who in the tradition of reform failed to link the preparation of plans with the vital implementation and legislative forces. All these weaknesses set the conditions for new possibilities. Perhaps the openness of planning, allowing anyone with a variety of qualifications to enter the planning discourse, caused the closure of this discipline. Insufficient financial support, untrained advocates, and segmented voluntary implementation powers had proved to be inadequate to preserve and protect American cities. Federal tutorship, with its stress on national planning, had been able to demonstrate the success of administrative planning. (532)

If city and regional planning was to be justified and to attain a permanence and influence within official legislative action, then the responsibility for coordinative planning must be placed within a single centralized agency, close to responsible officials and with a staff of researchers and technicians. On the other hand, if the entire ensemble of planning discourse continued to take place outside of the governmental structure of the American city, then planning would remain a scattered and irregular practice; jealousies, suspicious resistances, and territorial jurisdictions would persist to constrain the spontaneous melding of administrative and planning perspectives. Planning as a function of government must reject its critical propagandizing role. No longer being a civic body watching over the actions of public officials, its research, publications, and advice must fall under the control of executive administrative authority, offering information only upon request and restricted to studying questions and areas that the official staff deemed important. Increasingly bureaucratic rationality demanded the coordination of each administrative part so they could work together in concerted effort. Planning would be central, aiding officials to hold a comprehensive view of urban problems, drawing all the activities of different governmental departments to one central focus, systematically monitoring relevant urban processes through a series of information flows. (532)

If planning was to become an administrative process, restrictions must be placed upon the profession as well. Planners must build a temporary fence around a specific field that they could call their own. Without this identification of a unique and specific base, differentiated from other fields and professions, the breadth of planning efforts would dissipate their energy and weaken their resistance against the invasions of the unskilled and uninsightful. (69:144) Planners should remain masters of the physical field and ensure the improvement of economic and social conditions by promoting order in physical arrangements. (7) In this modification of the planning discourse, an official institution, the *Journal of the American Institute of Planners*, arose in 1935 to help distribute and clarify the diverse forms and configurations of planning. It was a vehicle of discourse through which planning formulation would be described, commented upon, reiterated, clarified, and reordered in an effort to identify and then systematize the specific procedures and objects of planning.

The first volume of the *Journal* began with the question, What is planning? A discourse had arisen to examine the basic premise of planning. Who were the planners? What were they trying to do, and with what information and what decision-making techniques? The most important properties of planning had always been those that remained constant; social and economic conditions were perpetually changing while the constant remained the physical conditions of land within the American city and its metropolitan whole. The flux of these larger economic and social influences set the order of the physical forms, but it was the constant relationships within the physical order of the American city upon which the planner's dialogue must rest. (69, 139, 519) Administrative planning, on the other hand, was the device to define distant goals, to formulate efficient means of attaining public purposes strategically drawn from alternative policy choices. It represented the intellectual work of forming programs and policies. (519)

We may have national, state, regional, county, town, and city planning, but it is the physical world that remains constant within these delimitations, and it is to this that planners must give sharpest attention. (139) The physical plan, upon which all actions of the planner should be based, still prevented them from doing two different things in the same location at the same period of time. It also betrayed the places where nothing had been done. It thus revealed both the foreseen and unforeseen advantages and disadvantages in the physical order of the American city. If these ideals and information were only expressed in words, then, it was feared, they would not appear so self-checking. (240)

Planners draw upon the exactitude of the fundamental sciences, but they add what they believe are desirable aims and objectives. They become advocates for a disciplined order for the American city and cease to be scientists. (84) The education of a planner still relied more upon practical experience and a blending of various threads of common sense than it did upon a rigorous university training. Thus, Russell Black proposed, the recipe for a good planner was one part personality, two parts drive, five parts common sense and good judgment, three parts social point of view, and only one part education. These must be mixed well and placed carefully in the field for a few years of proper exposure. (69:144)

No matter how much it was warned that the planners should hold to their physical land base, another set of abstract categories gained strength as it questioned the formalization of decision-making procedures and administrative practices to be allowed within the province of planning. (494) On this basis Lawrence Orton told the annual meeting of planners in 1940 that "planning should be conceived as a *process*, not as a given field of subject matter, nor as a given set of procedures, nor as a stereotyped form of organization." (396:6) Planning had finally cracked its static deductive mold. Now it referenced the dynamic arrangement of alternative means and fluctuating ends in the search for stabilizing action. Planning had to develop quantitative methods by which to weigh the merits of different governmental policies, to arrange in matrix form the various factors that must be brought together to avoid a clashing of programs. (343, 398) Planning had been formed to bring physical order out of urban chaos, to allot each land use and infrastructure provision its appropriate and co-ordinated space. These disciplinary principles were still embedded within planning but now must be added the further recognition that the dynamic nature of the city demanded constant administration and preventative state intervention. Federal policies that would underwrite the stability and growth of an urban economy brought a new imperative for this rational form of administrative planning. Thus the steps of strategic choice must be added to the logical process of physical planning: first, the determination of objectives; second, research to understand the problem; third, the discovery of alternative solutions; fourth, a strategic choice among all the alternatives; and fifth, a detailed execution of the chosen direction. (188)

Embedded within bureaucratic structures, effective planning meant the skillful coordination and balance of technical plans and political processes. Its success in a democracy, however, still depended upon the creation of a popular sentiment, a public will, that would invite and support official action. "A democracy must plan, but the execution [was] subject to the veto of the people." (541:253) Thus as planning enclosed itself within administrative bureaucracies, a void was opened, one that a series of statements struggled to close. "Planning in a Democracy," "democratic planning is not socialism," "planning needs the man in the street," were titles of a new style of discourse, which began just as the source of legitimation across society was being reformulated, as labor and the poor had won certain political rights, as the reactions against fascism were spreading around the world, as the fears of socialism gained strength. (87, 343) A discourse began in the 1930s that would increase in vigor in the postwar years as technical rationality and political legitimation needs of the American city and democratic state became more apparent. (87, 274) They grew in importance in the planner's dialogue as well when administrative planning tied itself to federal sponsorship. When that happened, the procedures of physical planning lost their sway over planning.

Some of the recent definitions of planning, it was argued by 1942, had become so broad that this scope was rivaled only by that which philosophy held in the early days of science when it embraced all scientific knowledge in every field of endeavor. Instead planners were once again told that they should become more conservative and restrict their sense of planning to the guidance of physical development, for this definition was extremely broad. To effect any change within this scope, plans must dig far deeper than planners had yet realized. First they must make fundamental studies of a community's present conditions and future trends, and then based on these studies they must make reasonable assumptions about the functions the community could hold in the future. Then they must establish physical, social, and financial criteria for the guidance and selection of specific proposals for physical development. Yet planners still lacked the necessary exact information, the technology with which to select the best solution. They had no methods of measurement to make quantitative comparisons of different policies and procedures. These must be the realm of the planner's future focus if the science of community planning was to be lifted further from the realm of conjecture or personal opinion. (398)

The Urbanism Study brought central focus back to the core of the city. Since property taxes and municipal revenues could no longer support public infrastructure and service expenditures in the American city, it was assumed that the federal state must now provide adequate financial support and investment incentives. Urban redevelopment and low-income housing programs would become the financial responsibility of the federal state and would be accepted as permanent interventions. In consequence new state laws were needed to enable the American city to distribute these revenues as fast as possible and to utilize them by inducing private capital to reinvest in the center of the cities. Hence a permanent system of federal public works, faster procedures of land assembly and tax foreclosures, and expanded concepts of eminent domain were suggested by the Urbanism Committee. If planning was to aid in the strategic allocation of federal revenues, it must become a permanent administrative activity subordinated to local political interests. These lessons echoed the voices of the new urban lobby, for if the federal government's Urbanism Study had set the tone and strategy for urban redevelopment and center city revitalization, this lobby would perfect the instrumentation of these policies within the American cities.

10

To Reconstruct the American City

Another strategy began to merge with this movement to save the cities. To forestall the complete bankruptcy of the American cities, two great elements of the metropolitan problem were simultaneously related: comprehensive city planning and the provision of minimum standards of housing for every American. Recovery without a sound economic policy to stabilize property values throughout the city was impossible as long as blighted rotten centers endangered their total economic life, as long as they failed to provide minimum standards of living and a diverse variety of residential units in different areas. (46, 251) The planning dilemma would be how to provide profitable housing for one family where two were before, how to reverse speculative market practices and plan the best use for each parcel of land from the point of view of the metropolitan whole. A disciplined order for the American city would have to struggle against real estate interests, the construction industry, and local municipal officials, all intent on their own desires to reconstruct the center of the American cities. In the end a strangulated housing program would be dominated by urban redevelopment schemes where slum-clearance projects would be divorced from low-income housing programs and the order of physical planning would be reduced to a memory.

Obstacles to Slum-Clearance Programs

As early as 1929, housing reformers had turned to the problem of blight and the solutions of slum clearance and low-income housing projects. Speaking in medical terms, they said that blight was "a civic cancer which must be cut out by the surgeon's knife. . . . It can be cured by radium if taken in time but after it has gotten to a certain stage, it infects the body politic, and the only cure for it is to cut with the surgeon's knife." (528:75) The problem remained how? No American city had ever done anything to eradicate blighted neighborhoods. No legal powers existed to clear slums because they were blighted or because they menaced real estate values in the center of the city. In the 1930s housing production continued to fall way below consumption needs. Since most of the new construction during the 1920s had been in the outlying suburbs, the hardest hit by this current housing shortage was the supply of low-income dwellings in the city center.

In every American city blighted areas threatened the economic stability of the whole. Hence planners advised the building industry and real estate interests to consider the stock of existing tenement houses much as the motor industry viewed the supply of used cars. A program must be developed to take the hopelessly depreciated and obsolete structures off the streets. A slum-clearance scheme seemed to be the only approach.

At the turn of the century New York City had sporadically condemned and cleared a few blocks of congested neighborhood sections, turning them into small parks and playgrounds. In Boston, Washington, and Cleveland as well, a few houses or sections of blocks had been condemned and cleared. (528) Beyond that there had yet to be a broad-scale slum-clearance program in any American city, and no instance of slum clearance with rehousing had yet appeared. Now, however, there were so many unsanitary, dilapidated, and obsolete structures that it was not profitable to continue to deal step by step with individual houses in hopes of bringing them up to health and safety standards. Rehabilitation would no longer work. The costs of labor expended on the operation were excessive, and the progress of modern architecture had made the plans of these old buildings obsolete, causing their maintenance and operation costs to rise far above those of new construction.[1] Piecemeal rehabilitation of housing in the older sections of the American city was no longer financially reasonable. (528) Only if an estimated $30 billion to $40 billion were offered and five years of steady concentration on the production of new low-income housing on slum-clearance sites took place might the building industry answer the housing needs of the bottom one-third of the nation. (21:153)

Early in the 1930s slum-clearance and low-income housing projects were promoted as the way to eliminate decay and to save investments already committed to the center of the American cities. But these were areas still held as the territory of private capital. Nowhere had the state entered into the provision of housing except in the sense that the cooperative state of the 1920s mounted an "Own Your Own Home" campaign, helped to create zoning ordinances, and reorganized building standards and construction techniques. Until the 1930s the federal government neither built nor operated housing, nor did it provide tax subsidies for workers' housing or control rents. (524)

The President's Conference on Home Building and Home Ownership in 1931 brought a new emphasis to the problem: private enterprise alone could not profitably provide low-income housing for the American city. From the early 1900s until the 1930s, housing reformers noted, limited-dividend housing corporations had been the only method utilized to draw private capital into this investment area. Able to demonstrate new ideas with respect to model tenement designs or to demonstrate new building procedures, these efforts were unable to meet the accumulating housing needs of low-income residents. Only government and business cooperating together, they now claimed, could both eliminate the slum and produce large-scale housing operations. (207, 559)

When the conference delivered its reports, the Committee on City Planning and Zoning maintained that until city planning was conceived in relationship to the provision of housing, there would continue to be a lack of stability in real estate values and population would continue to shift from one district to another; hence there would remain an inadequate demand from potential home owners. A committee on large-scale operations proclaimed that the successful development of large construction companies depended upon a readjustment in present laws, codes, and restrictive measures that previously had been based on individual and small-scale methods of building. When building codes, antiquated building trades, difficulties in land assembly, and inadequate methods of financing had been reassessed, then large-scale construction operations producing quantities of low-income housing would result. A committee on finance reported that a permanent fact-finding bureau within the Commerce Department must aid the building industry and tabulate and distribute information periodically regarding occupancy surveys, mortgages and trust deeds recorded, real estate transfers, new subdivisions opening, rates of new construction, construction costs, rental trends, land values trends, interest rates, and foreclosures.

Basically steering along the middle of the road, these 31 committee reports reflected the status quo in the home building industry, although there were some significant divergences. For example, Richard Ely suggested investigating the desirability of making housing for the poor a public function. This proposal was offered only as a personal opinion and phrased as a question, neglecting to suggest a solution, but Ely had raised the issue of how to provide the lowest-income workers with adequate housing. (88)

Hoover's conference nevertheless outlined a comprehensive slum-clearance program for America. First, American cities had to be given the power through their state legislatures to clear slum areas because they were unsanitary and because the public interest required it. Second, a special clearance authority must be established in every city undertaking such programs in order to survey the community, finding out the areas that needed to be cleared, determining the new uses to which these areas should be reconstructed, seeing that they were in harmony with the city's master plan, obtaining appropriations and public support for these projects, and finally overseeing the actual work. Third, there must be a means through which to obtain compensation for the property owners whose land has been taken at an equitable basis, one that was fair to the taxpayer as well. This last would be the major obstacle that every city must face. Even after they had created a slum-clearance program, extremely heavy costs would be imposed upon each city, for although it might be possible to use the police power to condemn houses unfit for human habitation, still "there is nothing in the decisions of the courts in any of our states that would lead to the conclusion that they would look with favor . . . of paying no compensation for buildings taken and destroyed on the ground that they are unsanitary, or of paying merely for the land its value as a site for certain limited purposes." (207:46–48) Thus the American city would have to place the costs of acquiring the land and buildings that were to be scrapped in slum-clearance programs upon the backs of its taxpayers.

Another major obstacle for any slum-clearance program was the cleared site. Common practice in Europe was to redevelop the area with housing for the displaced population or substitute groups, approaching both socially and economically the characteristics of the population that formerly lived on the site. There were in 1932 insuperable legal and constitutional blockages, not to mention economic and political ones as well, standing in the way of governmental housing or government-aided housing in the American cities. The case rested simply on the constitutional provision in each of the 48 states that "private property shall not be taken for other than public use, and to this date the courts have uniformly held that a public use is one in which *all* of the public may participate." Housing of any form stood outside this understanding. (207:49, 50)

Housing at Public Charge

Established housing reformers were also conservative in their suggestions for rehousing America. John Ihlder took the slow planner's approach by announcing that we must look at the trends that created the city slum: a diminishing rate of population growth and even a shrinkage in some areas of the city; a dramatic decline in payrolls of industry and commerce; a spreading of the urban population over the metropolitan district in order to relieve the problems of congestion; and the resulting almost completely deserted districts of the center cities. Thus the planning problem was to reconstruct the American city, providing profitably for one family where before there were two, the reverse of our common practice of crowding as many families onto a lot as could be obtained under meager restrictive building codes and zoning ordinances. Ihlder noted we faced yet another problem: we commonly assume that new housing will reach those who currently reside in city slums. From this group, however, we must descend in classification until we meet a residue that cannot pay any rent at all. Somewhere along this line, therefore, we must accept a new premise: "There must be housing at public charge. The choice is between continued degradation and recognition that this residue are dependent who, because of their children and because sub-standard living is a menace, must be provided with decent housing." (251:34)

The census of 1930 revealed that at least 6 million nonfarm homes and 5 million farm homes were substandard, the two together constituting 36 percent of the total housing in America. Once again the housing reformers brought out their lists of evils that bad housing created: the lack of light upon the resistance to disease; the lack of fresh air on well-being and vitality; overcrowding, which enables disease to spread, and its adverse effect on the nervous system; dampness often found in basement and cellar dwellings, producing rheumatism and favoring the development of colds, pneumonia, or even tuberculosis; and the lack of pure water or running water so necessary for cleanliness of persons and of the home, as well as the lack of sanitary flush toilets and a comprehensive sewer system. Morals as well still suffered under these conditions, for areas of bad housing correlated with statistics of high truancy and delinquency rates, and bad habits were closely connected with overcrowded housing lacking a sense of privacy. Safety and fire hazards were another common feature of bad housing, and under the effects upon the general welfare could be classified those of industrial efficiency, quality of our citizenship, standards of family life, and the intangibles of contentment and happiness. (559:4, 7–15)

Edith Elmer Wood continued to advocate the series of disciplinary concerns that housing reformers had developed in earlier years. Slums, she reiterated, evolved from several conditions. The shack type springs up within a shantytown just outside the city limits where no building codes or health ordinances exist to thwart them. Then there were rows of inadequate housing, erected years ago when housing standards were lower and could easily be rented to working-class families. The alley houses of Washington, D.C., and old Philadelphia were of this type, as was much of the housing in New England mill towns. But the basic type of slum, the one most prevalent and that was growing faster, was the neighborhood of mixed use and occupancy located in close proximity to the central business district, a neighborhood that once must have been for higher-class residences but shifted its use as businesses invaded and the original residents moved to the suburbs.

These slum areas used to be taken for granted; they were simply the natural effects of rapid city development. Only now, with depression conditions, the owners, mortgage holders, and real estate operators had begun to realize they represented wholly different effects. Immigration had stopped, the birthrate was falling, the drift from the farms to the cities seemed to have been reversed, and the development of skyscrapers pushed the business centers up vertically rather than horizontally: all these had produced a void in the city center. Zoning had often overzoned for business or industrial needs, which created blighted districts because it reserved too much land for these purposes, land that developers refused to turn to another use. (559:17–18) A new cooperation between government and real estate interests had to be forged if American cities were to answer their housing problems.

With the passage of the Emergency Relief and Construction Act of 1932, a tremendous new surge of interest in low-cost housing and slum-clearance projects took hold. With agricultural, manufacturing, and business at a standstill, the federal government became interested in merging public works as a relief measure and slum-clearance projects as a step toward economic recovery. It was not obvious what would be done with these cleared areas. Some thought they should be replaced by new skyscrapers; others saw the solution in quantity production of mass housing projects; others looked to the successful housing projects that European cities had already provided. Whatever the form the solution took, Kohn spoke to a group of planners in 1932, we must provide housing for all our people and accommodate them in areas with economic diversity and a variety of housing types. The real estate and banking obstructionists will dissolve, he hoped, when they realize that their existing properties cannot be saved without saving the whole American city. (277)

In 1934 governmental forces mobilized behind the provision of housing; they included the Housing Division of the PWA, the Public Works Emergency Housing Corporation, the Subsistence Homestead Division, fifteen state boards of housing, and twelve local housing authorities recently authorized to acquire land and construct and operate low-cost housing projects. For a few months in 1934 the Civil Works Administration had developed a real property inventory supplying necessary information on housing needs. (25:433) In addition the Federal Relief Administration had begun a campaign for the demolition of unsafe housing; the Reconstruction Finance Corporation made loans to cities for slum-clearance projects; and the Home Owners Loan Corporation and the Home Loan Bank Board aided home owners and home finance agencies in securing mortgages. (252) Some eight hundred American cities, Carol Aronovici noted in 1933, looked to the hundreds of millions of dollars that the Public Works Administration was making available for new housing.

With the market of high-rental housing overstocked, over-capitalized, and increasingly non-productive, reviving a dead building industry and saving the land speculator and the non-productive slums from the sheriff's hammer becomes a new passion with the realty interests. (21:148)

Although the Home Loan Banks and the Home Owners Loan Corporation were initially established to place federal money in the pockets of foolish and overambitious real estate investors, including the banks, they were unable to act constructively and stem the swelling tide of foreclosures. More recently, Aronovici noted, the real estate interests, especially organized investment companies such as banks, insurance companies, and mortgage companies, had pressured the government to tie the needs of low-income housing to slum-clearance programs:

This is the last resort of the avant garde of the slum owners, the investor in dead mortgages, and the hereditary slum owners. It is designed to save the skins of those who have been exploiting the slums as a matter of sound business practice and to keep the supply of housing down to the present level so as to avoid competition in quantity of accommodations, if not in quality. (21:150)

In an effort to aid the building industry, a real property inventory of 64 representative American cities was undertaken in 1934. This survey was intended to provide information to real estate men, operative builders, dealers in building materials, and mortgage-lending institutions in order to show them the extent and location of potential markets either for new building or for rehabilitating and upgrading the existing housing stock. Edith Elmer Wood claimed that the survey figures also held social, economic, and health significance, for they showed the extent to which communities shared in the type of bad housing always proclaimed to be an adverse effect on the health, family life, and citizenship of Americans. (559:78)

With both population and industry stationary and with production methods remaining approximately the same, Edith Wood continued, we can always expect to find the same number of skilled and unskilled, white-collar, and professional jobs. Hence we shall always have about one-third of the nation badly housed, and we know as well that the operative builder will make no effort to supply the needs of those unable to pay for standard housing. The country had experimented with limited-dividend housing, but its help had been disappointingly meager. "They have demolished no slums and have emptied no slums, and in no country have they reached the really low-income groups." (559:102–104) There must be a new recognition that the poor can be housed only if government and business cooperate and if the stimulus for private action comes from government subsidies.

No matter how much activity there seemed to be behind the production of low-income housing, the objective of the federal government remained economic recovery. Housing programs were simply a method to unlock the stagnating building industry and with the employment of laborers, architects and planners, to put money back into consumption and hence production. Home building was ideally suited for recovery needs. Being the least mechanized of trades, it offered a volume of work and stimulated a variety of related industries; there existed as well a large number of unemployed tradesmen; and the product did not compete with other consumer items. It was warned, however, that no matter how much federal stimulus was needed in housing, the actual work must be carried out and controlled by the localities, and private enterprise must be allowed to carry the heaviest load. Federal stimulus was needed only because private capital had withdrawn from decaying and blighted inner-city neighborhoods and because these areas had become so pervasive that they threatened many American cities with bankruptcy. (252)

A Government-Business Housing Alliance

Vague policies, conflicting strategies, uncertain financial arrangements, and uncharted routes plagued the housing activities of the federal government. The National Housing Act of 1934 tried in vain to stimulate the private market through the provision of mortgage insurance and building and home improvement loans. They hoped in this manner to bail out real estate capital in deteriorating inner-city neighborhoods and to keep home owners from abandoning their mortgages or allowing their properties to fall into tax arrears. In order to relieve unemployment in the building trades, $20 million was allocated to the Housing Division for limited-dividend housing corporations, and another $129 million was set aside for use by the Emergency Housing Corporation, which directly or indirectly constructed and operated housing projects accompanying major slum-clearance projects. (349:197)

Those low-income housing and slum-clearance projects in the early New Deal years were accepted by the state as necessary for putting the unemployed back to work as fast as possible, but as regulatory disciplines

against the unraveling processes of urban blight and the economic de-
stabilization of metropolitan areas, they received slight attention. By 1935
the national construction indicator had fallen 92 percent below its level
of 1925; residential building alone had declined 88 percent. (542) One
housing expert surmised that the housing deficit by the end of 1933 was
over 800,000 dwellings, and it continued to climb based on an annual
need of 300,000 new dwellings. (21) Even so the slow operation of the
federal agencies' demonstration projects, the mounting costs and delays
of relief work on federal projects, and the failure to provide even roughly
adequate levels of subsistence did not succeed in stimulating economic
recovery. (89) By 1937 only 50 housing projects had been started in 35
different cities, 45 percent of whose total costs were federally subsidized.
(406)

Urban real estate capital resisted the state's efforts to provide low-
income housing, viewing this action as a direct threat undermining small
property investors, disastrous to economic stimulation, and destructive of
the rights of private property. (252, 406) One of the most controversial
aspects of the Public Works Administration was its Housing Division. To
meet the obligation of housing projects, critics complained, cities were
saddling themselves with unprecedented maintenance and operating debts.
It was predicted that federal housing would lower the return on all existing
property in the American cities and thus was open to challenge with respect
to its constitutionality. (435) Indeed a court order ruled in 1935 that
federal use of eminent domain to acquire sites for public housing was an
unconstitutional use of its authority. The federal government could help
to finance low-cost housing, but the building, planning, and maintenance
work must reside at the local level within state or municipal housing
authorities. These quasi-government authorities, which existed in only a
few states, had been delegated the power to acquire land and construct
and operate low-cost housing projects financed by federal money or through
local municipal bonds.[2]

Nevertheless there was general agreement that if low-income housing
was to be provided on cleared sites, land acquisition costs must be held
to a minimum if rents were to remain reasonably low. In the early years
of the depression it was hoped that limited-dividend housing corporations
would quickly provide new housing construction opportunities. To enable
these corporations to assemble land, states had given them expanded
powers of eminent domain. But condemnation procedures were slow,
taking weeks and sometimes months to establish the value of land and
its fair conpensation price. Such cumbersome procedures could answer
neither relief employment nor low-income housing needs. Housing experts
proposed that the Public Works Emergency Housing Corporation might

acquire land for federal public purposes by filing in a federal court a declaration of taking, and setting down the purpose for taking, the area to be acquired, and the compensation to be paid. The courts could then set the time and terms for the surrender of private property. (560) The courts decided instead that housing was not a constitutional function of the federal state and must remain under local control.

Even so, the acquisition of land for the rebuilding of blighted areas by municipal authorities had not yet been recognized by the courts as a public purpose that cities could pursue. No court had decided whether housing constituted a public use of private property. Acquiring parcels of land for large-scale developments had to be done by piecemeal efforts without any kind of state aid. Slum clearance, it was argued, was a land salvaging operation as well as a housing effort; thus the city should be able to acquire inner-city property in slum and blighted areas and sell portions or all of it to private building corporations, which could develop the area. (207:8–12)

To eradicate the slum problem, the 1931 President's Conference on Home Building and Home Ownership had recommended the removal of these constitutional obstacles. They proposed that municipalities acquire and clear slum properties as an exercise of the flexible police power in the interests of the health, safety, and general welfare of the people and that these municipalities should be given the right to sell, to private corporations or individuals, parcels of the cleared land to be redeveloped for residential purposes. By selling off strips of land not in excess of 32 feet to limited-dividend corporations, low-income housing of two rooms' depth could be constructed, with the city reserving the interior of the blocks for small parks, walks, trees, and shrubbery. (207:54) Already in 1929 the Prudential Insurance Company had acquired two such city blocks of blighted housing, and the city of Newark had agreed to provide a park running through the middle of the area. The courts had accepted that city's action as a proper use of public funds aimed at promoting private housing by taking a portion of the land costs off the shoulders of the real estate developers. Could not cities, in reverse order, provide builders with cleared land at minimal cost in an effort to reduce the overall expense of private redevelopment? (560:222)

Aronovici had warned that housing the poor under the control of private capital might be a mirage. At first the state was persuaded to establish the Home Loan Bank and the Home Owners Loan Corporation to save overambitious housing investors, but these institutions failed to stem the crisis. Then came the Public Works Administration with its Housing Division and the Emergency Housing Corporation, and a stampede began by which private capital rushed to capture some of the $100 million set aside for low-income housing construction. To mediate the problems of land assembly and to facilitate federal and municipal financing credit for these housing operations, local housing authorities had been created. But every private property interest in the American city was out to wage war against any constructive effort of these new authorities. Toward this end a new pressure group came forward—the organized real estate interests, bankers, insurance and mortgage companies, and even the conference of mayors—which fused the provision of low-income housing with slum-clearance propositions. They secured legislation restricting the type of slums to be condemned and publicly acquired and allowed new construction to replace only dwellings that had been demolished. As well the sum of money apportioned was so meager that the whole federal housing movement could not mount even an adequate demonstration project. Thus urban real estate interests and local construction concerns had taken every precaution to keep to a minimum the supply of new low-income housing in order to avoid competition and to inhibit an overzealous utilization of the power of condemnation. (21:148)

This tentative housing discourse contained repetitive statements about the need for a new government-business alliance if low-income housing was to be provided. At one end of the debate opinions were offered to classify and examine the city's peculiar needs for housing its poor; somewhere in between preventative governmental policies were documented and proposed; yet at the opposite end of debate, the strategies of action confronted the prohibitions raised against state intervention. In this dialogue every legal, economic, and political device curtailed and redirected preventative action. Folded back upon itself, the planners' documents and dialogue continued to stress the needs, the desire, the hopes for housing the poor and erasing the slums, while the new urban lobby perfected its control over the strategies involved in a rehabilitated order of the American city.

The Cost of Slums and Blight

The dramatic collapse of the economy in the 1930s brought an end to the concept that the American city could grow without any bounds. Fiscal crisis carried with it a sudden realization that suburban development had required costly and overexpansive subsidies. In New York City, for example, the expenditures for the subway system had reached $25 billion, not counting the cost of additional sewer systems, streets, parks, playgrounds, and schools. (468) It became obvious that low-cost land in the inner suburbs was a myth of the 1920s. Now it ws felt that perhaps the major lending institutions would give some attention to the argument that the older parts of the city, the blighted areas, were menacing hundreds of millions of mortgages invested in the better parts of the American city. As blight spread out from the central core, unable to carry its share of the mounting taxes, the stable areas of the city were compelled to adopt a disproportionate amount of this burden. Because mortgage credit and the boomer spirit of private enterprise had overbuilt the suburbs, inner-city tenants were hard to find, vacancy rates were on the increase, and rents were necessarily reduced. It was therefore hoped that the major banks and mortgage holders would favor redevelopment within the heart of the American city as soon as they could be convinced that new methods of building, new neighborhood planning and rehabilitation schemes, and large-scale operations and mass production procedures could develop new market demands. (293)

It was becoming apparent to the planners during the 1930s that a blighted area of a city was an economic liability to the whole and that the community paid for this expensive form of housing. However great the cost of replacing these slums, it was not so great as the cost of maintaining them. The direct expense for supporting a slum in Cleveland, for example, was estimated in 1934 to be $2 million against an annual income drawn from that same area of $250,000. Similarly in Birmingham, nearly half of the city's budget was required for the maintenance of slums, which comprised one-fifth of the city's area. Of $1,191,352 of taxes to be raised from a blighted area in Chicago in 1932, only half had been collected three years later, and the city's expenditures for the same area in one year was more than $3 million. As the American cities began to age, the costs for fire, police, health, and other municipal services steadily mounted, while their revenues from taxes dramatically declined. (372)

Why were these older residential neighborhoods in the center city becoming blighted? The answers given were various: encroachment of business and other undesirable uses, which brought with them noise, dirt, and nuisances; the plan and arrangement of the street systems and lots, which led to an unfortunate practice of back or alley housing or an undesirable mix of stores and multiple dwellings; indirectly the automobile and other means of rapid transit, which enabled a quick escape for the more well-to-do residents and left a vacuum in the inner city to be filled by the less economically able. In consequence the small, blighted areas of old rooming houses and tenement dwellings, which had extended only a few blocks beyond the business center, now stretched out for miles in larger American cities. (207:1–13)

As land values declined in these neighborhoods, many investors liquidated their holdings. The holders of heavily mortgaged properties, however, could not dispose of their investments so easily. A study of the Lower

East Side of New York City discovered that over 90 percent of the properties in that area were heavily mortgaged. In Chicago a similar study of two blighted districts showed that two-thirds to four-fifths of the properties were so mortgaged. Many might argue that such were the results of economic advancement. The automobile industry had bankrupted the carriage manufacturing industry, and so new suburban land uses would bankrupt older residential areas. Urban real estate interests felt otherwise. Perhaps, they argued, these inner-city landowners were but one victim of the ballyhoo for home ownership sponsored by the cooperative state in the 1920s. Hence any acquisition of these lands or rebuilding of inner slums without adequate compensation to property owners would cause undue hardship and place unfair burdens upon innocent investors. Some accommodation must be made between the needs for urban redevelopment and the mortgage holders and home owners who faced losing their investments. (560:228–229)

Thus the American city was experiencing a redistribution of economic resources that corresponded approximately to the shifting structure of consumption. If the building industry had saturated the market for single-family homes in the suburbs, then a new urban market awaited development.

The luxury type of housing, including the single-family home was overbuilt and it [would] be years before we catch up with our surplus of high-grade apartments, office buildings, factories and warehouses. If the buiding industry [was] to survive, it must recognize its force and taking advantage of current technology and sociological ideals of housing, prepare itself to undertake large scale operation of a type never dreamed of before. (468:4)

To rebuild blighted inner-city neighborhoods and secure their investments against future deterioration would require governmental reorganization and innovative legal powers before large-scale operations, mass production techniques, and new forms of group housing could be launched successfully. There were financial, legal, and planning obstacles that the American city had to remove as well before private investment capital would be induced to return to the center.

Who Should Pay for City Services?

The collapse of rural land values in the 1920s and urban property losses in the 1930s gave sufficient evidence that the burden of taxes levied on private land could no longer be expected to finance the permanent provision of public services and infrastructure, much less the redevelopment of the center cities. In the midst of rising expenditures for unemployment relief, drastic limitations were placed against the tendency to raise the tax on property. A genuine tax revolt faced each American city: property owners refused to submit to greater taxation, with factories idle and profits reduced, industries said they could pay no more; taxpayers' associations, home owners' organizations, business groups, and many other civic interest groups were united against the hardships of property taxation. (230:249) Reductions in local tax assessments coupled with poor collection methods and taxpayers' strikes meant that city revenues continued to shrink. (37) An overindebted municipal bond market in 1932 and insurmountable relief needs by 1934 had forced cities to turn to the federal government for financial aid. By 1936 it was advised that these new federal-city relationships must not be pictured as merely emergency measures; probably they were permanent. (435:452) Thus two new sets of relationships and disciplinary controls had to be arranged against this background of permanent state intervention if capital investors were to return to the center of the American cities. The first began to question the tax base on which municipal revenues had been gathered and to reorganize legal concepts that inhibited municipal ownership of land. The second concerned itself with the appropriate governmental unit and administrative procedure that could effectively distribute to urban redevelopment interests a major proportion of the new federal revenues.

The history of property tax, it was pointed out, had been a history of escape for one form of property after another: first the railroads exited, then corporate stocks, bonds, and intangible property took their leave, and finally inadequate assessment procedures on railroads, public utilities, and large-scale corporations enabled them to evacuate entirely. Meanwhile property taxes on urban real estate, it was said, had prolonged and even aggravated depression conditions. Taxes were levied without regard to the level of earnings or financial status of property owners, and this was exacerbated by an official reluctance to reduce assessments when property values declined. Hence the property tax had forced a heavy delinquency rate, crippling the finances of local government and producing a heavier burden on those property holders who were still able to pay. (489:459)

American cities were experiencing a crisis of capital credit. Too many accumulated debts meant that cities could no longer pay interests at a level sufficient to attract new capital investments. As a result city infrastructure developments could not be built nor local employment needs met. (62:156) During the years of prosperity and accelerated capital growth the American cities had paid for their expanding infrastructure base through municipal bonds. The provision of new parks, schools, and street widening or extensions had been accepted as profit-yielding exercises self-financed by increasing property values and property taxes. By the 1930s, however, some of these projects began to take on the appearance of salvage services. If the original water system was a capital-creating infrastructure, the provision of unemployment relief was not. Without subsidization capital investment in infrastructure or services no longer yielded a profit. Depression was thus a debtor's pathology in which overextended loans, overproduction on borrowed capital, and inability to meet financial obligations forced the liquidation of holdings, distressed sales, and deflated property values still further. (489)

The depression had shown American cities that real estate could no longer be treated as a source of unlimited revenue. Coupled with the growing awareness that much of the wealth of the country had passed out of real estate and into such forms as personal income or corporate stocks, some new mode of taxation and a new basis for the sharing of revenues seemed inevitable if the increasing demand for public services and redevelopment needs within the city were to fall within the boundaries of municipal fiscal accounts, if the provision of needs was not to be correlated directly with a locality's ability to pay. (66, 489)

Wasteful overlapping governments with excessive expenditures and unneeded employees also exacerbated the burden on local property taxes. A shift away from this weighted taxation, a move toward a more scientific system of federal and state income, business, and consumer taxes, would necessitate a realignment of governmental responsibilities. Cities, counties, and regions needed to consolidate. Still they depended upon 166,000 structures of government, each with its own administrative machinery and its ability to borrow money and levy taxes. (13, 230) Inevitably it was asked, Which unit of government should bear the financial burden for public services and infrastructure, and who should specify the disiplinary criteria by which to control these expenditures?

The new urban lobby felt that only if the federal government paid for all of these functions would the burdens be equalized across the states yet allocated equitably to areas of greatest need. During periods of economic expansion and prosperity there may exist conflicts between new service and infrastructure programs and additional property tax assessments. A far-reaching public service program may be destroyed by local fears that the property tax burdens would discourage capital and industry from locating in their city. For the nation as a whole, the urban lobby pressured, no such conflict existed. (73)

Consequently as local control over the levying of taxes and the collection of revenues began to blend with new federal allocations, local politicians and urban real estate interests started to confer about the nature of this new federal aid. Whenever the city had shown itself to be ineffective in answering local problems and crises, then the tendency had always been to centralize directive powers at higher levels of administrative control. If the basic question was one of efficient and economic allocation of resources, as it had been in those days, then centralized control was the only recourse. Here, they proclaimed, the issue was one of expenditure control over new public funds. Now, the urban lobby argued, there existed a reason for intimate contact between the service deliverers and the consumers, in which the local government unit must hold operational control. (314:168) Economic planning for redevelopment, the overall policy guidelines, and financial controls might be held by a federal directive power, but the administrative management of these projects must fall to state and municipal authorities, while the specification of physical plans and project operations could be done only by the city. (188, 541) Municipal autonomy within the presence of permanent state intervention required recognition of local real estate and redevelopment interests, an urban point of view specifically different from those represented by state or federal accounts. (73, 534)

Superblock Redevelopment

Land investments in blighted city centers had become completely unproductive. If public housing activity was to be kept to a minimum yet the cities redeveloped, new uses for this land must be found to encourage private capital to reinvest in the heart of the city. Focusing on the problems of the Lower East Side in New York City can show the procedures that urban real estate interests and construction concerns began to develop for capital reinvestment. Since rapid-transit systems produced excessive decentralization, which was as economically wasteful as excessive congestion, planners in the 1930s began to profess that it was reasonable to expect a return of population to the center city. Middle-class dwelling areas near the center of commerce and trade and industrial activity were logical propositions to consider. (468) Since 1910 the Lower East Side had lost 53 percent of its population, a loss produced by antiquated dwellings, easy access to the suburbs, the cessation of immigration, the removal of industries to the outskirts of town, and all the other shifting land uses. An almost universal obsolescence of physical improvements had drastically reduced residential values. (47)

On the Lower East Side the city of New York faced a new and difficult problem. Social and economic instability and obsolescence existed on such a large scale that it threatened the soundness and stability of the entire municipal structure. Thus banks, title and mortgage companies, real estate firms, and civic organizations banded together in 1934 to try to save this slum area. Forming the Lower East Side Planning Association, they called upon Harlan Bartholomew to develop a rehabilitation scheme overhauling the entire district. Already they felt that the area's investments, both public and private, were too great to warrant further commitments unless redevelopment was soundly conceived and rationally planned. (47)

Joseph Platzker's study of the 3,029 "old law" tenements on the Lower East Side (those erected before 1901) showed that over 60 percent were built before 1887, and 25 percent of these before 1856. Widely scattered throughout the area, deteriorated beyond the stage that warranted rehabilitation, the only alternative was for the area to be demolished and modern new developments constructed in their stead. (417:3) Homer Hoyt also pointed out in an analysis of land uses on the Lower East Side that in 1934 there were 303 vacant and abandoned buildings and more than 80 vacant lots scattered across the district. By 1938 more than one-eighth of the area consisted of non-income-earning properties, tax delinquencies had increased, and most of the residents were on public relief. It seemed obvious to Hoyt that rehabilitation of the Lower East Side for its current residents was no longer economically feasible. (239)

On the other hand the land uses that remained anchored in Lower Manhattan were the Stock Exchange, the corporation offices and banks of Wall Street, the public utility offices, and state and municipal office buildings. But even with all of this activity, Hoyt noted, there was still an 18 percent vacancy rate in office space in the Wall Street area. Hence it was unlikely that the Lower East Side could be redeveloped for new office uses. The existing employment center of Wall Street did present, however, a potential demand for residential redevelopment. Almost 70 percent of all the workers in the Wall Street area commuted for at least 40 minutes per day, and many two hours while the Lower East Side lay within walking distance from their places of work and could be redeveloped as a middle- and upper-income residential area. (239)

Hence a disciplinary plan of control was essential in which the whole neighborhood could be redeveloped. Why not demolish the 300 vacant houses that stood on valuable land? Why should these ugly wrecks be allowed to remain as fire hazards, pest houses, depreciated structures that blocked the path of redevelopment? (468) The New York Building Congress called for modern district planning to enable such redevelopment: "The legal consolidation of many blocks into neighborhood units and the rezoning of a vast area for residential use are a prime necessity for the encouragement of new housing capital to again open its doors to Lower East Side development plans." (417:3)

The approach taken by the Lower East Side Planning Association was similar and emphasized the layout of a system of self-contained residential units, each large enough to create a neighborhood environment of its own. At the heart of every redevelopment plan lay the creation of a superblock. To pour public improvement money into new roads, playgrounds, and public utilities in a project area yet leave parts of the district spotted with blight and decay was to miss a spectacular opportunity. Instead the city should condemn the blighted area, acquire the land, erase the city streets, and then, after careful rezoning, sell the assembled land at public auction. In this manner the provision of new superblock redevelopment might save the city from financial disorder. (318)

For two different reasons, it was argued, housing redevelopments must be planned on a large scale: to enable site planners and architects to create appropriate neighborhood settings and because the degree of housing obsolescence and social and economic decay required reclamation of the entire area. (560) Thus rebuilding the city center should take place by cellular division, the idea promoted by Clarence Perry that cities should be broken down into manageable units in which normal, healthy family living could exist. Only such self-contained neighborhood districts carried with them a strategy of defense against future deterioration. (138) The cellular city is coming, proclaimed Clarence Perry in 1930, continuing to advocate his scheme of neighborhood units that he had carefully worked out for the Regional Plan of New York. In the future residential districts will be walled cities, enclosing a standard set of institutions and services designed for families with children. The automobile is determining that neighborhood units be built with walls, islands of quiet surrounded by streams of raging traffic. About four city blocks or 160 suburban acres constituted one of these neighborhood preserves, and it is these units that Perry foresaw as the basis for rebuilding the deteriorated areas of the center city. (412:459)

Housing, Henry Wright noted, meets city planning in the blighted areas of our cities, for here some form of group housing must be used to replace these useless districts. No longer can we hold out the ideal of the bungalow for every working man, for this falls far below his earning ability. Nor should we continue to allow the speculative practice of crowding even generous lot sizes with as many row houses as possible. To meet the needs of moderate-income workers, some form of group housing, a hybrid of the row house and the flat, must be provided; this is imperative to the economic rehabilitation of the American cities, and only this will forestall its bankruptcy. (569) The plan depended upon abandoning individual lot lines and eliminating the narrow side lots between houses, thus enabling more than two dwellings to be erected in a continuous stretch. These houses, from one to three stories high, had a shallow site plan, so no house was more than two rooms in depth. Already in the 1920s, Wright noted, Europe, especially Germany and Holland, had experimented with the provision of group housing for its working classes. (570) The German scheme consisted of parallel rows of buildings, oriented at will by the site designer and opened at either end of the block. Their orientation, rhythm, and sequence represented an organic form from enclosure to enclosure. (155)

In order to develop this kind of group dwelling, the practice of selling subdivided lots to private owners who then held them out of development while they acquired the money to build or waited to resell their vacant lots when land prices had risen must be stopped. The promise for the future of American housing, Henry Wright prophesied as early as 1931, lies in developing huge operating companies that can purchase large tracts of land, plan and subdivide them for private homes, and manage or control their operations. (568)

Any new construction must therefore take advantage of the economies of large-scale production.

Satisfactory environment is the first prerequisite of good dwelling areas, and the present conditions in the Lower East Side are outstanding examples of the fact that good environment cannot be achieved by uncontrolled buildings on small lots, constructed merely in response to short-lived speculative demands. (47:15)

Thus areas lying between main thoroughfares on the Lower East Side should be reconstructed as self-contained neighborhoods. The first problem was to recognize that in a predominantly residential use district, there were too many streets: 41.6 miles of streets must be reduced to 16.1 miles. Many of the new streets, moreover, would be restricted for pedestrian use or redeveloped as public parks when high acquisition costs prohibited housing. Residential buildings would be located around the perimeter of each superblock, and a community center would dominate the heart of each neighborhood. Schools, churches, and recreational facilities were planned for the ground floor of buildings, and shopping areas were confined to the boundary streets and to the intersection of the pathways within the interior space. (47)

These early redevelopment plans for the Lower East Side outlined the basic methods that would be utilized later for the redevelopment of city centers. New land uses eventually would be found to turn slum districts into capital assets, and many of these new uses would be moderate- or upper-income residential projects contained within their own stabilized neighborhood. But without the legal powers to condemn and raze whole districts and with few financial incentives accompanying these plans, nothing came of the proposals for the redevelopment of the Lower East Side. Although a great number of inner-city properties reverted back to the banks through mortgage foreclosures and idle capital began to accumulate in these lenders' hands while new investment areas were difficult to find, reinvestment in redevelopment projects still was not forthcoming. If these banks invested their idle capital in new mortgages within the same city districts experiencing disinvestment, then this, they felt, would only further devaluate their previously committed but obsolete investments. Hence investors in the American city were taking a position of watchful waiting. (536:2)

Not surprisingly demolition gained momentum while redevelopment plans were stalled. In 1934 the New York Housing Authority proclaimed, after an extensive survey, that there were 17 square miles of slums in New York, of which 10 square miles required immediate evacuation as they were unfit for human habitation. A large-scale government-subsidized housing program was the only answer. (376) While awaiting new powers and legislation that would enable municipalities to demolish slum areas, more-stringent tenement laws were passed in New York City. This simply sped up the process of abandonment. In general the problem of abandonment and vacancy of obsolete buildings had become so serious that under the impetus of federal relief money, cities began to formulate demolition projects as part of their public works programs. Demolition manpower was paid for by the federal government as an inducement to property owners to assent to demolition without cost and to enable wrecking contractors to undertake the jobs in return for the payment of salvage. The overall shrinkage of income from obsolete properties during the depression, the spiraling costs of rehabilitation and repairs on obsolete buildings, and the increasing tax and insurance rates were further incentives that compelled many property owners to volunteer to demolish their buildings. So successful was this demolition program that in New York City more than 7,000 dwelling units were destroyed between 1934 and 1936.

Neighborhood Improvement Districts

The American city used other means to protect good real estate investments from poor ones while they awaited broader redevelopment powers. The neighborhood district would be the key to urban redemption. No well-planned, properly functioning city, the planners warned, could exist without good neighborhoods. (43) Hence early in the 1930s the National Association of Real Estate Boards began to pressure for legislation that would enable property owners in decayed and depopulated inner-city districts to fight for the preservation of their own neighborhoods. They asked for state enabling legislation authorizing municipalities to create neighborhood improvement districts if so requested by more than half of the property owners representing more than half of the assessed value of property in the district. Boundaries were drawn around the improvement districts, and a rezoning plan prepared and submitted to the city council. Such a district would then be able to reserve all of its land for residential purposes with the exception of a few lots to be set aside for neighborhood activities and local businesses. They could require all nonconforming uses to cease operation within ten to fifteen years. Moreover the district could acquire by purchase or condemnation any properties devoted to nonconforming uses, properties that were obsolete and detrimental to neighborhood property values, and any vacant areas needed for replanning or replotting the district. As well the improvement district would hold the power of design and site approval over all new buildings and reconstructions proposed for the area. It could provide neighborhood services, such as garbage collection and park maintenance, in addition to those already provided by the city. (374)

During the depression years the Home Owners' Loan Corporation developed hundreds of maps of American cities showing neighborhood areas that could be saved if organized into neighborhood improvement districts. Waverly, Baltimore, was a pilot project undertaken by the Federal Home Loan Bank Board in 1939 to demonstrate the techniques of neighborhood conservation. First settled in 1830, this residential neighborhood near the central business district of Baltimore was an area of 39 city blocks and housed some 7,000 people where four out of five families owned their own homes. Without parks or open spaces, with lot sizes that varied, narrow and ragged street patterns, an absence of any standard building line, and so on down the list of defects, this area of the city was improperly planned. Most of the structures were old, detached frame houses dating back some 75 years or more, none in a condition of advanced decay and most in generally good repair. About one hundred of these structures, however, were badly deteriorated. (324)

The improvement approach began by studying individual structures, developing reconditioning and remodeling plans, and estimating the costs of rehabilitation work and the anticipated changes to property values. Studies were also made of the street and alley pattern, public utilities, and traffic flows. An overall improvement plan for the neighborhood focused on restoring depreciated structures and implementing a maintenance program. The next phase adjusted zoning regulations, developed playground facilities, and undertook street widenings and developed a plan for the voluntary demolition of blighted structures, to be coupled with their gradual replacement by municipally subsidized housing. As far as the Home Owners' Loan Corporation was concerned, the Waverly experiment was a success. In its second year of operation the number of paid-in-full rehabilitation and refinancing loans nearly doubled while borrowers in default dropped by over a half. Although one of the results of this program had been the untoward displacement of a family on relief, the corporation claimed "that a relief family really had no business in the neighborhood. It was the presence of such marginal families that was pulling down neighborhood values and discouraging the necessary repair and reconditioning work." (324:13)

Another scheme of neighborhood conservation promoted by the New York Building Association in 1936 was first offered as a solution for the redevelopment of the Lower East Side. Real estate interests, suffering from a shrinkage of income on blighted inner-city properties, knew they could not bear the costs of land assembly that would be necessary for wholesale redevelopment. Hence they proposed a start be made by considering the city block as the unit of design and management. Having decided upon standards for the maintenance of real estate values, properties on this block could then be controlled to conform to these standards. In blighted areas or areas experiencing trouble, renters were difficult to find and thus improvements economically unfeasible. If individually owned properties were collectively placed under the management of one realtor, tenants could be found and the economics of such cooperation would be obvious. First, the manager could suggest savings and increased earnings to the block if they rid themselves of certain nuisance uses. Second, each owner could deposit the deed of his property with the block corporation and receive in exchange stock representing the same ratio of value to the total shares of the whole. Third, mortgages could be consolidated and placed in the hands of a trustee. Special legislation, already being created in New York State, would enable this trustee to act in the general interest of the group. The block corporation was thus in the position to acquire land by demolishing obsolete structures without the need for land-acquisition fees. Hence a gradual replacement and upgrading program could take place that would be self-financing. Next the block could use its credit to finance redevelopment on the first demolished lot and then step by step proceed until all obsolete buildings were replaced by modern income-generating structures. Thus block preservation and group management could proceed in tandem without erasing investments in private property and by avoiding the pitfalls of eminent domain and public housing. (231:4)

By 1938 many housing reformers had joined the real estate interests in their search for means to retard the deterioration of neighborhoods that remained suitable for residential use and retained social and economic values worth conserving. The logical step for these advocates was a community improvement corporation. Like the improvement districts these corporations would provide a package of services to neighborhood home owners, surveying the physical conditions of buildings and securing information about their tax status and possible reassessments. A community trust, operating as a revolving fund, would be able to hire architectural teams, finance remodeling and modernization studies, and draw up economic prospective structures in need of rehabilitation. This trust could also purchase or lease and improve properties whose condition had fallen below the standards of the surrounding neighborhood. (352)

Most residential neighborhoods, the planners added, were by 1938 showing signs that they needed to revise their zoning ordinances if they wanted to eschew decay. Superspeculative practices of the 1920s, which had overzoned for business and commercial property, now left these neighborhoods open to blight and stopped the flow of improvement dollars. Unless nonconforming uses were gradually eliminated from these residential districts, even the higher-class districts might succumb to decline and abandonment. Thus neighborhood planning was becoming an additional item on most city planning agendas. St. Louis was one of the earliest cities to divide its residential areas into 81 neighborhood units in an effort to stimulate citizen action in the improvement and preservation of these areas. (352) New York City also concerned itself with neighborhood conservation, recommending a city-wide division of neighborhoods into redevelopment, rehabilitation, and conservation districts. (315) Cleveland began to plan for rehabilitation and redevelopment by dividing the city into areas that were seriously blighted and therefore in need of redevelopment, areas becoming or nearly blighted that required neighborhood conservation, and areas that eventually would be endangered and hence needed protective measures. Rehabilitation, redevelopment, conservation, and zoning code compliance began to be new classificatory tools by which neighborhood blight might be disciplined and stopped.[3]

City Planning Requirements

Everyone seemed to jump from the conclusion that to clear a slum area meant subsequently to rebuild it with good housing. But Bettman asked as early as 1934 how we know if a given blighted area is the appropriate place for new housing developments. Might the population continue to decline and devaluation of property values reoccur because the area is an inadequate location for residential uses? The cleared sites might be better used for industrial or commercial development. Before jumping into new housing projects, Bettman warned, we need thorough analysis and city planning. Investment value in new housing is dependent not only on the design and character of the development plans but on the supply of public services, the infrastructural connections to other parts of the city. Rebuilt areas can be protected from future decline only if they are well planned and integrated with other parts of the city. (64)

Before deciding what to do with slums and blighted areas of the American city, Bettman suggested, thorough city planning must be undertaken. The community needs to know the population and industrial trends in the area. What should be the pattern of alloction of residential, trade, industrial, public, and transportation land uses that will produce an economical and stable development for the entire city? (65) Bettman also argued that both of the constitutional issues that confronted the movement for large-scale housing redevelopments on cleared sites—those of the appropriateness of applying public funds for private redevelopment and the use of eminent domain to acquire land for housing projects—could be answered through the process of planning. A careful and thorough city planning investigation would demonstrate whether a proposed slum-clearance and housing project was justified as a matter of good city layout and development because the project was related to other public services, because the necessary housing was not likely to be provided by private capital without public assistance, and because it promised to reduce crime and disease. Thus planning might provide courts with proof that the clearance of slums and the provision of housing would be a direct public purpose or public use in the constitutional sense of the phrase. (64)

The cost and slow process of land acquisition still inhibited redevelopment. Courts held that land must be valued according to the use for which it is most appropriate and that public acquisition of private land must pay such compensation fees. Once again Bettman argued, the functional use of the land in question could be determined by the city plan. If a city plan designated an area suitable for redevelopment as low-income housing, then comparative compensation could be measured accordingly by the courts. (64) In line with these suggestions, Frederic A. Delano, vice-chairman of the National Resources Committee, suggested that the federal government might simultaneously promote the home building industry and sound community planning:

The federal government might properly offer to pay a certain percentage of the cost of acquisition of land by municipalities, on the condition that the municipality, in using such land, should take suitable precautions to insure the sound development of the neighborhood. The federal government should be careful not to subsidize the development of neighborhoods of jerry-built houses nor of surplus residential sections, nor of poorly planned communities. It should offer financial assistance only when municipalities follow a proper and well considered housing and land use policy. (226:565)

Suddenly the movement to redevelop the inner-city slum had taken hold; every city was in a hurry to put its scheme into action without waiting for planning forethought. If blighted areas are the effects of long-term decline and show transformations of housing style and residential preferences, then, the Committee on Urban Redevelopment for the National Conference on Planning argued, their removal or reduction will require long periods of careful thought, not emergency action. Many of the causes that created stagnation and depopulation of inner cities were nationwide trends, which planners could do nothing about. Each locality, however, reacted to these universal trends differently. This, the committee offered, was the area for planning investigation. If a blighted neighborhood is not related to the rest of the city through adequate transportation networks, employment opportunities, and commercial access, then it may not provide an economic justification for redevelopment or might be an area that is premature for conservation. (65)

Many blighted residential areas happen in conjunction with the decline of the central business district, so their problems must be solved simultaneously. Perhaps these areas should be redeveloped for other than residential uses or for higher-income groups than currently reside in them. Redevelopment, the planners began to stress, must not automatically mean low-income residential construction. (65) Although the justification for winning an expanded power of eminent domain, securing tax exemptions on redevelopment projects, and developing other forms of financial aid was overtly the provision of low-income housing, even the planners agreed that redevelopment must be able to attract private investment capital and offer a return on investment, which low-income housing uses alone might not always provide. Hence the last pieces in the redevelopment game were being forged out of the depression experience.

Securing Redevelopment Legislation

Limited-dividend housing operations, tax foreclosures, and land assembly methods were cumbersome devices to revitalize the heart of the city. Slowly forces were building up for a greater liberalization of state laws in order to permit urban authorities the right to acquire, hold, and dispose of land as they saw fit and as they might more broadly interpret public use. First, in the line of new legislation, the 1937 United States Housing Act established the U.S. Housing Authority (USHA) empowered to distribute $500 million in repayable loans and annual subsidies to municipal housing authorities for the purpose of slum clearance and low-income housing. To be eligible for these funds, a local housing authority had to raise 10 percent of the redevelopment costs and match at least 20 percent of USHA annual subsidies. The local 20 percent contribution usually took the form of exempting the housing project from taxation for ten years. When it was noted that housing in a slum area had long been in tax arrears and that land acquisition costs included the payment of these back taxes, it was argued that tax increases were less of a loss than at first appeared. Coupled with savings on extra municipal services for blighted areas such as health and police and with an increase in neighboring property values, these projects might be thought of as revenue generating. Loans from USHA were evidenced as bonds of the local housing authority and issued by USHA at 3 percent interest. These bonds, which were the authority's 10 percent share, were exceedingly attractive to investment houses. Thus USHA, it was argued, would slowly draw private capital back into inner-city real estate investment. As economic prosperity returned, it was hoped that private capital would invest in 20, 30, or even 50 percent of the redevelopment costs, consequently enabling USHA to reduce its own contribution. (271)

By 1938 155 of the 236 housing authorities in American cities were being assisted by federal aid. So great were the demands upon USHA funds that only a year after its birth, its entire source had been committed. Still the overall impact of the program was minimal. Jealous real estate capital would see that no renewal of funds would follow the initial apportionment. Fearing that public housing might compete with private housing, they required that no more than 10 percent of the total aid be committed to any one state and nearly 50 percent of this be allocated to small cities and towns with populations less than 49,000. (542) By 1941 there were 629 urban housing projects, of which only half were located in blighted neighborhoods on cleared sites. By this time, moreover, USHA was preoccupied with its defense housing programs. Slum redevelopment and low-income housing projects were held off to await returning postwar prosperity. (228)

The city continued to search for other ways to enable private capital to exploit redevelopment. Nevertheless low-income housing could not be made profitable for capital investment. The three private developments involving large-scale housing and slum clearance, two in Chicago and one in Newark, had demonstrated extremely low rates of return on investments. (43) In spite of elaborate redevelopment plans, the real costs of clearance and low-income housing tended to be ignored. Not one case study existed to show what could be done with a blighted neighborhood. How much would it cost for land to be acquired? What were the expenses of reconstruction? Who would pay the initial subsidy? Who would benefit from neighborhood redevelopment? A warning was raised once more that redevelopment should not be thought of as primarily a low-income housing program if prosperity was to return to the city. (228)

New York State began to develop experimental legislation. As early as 1934, a trial bill was introduced in Albany to aid group planning of deteriorated areas. In 1939 the Merchants Association of New York drafted a bill for slum redevelopment, which the governor vetoed. Other legislation, however, enabled the Savings Bank Trust Company and other types of financial trustees to exchange defaulting mortgages for securities issued for the consolidated mortgage debt. The road was beginning to open for implementing the group and neighborhood improvement plans designed by architects and real estate interests in New York City. By 1941 a revised Redevelopment act was enacted for the state. (228) The enthusiastic response that met this act was based on the hope that volunteer corporations would use these new legal methods in order to fight neighborhood blight. The act was intended to protect property owners and real estate investors from losses suffered during public acquisition and redevelopment and thus enable them to maintain their control over eventual improvements. This pioneering new law, which other states began to copy, authorized tax exemptions as an investment enticement to redevelopment corporations for ten years. (123)

These new corporations were empowered as well to assemble land through condemnation or, alternatively, a city could condemn land and then turn it over to these redevelopment corporations. In order for an investment group to assemble an area large enough to secure its improvements, they had to negotiate with many slum property owners, many of them absentee landlords, many unwilling to sell, and many demanding unrealistic prices. After the redevelopment corporation acquired 51 percent of the site, however, it could utilize the powers of condemnation for the remaining plots in the area. Every redevelopment plan would bear the planning commission's approval and would be located in an officially designated "substandard or unsanitary area." In turn the redevelopment plan must declare for the commission's approval every building it was going to demolish, its site, size, use, intentions stated about playgrounds, parks, and number of dwelling units, their rental levels, and so forth. The planning commission as well was responsible for observing that there was adequate housing within the city with substantially similar rental costs for the displaced residents. (140)

Slowly cities began to secure legislation that would enable private capital to undertake comprehensive redevelopment of its blighted districts. The aim was to secure the highest and best use of these areas according to the city's overall needs. Hence redeveloped land uses did not necessarily have to be for low-income residential purposes; they could be for upper-income residential needs, commercial developments, or public utilities.[4]

It seemed more and more apparent that new investment access had to be made to draw the quasi-public reservoirs of capital, that of the banks and insurance companies, into the renaissance of real estate in the American city. Thus in 1942 New York State passed the Redevelopment Companies Act, which enabled insurance companies to invest in redevelopment projects. Although slum clearance and its redevelopment for low-income housing initially was the persuasive item that relaxed the boundaries drawn around the constitutional power of eminent domain, the limited concept of public purpose, and the provision of various tax and financial incentives, now redevelopment legislation cropping up in state after state no longer restricted redevelopment to low-income housing.

Slum-clearance concepts and redevelopment techniques had crystallized just when attention was drawn away into defense preparation and entry into World War II. Nevertheless the city now held the mechanisms through which redevelopment of the urban core for new commercial, administrative, governmental, cultural, and educational uses, as well as the all-but-forgotten low-income housing projects, would secure new urban investment areas and stabilize already committed real estate equities during the long wave of economic development after World War II.

11

Planning for Postwar Regional Cities

As urban redevelopment projects were terminated before and during the war, the emphasis once more was to attain national economic stability through purposively planned action. During the 1930s two elements had struggled with each other: the recognition by national planners that federal intervention was essential for economic recovery; this force stood against real estate interests and local politicians within the American city who were fearful of state competition in such areas as public housing and disliked the mounting taxes levied on private property. (109, 222) By 1939 this struggle had kept total federal expenditures in both welfare payments and direct subsidies to threatened property owners from being of sufficient magnitude to end the depression. World War II, however, resolved the economic and fiscal crisis. Federal expenditures on rearmament and war preparation finally absorbed the dislocated surplus and answered the problem of unemployment. (39)

The war was a homogenizing experience for American society. Having reluctantly dragged big business into rearmament in 1941, the federal tax incentives and lucrative war contracts propelled the concentration and nationalization of capital across the country. Fifty-six of the largest and best equipped companies received 80 percent of all the war contracts, and 40 percent of all research contracts went to the ten largest corporations. (41) Bound together in self-supporting linkages, this corporate-government cooperation was the final articulation through which the state would consolidate and organize its dominance over the cities. On the one side of this cooperation, government realized that it must protect large corporations from depression and develop a network of subsidies and investments to ensure rapid economic growth, high rates of employment, and increasing standards of living for the majority of Americans. On the other side, the main question that large-scale capital would have to answer within this alliance was how to affect national economic policy in its own best interest, how to weave a general overriding capitalist interest subordinating the urban lobby and local capital interests within this consolidating spirit. This meant that more adequate political and administrative structures would have to be built; a reorganization and redistribution of local political power would have to occur so that a more direct route could open between national corporate policy and local urban implementation. Thus large corporations turned toward the equilibrating strategy of regional government. One more attempt would be launched to create intermediary political and ideological institutions that could moderate and temper local interests in struggle with the growing economic dominance of monopoly capital.

In the six largest metropolitan areas of America during the 1930s, population growth was confined to the regions outside the center cities, and in four of these areas it more than surpassed positive declines in the center city. (433) Loss of population in the center and sprawling residential growth in the suburbs once again made a new effort for governmental merger a possibility. The number of incorporated cities and villages in the counties surrounding St. Louis, for example, had doubled or trebled during the 1930s until they constituted a solid ring around the city. Under the impetus of the Federal Housing Administration's home financing policy, new subdivisions and random clusters of dwellings had sprung up throughout the counties. Thus a new authority for county planning and zoning under an officially binding master plan was created, while the center city's plan remained unofficial. (50)

Chicago was experiencing the same shift in its population. Recognizing the drift of former city residents to the unincorporated areas outside the city limits, Cook County had enacted a system of county-wide zoning. But with ineffective implementation controls and nonexistent county-wide health and firefighting services, a toll had already begun to be paid in these suburbs.[1] Cleveland as well had lost population during the 1930s to the second ring of villages and towns outside the incorporated areas. Within this metropolitan area taxpayers were supporting 61 police departments and providing inadequate and independent systems for fire protection, planning, public works, and courts. (287) The location of war plants added to this metropolitan sprawl for it became apparent by 1942 that most of the new plants would be located within commuting distances of cities with populations of 100,000 or more. Clearly postwar growth within these metropolitan areas would fill in vacant areas between the old city center and the outer ring of these new industrial plants. (206:4)

The administrative and financial problems of both central cities and their suburban satellites had intensified to such a degree that Thomas Reed, an advocate of and counselor for regional governments since the

1920s, believed that the way was open finally in 1941 for a new order in metropolitan government. New allies in the suburbs and central cities, as well as among the planning professionals, stood ready to fight against the organization of local governments so out of phase with social and industrial reality. A loss of population and taxable values had brought a well-publicized fiscal crisis to the central cities, while simultaneously a less noticeable but similar crisis erupted in the suburban satellites. There hundreds of thousands of families were almost poverty-stricken by their move to the suburbs, demanding and expecting the provision of quality schools and municipal services yet unable to pay increasing taxes. This overload of revenues divided between the suburban towns where most families lived and the municipality where they traded, worked, and entertained themselves was the most apparent fault of urban decentralization. (433) As it had been suggested since the 1910s, only a reorganized structure of governments would offer a more equitable service and resource base. The plans for these metropolitan cities were to redescribe and renew accounts of the interdependencies and interrelations of the regional unit: the area from which the city drew its raw materials, its retail and wholesale market area, its areas of labor supply and communications. (557) Again it was stressed that only a regional development plan would provide the necessary economic stability and security for future prosperity.

The imperatives of national defense and the need for postemergency planning both coalesced around the effort to rationalize and centralize governmental functions over entire metropolitan regions. The pressures of rearmament with its imperatives for fast and efficient delivery made the costly and chaotic nature of local government organization an available target. In the competition for government war contracts and the successful meeting of emergency housing and military service needs, so many fragmented parts to local government which made a given geophysical unit unable to function as a united governmental force, or failed to present any overall service plan or policy for economic and regional development, all added up to a wasteful loss of resources and wartime efficiency. But how in the face of political and economic opposition that had lasted for years would it be possible to sew together various layers of government into one functional region? The creation of one metropolitan government where before there had been many meant the abolition of jobs, the destruction of local political interests and economic controls, and the abandonment of long-established patterns of local identification.

The standard remedies for regionalization were few. City-county consolidation, the merger into a single unit of government, had been at a standstill since 1922. This had been only a partial answer to metropolitan problems since population could always outgrow the county's boundaries.

Besides this merger movement usually failed when rural county residents realized their properties would be reassessed at urban levels, and when city residents feared new tax obligations in the extension of city services to rural areas. The inability to transcend these obstacles had led many regions to the idea of a federated type of metropolitan organization, but this too had met with little success since 1930. Here metropolitan government was given control of certain functions of general concern to the whole region, while local authorities maintained their autonomy in special areas. The danger with this form of metropolitanization was its tendency to add an overlapping complexity of areas and jurisdictions more costly and cumbersome than unified government.

Under recent federal impetus, however, a form of special metropolitan districts embracing one public service such as power, water, or parks had arisen, often displaying spectacular results, such as the metropolitan water district of southern California, which coordinated thirteen cities within its comprehensive water scheme. But providing one district service, one more overlapping set of controls, lay far from a practical solution for the interrelated complexities of the metropolitan problem. In sum it appeared that the only major progress lay along the lines of functional consolidation. (433) One unit of government received the authority to perform a function previously allocated to several units within the region such as the county administration of social security assistance, or municipal and county sewer and disposal services. While scarcely solving the issues of regional inefficiency, at least this form of reorganization refrained from increasing the complexities of local governmental areas while it slowly moved toward regional consolidation. (316)

As the federal arm of administration stretched across the country, the problems of local government kept pace. Planners began to ponder what would be the effect of mass bombing upon the trend toward suburbia. What schemes of metropolitan government would emerge from the victory of fascism or the collectivism of an embattled democracy? After the war what would be the impact of continued federal grants-in-aid? What force would federal regional authorities, the federal politics of decentralization through regional administrative units, put behind metropolitan and regional trends? And who could foresee the technological effects of swifter transportation modes, new alloys and plastics, and long-range transmission of electric power?[2] To deal with these questions and to prepare for postwar emergencies, local planning councils and regional metropolitan planning authorities began to spring up in many cities.

The American Society of Planning Officials sponsored a nationwide contest in 1943 for proposals leading to regional councils of governments. (68) But regional development for wartime efficiency could not hold back while the appropriate metropolitan administrative and legislative apparatus evolved. Thus planning alone began to align its disciplinary framework to the renewed concerns of metropolitan efficiency. A new crystallization around a regional master plan began to emerge. The master plan had always been an arrangement of maps, charts, and analytical interpretations of social, economic, and financial data, which articulated the physical structure for municipal development. Now to speak of regional economic growth and industrial stability and to rebuild the obsolete sections of slums and counteract the influence of blighted areas, a regional master plan was required.

The functional disciplinary order of the planning discourse unfolded its scope to reembody the constant analysis and adaptation of each community part to its social and economic regions. (65) Overlaying a twenty- to thirty-year plan projecting the physical structure and development of the regional area, a coordinated system of transportation terminals and lines was drawn, so related to the visible pattern of land use that traffic congestion and parking nuisances were to be avoided in advance. Against these maps another was held in parallel, one depicting the detailed conditions of every town and city in the regional area. In the space between the ideal and the real were placed the locational grid of projects that would draw physical reality in closer conformance to the ideal regional plan. (280) New series of data and new collaborative institutions coalesced around the regional master planning agency responsible for development and replanning. Sewerage and water programs, airport and highway locations, race frictions, needs of returning servicemen, problems of social maladjustment and crime, population migrations, health and welfare considerations were linked together through the composite studies of postwar planning councils, metropolitan and county planning commissions, and citizens' defense groups. (286, 433)

All of these marks upon the regional plan summoned forth a secondary description: the process of publication, explanation, and discourse through a network of official and citizen groups. In many cities community-wide citizens' councils arose. These groups, it was felt, might succeed with metropolitan planning where regional governments had failed; they might call together and promote officials and citizens to think in terms of the regional whole and act as a clearinghouse and propagandizing effort that could move pragmatically toward the promotion and establishment of regional governments. (286, 501)

Within this regional perspective the National Resources Planning Board set out by executive order in 1941 to serve as a clearinghouse and promotional agency for postwar planning. Calling for metropolitan planning and regional development programs, its purpose was to decentralize national policy making to nine regional offices, to consider the regional contingencies of national prosperity and full employment, and to establish a plan by which to avert recycling postwar depression. Executive and congressional jealousies in 1943 caused this national planning effort to end, thus removing the only interagency-intergovernmental planning effort that could have effectively coordinated corporate interests at the federal level and carried them across to the regional base.

With its demise a vacuum was created between national corporate policy and economic regional development. Motivated by the fear of economic instability and renewed depression, corporate planners extended their control wherever possible over critical resources, market areas, access to supplies, transportation and distributory networks, governmental services, and investments. Into the field of postwar planning, therefore, many private corporate groups began to join the regionalization effort. Central among these was the Council for Economic Development (CED), the Rockefeller Brothers Fund, and the Ford Foundation. By 1943 CED announced it had created a network of 34 local groups lobbying for regional governments and the stimulation of postwar planning within metropolitan American cities. (342)

The public powers to be embedded within any authority attempting to reconstruct the metropolitan regions stood however against the values of liberty and private property so crucial to a democracy. Corporate interests would continue to establish voluntary regional commissions after the war, but the foes of central planning returned the focus once again to local initiative and local control over planning for the reconstruction of the American cities. This parochialism would leave its mark upon planning, for real estate groups in the early 1940s began to block the efforts of comprehensive planners by undertaking their own plans for public works, revising antiquated building codes, developing more equitable tax formulas, and initiating local proposals for slum-clearance projects. (187)

Planners saw housing and slum-clearance programs as only one element in a comprehensive effort that would socially, economically, and physically reconstruct the central cities and their metropolitan regions. Still the basic requirement for planners, Russell Black tried to convey in 1944, was the appreciation of form and a knowledge of how to design because the order of the American city extends far beyond the realm of ideas to the molding and disciplinary control of land and structures for multiple uses and purposes. In this form determination, planners must learn to deal with large spatial relationships that extend toward the region. They must also learn the mechanics of plan making and plan presentation. Then they must have a solid understanding of statistics in order to know which acts are important and which are not, and they must have a basic understanding of urban law, economics, and public finance. (68) Local interests, however, would forget this regional avenue; they would divorce their efforts from comprehensive and regional planning in the American cities. Instead their efforts to obtain slum-clearance legislation, powers of eminent domain, and housing subsidies were all assigned the function of attracting private capital and local real estate entrepreneurs back to the center city. They equated publicly subsidized redevelopment projects with plans for clearing the slums. Private enterprise, not public authorities or disciplinary planners, was to be given the first opportunity to reorder the postwar American city. (187)

Bartholomew would lament in 1949 as he reflected on the twentieth-century experience in city planning that a chasm still existed between broadly conceived plans and their effective implementation. Two obstacles stood in the way. The larger was the constantly fluctuating and disturbed worldwide and national economic conditions, which restricted local vision and action. But the second obstacle presented the basic dilemma. The achievement of planning in a democracy could be accomplished only through mass understanding and united action. "So battered and buffeted by wars and economic upheavals have been our citizens that day to day problems are paramount, and there is little time and energy left for other considerations. Long-range community planning becomes a secondary, unimportant consideration."[3]

Planning would stand by itself, apart from political authority and local controls in the postwar American city, whispering suggestions rather than uttering commands. Charles Merriam claimed this was natural for the data upon which the disciplinary controls of planning were based were too incomplete to offer absolute directives. Instead more research was required if planning was to become a science. But in those areas where planning interfered with political power, the planners must be warned, they did so by damaging the democratic order. "The very purpose of planning," Merriam claimed in 1944, "is to release human abilities, to broaden the field of opportunity, and to enlarge human liberty. We plan primarily for freedom, the ways and means and instruments are secondary to the main purposes. The right kind of planning—democratic planning—is a guarantee of liberty and the only real assurance in our times that men can be free to make a wide range of choices." (341:1086–1087)

An Architecture of Complexity

Most of the content that the field of planning would elaborate upon during the postwar era had already been defined during the years of depression crisis. Metropolitan area-wide planning and governmental control linked to the problem of uneven suburban, urban, and rural development; the urban research and analysis needed to redefine the planning process and to focus on the urban problem; the domain of urban housing and slum clearance, which would restrict the structure and location of planning thought; the modes of physical, administrative, and socioeconomic planning; the permanency of state intervention with its requisite intergovernmental and fiscal reorganizations: these groups of statements would once again mark out the internal configuration of the planning discourse in the postwar era of metropolitan development as much as they had previously.

We have examined the spiraling movement of planning, analyzing in turn the repetitive tensions of centrifugal-centripetal urban development forces, centralized-decentralized governmental control, and comprehensive-fragmented planning domains, seeking to explain how the theories of planning and its reform practices reflected the boundaries and limits within the structure of American capitalism. I have advocated a dialectical view of the genesis and structure of planning theory, one in which development occurs in response to contradictions and problems within the system of American cities. In turn these dilemmas have been inserted into the theory of planning around the opposing forces of centralized state intervention necessary to secure and maintain the growth and stability of the economic system and decentralized tendencies of local control or citizen participation necessary for legitimating governmental intervention and compensating unmet social needs and services. The possibility of national economic planning, a consolidated and institutionalized state power, thought to be crucial for solving the crisis of depression, represented an exterior or absolute limit to planning, a practice that would not be satisfied under the notion of democracy and the private economic demands of local municipal interests. In consequence the state formation of urban social and economic policies in the postwar era would continue to struggle against this demarcation line. Instead state planning policies would present a separate complexity. The postwar state would be seen as one part among an ensemble of groups sharing decision-making power, standing in equilibrium one against the other within an integrated social system. With its administrative apparatus, the state would appear to function as a rational organizer and director of cooperative efforts among a pluralistic array of interest groups. (117, 242)

Within this complexity with its multiple levels of demands and interests, technocratic postwar planning formed its ideological mold. Rational styles of decision making and projection, adaptive behavioral control of systems, and efficient administrations of programs and budgets became a union of interdependent planning functions within a stage of advanced capitalism where science and technology were the leading forces of production and where economic growth depended upon the accumulation of information and elaborate problem-solving techniques. (212) The discourse on the order of the American cities of the late 1940s revealed the same expression of hierarchical complexity. The urban complex has three spontaneous groupings: the neighborhood grounded in family life and face-to-face communication, the natural community areas dependent upon the same socioeconomic institutions located within their city centers, and the region defining a social-economic and cultural unit. (130) The process of planning must reflect the horizontal and vertical integration of these three components. As Melville Branch explained later in 1950, "coordinative planning" meant that planning decisions embodied in lower levels culminated in higher more complex forms of analysis and projection than were possible within the simpler, lower-level elements. (77)

Rational planned action formed the same unity of functional statements, the same divisions and linkages connecting one step to another in search of a common disciplinary strategy: the selection of goals, the analysis of these goals based on the community's needs and resources, their order of priority, their implications and probable consequences, and the selection of the most efficient and acceptable means for attaining them. Now however the sequence of rational components had to be organized to include a community plan; each individual action had to be coordinated and articulated into an overall general strategy. (558) Norbert Wiener told the planning conference of 1954 that "all good planning is in the nature of what is called 'feedback' in the field of communication engineering and the design of control apparatus," a process of continual self-regulation by which the information relating to the success or failure of plans and planned components was carefully evaluated and used to perfect the process of goal attainment. (550:1)

Not more than 25 years later Webber and Rittel observed that the urban complexity, which they called an open societal system, constituted "wicked problems," ill defined and without definite solution. Planning solutions would arise only from the complexity of discovery procedures that dealt with multileveled contexts and incomplete causal relations. Wicked problem solving contained an argumentative process in which the problem and proposed solution were mutually dependent and in which some of the ramifications and waves of repercussions with long-term effects might never be appraised. Thus planning solutions could always be perfected without a stopping point. Whatever solution was finally arrived at, it was only the beginning of another more complex problem to be re-solved. (448)

Understanding this architecture of complexity was the challenge that the abstract process of planning accepted for its standard during the postwar era. Stemming from the World War II production of missile-control devices and computers to track their firing patterns, the theory of information and systems stability began. From that starting point it spread across the physical and human sciences. This systems logic and theory of information also must be examined against the background of advanced capitalism.

After World War II and until the late 1960s, the United States experienced a sustained period of economic expansion. A burgeoning public sector, increasing state regulation in pursuit of fiscal policies, and the provision of a vast array of social services were state practices with which the postwar American public would be confronted. The accumulation of information, the use of computers, and rational management and administration schemes were organizational devices that coordinated the multiple levels of services and needs presented by a nation of cities.

Postwar state expenditures were characterized by economic stimulation and political legitimation. State investments in infrastructure such as highways, airports, and industrial parks increased the rate of productivity of private capital units, while social services such as social security and health insurance indirectly aided productivity by increasing the reproductive power of labor and simultaneously by absorbing some of the increasing costs of labor. As James O'Connor has shown, these expenditures primarily benefited the monopoly sector, in which production was more specialized and interdependent, and in consequence it necessitated the simultaneous expansion of the state sector providing a coordinating mechanism. Increasing productivity rates in large manufacturing industries, however, were not accompanied by a subsequent growth of employment. Quite the reverse occurred.[1] To absorb the surplus of labor pushed out of traditional manufacturing industries, the low-wage but fast-growing service, clerical, and retail occupations along with the slow-growing nonunionized and small-scale manufacturing industries were stretched to their limits. But expansion in this sector was never fast enough to absorb the necessary employment or provide wages at sufficient subsistence levels. Thus the numbers of unemployed and minimally employed tended to grow as prosperity within the public and monopoly sectors increased. (388) The American postwar economy can be characterized dichotomously: a rapidly expansive monopoly sector juxtaposed against the opposite pole where impoverishment and degradation increased among the minimally employed and surplus populations.

Planning in the postwar American cities was drawn inevitably toward a recognition and acceptance of the social costs produced by this expansive but uneven economic development. In order to offset the opposition among those not directly enhanced by state economic policies, such as the blacks and the urban poor, and to increase its legitimate authority for spending social revenues on urban renewal projects where real estate entrepreneurs gained more than the targeted areas, the state provided a second category of expenditures whose function was to maintain social harmony through the welfare system, public housing and poverty programs, or environmental protection. (388) But the dual functions of state expenditures—to maintain economic accumulation and provide political legitimation—were often diametrically opposed. Drawing revenue into unproductive personnel training programs for ghetto residents or providing public housing subsidized way below market levels meant limiting the revenues needed for capital outlays. Caught in a struggle between a stable economic base and a harmonious social order, the postwar planning apparatus in cities innovated with administrative operations, experimented with citizen participation, and rationalized budgetary procedures, governmental reorganizations, and revenue allocations in order to provide the most efficient state services, projects, planned development, and growth at least expense.

Themes of the planning discourse began to articulate these tensions by embedding their dialogue within the problem of democracy and planning. Fearing a retrenchment in budget allocations, personnel, and services of government after World War II, Louis Wirth proclaimed to the Planning Conference in 1947 that the pervasive nostalgia for simplicity, a laissez-faire economy without public controls, was an "obstinate refusal to face fundamental issues." (558) Planners, he alerted, must be aware of this negativistic opinion, for as long as it questioned the functions of government, planning itself would remain sheer fantasy. The system of private enterprise depended upon planning. In an extremely complicated society with worldwide ramifications, planning was essential to maintain and sustain the conditions for private enterprise. (558)

"Freedom exists as a balanced condition . . . the maintaining of this balance is the principal function of government," William Jewell told planners in 1960. (260:45) Planning, strategically located between the public and governmental bureaucracies, consequently stood as close as possible to the tensions of freedom and order, for in the creation of a plan, the planner must mediate between the forces of innovation and individual expression and the simultaneous development of a balanced and orderly community. Only by drawing upon both public involvement and technical competency would the balance between diversity and order be democratically weighed. (27, 478)

Administrative policy planning pointed toward this conjunction, for its purpose was to draw "more wholesome relationships between the planner and democratic authority," welding together the various groups and subgroups with their volunteer participatory directives against the democratically elected powers of decision. (190) "Civic ignorance," against which progressive reform had always struggled, was still the flaw in the political action of planning theories. Therefore an interpretative picture of community development based on surveys and information brought together by elite representatives and drawing a comparative matrix in balance against the development standards of other communities was proposed to educate and motivate citizens to participate. Juxtaposing technically exact and specialized studies with the training and public discussion of a few key people, the old communicative theories of planning were restored and revitalized. (558) Again we find produced the dual themes of empirical evidence and public awareness. It is here, where technical information and political pluralism join, that we must look for the ideological form of planning in the postwar American city. Knowledge, which is neutral, objective, technical, and scientific, beyond the domain of special group and class interests, became the ideal motivator for social change. It was an empirical screen behind which the basic contradictions of uneven economic development within the order of American cities would withdraw. Planners, public elites, rational men were to be the overseers of this new positivity, the neutral theoreticians of the planning mentality in a nation of cities. Wirth had explained, "Policy-making functions of government [require] increased technical knowledge for their adequate performance. It is at this point that some of our most acute problems of reconciling democracy with efficiency arise." (558:9)

Modern technology had transcended the tradition of localism and stood against the pressures that had so long opposed more comprehensive governmental organizations and controls. Yet planners were to be more than mere technocrats in this new governmental complex, for their role was to draw all the relevant specialists to focus on the urban complexity and to enunciate more comprehensive, broader concerns. Since each need served by urban government was interrelated yet complex enough to require specialized and professional treatment, it was to be the planner who must draw the circle of logic around the technically competent parts. (506) But efficient decision-making processes controlled from centralized governmental structures also required the participation of community groups. These groups in turn would constitute forums reflecting the needs, values, and operational problems within isolated subgroups of the community. (358, 473) A citizens' planning agency could stimulate operational procedures only if it too, like the technical experts, maintained a neutral stance, exercising independent judgment on the basis of objective and accurate facts. Providing a meeting ground for diverging rational opinions, the citizens' organization and public review were the reformist location in which the technical plan was logically tested and interpreted, where opposing reactions were understood and reconciled into a consensus of planned objectives and community tolerance.

The challenge for planning in a nation of cities was clear: the simultaneous juxtaposition of community planning and local participation with the objective competence and neutral authority of technical knowledge and policy directives from governmental bases. In other words planning would come to reflect the same contradictory functions of the state under advanced capitalism: those of political legitimation and capital accumulation. In addition both community participation and rational decision making were processes. Consequently second-order abstractions about democratic and technical processes of power were the measures against which planning in postwar urban America would stand or fall. The older concerns of physical planning, land-use maps, real estate developments, and architectural embellishments lost their control over the exercise and focus of the planning mentality.

These rationality and participatory functions of planning must also be linked to the dynamics of capitalism during the long phase of economic growth from 1945 to roughly 1968 and to its period of inflation and stagnation in the 1970s and 1980s. During the phase of growth planning policies were aimed primarily at organizing and guiding private capital as it exploited and invested in urban redevelopment and metropolitan expansion. If planning attended to participatory needs, it was only as they were created or affected by private development. During the downswing of the economy after 1968, however, the state began to prune away inefficient governmental programs, reorganized its administrative structure, cut back on fiscal expenditures, and tightened regulative controls, all in an effort to clear the path toward its next cycle of economic growth and stagnation. But in neither its period of expansion nor contraction did planning hold onto the process of physical land-use planning.

Let us look more specifically at the demise of physical planning during the economic phase of accelerated growth in which urban redevelopment was the dominant planning activity. As Melvin Webber related in 1963, urban complexity had brought a new depth to comprehensive physical planning. Simple linear relationships that had once tied neighborhoods to the metropolitan whole were now understood to be embedded in complex causal networks and subtle behavioral relationships that marked the human and material systems that the city mirrored. It was no longer understanding the urban physical form but the interdependent processes that linked yet one more element to another that directed the planner toward more effective interventions in urban development. Each municipal agency was to follow the effects that its programs outlined for neighborhoods, to evaluate bundles of policies and thereby measure their results, to establish flows of data monitoring the state of urban populations, the city's economy and physical form. (538) The role of systematician—someone to look over and be responsible for federal directives and to integrate the variety of social and public services every municipality provided—fell to the comprehensive planner; he could point to and clarify the refurbished central cities, the expanding housing stock, the social relations of ethnic neighborhoods, all the elements and levels compounded in the metropolitan urban whole.

Yet already surfacing from within the difficulties of comprehensive physical planning was the desire among many planners for political power and practical effectiveness. For too long planning had been held to the threshold of utopia and had floundered on ill-conceived principles and half-formed conceptions. The world of practice and political choice where cities were structured and formed in reality—the world of the banker, the builder, the construction union, the political elites and public bureaucrats—these were the forces the planners longed to join. It is the distortion of these ideas of practice no longer compatible with the mold of physical planning that began to modify and politicize the planning mentality. The rational process of planning, it was stated, was no more than a calculus of decision formulations that must be juxtaposed to political action. The decisions of the mayor, the merchant, the urban renewal director, even the homebuilder and developer were lost among the conflicts and alternative choices of urban development. (347) Comprehensive planning must provide governments and private citizens with public agendas for action and political theories with their own style of implementation, recognizing that plans were political agendas that affected differently various groups and interests. (304)

Beginning with the Housing Act of 1949 the state began to intervene significantly in the financing of center city construction: first by purchasing, demolishing, and thereby liberating the land from objectionable and unproductive uses, and second, by assuring long-term prefinancing of construction operations, a rapid turnaround time for private capital was created. (513) With one major realignment private investment was drawn into redevelopment schemes. While claiming to be low-cost housing programs, urban renewal projects during the 1950s and 1960s demolished more homes than they built and displaced more neighborhood residents and activities than they relocated. New luxury apartments, university expansions, commercial and civic centers, governmental and cultural buildings, and new barriers of cleared and renovated land cordoned off productive land uses from slums. (96)

Of interest to planners was the new valuation of renewal entrepreneurs. Due to the separation of public financing and private production, governmental promoters of development projects not only had to generate the necessary capital but also coordinate the people and institutions linked to urban renewal projects. These entrepreneurs became the guardians against the financial risks of renewal ventures; they attracted the capital, determined the role of the enterprise in the market economy and built and maintained an efficient and technical staff to oversee the redevelopment plans. (56) As the number of renewal projects increased, the administrative activities of decision and control began to predominate, and here within the context of financial uncertainty and risk was a functional position for the urban planner.

Urban renewal projects involved middle-range objectives demanding both autonomy of action in limited fields and centralization of responsibility in local governments. (141) So it is that Martin Meyerson explained to the profession of planners that a middle ground was needed: an intermediate set of planning functions performed on a sustained and comparative basis as a framework for the investments of private homebuilders, the social expenses of governments, the public infrastructural decisions of municipal commissioners, the corporate investors in real estate transactions, and the slum-clearance projects of renewal authorities. Middle-ground community planning functions were to coordinate a set of interrelated processes: the regular preparation of market analyses to facilitate housing, commercial, and industrial operations; periodic reports on dangerous signs of blight and economic and population transformations; policy clarifications by which to revise community development objectives; short-run ten-year development plans spelling out specific actions; and review, research, and evaluation on the consequences of development projects. (347)

Other issues as well perturbed the physical planning ideal. To direct all planning endeavors over a seven-year period toward the publication of a static univalued document meant that private market actions dominated urban development. Urban sprawl, neighborhood blight, and strip commercial development should be the planners' concerns, Constance Perrin claimed. Comprehensive planning with its compulsion to consider every variable and embed its recommendations in physical analyses could not supply the legislators and politicians with the information they required. Federal programs of the 1950s and 1960s such as health care, education, highways, and urban renewal needed concrete policies and short-range directives. (408)

By 1959 the concerns of the middle-range pragmatic planners had been institutionalized within the Community Renewal Program (CRP), bringing with it a basic shift upward in the rationalization of the planning process. It was no longer sufficient to draw a comprehensive picture of the American city and then adjust each short-range program to conform to this idealized pattern. Now the planners' observations must be limited to public and private action, which over time structured this urban complexity. (348) When one designed a community program, all the possible public policies were mixed together according to their effects over time and in relation to various levels and rates of investment. Program evaluation necessitated a framework by which to measure and compare the consequences of future results, and this in turn assumed a statistical base providing accounts of the state of the system and a descriptive account of the system's operations. Careful analysis would thus identify the major problems and then adjust, monitor, and evaluate the policies as they affected community development.

Information has always been the basis of planning. Now computer simulation models and urban data banks were going to provide the predictive ability so absent in earlier plans. Urban development models, in part supplied through CRP grants and in part by transportation studies, reduced the structure of urban land uses to the arrangements of decisions representing the real estate market. Data correlating land-use activities, population choices for residential areas, types of residential developments, transportation corridors, and population flows either simulated the supplies and demands of residential activity across an urban field, accessed the optimal location of transportation routes throughout the metropolitan area, or foretold the structure and development of future land uses.

One of the purposes of planning in a nation of cities was to reduce contingencies in the planning environment and thus secure control over multilevel complexity. This offered a legitimate basis upon which the state could intervene within the economy. Decision theories or efficiency techniques deal with uncertainty and complexity at an abstract level. They can avoid a legitimacy crisis as long as the public remains depoliticized. (212) Thus when the pressures of legitimacy first approached the process of planning in the American city, there were modifications within the structure of technical decision-making control before there were changes within the political process of public accountability.

In the process of public decision making, planning had to learn to buttress its rational techniques with normative statements and values that could act as objective standards for choice. In a democratic society in which community groups can pursue a plurality of conflicting or congruent goals, effective plans must express the variety and sometimes inconsistent conceptions of community interests. (538) Diversity must be the planner's framework; he must seek his clients' preferences, draw them out into open debate, and make them objective standards for evaluating community goals and programs. "Client analysis" was thus to be an empirical study—a market research of the behavior, wants, preferences, and needs of participant residents in community programs. (142) To close the gap between the bureaucratic planner and the community group, it became the planner's responsibility to assist in the discovery and empirical objectification of these community values and needs.

Thus by focusing on objectifiable value statements, a choice theory of planning emerged. Endowed with arbitrary priorities, arranged in hierarchical matrixes, these values became the measures upon which effective bargaining among preferences, an instrumental exchange of valued positions, was brought into play. The planner's role was to facilitate choice in society, to accord values a position not given weight before, to differentiate the futures that correlated best with a community's interests. So it was to be the planner who would draw us closer to a fully competitive political market by widening participatory opportunities in the arena of choice. (118)

Decision making under conditions of competing interests, in a planning environment where different value preferences evaluated choices in different styles, moves the calculation of strategic action to an expansive level of rationalization. (214) In a context of incomplete information where the behavior of one's opponent can never be empirically known, to gain control over conditions of indeterminacy bends the matrix of values and the organization of choice to the strategy of survival. Values that conflict or stem from different preferences become functional choices to be exchanged. From cost-benefit analysis, to goal achievement matrixes, or program budgeting, the same problem arose: how are values to be traded off to achieve the programmed goal? What is to be their criterion of exchange, their weighting of gains and measurements of losses within which stability can be obtained? In the many criticisms flung against these rationalized decision procedures, we find the vertical limits of technical rationality to have been met: questions that test the relevancy of measurement scales, the bias of evaluators, the superiority of the marketplace and social welfare aggregations; problems with unmeasurable social costs and interdependent externalities; the failure of bureaucracies to achieve the necessary levels of technical expertise or leadership or the correct information; the relevant data by which to operationalize computerized models, data banks, and procedures. (477, 553) The continual substitution of rational norms and decision techniques for political disputes eventually leaped over acceptable or legitimate boundaries. When this occurred, planning in the American cities learned to experiment with the political process of participatory planning.

Precisely as the state and the economy were cojoined in postwar development, the state was confronted with a plurality of publics and the need to ascertain their values and incorporate their interests in the implementation of state goals. As the state does so, however, its own stability is undermined by politicizing more contradictions, by creating interests that cannot be subordinated to programmed steering control and that demand the expansion of fundamental civil rights and socialized services.

Legitimation expenses increasingly dominated the state's domestic expenditures during the 1960s, not as a means by which to eradicate poverty but to integrate and contain those with the most militant and disrupting demands. Thus the poverty programs of the state, inaugurated under the Equal Opportunity Act of 1964 and the Housing Act of 1964, and continued with the Demonstration Cities and Metropolitan Development Act of 1966 and the Housing and Urban Development Act of 1968, set a new dialectic in motion: not only was it to produce a social order among the poorest classes, but as these classes pressed more vigorously for their own civil and political rights, more areas of society subsequently became politicized and this heightened social and political awareness in turn threatened the legitimate aims and programs of the administrative state. As the threshold of legitimacy rose, the state began to experiment with pluralist participatory politics, but as it did it sometimes triggered explosive demands that it could not always control and that set off adjustments to the threshold of acceptability. Planning recognized these legitimate pressures of fragmented and isolated publics and absorbed them into its own procedures.

The basic state interventions in the city during the 1950s had promoted the stabilization and accumulation of private real estate capital. But these interventions were also social in nature. State allocations for urban renewal to private real estate entrepreneurs affected areas such as the relocation

of ghetto residents, the cordoning off of slum territories from more profitable center city land uses, the dependencies of construction workers on
public contracts, the liberal citizens' awareness of social inequalities. These
distortions in the physical base of the American cities brought a new
politicization to planning during the 1960s.

The principle upon which planning had been formed had always been
the use of land—the physical arrangement of space that reflected production and circulation needs. The grid that divided the experiences of
planning one from another had undergone many transformations. Although
their orientation since the 1930s had turned increasingly toward social
and economic development, planners still held the translation of these
goals into a physical plan to guide public and private investment as the
epicenter of professional activity. (410, 411)

Complexity, however, marked the fragile construction of this planning
mentality, for as Dyckman stressed, it was out of the interdependencies
of the social fabric that the necessity for social planning emerged, for one
could not intervene in any given portion of the social web without disrupting
the structure and entangling oneself in the consequences. Remedial social
planning or ad hoc solutions for specific social problems were the necessary
reactions against major unplanned forces that shaped society but that no
planner could predict or control. (142) If physical planning had been the
stable mark upon the land-use map, then social planning would resemble
the conflicts and variations from which it must grow. (409) Beneath the
older physical symptoms of land disarray lay a realm of unfathomable
social disorders. The problems of urban renewal had created unintended
consequences. Primarily planned to restore community development, it
had unexpectedly created residential relocation difficulties, dislocating
small merchants, and completely disrupting neighborhoods, stresses borne
primarily by poor and minority families. (142) The Harlem and Los Angeles
ghetto riots in the summers of 1964 and 1965, the withdrawal into two
separate and unequal societies, seemed to make comprehensive planning
that saw physical development and land-use order as ends in themselves
irrelevant and anachronistic. (81)

That community economic development, political values, and territorial
control should have become the dominant object of the planning discourse
during the 1960s can be seen as the crystallization of an ensemble of
events: pressure from the lowest strata of the working class, consolidating
controls of monopoly capital, state interventions for the purpose of social
integration and order. An imbalance was bound to prevail, for while the
community under study itself might offer evidence of the need for development, this was treacherous ground, as Dyckman declared, for the
expert determination of these community needs, the creation of reasonable

professional demands, the linkages back to appropriate state services might be the facade under which class and professional prejudices would prevail. (142) Planners offered an ideological resolution: the community's own acquisition of knowledge, their possession of a technical language to rationalize their demands, was equated with the power to manipulate state directives. (407)

As planning dissociated itself from a physical base, it descended toward a particular disorder. First the overriding concept of a public interest disintegrated and then the ideal of comprehensive planning as the profession immersed itself in political participation. Throughout the 1960s the profession registered a growing awareness that the ideal of master planning never had been achievable. A comprehensive viewpoint of the urban totality justified in the name of the public interest implied a top-down autocratic approach. New values and choices were always arising, making it unrealistic to measure short-range changes against the long-term development goals embodied within a master plan. Thus in a pluralistic environment the focus must rest on the interactions between elements of the system, on facilitating more decision components and looser organizational arrangements without necessarily changing the system's directions. A planner, Herbert Gans explained, had the right to tell a community what was good for it only when this advice was relevant to the goals of the community, and especially if the community was not even aware of the relevance. But the community in a pluralistic society always held the right to reject this advice, for no suprapolitical authority stood higher than the desires of the community itself. (189) This kind of disorder reflected deep-seated turbulence within planning.

The aim of citizen participation was to provide interest groups with the resources they needed in the democratic process of decision making. Since the New Deal, and even earlier in Hoover's contending powers among the state, labor, and capital, the federal government had facilitated the process of countervailing powers. "Creative federalism" of the 1960s meant that local groups and organizations had to bargain directly with federal powers invested in state and local bureaucracies. Increasing the number of official participatory groups yet allowing local governmental units the veto power and leverage over neighborhood proposals placed a premium on a liberal expectation of cooperation and consensus in participation, shared powers, balance of rights, and partnership. (407)

Participatory pluralist planning was a principled response to aid in both the achievement of social justice and the reformulation of planning. Years of community disruption and dislocation by urban renewal projects and federal highway programs, the damage inflicted upon minority interests by planners whose traditional support lay with downtown business interests, the pressure of civil rights, the tensions of racial discrimination—these were part of the context in which American pluralist politics offered a new style of conditional action: to do away with the ideal of comprehensive physical planning, which separated planning from politics and placed long-range plans as nonpolitical agendas against the pressures of community interest groups, and to substitute public participation of groups in the process of redistributive planning. Fragmented into isolated neighborhood groups, pitted against an array of partially responsible urban bureaucracies and through the acceptance of a position in this participatory game, these groups placed themselves directly within the technical process of abstract planning in a nation of cities. Institutionalized and reified, citizen participation of the 1960s remains an example of the political misunderstanding by participatory planners of the stability and legitimation needs of the state, of the tactics by which mass protest policies were carefully contained, and comprehensive physical styles of planning completely eclipsed.

13

The City of Collective Memory

Although this book traces the discourse of city planning, it has also been in the end a book considering the crisis of modernism and its impact on physical planning. Industrial development in the nineteenth century, which heedlessly devastated the urban environment physically and socially, produced within planning a reaction to escape from the meanness of this city chaos, to enshroud itself in the promise of technical utilitarianism and functional organization, above all to be liberated from the tyranny of tradition represented by the nineteenth-century metropolis and to build anew a brave, rational city. In the twentieth century modern man and urban life were inseparably and nihilistically joined, for urban life distilled both the alienating man-machine domination as well as the utopian promise of material advancement.

Here the tendency to seek a formal order for the city can be aligned with the modernist gesture to reappropriate a fragmented and compartmentalized modern reality by transforming it into a personal aesthetic style and a private abstract language. This urge to aesthetic abstraction reveals an inability of modern man to establish a rapport with material reality. Thus is created a gap between those concerned with stylistic order and those dependent upon social conditions, as well as a situation that reflects the alienation and separation of modern reality.

This is what Siegfried Kracauer captured when he claimed that "capitalist thinking can be identified by its abstractness." It is not capable of grasping the actual substance of life. We may gain through science a more rational mode of thought, but this is at the expense of our abilities to depict the material world. (280:63) The more that material reality is reduced the more removed our consciousness of forming it becomes. Abstraction obstructs a dialogue with images and meanings; we remain above and elusive of physical reality. In the end functional and rational precision exude a cold and sober aesthetic.

In the 1980s the two professions of the built environment, the process planner and the formalist architect, can no longer discuss together the form or future of the American city, a fact we must blame on the antiurban and ahistorical mentality of both of them. Manfredo Tafuri has suggested that perhaps the disintegration of the concept of form corresponds to the creation of the modern metropolis, for "the secret of form is that it is boundary." (503:60) Instead an antiurban ideology pervaded the mentality of the architects and planners of the modern movement. Their concept of a global machine city in which spatial organization was fragmented and development abstracted revealed an inherent negativity to the large metropolitan whole. The only way that the city could be experienced was mechanically.

The aesthetics of the machine produced an outburst of abstractions, where the machine city could be understood only in terms of its logic of functional ensembles and technical operations. For this new style, the laws of assemblage and disassemblage became essential. This modern imagination, however, required looking at urban form and texture through a particular set of lenses that occluded the ability to engage in social reality.

In 1903 Georg Simmel wrote, "The deepest problem of modern life arises from the claim of the individual to preserve the independence and identity of his being against the super-powers of society, of his historical inheritance, and of the external culture and technique of life." (404:170) This attempt of the individual to make sense of personal existence often leads to a withdrawal from experience. Lukács, following Simmel's lead, wrote that in the theory and practice of modernism, the image of man is by nature solitary and asocial. Man is unable to establish relationships with things or persons outside of himself. So defined he becomes ahistorical; there is neither a reality beyond the self nor a personal history formed through contact with that reality. Thus the unchallenged assumption is the status quo, obscuring political overtones and denying an engagement with social reality. This position saps the vitality of criticism and opposition to the state of existence. In any critique of social conditions, Lukács continued, it is these very conditions that must hold the central place. The modernist position, however, holds no standard against which it can compare the pathological and distorted condition of human existence. Instead technique is isolated from content, its importance amplified in order to avoid significant commentary on social conditions. "The denial of history, of development, and thus of perspective, becomes the mark of true insight into the nature of reality." (312:20–21, 28, 33, 34)

Modernism led to the destruction of traditional modes of physical planning and the abandonment of conventional forms of the American city.

Edmund Bacon's comment on the urban process in 1969 can draw our perspective back to the city, for he blamed the failure of cities on the intellectuals' inability to bring about a viable concept of a modern city, as well as their refusal to create a vivid and driving concept toward which we could plan the urban totality. Instead, Bacon claimed, postwar planners were content in devaluing the importance of the traditional urban form and ahistorically were locked into perpetuating the New Deal structure of assumptions. Thus planners still responded to the belief that "one third of the nation was ill-housed, ill-clothed, and ill-fed" and automatically collapsed their vision to focus on the "poor" as an abstract group that never existed. So removed from the contextual situation had the planners become that vast public housing projects sited on open space wastelands were designed to destroy the slums and to eradicate the connective tissue in the historical centers of the American city. Yet another borrowed concept from the 1930s was the demonstration project embedded in such subsidized projects as the greenbelt towns, rural resettlement policies, and slum-clearance programs. Here, Bacon noted, the planner dealt only with a fragment of the urban dilemma and abandoned the old, comforting, but outmoded modes of the familiar "good neighborhoods" and created entirely new ones out of environment and process. (33:130)

In 1946 Max Horkheimer, considering the domination of nature by rational processes of thought in a different critical context, underlined this failure of modern man to provide a grounding in social reality that would produce a sense of time, history, social change, and perspective:

If reason is declared incapable of determining the ultimate aims of life and must content itself with reducing everything it encounters to a mere tool, its sole remaining goal is simply the perpetuation of its co-ordinating activity. . . . Yet the more all nature is looked upon as . . . mere objects in relation to human subjects, the more is the once supposedly autonomous subject emptied of any content, until it finally becomes a mere name with nothing to denominate. The total transformation of each and every realm of being into a field of means leads to the liquidation of the subject who is supposed to use them. This gives modern industrial society its nihilistic aspect. (232:92–93)

Frozen into a rigid position, modern man, without perspective, has no power of decision, no ability to change the social situation.

Richard Bolan's summary of the attack during the 1960s on the classical model of physical planning stressed this nihilistic perpetuation of planning's coordinating activity and the demise, indeed eclipse, of any physical content or formal expression for process planners. (74) Reality, Bolan proclaimed, never measured up to the ideal. An advisory planning commission, with its comprehensive view of the city and the public, capable and responsible for the development of long-range growth goals, was a fragile illusion. A master plan, intended to impose order upon the physical form of the American city, was a chimera on the backs of planners, which the priests of rationality must now exorcise. Political scientists, economists, local politicians, and planners agreed that the urban future could never be accurately predicted, that community goals in a turbulent world remained elusive, that information would always be indeterminate, that a decentralized democratic political system made comprehensive planning from a centralized authority impossible. The ideal of a public interest embodied in a comprehensive plan, moreover, conflicted with the reality that private interests directly influenced public policy formation and that political decision making operated on fragmented choices, not integrated wholes.

Allowing private interests to penetrate the public sphere excused traditional physical planning from engaging in battle over urban space and form. It weakened as well the critical reasonings of planning over state directives and policies as they affected the form of the American city. If planners believed that they were redressing the inequities of the private market by extending the process of planning beyond the physical environment, they did so at the expense of keeping these issues before the gaze of the urban formalists or architects. (186) No doubt this split between the architect and the planner goes back to the introduction of the modern movement to America in 1932 when Henry-Russell Hitchcock and Philip Johnson organized an exhibition at the Museum of Modern Art on modern architecture. In their accompanying book they stressed the weaknesses of the European concept of social planning and the new aesthetic directions to be forged from the American experience.

The Siedlungen [group housing] of the European functionalists generally reach the neutral aesthetic level of good building. . . . We must not be misled by the idealism of the European functionalists. Functionalism is absolute as an idea rather than as a reality. As an idea it must come to terms with other ideas such as that of aesthetic organization. . . .

The Siedlungen implies preparation not for a given family but for a typical family. This statistical monster . . . has no personal existence and cannot defend himself against the sociological theories of the architects. . . . [The] Europeans build for some proletarian superman of the future. Yet in most buildings the expressed desires of a given client are the most explicit and difficult functions. Architects whose discipline is aesthetic as well as functional are usually readier to provide what is actually needed.[1]

While Hitchcock and Johnson pushed the American architect to stress formal style over social function, the planners were left as the sole advocates for social concerns. In consequence architects and planners, each intent on expressing a different set of needs, no longer had a language with which to communicate. As a result the postwar American city suffered an incredible shock for no one paid attention to urban form.

Leon Krier, speaking about the disintegrated form of the European city, claims that zoning, which destroyed the complex urban codes of the nineteenth century, must be the root cause for the broken dialogue between the architect and urban form. (282) In segregated functional cells industry was divorced from cultural centers, offices from residential zones, public from private spaces, and monumental architecture from anonymous buildings. Le Corbusier, Krier states, an unwitting culprit, designed in elegantly artistic forms the contradictions of an industrial society intent on destroying the city. Next Walter Gropius and then the Charter of Athens through their dedication to fresh air, sunlight, health, and recreation devalued still further the memory of the nineteenth-century city. So modern architecture, with its disturbed communication with everyday life and enclosed within a rhetoric of styles, attained complete autonomy from history, urban form, and social concerns.

More recently a new awareness of history in the context of urbanism has been imported from Europe, where the reexamination of the modern movement's betrayal of history is directed toward the creation of a new program for urban form. Manfredo Tafuri, Carlos Aymonino, Aldo Rossi, and Leon Krier are among the members of this dialogue on the postmodern European city. It is to their discourse, but not to their two-dimensional architectural forms, that we turn in order to draw a sharper focus on the city and its morphological form. Now the city is brought once again onto the center stage, for without the city, they claim, architecture would not exist. The city becomes the "ultimate scope of [architecture's] striving for form." (302:86)

The past failures of the architect-planner to build images of the city reflect the refusal to allow the past to be experienced with the present in a new constellation. In consequence our modern cityscapes show little awareness of their historical past. New architectural structures, spaghetti highway interchanges, and historic preservation projects are seldom integrated with the existing urban texture. Instead the historical centers of the city were dangerous to modern life; they had to be completely removed or reduced to museum pieces. (503:48–49)

In this manner the modern architect and urban planner failed to allow a clash, a collage of the new with the old. Indeed the dialogue between planning and history was silent, so that the structural elements of the traditional street, district, or public square were not allowed to aid the reshaping and reorganization of the modern order of the American city. A new modern city of functional components negated and emptied its valueless historical centers. Since architects and planners had given up trying to understand the structure and morphology of urban form and the overlaying of historical and interpretive elements, they thus inserted new functional components randomly into the existing fabric.

Tafuri requests that history be allowed to preside over planning, and planning then must become a programmatic guide for architecture and urban design. (503:40, 45, 57, 58) The entire urban context that configures architecture must be drawn into critical awareness: the regulatory controls, the political and economic conditions, the technical and social means of production, the cultural milieu. To reinterpret the spatial and historical elements of the city in this manner decodes the very meaning of the verb "to plan."

Nevertheless, only after careful consideration will history find its proper place within planning, for the current rescue of "history" from the warehouse of society can be a farce. On one hand we often have historic preservation that looks like a near equivalent to stage designing or an emotional remembrance of a nostalgic past; and on the other hand postmodernism turns toward a past without any idea of how to use it.

The planners for the most part are silent, as if they refuse to create a place for their voices in the historical process and accept instead the sealed empirical world to which they have condemned themselves. When they do find a voice, they attempt to offer a structural analysis of urban form best exemplified in the work of Kevin Lynch. Searching for a way to describe urban form, he isolates landmarks, nodes, paths, edges, and districts in order to offer the user a behavioral image of the city. Thus the sense of a settlement becomes "the clarity with which it can be perceived and identified, and the ease with which its elements can be linked with other events and places and that representation can be connected with nonspatial concepts and values." (313:131) Lynch includes in this analysis the sense of identity or place, the sense of how the parts fit together or offer a sense of orientation, the congruence of environmental structures to nonspatial demands, the transparency with which one perceives the operations of various technical functions and social processes. These formal concerns are motivated by behavioral needs, for "sense is an important functional concern, since the ability to identify things, to time behavior, to find one's way and to read the signs, are all requisites of access and effective action." (313:144) But in this case the history of place is broken up, and only in fragments as palatable remnants of the past is it allowed to fit into the functional reordering of the city.

An analysis of urban form and a sense of the city must emerge from a dialectical understanding of historical permanence and morphological change. A physical plan of the city would analyze the manner in which the city has been structured, and this would define the method and means for the reorganization of architectural complexes and urban sectors. In a famous essay on James Joyce's *Ulysses*, T. S. Eliot wrote that "one can be 'classical,' in a sense, by turning away from nine-tenths of the material which lies at hand and selecting only mummified stuff from a museum . . . or one can be 'classical' in tendency by doing the best he can with the material at hand." (418:222) What becomes important now is the texture of memories already embedded in the city and how the architect-planner uses these elements to structure and reorder the city with a classical tendency.

John Ruskin too drew our attention to the memory of the city, for he realized in 1849 the modern dilemma: that the vitality of nations was crowding in upon city gates, that modern life would be acted out upon the urban stage. The only influence that could possibly offer the healing inspiration of wood and field from which these urban crowds had fled would be the "power of ancient Architecture." He advised, "We may live without her, and worship without her, but we cannot remember without her," and wisely he warned, "Do not part with it for the sake of the formal square, or of the fenced and planted walk nor of the goodly street nor opened quay. The pride of the city is not in these. Leave them to the crowd." (474:187)

More recently Carlos Aymonino has reminded us that to begin to unravel the process where building typology and spatial morphology confront one another and transform urban development, we must return to the economic and political, the cultural and social context that are important to both the spatial morphology and building typology of the city. For example, he points out, when it first became possible to sell land for cash as a good upon the open market, land took on a new form. Privileged zones of development were valued for their high market prices. Thus diverse architectural pastiches and eclectic styles developed, more in response to commercial needs and less as a solution to architectural problems. Uniform block and lot divisions were primarily a response to market exchange, yet they too limited architectural freedom and diversity. As the number of private land investors increased, the allocation of streets, sewers, and railway lines became the only way to control the order of this developing new city. The "readability" of urban form, once grasped through the structural relationships between building types and spatial form, began to decline, and it was only in the ancient quarters of the city where formal completeness remained. (32)

So we must once again look upon these older city centers to draw upon the resources of collective memory. Aldo Rossi claims that the old city is a repository of history where memory becomes the conducting thread of the entire structure. He envisions the city as the finest and most complete expression of architecture, and he places the responsibility upon the architect to explain the form of the city and the principles of architecture governing that form. "In the city there are urban facts that withstand the elements of time . . . these facts are the monuments that constitute, make up, configurate the city. They give meaning to the life of the city." (354, 470, 495) These historical traces are expressed through the city plan, which records the way the city is first impressed upon our minds. Certain features of the city, such as a piazza or an arcade, pass from being instrumental in the development of urban space and become fixed attributes of the city. In consequence Rossi is intent on defining a typology of buildings and urban spaces in their relationship to the city whole, to the division of land, to the motivational forces behind their development. But these must not become frozen attributes outside of the historical context in which they were born, for then these spatial typologies would become memories out of place. Rossi optimistically claims, on the other hand, that these typologies must be seen as a tool not only in the manipulation of aesthetic form but in the critical act of disrobing reality. The act of quoting familiar types then becomes a radical stance, for these categorical types come polluted with political meanings and burdened with cultural memories. Thus it is expected that in the collage effect of the old and the new parts of the city, a criticism of architecture is offered by referencing these contextual meanings. This can be like walking on a thin tightrope, however, for decorative pastiches do not necessarily arouse our collective memory.

Another approach, with similar intent, is seen in the work of Leon Krier, who focuses on the destruction of the public realm in the modern European city. Again deference is given to the traditional urban elements such as the street, the squares, the colonnades, the arcades and courtyards as the connecting tissue of memory. Building typologies and morphological analyses are then used to reconstruct the city and to reestablish the impoverished public sphere. "The building block," Krier explains, "must be isolated as being dialectically the most important typological element to compare urban space, the key element to any urban pattern." Traced over time the agony of the urban block witnesses its displacement as the keystone of urban form to its complete domination by larger building programs in the modern metropolis. If the future is to allow for a new urban form, then the block must be the basic instrument in forming the public realm of streets and squares. (283) The re-creation and the design of this public realm take on the vision of a future urbanism: a design program that allows the architect to foresee how to reconstruct the damaged urban form out of old pieces of fabric and new public spaces, recently constructed buildings and a catalog of memories. (282)

From within architecture and pointing toward the direction of a new physical planning, these European architects preach of a day that the city will be redeemed from the reputation it has suffered since the emergence of modernism. They have, in the manner of Michel Foucault, tried to show "based upon their historical establishment and formation, those systems which are still ours today and within which we are trapped. It is a question, basically, of presenting a critique of our own time, based upon retrospective analyses." (484:192) Thus the formation of a humanistic order to the American city still lies in the future, for the characteristic features of the modern city—its alienating abstractions, rational efficiency, fragmented and malign configuration, ruptured tradition and memory— are still very much with us in the present.

Notes

Chapter 1

1. For the role of metropolitan financiers, businessmen, and politicians in the creation of the ethic of economic expansionism, see W. A. Williams, "Imperial Anticolonialism," *Tragedy of American Diplomacy*, 18–57.

2. For lengthy descriptions of the social instability of cities in this era, see Gabriel Kolko, *Main Currents in Modern American History*, and Stephan Thernstrom, *The Other Bostonians*.

3. To transcend does not imply that the rural-urban opposition evaporated but that it lost its absolute validity and became absorbed into a new totalization.

Chapter 2

1. The distinction here is between a preevolutionary concept of environment as a static milieu that surrounded an organism and in which the organism survived or perished and the more evolutionary and dynamic concept of an environmental space in which both the organism and the environment acted upon and reacted to each other. See Francoise Jacob, *The Logic of Life: A History of Heredity*, 138–139, and Jean Piaget, *Biology and Knowledge*, 106, 110–111.

2. Michel Foucault makes a similar point with respect to medical doctors and the fears of madness in the eighteenth century which summoned doctors to protect the rest of society from these vague dangers. See Michel Foucault, *Madness and Civilization*.

3. Olmsted's first report of the Bull Run battle placed more emphasis on the disciplinary problems of deserters than on sanitary conditions or care of the wounded. George M. Frederickson, "The Sanitary Elite," *The Inner Civil War: Northern Intellectuals and the Crisis of the Union*.

4. The expanded interest of intellectuals in social science in the postwar years was prompted by a desire to discover the underlying truths that would produce such an ordered and disciplined society. Olmsted was a member of a local social science association in the 1870s and 1880s.

5. For an example of tenement-house surveys, see Robert W. de Forest and Lawrence eds., *The Tenement House Problem* (New York: 1903).

Chapter 3

1. See p. 238 of Carol Aronovici, "Suburban Development," *Annals of the American Academy of Political and Social Science* 51 (January 1914), 234–238.

2. Some architectural critics looked at this tradition of the Ecole des Beaux-Arts as a crushing assault upon the development of American architecture. For example, see William H. Jordy and Ralph Coe, eds., introduction to *Montgomery Schuyler: American Architecture and Other Writings*.

3. America of the 1890s had just become a world power pursuing imperialistic expansion in South America and the Pacific Islands. Economically, America was in pursuit of new markets, but it used the ideological gloss of a Christian duty to civilize and uplift the poor people of the backward nations. See Charles and Mary Beard, "World Mission Under Arms," *The American Spirit*, Chap. 10.

4. See p. 1 of "Report on Rapid Transit in New York City," *Bulletin of the Municipal Art Society of New York* 14 (1904), 1–46.

Chapter 4

1. Michel Foucault speaks of disciplinary order as an integrated system not meant to be seen but infused across an apparatus of observation, recording, and tracking. In similar fashion we can view city planning as a disciplinary mechanism watching over and regulating urban development in order to create the correct and ideal spatial order.

2. John Nolen, *New Ideals in the Planning of Cities, Towns and Villages* (New York: American City Bureau, 1919), 25.

3. Some states had already recognized the theory of local assessments according to local benefits. A 1787 New York legislative act was the first such legal recognition. Kansas, Mississippi, the City of New York, and Chicago were nineteenth-century additions. Nelson Lewis, *The Planning of the Modern City*, 367, 375–381.

Chapter 5

1. As Marx (*Grundrisse*, 510) reminds us of history, " . . . the merchant induces a number of weavers and spinners, who until then wove and spun as a rural, secondary occupation, to work for him, making their secondary into their chief occupation; but then has them in his power and has brought them under his command as wage laborers. To draw them away from their home towns and to concentrate them in a place of work is a further step. In this simple process it is clear that the capitalist has prepared neither the raw material, nor the instrument, nor the means of subsistence for the weaver and the spinner. All that he has done is to restrict them little by little to one kind of work in which they become dependent on selling, on the *buyer*, the *merchant*, and ultimately produce only *for* and *through* him."

2. John Nolen, "The Factory and the Home: Shall the Homes of Factory Employees Go To The Outskirts with the Factory?," *Proceedings of the National Housing Association* 2 (1912): 105–120; Graham R. Taylor, *Satellite Cities: A Study of Industrial Suburbs* (New York: Appleton, 1915).

3. "Report on Rapid Transit in New York City," *Bulletin of the Municipal Art Society of New York* 14 (1904): 10.

4. Daniel L. Turner, "Rapid Transit Development," in *Development and Present Status of City Planning in New York City* (New York: Board of Estimate and Apportionment, 1914), 40–41.

5. Turner, 50.

6. Turner, 51.

Chapter 6

1. By the end of the 1890s, although 15 states had constitutional provisions against monopoly formation, only national legislation controlling a national market could effectively move against this trend of consolidation. See, for example, Edward C. Kirkland, "The Attack on Wealth," *Industry Comes of Age*.

2. Progressive reform followed two lines of innovative development. One involved the technical and functional improvement of certain areas such as land management, housing projects, and public transportation facilities, all of which were embedded in a comprehensive plan. The other innovation lay along the route of governmental or bureaucratic reorganization and planning. Ernest Griffith has also noted that the business community began, after the 1890s, to pay attention to both the efficiency of public service functions and the material conditions of the urban environment as a place to live and work. Ernest S. Griffith, *A History of American City Government*.

3. Roy Lubove claims in *Twentieth Century Pittsburgh* that these failures were the result of a split between nationally oriented monopoly corporations and locally concerned small entrepreneurs and tradesmen. Overall rationalization and centralization of decision-making power always presented a threat to the smaller speculative business interests.

4. In 1909, Harvard College established a city planning course within its landscape architecture program. See Arthur Shurtleff, "Six Years of Planning in the U.S.," *Proceedings of the Seventh National Conference on City Planning*. In 1929, Harvard University was the first to create a school of city planning. See Mel Scott, *American City Planning Since 1890*, 266.

5. The First National Conference on City Planning and the Problem of Congestion met in Washington, D.C., in 1909. See Mel Scott, *American City Planning Since 1890*, 95. The National Housing Association was founded in 1909 and began having annual conferences shortly thereafter. See Scott, 129.

6. City planning legislation had four characteristics: first, laws usually asked planning commissioners to serve without remuneration; second, there were ex officio members of the commission, who represented existing administrative bureaucracies; third, the planning commission's powers tended to be only advisory; and fourth, the members who were not ex officio were appointed and usually fewer than nine. Connecticut was the first state to pass city planning legislation, creating a City Planning Commission in Hartford in 1907. Around 1913, California, Massachusetts, New York, Ohio, Pennsylvania, and New Jersey had legislation enabling towns of certain classes to create City Planning Commissions or Departments of City Planning. For further details, see Charles M. Robinson, *City Planning*, 315–325; and Frederick Olmsted, Jr., "City Planning Program."

Chapter 7

1. The scientific management reform movement swept the country between 1910 and 1919. Although they initially focused on industrial management, scientific

management advocates claimed its universal application to other areas such as schools, philanthropic institutions, professions, governments, and cities. In short, it could be applied to any activity that sought to combine the values of efficiency with functional organization. At the base of these principles stood the intention to extract greater productivity from human labor. It was maintained that there existed only one best method for accomplishing any particular task, and that it was management's responsibility to scientifically analyze and plan the most efficient organization of work and to discipline these movement and work tasks into a functional hierarchical order.

2. Hawley has referred to this cooperative state as the "associative state," but the term *cooperative state* underlines the voluntary spirit embedded within its reform methodology. Ellis Hawley, "Herbert Hoover, the Commerce Secretariat and the Vision of an 'Associative State,' 1921–1928," *Journal of American History*.

3. A 1921 Supreme Court case said the government could be the supplier of business statistics, but it must return the data to the industry without performing any analysis of the data. See Peri Arnold, "Herbert Hoover," 537–539.

4. In 1921 a Bureau of Housing and Living Conditions in the Department of Labor was proposed. Its purpose was to increase the productive capacity and well-being of workers, to promote good citizenship, to investigate housing and living conditions among the industrial population, to research and experiment with programs that might eliminate slums, to prompt localities to deal with housing shortages without federal aid, and to serve as a clearinghouse of information on housing and living conditions.

5. The Department of Labor held an Own Your Own Home campaign in order to stimulate the building industry in the early 1920s, but economic stagnation was too strong at this time for the campaign to produce any results. See Lawrence Veiller, "Housing Progress."

6. Thomas Adams, "Modern City Planning," *National Municipal Review* 11, no. 6 (June 1922).

7. *Ambler Realty Co.* v. *Village of Euclid*, 297 Fed. 307 (1924).

8. Edward Bassett, "Constitutionality of Zoning in the Light of Recent Court Decisions," *National Municipal Review* 13, no. 9 (September 1924), 492–497.

9. Bassett, "New Court Decisions on Zoning," *National Municipal Review* 24, no. 6 (June 1925), 346–349.

10. Bassett, "New Court Decisions."

11. Bassett, "New Court Decisions."

12. Bassett, "Constitutionality of Zoning."

13. Bassett, "New Court Decisions."

14. Bassett, "New Court Decisions."

15. Bassett, "New Court Decisions."

Chapter 8

1. For the debate between Lewis Mumford and Thomas Adams over differing conceptions of regional planning, see *Planning the Fourth Migration: The Neglected Vision of the Regional Planning Association of America*, ed. Carl Sussman, 224–267.

2. For example, the city plan for Harrisburg which H. S. Swan completed in 1925 was a ten-year program for traffic and thoroughfare improvements. Swan pointed

out that the city should immediately outline a major thoroughfare plan on the city map, adopt new traffic regulations and enact new parking rules, reroute some trolley lines, and propose new street widenings; that in the succeeding five years the city should synchronize its traffic control in the business section, reconstruct its Market Street subway, and eliminate all street grade crossings; and that in the following five years additional bridges were to be built, more trolleys rerouted, and more streets widened and extended. For further details, see Dean Hoffman, "Harrisburg's City Plan," 501.

3. For further information about the regional attitudes of Mumford and Stein, see Lewis Mumford, "The Fourth Migration," *The Survey* 54, no. 3 (May 1, 1925):151–152; and Clarence Stein, "Dinosaur Cities," *The Survey* 54, No. 3 (May 1, 1925):134–138.

4. Carol Aronovici, "The Planner's Five-Foot Shelf," *Century* (October 1932): 476.

Chapter 9

1. Paul V. Betters, "Federal Aid for Municipalities," *National Municipal Review* 22, no. 4 (April 1933):174–178.

2. George C. Mowry, *The Urban Nation, 1920–1960* (New York: Hill and Wang, 1955).

3. The real test came in 1934 when the Supreme Court ruled that governmental code setting was an unconstitutional delegation of legislative power, that the regulation of business lay beyond the scope of federal authority. See Ellis W. Hawley, *The New Deal and the Problem of Monopoly.*

Chapter 10

1. Harold S. Buttenheim, "Slum Clearance by Private Effort," *Proceedings of the Tenth National Conference on Housing* (January 1929), 85–95.

2. By 1934, Ohio, New York, New Jersey, Michigan, and Maryland had passed similar laws. See John Millar, "Housing under the New Deal."

3. Terminology in this field has never been precise. First, *slum clearance* and *rehabilitation* meant the demolition of blighted areas and their replacement by new low-income housing projects. Next, *rehabilitation* was replaced by *redevelopment*, while *rehabilitation* itself took the meaning of reconstruction and preservation of older structures. *Neighborhood conservation* then began to refer to the selected implementation of redevelopment and rehabilitation, plus rigorous code enforcement. See Edmond Hoben, *Housing in Neighborhood Rehabilitation: A Summary of Activities and Proposals.*

4. In 1941, the Metropolitan Life Insurance Company announced it would undertake a huge new housing project on the Lower East Side of New York City; this was to become Knickerbocker Village. See Paul Wundels, "Private Enterprise Plan in Housing Faces First Test."

Chapter 11

1. Albert Lepawsky, "Chicago—Metropolis in the Making," *National Municipal Review* 30, no. 4 (April 1941), 211–216.

2. Lepawsky, "Chicago."

3. Harland Bartholomew, *Development and Planning of American Cities* (Pittsburgh: Carnegie Institute of Technology, 1949), 22.

Chapter 12

1. Between 1947 and 1964 the output of textile industries grew by 40 percent but their employment was cut by one-third; iron and steel foundries, lumber and wood production, and shoe manufacturing all showed production increases of 15–40 percent while employment dropped 10–20 percent; and the construction industry, slowest of all to absorb technical innovations, doubled its productivity without significantly increasing its employment rates. Douglas Dowd, "Accumulation and Crisis in U.S. Capitalism."

Chapter 13

1. Henry-Russell Hitchcock and Philip Johnson, *The International Style* (New York: Norton, 1932), 91–93.

Bibliography

1. Ackerman, Frederick L. "The Architectural Side of City Planning." *Proceedings of the Seventh National Conference on City Planning*. June 1915.

2. Adams, Thomas. "The American Community in Fifty Years." *Proceedings of the Twenty-Fourth National Conference on City Planning*. 1932

3. Adams, Thomas. "Housing and Social Reconstruction." *Proceedings of the Seventh National Conference on Housing*. November 1918.

4. Adams, Thomas. "Objections to Zoning Considered." *National Municipal Review* 14, no. 2 (February 1925): 74–77.

5. Adams, Thomas. "Regional and Town Planning." *Proceedings of the Eleventh National Conference on City Planning*. May 1919.

6. Adams, Thomas. "Regional Planning in Relation to Public Administration." *National Municipal Review* 15, no. 1 (January 1926): 35–42.

7. Adams, Thomas. "Town and Country Planning in Old and New England." *Journal of the American Institute of Planners* 3 (July–August 1937): 91–98.

8. Adler, Felix. "The Ethics of Neighborhood." *University Settlement Studio* 2 (July 1906): 27–33.

9. Adorno, Theodor. "Commitment." *New Left Review* 87–88 (September–December 1974): 75–89.

10. Allen, Walter S. "Street Railroad Franchises in Massachusetts." *Annals of the American Academy of Political and Social Science* 26 (January 1906): 91–110.

11. Alony, Frederick. "The Economy of a Municipal Labor Test." *Charities Review* 4, no. 7 (June 1895): 440–445.

12. Altvater, Elmar. "Notes on Some Problems of State Intervention—II." *Kapitalistate* 1 (1973): 96–108; 2 (1973): 76–83.

13. Amy, Henry J. "Tax Relief for Real Estate." *National Municipal Review* 28, no. 1 (January 1939): 36–43.

14. Anderson, Alan D. *The Origin and Resolution of an Urban Crisis: Baltimore, 1890–1930*. Baltimore: Johns Hopkins University Press, 1977.

15. Anderson, William. "The Federal Government and the Cities." *National Municipal Review* 13, no. 5 (May 1924): 288–293.

16. Andrew, John B. "Reducing Unemployment by Planning Public Works." *National Municipal Review* 10, no. 4 (April 1921): 215–220.

17. Arnold, Peri E. "Herbert Hoover and the Continuity of American Public Policy." *Public Policy* 20, no. 4 (Fall 1972): 525–544.

18. Aronovici, Carol. "Constructive Housing Reform." *National Municipal Review* 2, no. 2 (1913): 210–220.

19. Aronovici, Carol. "Housing and the Housing Problem." *Annals of the American Academy of Political and Social Science* 51 (January 1914): 1–7.

20. Aronovici, Carol. *Housing and the Housing Problem.* Chicago: McClurg, 1920.

21. Aronovici, Carol. "Housing the Poor: Mirage or Reality?" *Law and Contemporary Problems* 1 (1933–1934): 148–157.

22. Aronovici, Carol. "Let the Cities Perish." *Survey* (October 1932): 437–440.

23. Aronovici, Carol. "Regionalism: A New National Economy." *Columbia University Quarterly* 28 (December 1936): 268–278.

24. Aronovici, Carol. *The Social Survey.* Philadelphia: Harper, 1916.

25. Ascher, Charles S. "Mobilizing Our Housing Forces." *National Municipal Review* 23, no. 8 (August 1924): 433.

26. Ascher, Charles S. "Regionalism—A New Approach to the Good Life." *National Municipal Review* 20, no. 10 (October 1931): 592–596.

27. Aschman, Frederick T. "The 'Policy Plan' in the Planning Program." *National Conference on Planning.* 1963.

28. Atterbury, Grosvenor. "How to Get Low Cost Houses." *Proceedings of the Fifth National Conference on Housing.* 1916.

29. Atterbury, Grosvenor. "Model Towns in America." *Scribner's Magazine* 52 (July 1912): 20–34.

30. Augur, Tracy B. "Land Planning for States and Regions." *Journal of the American Institute of Planners* 2, no. 1 (January–February 1936).

31. "The Awakening of the Cities." *World's Work* (June–October 1911): 14494–14506, 14612–14618, 14725–14733, 14831–14837, 15000–15005.

32. Aymonino, Carlo. "Le role des capitales due XIXe siècle." *Les Cahiers de la recherche architecturale*, no. 1 (December 1977): 57–71.

33. Bacon, Edmund. "Urban Process: Planning with and for the Community." *Architectural Record* 145, no. 5 (May 1969): 129–134.

34. Bailey, William L. "The Twentieth Century City." *American City* 31, no. 2 (August 1924): 142–143.

35. Bailie, William. "Comprehensive City Planning: What a Planning Board Means for Boston." *New Boston* 2, no. 6 (October 1911): 229–232.

36. Baker, Charles W. "A Federal Department of Public Works: A Move for Economy." *National Municipal Review* 9, no. 4 (April 1920).

37. Bane, Frank. "Extent of the Relief Problem." *National Municipal Review* 24, no. 4 (April 1935).

38. Bane, Frank. "Feeding the Hungry." *National Municipal Review* 21, no. 11 (November 1932): 628–633.

39. Baran, Paul, and Sweezy, Paul. *Monopoly Capital.* New York: Monthly Review Press, 1966.

40. Barker, Henry A. "The Park in Its Relation to Physical Geography and the City Plan." *Charities and the Commons*, February 1, 1908.

41. Barnet, Richard J. *Roots of War*. New York: Atheneum, 1972.

42. Bartholomew, Harland. "Is City Planning Effectively Controlling City Growth in the United States?" *Proceedings of the Twenty-Third National Conference on City Planning*. 1931.

43. Bartholomew, Harland. "The Neighborhood. . . . Key to Urban Redemption." *National Conference on Planning*. (1941).

44. Bartholomew, Harland. "The Principles of City Planning." *American City 26*, no. 5 (May 1922): 457–461.

45. Bartholomew, Harland. "A Program to Prevent Economic Disintegration in American Cities." *Proceedings of the Twenty-Fourth National Conference on City Planning*. 1932.

46. Bartholomew, Harland. "Technical Problems in Slum Clearance." *Proceedings of the Twenty-Fifth National Conference on City Planning*. 1933.

47. Bartholomew and Associates. *Plans for Major Traffic Thoroughfares and Transit, Lower East Side, New York City*. 1932.

48. Bartlett, Dana W. "Los Angeles—1915." *New Boston 1*, no. 6 (October 1910).

49. Bassett, Edward S. *Constitutional Limitations on City Planning Powers*. New York: Board of Estimate and Apportionment, Committee on the City Plan, 1917.

50. Baumhoff, Richard G. "St. Louis Struggles for Metropolitan Solution." *National Municipal Review 29*, no. 9 (September 1940): 575–578.

51. Beard, Charles A. "Conflicts in City Planning." *Yale Review 27* (October 1927): 65–77.

52. Beard, Charles A. "The Control of the Expert." In *Experts in City Government*, ed. Edward A. Fitzpatrick. New York: Appleton, 1919.

53. Beard, Charles A. "Recent Activities of City Clubs." *National Municipal Review 1*, no. 3 (1912): 435.

54. Beard, Charles A. "Some Aspects of Regional Planning." *American Political Science Review 20*, no. 2 (May 1926): 273–283.

55. Beard, Charles, and Beard, Mary. *The American Spirit*. New York: Collier, 1942.

56. Bellush, Jewel, and Hausknecht, Murray. "Entrepreneurs and Urban Renewal." *Journal of the American Institute of Planners 32*, no. 5 (September 1966): 289–297.

57. Benjamin, Walter. *Illuminations*. Tr. Harry Zohn. New York: Schocken, 1969.

58. Bennett, E. H. "Planning for Distribution of Industries." *Annals of the American Academy of Political and Social Science 51* (January 1914): 206–212.

59. Bennett, E. H. "Zoning Chicago." *National Municipal Review 2* (March 1922): 69.

60. Bennett, March G. "Metropolitan Boston: What It Is and How It Should Be Governmented." *New Boston*, no. 3 (July 1910): 107–112.

61. Bennett, March G. "What Federation Could Do for Metropolitan Boston." *New Boston 1*, no. 12 (April 1911): 526–528.

62. Berle, A. A. "Municipal Credit in National Affairs." *National Municipal Review 24*, no. 3 (March 1935): 156.

63. Bettmann, Alfred. "City and Regional Planning in Depression and Recovery." *Proceedings of the Twenty-Fifth National Conference on City Planning.* 1933.

64. Bettmann, Alfred. "Housing Projects and City Planning." *Law and Contemporary Problems* 1 (1933–1934): 206–212.

65. Bettmann, Alfred. "Report of the Committee on Urban Redevelopment." *National Conference on Planning.* 1941.

66. Biesen, Chester. "Cities Get 'Out of Red' Together." *National Municipal Review* 33, no. 3 (March 1944): 132–178.

67. Bird, Frederick L. "American Cities and the Business Depression." *National Municipal Review* 20, no. 11 (November 1931): 630–634.

68. Black, Russell Van Nest. "The Composite Profession of Planning." *Journal of the American Institute of Planners* 10 (Autumn 1944): 14–17.

69. Black, Russell Van Nest. "Planning as a Professional Career." *Journal of the American Institute of Planners* 2 (November–December 1936): 144.

70. Black, Russell Van Nest. "Planning Considerations in Various Kinds of Public Works." *Proceedings of the Twenty-Fifth National Conference on City Planning.* 1933.

71. Black, Russell Van Nest. "Planning Problems V." *National Conference on Planning.* 1941.

72. Blanchard, John. "The National Government Surveys Urban Life." *National Municipal Review* 26, no. 10 (December 1937): 479–483.

73. Blough, J. Roy. "Financing the Welfare Provisions of the Social Security Program." *National Municipal Review* 25, no. 4 (April 1936): 215–223.

74. Bolan, Richard S. "Emerging Views of Planning." *Journal of the American Institute of Planners* 33, no. 4 (July 1967): 233–245.

75. Book, William H. "How Indianapolis Combines Poor Relief with Public Work." *National Municipal Review* 20, no. 9 (September 1931): 513–517.

76. Boyd, D. Knickerbacker. "Standardization of Parts in House Construction." *Proceedings of the Eighth National Conference on Housing.* December 1920.

77. Branch, Melville C. "Concerning Coordinative Planning." *Journal of the American Institute of Planners* 26, no. 4 (Fall 1950): 163–171.

78. Brandt, Lillian. "Wanted: A Breathing Space." *Charities Review* 11 (1903): 201–205.

79. Bremmer, Robert H. *American Philanthropy.* University of Chicago Press, 1960.

80. Brigham, Henry R. "How to Meet the Housing Situation." *Atlantic Monthly* 75 (March 1921): 404–413.

81. Brooks, Michael P., and Stegman, Michael A. "Urban Social Policy, Race, and the Education of Planners." *Journal of the American Institute of Planners* 34 (September 1968): 280–286.

82. Brooks, Robert C. "Businessmen in Civic Service: The Merchants' Municipal Committee of Boston." *Municipal Affairs Review* # 1 (September 1897): 491–508.

83. Brunner, Arnold W. "The Meaning of City Planning." *Proceedings of the Fourth National Conference on City Planning.* May 27–29, 1912.

84. Burdell, Edwin S. "A Sociologist Looks at Planning Education." *Journal of the American Institute of Planners* 3, no. 6 (November–December 1937): 147.

85. Burnham, Daniel H. "White City and Capital City." *Century Magazine* 63 (February 1902): 619–620.

86. Buttenheim, Harold. "Hoover Conference Spurs Local Efforts for Traffic Control and Facilitation." *National Municipal Review* 15, no. 6 (June 1926): 336.

87. Buttenheim, Harold S. "Planning Needs the Man in the Street." *National Municipal Review* 28, no. 12 (December 1939): 832–838.

88. Buttenheim, Harold S. "The President's Housing Conference—and Later." *National Municipal Review* 21, no. 2 (1932): 83–87.

89. Buttenheim, Harold S. "Uncle Sam or Boss Sam?" *National Municipal Review* 23, no. 12 (December 1934): 655–659.

90. Buzelle, George B. "Charity Organization in Cities." *Charities Review* 2, no. 1 (November 1892): 3–10.

91. Byrd, Harry. "Too Many Governments." *National Municipal Review* 22, no. 9 (September 1933): 431.

92. Caffin, Charles H. "The Beautifying of Cities." *World's Work* 3 (November 1901): 1429–1440.

93. Caffin, Charles H. "Municipal Art." *Harper's New Monthly Magazine* (April 1900): 655–666.

94. Calrow, Charles J. "The Planners Face a New Job." *National Municipal Review* 25, no. 10 (October 1936): 613.

95. Carlton, Frank T. "Urban and Rural Life." *Popular Science Monthly* 68 (March 1906): 255–260.

96. Castells, Manuel. "La Renovation urbaine aux Etats-Unies." *Espaces et société* 1 (1970): 107–135.

97. Castells, Manuel, and Godard, Francis. *Monopolville: L'Entreprise, l'etat, l'urbain*. Paris: Moutan, 1974.

98. Chase, Stuart. "The Future of the Great City." *Harper's Magazine* 160 (December 1929): 82–90.

99. Cheney, Charles H. "Zoning in Practice." *National Municipal Review* 9, no. 1 (January 1920): 31–43.

100. "The City and the Citizen." *Outlook*, May 9, 1903.

101. *A City Plan for Saint Louis*. Civic League of Saint Louis, 1907.

102. "A City Planning Primer." *American City* 36, no. 1 (January 1927): 89–95.

103. Ciucci, Giorgio; Dal Co, Francesco; Manieri-Elia, Mario; and Tafuri, Manfredo. *The American City: From the Civil War to the New Deal*. Tr. Barbara Luigia La Penta. Cambridge: MIT Press, 1979.

104. "Civic Nerve Centers." *New Boston* 1, no. 1 (May 1910): 35–36.

105. Clark, John M. *Economics of Planning Public Works*. Washington, D.C.: U.S. Government Printing Office, 1935.

106. Closson, C. C. "The Unemployed in American Cities." *Quarterly Journal of Economics* 8 (January 1894): 207–210.

107. Coler, Bird S. "Mistake of Professional Reformers." *Independent* 53 (June 1901): 1405–1407.

108. Collins, J. A. "The Decadence of Home-Ownership in the U.S." *American Magazine of Civics* 6 (1895): 56–64.

109. Conkin, Paul K. *FDR and the Origins of the Welfare State.* New York: Crowell, 1967.

110. Coolidge, Randoph. "The Problem of the Blighted District." *Proceedings of the Fourth National Conference on City Planning.* 1911.

111. Corbett, Harvey W. "The Influence of Zoning on New York's Skyline." *American Architect,* 123 (January 1923): 1–4.

112. Corbett, Harvey W. "What the Architect Thinks of Zoning." *American Architecture* 125 (1924): 149–150.

113. Coudenhove-Kalergi, R. N. "The New Nobility: The Type of the Rustic and the Urbanite." *Century Magazine* 109 (November 1924): 3–7.

114. Creese, Walter. *The Search for Environment: The Garden City: Before and After.* New Haven: Yale University Press, 1966.

115. Crowell, F. Elisabeth. "The Housing Situation in Pittsburg." *Charities and the Common* 21, no. 19 (February 1909): 871–881.

116. Curran, Henry H. "Our Hundred Million Dollars in New Housing under Tax Exemption." *National Municipal Review* 10, no. 10 (October 1921): 502–505.

117. Dahl, Robert A. *Who Governs?* New Haven: Yale University Press, 1961.

118. Davidoff, Paul, and Reiner, Thomas A. "A Choice Theory of Planning." *Journal of the American Institute of Planners* 28, no. 2 (May 1962): 103–115.

119. Day, Frank Miles. "The Location of Public Buildings in Parks and Other Open Spaces." *Proceedings of the Third National Conference on City Planning.* May 1911.

120. Delano, Frederic A. "The National Resource Committee: A Review." *American Planning and Civic Annual* 7 (1936): 5–10.

121. Deleuze, Gilles, and Guttari, Felix. "Rhizome." *Ideology and Consciousness* 8 (Spring 1981): 67–68.

122. Deming, Horace E. *The Government of American Cities.* New York: Putnam, 1909.

123. Desmond, Thomas C. "Blighted Areas Get a New Chance." *National Municipal Review* 30, no. 2 (November 1941): 629–640.

124. "The Development and Coordination of Planning." *Journal of the American Institute of Planners* 2, no. 5 (September 1936): 125–127.

125. *Development and Present Status of City Planning in New York City.* New York: Board of Estimate and Apportionment, 1914.

126. Devine, Edward. "Social Ideals in Present American Programs of Voluntary Philanthropy." *American Sociological Society* 7 (1912): 177–188.

127. Dewey, John. *The Public and Its Problems.* Chicago: Holt, 1927.

128. Dickerman, G. S. "The Drift to the Cities." *Atlantic Monthly* 112 (September 1913): 349–353.

129. Dickinson, John. "The Real Property Inventory." *American Civic Annual* 5 (1934): 84–87.

130. Dickinson, Robert E. "The Social Factor in City Planning." *Journal of the American Institute of Planners* 12, no. 3 (1946): 5–10.

131. Diggs, Annie L. "Garden City Movement." *Arena* 28, no. 6 (1902): 626–633.

132. Donald, W. J. "Regional Planning in Motion." *Proceedings of the Eleventh National Conference on City Planning,* May 1919.

133. Donzelot, Jacques. *The Policing of Families.* Tr. Robert Hurley. New York: Pantheon, 1979.

134. Donzelot, Jacques. "The Poverty of Political Culture." *Ideology and Culture* 5 (Spring 1979): 73–86.

135. Dowd, Douglas. "Accumulation and Crisis in U.S. Capitalism." *Socialist Revolution* 5, no. 2 (June 1975): 7–44.

136. Dowd, Douglas. *The Twisted Dream: Capitalist Development of the United States since 1776.* Cambridge: Winthrop, 1974.

137. Downing, Andrew Jackson. "Letters to the Editor." *Horticulturist and Journal of Rural Art and Taste* 3 (October 1848): 1.

138. Downs, Myron D. "The Location of Housing Projects and the City Plan." *Journal of the American Institute of Planners* 4, no. 3 (May 1938): 58–59.

139. Draper, Earle S. "Levels of Planning." *Journal of the American Institute of Planners* 3, no. 2 (March 1937): 29–34.

140. Ducey, John M. "Criteria for Selection of Initial Development Areas." *National Conference on Planning.* 1948.

141. Duggar, George S. "The Relation of Local Government Structure to Urban Renewal." *Law and Contemporary Problems* 26 (Winter 1961): 49–56.

142. Dyckman, John W. "Social Planning, Social Planners, and Planned Societies." *Journal of the Institute of Planners* 32, no. 2 (March 1966): 66–75.

143. Dykstra, C. A. "If the City Fails, America Fails." *Survey Graphic* 26, no. 12 (December 1937): 663.

144. Dykstra, C. A. "Your City and You." *Vital Speeches*, April 1, 1937.

145. Dykstra, C. A., and Hoehler, F. K. "An Appraisal of Cincinnati's Efforts to Meet Unemployment." *National Municipal Review* 19, no. 11 (November 1930): 741–743.

146. Eliot, Charles W. II. "Does City Planning Assist Economic Planning?" *Annals of the American Academy of Political and Social Science* 162 (July 1932): 121–126.

147. Eliot, Charles W., II. "New Approaches to Urban Planning." *American Planning and Civic Annual* 6 (1935): 304–307.

148. Embury, Aymar, II. "New York's New Architecture: The Effect of the Zoning Law on High Buildings." *Architectural Forum* 35, no. 4 (October 1921): 118–124.

149. Ewen, Stuart. *Captains of Consciousness: Advertising and the Social Roots of the Consumer Culture.* New York: McGraw-Hill, 1976.

150. "Exposition in 1915." *New Boston* 1, no. 1 (May 1910): 36–37.

151. Fabricant, Soloman. *The Trend of Government Activity in the United States since 1900.* New York: National Bureau of Economic Research, 1952.

152. Fechter, Paul. "The Failure of American Architecture.'" *Living Age* 337 (November 1929): 274–277.

153. Feder, Leah Hannah. *Unemployment Relief in Periods of Depression: A Study of Measures Adopted in Certain American Cities.* New York: Russell Sage Foundation, 1936.

154. Fein, Albert. "The American City: The Ideal and the Real." In *The Rise of an American Architecture*, ed. Edgar Kaufmann, Jr. New York: Praeger, 1970.

155. Feiss, Carl. "Housing and the Urban Esthetic." *Magazine of Art* 37, no. 7 (November 1944): 258–262, 278.

156. Feiss, Carl. "One Nation Indivisible. *Survey Graphic* 29, no. 2 (February 1940): 104–105, 140.

157. Ferriss, Hugh. *The Metropolis of Tomorrow.* New York: Ives Washburn, 1929.

158. Filene, Edward. "Boston-1915 and Labor Unions." *New Boston* 1, no. 8 (December 1910): 360–364.

159. Fillebrown, Charles. "Taxation and Housing." *Proceedings of the Fourth National Conference on Housing.* October 1915.

160. Fogelson, Robert M. *The Fragmented Metropolis: Los Angeles, 1850–1930.* Cambridge: Harvard University Press, 1968.

161. Forbes, Elmer S. "Rural and Suburban Housing." *Proceedings of the Second National Conference on Housing.* December 1912.

162. Ford, George B. "The City Scientific." *Proceedings of the Fifth National Conference on City Planning.* May 1913.

163. Ford, George B. "General Statement with Regard to City Planning in Newark, New Jersey." *Preliminary Report of the City Plan Commission, Newark, N.J.* June 1912.

164. Ford, George B. "The Housing Problem 1–5." *Brickbuilder* 18 (1909): 26–29, 76–79, 100–104, 144–147, 185–189.

165. Ford, George B. "New York City Now Controls the Development of Private Property." Memorandum of Commission on Building Districts and Restrictions, 1916[?].

166. Ford, George B. "Planning the Attractive Town." *Proceedings of the Thirteenth National Conference on City Planning.* May 1921.

167. Ford, George B. "Recreation, Civic Architectures, Building Districts and General Summary of Present City Planning Needs." *Development and Present Status of City Planning in New York City,* 52–76, New York: Board of Estimates and Apportionment, 1914.

168. Ford, George B. "Regional and Metropolitan Planning Principles, Methods and Co-operation." *Proceedings of the Fifteenth National Conference on City Planning.* 1923.

169. Ford, George B., and Goodrich, E. P. *Preliminary Report of the City Plan Commission, Newark, N.J.* June 1912.

170. Ford, James. "How National Attention Was Directed to Better Homes." *American Civic Annual* 1 (1929): 37–43.

171. Foucault, Michel. *The Archaeology of Knowledge.* Tr. A. M. Sheridan Smith. New York: Pantheon, 1972.

172. Foucault, Michel. *The Birth of the Clinic.* Tr. A. M. Sheridan Smith. New York: Pantheon, 1973.

173. Foucault, Michel. *Discipline and Punish: The Birth of the Prison.* Tr. Alan Sheridan. New York: Pantheon, 1977.

174. Foucault, Michel. *Language, Counter-Memory, Practice.* Ed. Donald F. Bouchard. Ithaca: Cornell University Press, 1977.

175. Foucault, Michel. *Madness and Civilization.* Tr. Richard Howard. New York: Vintage, 1967.

176. Foucault, Michel. *Michel Foucault: Power, Truth, Strategy*. Ed. Meagan Morris and Paul Patton. Sydney: Feral, 1979.

177. Foucault, Michel. *Power/Knowledge: Selected Interviews and Other Writings, 1972–1977*. Ed. Colin Gordon. New York: Pantheon, 1980.

178. Foulke, William D. "Evolution in City Charter Making." *National Municipal Review* 4, no. 1 (January 1915): 13–25.

179. Fox, Kenneth. *Better City Government: Innovation in American Urban Politics, 1850–1937*. Philadelphia: Temple University Press, 1977.

180. Frankel, Lee K. "Financing the Small House." *Proceedings of the Second National Conference on Housing*. December 1912.

181. Franklin, R. S. *American Capitalism: Two Visions*. New York: Random House, 1977.

182. Frayne, Hugh. "The Cost of Labor." *Proceedings of the Ninth National Conference on Housing*. December 1923.

183. Fredrickson, George M. *The Inner Civil War: Northern Intellectuals and the Crisis of the Union*. New York: Harper and Row, 1965.

184. French, George. "New England Will Come Back." *New Boston*, 2 no. 3 (July 1911): 99–101.

185. Freund, Ernest. *Police Power*. Chicago: Callaghan, 1904.

186. Frieden, Bernard J. "The Changing Prospects for Social Planning." *Journal of the American Institute of Planners* 33, no. 5 (September 1967): 311–323.

187. Funigiello, Philip J. *The Challenge to Urban Liberalism: Federal-City Relations during World War II*. Knoxville: University of Tennessee, 1978.

188. Galloway, George B. *Planning for America*. New York: Holt, 1941.

189. Gans, Herbert. *People and Plans*. New York: Basic, 1968.

190. Gans, Herbert. "Planning and Political Participation." *Journal of the American Institute of Planners* 19, no. 1 (Winter 1953): 3–9.

191. Gates, Earl F. "Boston's Need for a City Plan." *New Boston* 2, no. 3 (July 1911): 108–110.

192. Geddes, Patrick. *City Surveys for Town Planning*. Edinburgh: Geddes and colleagues, 1911.

193. Geddes, Patrick. "The Survey of Cities." *Sociological Review*, (January 1908): 1–6.

194. Gelfand, Mark I. *A Nation of Cities: The Federal Goverment and Urban America, 1933–1965*. New York: Oxford University Press, 1975.

195. "The Genesis of Boston-1915." *New Boston* 1, no. 1 (May 1910): 5–7.

196. Goetze, Siegfried. "The Housing Situation in Los Angeles." *National Municipal Review* 13, no. 4 (April 1924): 197.

197. Goldmann, Lucien. "Dialectical Materialism and Literary History." *New Left Review* 92 (July–August 1975): 59–81.

198. Goldmann, Lucien. "Dialectical Thought and Transindividual Subject." In *Cultural Creation*. Tr. Bart Grahl. Saint Louis: Telos, 1971.

199. Goldmann, Lucien. *The Philosophy of the Enlightenment*. Tr. Henry Mass. Cambridge: MIT Press, 1968.

200. Gould, E. R. L. "Civic Reforms and Social Progress." *International Quarterly* 3 (March 1901): 344–358.

201. Gould, E. R. L. "The Housing Problem in Great Cities." *Quarterly Journal of Economics* 14 (1899–1900): 378–393.

202. Gould, E. R. L. "Park Areas and Open Spaces in Cities." *American Statistical Association Publication* (1888–1889): 49–61.

203. Gray, John H. "The Gas Commission of Massachusetts." *Quarterly Journal of Economics* 14 (1899–1900): 509–536.

204. Gray, John H. "Giant Power." *National Municipal Review* 15, no. 3 (March 1926): 165–172.

205. Gray, L. C. "Large Scale and Rural Land Planning." *Proceedings of the Twenty-Fifth National Conference on City Planning.* 1933.

206. Greer, Guy, ed. *The Problem of the Cities and Towns: Report of the Conference on Urbanism.* Cambridge: Harvard University Press, 1942.

207. Gries, John M., and Ford, James. *Slums, Large-Scale Housing Decentralization, The President's Conference on Home Building and Home Ownership.* Washington, D.C.: National Capitol Press, 1932.

208. Griffith, Ernest S. *A History of American City Government: The Conspicuous Failure, 1870–1900.* New York: Praeger, 1974.

209. Haan, Hugo. "International Planning: Its Necessity and Its Special Features." *Annals of the American Academy of Political and Social Science* 162 (July 1932): 36–42.

210. Habakkuk, H. J. *American and British Technology in the Nineteenth Century.* New York: Cambridge University Press, 1962.

211. Haber, William. "Economic and Social Factors in City Planning." *Planning for the Future of American Cities, Proceedings of the Joint Conference on City, Regional, State and National Planners.* May 1935.

212. Habermas, Jürgen. *Legitimation Crisis.* Tr. Thomas McCarthy. Boston: Beacon, 1975.

213. Habermas, Jürgen. "The Public Sphere." *New German Critique* 3 (Fall 1974): 48–52.

214. Habermas, Jürgen. *Theory and Practice.* Tr. John Viertel. Boston: Beacon, 1973.

215. Haldeman, Antrim B. "The Control of Municipal Development by the 'Zone System' and Its Application in the U.S." *Proceedings of the Fourth National Conference on City Planning.* 1912.

216. Haldeman, Antrim B. "Report on Regional Planning." *Proceedings of the Twelfth National Conference on City Planning.* April 1920.

217. Hamlin, A. D. F. "Our Public Untidiness." *Forum* 33 (May 1902): 322–332.

218. Hansen, Alvin. "The City of the Future." *National Municipal Review* 32, no. 2 (February 1943): 68–72.

219. Harder, J. F. "The City's Plan." *Municipal Affairs* 2 (1898): 25–43.

220. Hartman, Edward T. "Wherein Direct Housing Legislation Fails." *Annals of the American Academy of Political and Social Science* 51 (January 1914): 78–81.

221. Hawley, Ellis. "Herbert Hoover, the Commerce Secretariat, and the Vision of an 'Associative State,' 1921–1928." *Journal of American History* 61, no. 1 (June 1974): 116–140.

222. Hawley, Ellis W. *The New Deal and the Problem of Monopoly: A Study in Economic Ambivalence.* Princeton University Press, 1966.

223. Hays, Samuel P. "Reform in Municipal Government." In *The Urbanization of America,* ed. A. M. Wakestein. Boston: Houghton Mifflin, 1970.

224. "Henry Ford Dooms Our Great Cities." *Literary Digest,* November 15, 1924.

225. Herrold, George H. "Obsolescence in Cities." *Journal of the American Institute of Planners* 1, no. 4 (November–December 1935): 73–75.

226. Heydecker, Wayne D. "Public Ownership and Control of Urban and Suburban Land." *National Municipal Review* 26, no. 12 (December 1937): 561–571.

227. Higgins, Edward. "Municipal and Private Management of Street Railways." *Municipal Affairs Review* 1 (September 1897): 458–490.

228. Hoben, Edmond. *Housing in Neighborhood Rehabilitation: A Summary of Activities and Proposals.* Chicago: National Association of Housing Officials, 1941.

229. Hoffman, Dean. "Harrisburg's City Plan." *National Municipal Review* 15, no. 8 (August 1975): 501.

230. Hoffman, Harold G. "Solving Local Tax Problems." *National Municipal Review* 24, no. 5 (May 1935): 249.

231. Holden, Arthur C. "Some Famous Neighborhoods." *Land Usage* 3, no. 2 (February 1936): 4.

232. Horkheimer, Max. *Eclipse of Reason.* New York: Seabury, 1974.

233. "The Housing Problem." *Municipal Affairs* 3 (1899): 108–131.

234. "How the Cities Stand?" *Survey,* April 15, 1932, 71.

235. Howe, Frederick C. "The City as a Socializing Agency." *American Journal of Sociology* 17 (March 1912): 590–601.

236. Howe, Frederick C. "The Garden Cities of England." *Scribner's Magazine* 52, no. 1 (July 1912): 1–19.

237. Howe, Frederick C. *Privilege and Democracy in America.* New York: Scribner, 1910.

238. Howe, Frederick C. "The Remaking of the American City." *Harper's Monthly* 127 (July 1913): 186–197.

239. Hoyt, Homer, and Badgely, L. Darward. *The Housing Demand of Workers in Manhattan.* Confidential report, not for publication. November 1938.

240. Hubbard, Henry V. "A Planner Returns the Look." *Journal of the American Institute of Planners* 3, no. 6 (November–December 1937): 150–151.

241. Hubbard, Theodora Kinball, and Hubbard, Henry V. *Our Cities Today and Tomorrow: A Survey of Planning and Zoning Progress in the United States.* Cambridge: Harvard University Press, 1929.

242. Hunter, Floyd. *Community Power Structure.* Chapel Hill: University of North Carolina Press, 1953.

243. Hunter, Robert. "The Relation between Social 'Settlements' and Charity Organization." *Journal of Political Economy* 11 (1902): 75–88.

244. Hurd, Richard M. *Principles of City Land Values.* New York: Record and Guide, 1903.

245. Hurlburt, Walter C. "Municipal Aid for the Unemployed." *National Municipal Review* 20, no. 5 (May 1931): 275–281.

246. Hurst, James Willard. *Law and the Conditions of Freedom in the Nineteenth Century.* Madison: University of Wisconsin Press, 1956.

247. Huth, Hans. *Nature and the American: Three Centuries of Changing Attitudes.* Berkeley: University of California Press, 1957.

248. Ickes, Harold. "Federal Emergency Administration of Public Works." *Proceedings of the Twenty-Fifth National Conference on City Planning.* 1933.

249. Ickes, Harold. "Why Do We Need a National Planning Board?" *American Planning and Civic Annual* 6 (1935): 3–5.

250. Ihlder, John. "The City Plan and Living and Working Conditions." *Proceedings of the Thirteenth National Conference on City Planning.* May 1921.

251. Ihlder, John. "A Constructive Housing Program from the Community Point of View." *Proceedings of the Twenty-Fourth National Conference on City Planning.* 1932.

252. Ihlder, John. "A National Housing Program." *American Civic Annual* 5 (1934): 81–84.

253. Ihlder, John. "What Are the Best Types of Wage-Earner's Housing?" *Proceedings of the Second National Conference on Housing.* December 1912.

254. *Improvement Plan of Philadelphia.* Philadelphia: Fairmount Park Associates, 1908.

255. Isard, Walter. "A Neglected Cycle: The Transport Building Cycle." *Review of Economic Statistics* 24, no. 4 (November 1942): 149–158.

256. Jackson, Walter. "The Place of the Motor Bus." *National Municipal Review* 11, no. 2 (November 1922): 368–371.

257. Jacob, Françoise. *The Logic of Life: A History of Heredity..* Tr. B. E. Spillman. New York: Pantheon, 1973.

258. James, Harlean. *Land Planning in the United States for the City, State and Nation.* New York: Macmillan, 1926.

259. James, Harlean. "Lessons from Government Experience in Housing." *National Municipal Review* 10, no. 8 (August 1921): 427–433.

260. Jewell, William F. "Freedom under Planning." *Journal of the American Institute of Planners* 26, no. 3 (August 1960): 45.

261. Johnson, David A. "The Emergence of Metropolitan Regionalism: An Analysis of the Regional Plan of New York and Its Environs." Ph.D. dissertation, Cornell University, 1974.

262. Jones, Gareth Stedman. *Outcast London: A Study in the Relationship between Classes in Victorian Society.* London: Penguin, 1971.

263. Jordy, William, and Coe, Ralph, eds. *Montgomery Schuyler: American Architecture and Other Writings.* Cambridge, Mass.: Belknap Press of Harvard University Press, 1961.

264. Karl, B. D. "Presidential Planning and Social Science Resource: Mr. Hoover's Experts." *Perspectives in American History* 3 (1969): 347–409.

265. Kellogg, Paul U. "Boston's Level Best." *Survey* 22 (June 1909): 382–395.

266. Kellogg, Paul U. "Labor Planks in a Civic Platform." *New Boston* 1, no. 8 (December 1910):

267. Kellogg, Paul U. "The Pittsburgh Survey." *Charities and the Commons* 21, no. 14 (January 2, 1909): 517–528.

268. Kellor, Frances A. "How to Americanize a City." *American City* 14, no. 2 (February 1916): 164–166.

269. Kelsey, Albert. *The City of the Future*. Municipal Art Society of Baltimore, 1902.

270. Kemp, Norval D. "Lopsided Development." *Survey*, July 31, 1909.

271. Keyserling, Leon H. "Low-Rent Housing Builds on Sound Money." *National Municipal Review* 28, no. 8 (August 1939): 632–639.

272. Kimball, Theodora. "A Review of City Planning in U.S., 1920–1921." *National Municipal Review* 2 (January 1922): 27–32.

273. Kirkland, Edward C. *Industry Comes of Age: Business, Labor and Public Policy, 1860–1897*. New York: Holt, Rinehart and Winston, 1961.

274. Kline, Howard M. "Citizen Groups in Review (Part I)." *National Municipal Review* 30, no. 10 (October 1941): 574–578, 612.

275. Kneier, Charles M. *City Government in the United States*. New York: Harper, 1934.

276. Knox, William. "How Savings Banks Can Aid Housing." *Proceedings of the Ninth National Conference on Housing*. December 1923.

277. Kohn, Robert. "What Next in Housing?" *Proceedings of the Twenty-Fourth National Conference on City Planning*. 1932.

278. Kolko, Gabriel. *Main Currents in Modern American History*. New York: Harper and Row, 1976.

279. Kolko, Gabriel. *The Triumph of American Conservatism*. Chicago: Quadrangle, 1973.

280. Kracauer, Siegfried. "The Mass Ornament." *New German Critique* 5 (Spring 1975): 67–76.

281. Kriehn, George. "The City Beautiful." *Municipal Affairs* 3 (1899): 594–601.

282. Krier, Leon, ed. "Cities within the City." *Architecture and Urbanisme* 77, no. 11 (November 1977): 69–109.

283. Krier, Leon. Fourth Lesson: "Analysis and Project for the Traditional Urban Block." *Lotus International* 19 (January 1978): 42–55.

284. Lamb, Frederick S. "Municipal Art." *Municipal Affairs* 1 (1897): 674–688.

285. Landis, Benson Y. "The Controversy over Federal Unemployment Relief." *National Municipal Review* 21, no. 5 (May 1932) 305–308.

286. Larsen, Christian L. "Cleveland Plans on Area Basis." *National Municipal Review* 34, no. 5 (May 1945): 223–228.

287. Larsen, Christian L. "Cleveland—Potential City of a Million." *National Municipal Review* 30, no. 6 (June 1941): 335–340.

288. Larson, Magali Sarfatti. *The Rise of Professionalism*. Berkeley: University of California Press, 1977.

289. Lasker, Bruno. "The Atlanta Zoning Plan." *Survey* 98 (April 1922): 114.

290. Layton, Edwin T., Jr. *The Revolt of the Engineers: Social Responsibility and the American Engineering Profession*. Cleveland: Press of Case Western Reserve University, 1971.

291. Lesher, Robert A. "National Arteriosclerosis." *Survey* 38 (October 1932): 456–460.

292. Lespes, Jules. "Mainly about Words." *National Municipal Review* 25, no. 9 (September 1936): 490.

293. Lester, Orrin C. "The Attitude of Lending Institutions Toward an East Side Housing Program." Memorandum, Columbia University library, 1932.

294. Levine, Daniel. *Varieties of Reform Thought.* Madison: State Historical Society of Wisconsin, 1964.

295. Lewis, Nelson P. "The City Plan and What It Means." *Proceedings of the Municipal Engineers of the City of New York.* 1911.

296. Lewis, Nelson P. *The Planning of the Modern City.* New York: Wiley, 1916.

297. Lewis, Nelson P. "Sequence of Operations in City Planning Work." *Proceedings of the Thirteenth National Conference on City Planning.* May 1921.

298. Lewis, Oscar. "Getting Off the Bandwagon." *Harper's Monthly* 154 (January 1927): 168–172.

299. Lincoln, Alice N. "Improved Dwellings." *Charities Review* 4, no. 8 (June 1895): 425–433.

300. Lindeman, Eduard C. "Aspects of Community Organization in Relation to Public Policy." *Annals of the American Academy of Political and Social Science* 55, no. 194 (January 1923): 83–87.

301. Lindeman, Eduard C. "Planning: An Orderly Method for Social Change." *Annals of the American Academy of Political and Social Science* 162 (July 1932): 12–18.

302. Llorens, Tomas. "Manfredo Tafuri: Neo-Avant-Garde and History." *Architectural Design* 51 (July–August 1981): 83–94.

303. Logan, James. "The Public-Service Corporation and the City." *New Boston* 2, no. 5 (September 1911): 181–186.

304. Long, Norton E. "Planning and Politics in Urban Development." *Journal of the American Institute of Planners* 25, no. 4 (November 1959): 167–169.

305. Lowell, Lawrence. "The Need for Experts in City Government." In *Experts in City Government,* ed. Edward A. Fizpatrick. New York: Appleton, 1919.

306. Lubove, Roy. *Community Planning in the 1920's: The Contribution of the Regional Planning Association of America.* University of Pittsburgh Press, 1963.

307. Lubove, Roy. "Homes and 'A Few Well Placed Fruit Trees': An Object Lesson in Federal Housing." *Social Researcher* 27, no. 4 (1960): 469–487.

308. Lubove, Roy. *The Progressives and the Slums: Tenement House Reform in New York City, 1890–1917.* University of Pittsburgh Press, 1962.

309. Lubove, Roy. "Twentieth Century City: The Progressive as Municipal Reformer." *Mid-America* 41 (1959): 195–209.

310. Lubove, Roy. *Twentieth-Century Pittsburgh: Government, Business and Environmental Change.* New York: Wiley, 1968.

311. Lukács, Georg. *History and Class Consciousness.* Tr. Rodney Livingstone. Cambridge: MIT Press, 1971.

312. Lukács, Georg. *Realism in Our Time.* New York: Harper Torch Books, 1971.

313. Lynch, Kevin. *A Theory of Good City Form.* Cambridge: MIT Press, 1981.

314. McCombs, Carl E. "Local Self-Government and the State." *National Municipal Review* 26, no. 4 (April 1937): 168.

315. McCrosky, Theodore. *Residential Area Analysis: Prepared for the Mayor's Committee on City Planning.* New York, 1938.

316. McDiarmid, John. "Los Angeles Attacks Metropolitan Problem." *National Municipal Review* 29, no. 7 (July 1940): 459–508.

317. McFarland, J. Horace. "The Growth of City Planning in America." *Charities and the Commons,* February 1, 1908.

318. McGoldrick, Joseph D. "Can We Rebuild Our Cities?" *National Municipal Review* 34, no. 1 (January 1945): 5–9.

319. MacKaye, Benton. "End or Peak of Civilization?" *Survey* 68 (October 1932: 441–444.

320. McKelway, St. Clair. "Modern Municipal Reform." *Journal of Social Science* 34 (1896): 126–139.

321. MacLauren, R. D. "Does Zoning Protect Only the Aesthetic Sense?" *National Municipal Review* 12, no. 9 (September 1928): 504.

322. MacLauren, R. D. "Where Zoning Fails." *National Municipal Review* 12, no. 5 (May 1928): 257.

323. McLean, Francis H. "The Charities of Pittsburgh." *Charities and the Commons* 21, no. 9 (February 1909): 858–868.

324. McNeal, Donald. "Waverly—A Study in Neighborhood Conservation." *National Conference on Planning.* May 1941.

325. MacVeagh, Franklin. "The Businessman in Politics." *Proceedings of the National Conference for Good City Government.* 1897.

326. Magee, William A. "The Organization and Function of a City Planning Commission." *Proceedings of the Fifth National Conference on City Planning.* 1913.

327. Malin, James C. "Ecology and History." *Scientific Monthly* 70 (May 1950): 295–298.

328. Maltbie, Milo R. "The Grouping of Public Buildings." *Outlook* 78 (September 1904): 37–48.

329. Mandel, Ernest. *Late Capitalism.* London: New Left Review Books, 1972.

330. Marsden, K. Gerald. "Philanthropy and the Boston Playground Movement, 1885–1907." *Social Service Review* 35, no. 1 (March 1961): 48–58.

331. Marsh, Benjamin. "Can Land Be Overloaded?" *Annals of the American Academy of Political and Social Science* 51 (January 1914): 54–58.

332. Marsh, Benjamin C. *An Introduction to City Planning.* New York, 1909.

333. Marx, Karl. *The Eighteenth Brumaire of Louis Bonaparte.* New York: International, 1963.

334. Marx, Karl. *Grundrisse.* Tr. Martin Nicholaus. New York: Vintage, 1973.

335. Mattick, Paul. *Marx and Keynes: The Limits of the Mixed Economy.* Boston: Extending Horizons, 1969.

336. Maxwell, William Q. *Lincoln's Fifth Wheel: The Political History of the United States Sanitary Commission.* New York: Longmans, Green, 1956.

337. Meeks, Carroll L. V. *The Railroad Station: An Architectural History.* New Haven: Yale University Press, 1956.

338. Merriam, Charles E. "The Federal Government Recognizes the Cities." *National Municipal Review* 23, no. 2 (1934): 107–109.

339. Merriam, Charles E. "How Far Have We Come and Where Do We Go from Here?" *National Municipal Review* 20, no. 1 (January 1931): 7–12.

340. Merriam, Charles E. "National Planning in Practice." *American Planning and Civic Annual.* 1935.

341. Merriam, Charles E. "The National Resources Planning Board: A Chapter in American Planning Experience." *American Political Science Review* 8 (1944): 1086–1087.

342. Merriam, Charles E. "Make No Small Plans." *National Municipal Review* 32, no. 2 (February 1943): 63–67.

343. Merriam, Charles E. "Planning in a Democracy." *National Conference on Planning.* 1940.

344. Merriam, Charles E. "What Planning Can Contribute to Governmental Reorganization of Urban Areas." *American Planning and Civic Annual* (1935): 294–297.

345. Merrill, Harold. "How Planning Commissions Have Met the Emergency." *American Civic Annual* 5 (1934).

346. Metzenbuam, James. *Law of Zoning.* New York: Baker, Voorhist, 1930.

347. Meyerson, Martin. "Building the Middle-Range Bridge for Comprehensive Planning." *Journal of the American Institute of Planners* 22, no. 2 (Spring 1956): 58–64.

348. Michael, Donald N. "Urban Policy in the Rationalized Society." *Journal of the American Institute of Planners* 31, no. 4 (November 1965): 283–288.

349. Millar, John. "Housing Under the New Deal." *National Municipal Review* 23, no. 4 (April 1934): 197.

350. Miller, Joseph D. "The Futilities of Reformers." *Arena* 26 (November 1901): 481–489.

351. "A Minute on Charles Mulford Robinson." *Transactions of the American Society of Landscape Architects* 1 (1919): 7–9.

352. Mitchell, Robert B. "Prospects for Neighborhood Rehabilitation." In *1938 Housing Yearbook.* Chicago: National Association of Housing Officials, 1938.

353. Museum of Modern Art. *Architecture: International Exhibition.* New York: MOMA, 1932.

354. Moneo, Rafael. "Aldo Rossi: The Idea of Architecture and the Modena Cemetery." *Oppositions* 5 (Summer 1976): 31–34.

355. Moody, Walter D. *What of the City?* Chicago: McClery, 1919.

356. Moore, Charles, ed. *Plan of Chicago.* June 1909.

357. Moore, M. I. "Sanitary Oversight of Dwellings." *Charities Review* 4, no. 8 (June 1895): 434–439.

358. Morton, Frances H. "Clinic: Role of a Citizen Planning Agency." *National Conference on Planning.* 1954.

359. Movor, James. "The Functions of the Municipality, with Special Reference to Public Services." *Proceedings of the Conference for Good City Government.* 1904.

360. Mumford, Lewis. "Botched Cities." *American Mercury* 28, no. 70 (October 1929): 143–150.

361. Mumford, Lewis. "City Planning and the American Precedent." *New Republic*, June 11, 1924.

362. Mumford, Lewis. "The Intolerable City: Must It Keep Growing?" *Harper's Monthly* 152 (February 1926), 283–293.

363. Mumford, Lewis. "The Next Twenty Years in City Planning." *Proceedings of the Nineteenth National Conference on City Planning.* 1927.

364. Mumford, Lewis. "Social Purposes and New Plans." *Survey Graphic* 29, no. 2 (February 1940): 119–121, 128.

365. Mumford, Lewis. "Regions—To Live In." *Survey* 54, no. 3 (May 1925): 151–152.

366. Mumford, Lewis. "The Sacred City." *New Republic*, January 27, 1926, 270.

367. "Municipal Finance." *Harper's New Monthly Magazine* 69, no. 2 (1898): 779–787.

368. Munro, William Bennett. *The Government of American Cities.* New York: Macmillan, 1913.

369. Munroe, James P. "What Boston-1915 Is Doing." *National Municipal Review* 1, no. 1 (1912): 73–76.

370. Murphy, John J. "Some Effects of Housing Regulations." *Annals of the American Academy of Political and Social Science* 51 (January 1914): 99–103.

371. National Association of Housing Officials. *Demolition of Unsafe and Unsanitary Housing: An Outline of Procedure for a Comprehensive Process.* Chicago, 1934.

372. Navin, Robert Bernard. "Analysis of a Slum Area." Ph.D. dissertation, Catholic University of America, 1934.

373. "The Neighborhood Center—A Moral and Educational Factor." *Charities and the Commons* 19 (February 1, 1908): 1504–1506.

374. Nelson, Herbert. "The Share of the Realtor." *Proceedings of the Joint Conference on City, Regional, State and National Planning.* May 1935.

375. Neufield, Maurice F. "Shall Mr. Crockett Enter Planning?" *Journal of the American Institute of Planners* 4, no. 5 (September–October 1938): 125–128.

376. New York Housing Authority. *The Failure of Housing Regulations.* 1936.

377. Nichols, J. C. "Housing and the Real Estate Problem." *Annals of the American Academy of Political and Social Science* 51 (January 1914): 132–139.

378. Nolen, John, ed. *City Planning.* New York: Appleton, 1917.

379. Nolen, John. "City Planning and Civic Consciousness." *New Boston* 1, no. 1 (May 1911): 7–11.

380. Nolen, John. "General Planning Board for Metropolitan Boston." *National Municipal Review* 1, no. 2 (1912): 231–235.

381. Nolen, John. "Getting Action in City Planning." *Proceedings of the Thirteenth National Conference on City Planning.* May 1921.

382. Nolen, John. "The Housing Standards of the Federal Goverment." *Proceedings of the Seventh National Conference on Housing.* November 1918.

383. Nolen, John. "The Importance of Citizens' Committees in Securing Public Support for a City Planning Program." *Proceedings of the Sixteenth National Conference on City Planning.* Los Angeles, 1924.

384. Nolen, John. "Industrial Housing." *Proceedings of the Fifth National Conference on Housing.* October 1916.

385. Nolen, John. "New Communities Planned to Meet New Conditions." *Proceedings of the Eighteenth National Conference on City Planning.* 1926.

386. Nolen, John. *New Ideals in the Planning of Cities, Towns and Villages.* New York: American City Bureau, 1919.

387. Nolen, John. "The Place of the Beautiful in the City Plan: Some Everyday Examples." *Proceedings of the Fourteenth National Conference on City Planning.* 1922.

388. O'Connor, James. *The Fiscal Crisis of the State.* New York: St. Martin's, 1973.

389. Offe, Claus. "The Abolition of Market Control and the Problem of Legitimacy, I–II." *Kapitalistate* 1 (1973): 109–116; 2 (1973): 73–75.

390. Offe, Claus, and Ronge, Volker. "Theses on the Theory of the State." *New German Critique* 6 (1975): 137–147.

391. Olmsted, Frederick L., Jr. "Basic Principles of City Planning." *American City* 3, no. 2 (August 1910): 67–72.

392. Olmsted, Frederick L., Jr. "City Planning and Housing." *Proceedings of the First National Conference on Housing.* June 1911.

393. Olmsted, Frederick L., Jr. "A City Planning Program." *Proceedings of the Fifth National Conference on City Planning.* May 1913.

394. Olmsted, Frederick L., Jr. "Reply in Behalf of the City Planning Conference." *Proceedings of the Third National Conference on City Planning.* May 1911.

395. Olmsted, Frederick L., Jr. "War Housing." *Proceedings of the Tenth National Conference on City Planning.* May 1918.

396. Orton, Lawrence M. "What Is the Place of the Planning Function in Local Government?" *Journal of the American Institute of Planners* 6, no. 1 (January–March 1940): 1–9.

397. Osborn, Henry L. "A Mission of the Public Park." *American Magazine of Civics* 9 (July 1896): 171–190.

398. Osborne, Harold S. "Increasing the Depth of Planning Responsibility." *National Conference on Planning.* 1941.

399. Overstreet, H. A. "Arousing the Public Interest in City Planning." *Proceedings of the Twentieth National Conference on City Planning* (1928).

400. Palmer, Alice F. "Some Lasting Results of the World's Fair." *Forum* 26 (1893–1894): 520–523.

401. Panofsky, Erwin. *Idea: A Concept in Art Theory.* Translated by Joseph J. S. Peake. New York: Harper and Row, 1968.

402. Park, Robert E. "The City: Suggestions for the Investigation of Human Behavior in the City Environment." *American Journal of Sociology* 20, no. 5 (March 1915): 577–612.

403. Parker, G. A. "The Trend of the Park Movement." *Charities and the Commons* 26, no. 14 (July 1906): 407–408.

404. Parkinson, G. H. R., ed. *Georg Lukács: The Man, His Work and His Ideas.* New York: Vintage Books, 1970.

405. Patton, Clifford. *The Battle for Municipal Reform: Mobilization and Attack, 1875 to 1900*. Washington, D.C.: American Council on Public Affairs, 1940.

406. Peaslee, Horace. "Housing Program under the Public Works Administration." *American Civic Annual* 5 (1934): 90–93.

407. Peattie, Lisa R. "Reflections on Advocacy Planning." *Journal of the American Institute of Planners* 34, no. 2 (March 1968): 80–87.

408. Perlin, Constance. "A Noiseless Secession from the Comprehensive Plan." *Journal of the American Institute of Planners* 33 (September 1967): 337–346.

409. Perlman, Robert. "Social Welfare Planning and Physical Planning." *Journal of the American Institute of Planners* 32, no. 4 (July 1966): 237–241.

410. Perloff, Harvey S. "Education of City Planners: Past, Present and Future." *Journal of the American Institute of Planners* 22, no. 4 (Fall 1956): 186–217.

411. Perloff, Harvey S. "How Shall We Train Planners We Need?" *National Conference on Planning*. 1951.

412. Perry, Clarence Arthur. "The Cellular City—Why It Is Coming." *Survey*, January 15, 1930, 459.

413. Peterson, Jon A. "The Origins of the Comprehensive City Planning Ideal in the United States, 1840–1911." Ph.D. dissertation, Harvard University, 1967.

414. Phelps, Arthur S. "The Coming Exodus." *Arena* 35 (April 1906): 5.

415. Piaget, Jean. *Biology and Knowledge*. University of Chicago Press, 1971.

416. *The Plan of New York*. New York: Committee for Private Circulation, 1923.

417. Platzker, Joseph. "Sixty Percent of Lower East Side Needs Replacement." *Land Usage* 3, no. 3 (March 1936): 3.

418. Poggioli, Renato. *The Theory of the Avant-Garde*. Tr. Gerald Fitzgerald. Cambridge: Belknap Press of Harvard University Press, 1968.

419. Polanyi, Karl. *The Great Transformation*. Boston: Beacon, 1944.

420. Pollard, W. L. "Outline of the Law of Zoning in the U.S." *Annals of the American Academy of Political and Social Science* 155, no. 1 (May 1931): 15–33.

421. Pond, Irving. "Zoning and the Architecture of Big Buildings." *Architectural Forum* 25 (October 1921): 131–133.

422. Poulantzas, Nicos. *Political Power and Social Classes*. London: New Left Books, 1972.

423. Pratt, Edward E. Industrial Causes of Congestion of Population in New York City. *Studies in History, Economics and Public Law* 43. New York: Columbia University, 1911.

424. Pratt, Frederic B. "Work of the Brooklyn Committee on City Plan." *Development and Present Status of City Planning in New York City*. 1914.

425. *Preliminary Report of the Fifth Avenue Commission*. New York, 1911.

426. "Public Parks and Playgrounds: A Symposium." *Arena Magazine* 40 (1894): 274–288.

427. Puff, Charles F. "Relation between the Small House and the Town Plan." *Annals of the American Academy of Political and Social Science* 51 (January 1914): 148–153.

428. Purdy, Lawson. "The Districting of Cities." *Proceedings of the National Housing Association*. October 1916.

429. Purdy, Lawson. "What the Citizen Thinks of Zoning." *Proceedings of the Ninth National Conference on Housing.* December 1923.

430. Quincy, Josiah. "Playgrounds, Baths and Gymnasia." *Journal of Social Science* 36 (1898): 139–147.

431. Rajchman, John. "Nietzsche, Foucault, and the Anarchism of Power." *Semiotexte* 3, no. 1 (1978): 105.

432. Rauch, John. H. *Public Parks: Their Effects Upon the Moral, Physical and Sanitary Conditions of the Inhabitants of Large Cities.* Chicago: Griggs, 1869.

433. Reed, Thomas H. "The Metropolitan Problem." *National Municipal Review* 30, no. 7 (July 1941): 400–408.

434. Reed, Thomas H. *Municipal Government in the United States.* New York: Appleton-Century, 1926.

435. Reinhold, Frances L. "Federal-Municipal Relations—The Road Thus Far." *National Municipal Review* 25, no. 8 (August 1936): 452.

436. *Report of the Commission of Housing and Regional Planning to Governor Alfred E. Smith.* Albany: Lyon, 1976.

437. "Report of the Committee on Civic Centers." *Bulletin of the Municipal Art Society of New York* 15 (1905): 1–14.

438. *Report of the Fifth Avenue Association for the Year 1912.* February 1913.

439. *Report of the Fifth Avenue Association for the Year 1913.* February 1914.

440. *Report of the Fifth Avenue Association for the Year 1914.* February 1915.

441. *Report of the New York City Commission on Congestion of Population.* New York: Lecouver, 1911.

442. *The Report of the New York City Improvement Commission to the Honorable George B. McClellan, Mayor of the City of New York and to the Honorable Board of Aldermen of the City of New York.* 1907.

443. *Report of a Preliminary Scheme of Improvements.* New York: Staten Island Improvement Commission, 1917.

444. Report of the Urbanism Committee to the National Resources Committee. *Our Cities: Their Role in the National Economy.* Washington, D.C.: U.S. Government Printing Office, 1937.

445. Riis, Jacob. *How the Other Half Lives.* New York: Scribner, 1890.

446. Ritchie, Ryerson. "Commercial Organization and Municipal Reform." *Proceedings of the National Conference for Good City Government.* 1897.

447. Ritchie, Ryerson. "The Modern Chamber of Commerce." *National Municipal Review* 1, no. 2 (1912): 161–169.

448. Rittel, Horst, and Webber, Melvin. "Dilemmas in a General Theory of Planning." *Policy Sciency* 4 (June 1973): 155–170.

449. Robbins, Mary C. "Park-Making as a National Art." *Atlantic Monthly* 79 (January 1897): 86–98.

450. Robbins, Mary C. "Village Improvement Societies." *Atlantic Monthly* 79, no. 472 (February 1897): 212–221.

451. Robinson, Charles Mulford. *The Beautifying of Honolulu.* Oahu Hawaii Territory: Board of Supervisors, March 14, 1906.

452. Robinson, Charles M. *The Beautifying of San Jose.* San Jose: Outdoor Art League, January 1909.

453. Robinson, Charles M. *Better Binghamton: A Report to the Mercantile-Press Club of Binghamton, New York.* September 1911.

454. Robinson, Charles M. *City Planning.* New York: Putnam, 1916.

455. Robinson, Charles M. "Civic Improvement Possibilities of Pittsburgh." *Charities and the Commons* 21, no. 19 (February 1909): 801–826.

456. Robinson, Charles M. "Improvement of City Life." *Atlantic Monthly* 1,2,3 (April, May, June 1899): 524–537, 654–664, 771–785.

457. Robinson, Charles M. *The Improvement of Fort Wayne, Indiana.* Fort Wayne: Civic Improvement Association, September 1909.

458. Robinson, Charles M. *The Improvement of Ridgewood, New Jersey.* Ridgewood: Board of Trade, 1908.

459. Robinson, Charles M. *Modern Civic Art or the City Made Beautiful.* 4th ed. New York: Putnam, 1918.

460. Robinson, Charles M. *A Plan of Civic Improvement for the City of Oakland, California.* Oakland Enquirer Publishing Company, 1906.

461. Robinson, Charles M. *Proposed Plans for the Improvement of the City of Denver.* Denver: City and County Art Commission, January 1906.

462. Robinson, Charles M. *Report on the Improvement of Dubuque, Iowa.* Dubuque: Joint Committee Representing Dubuque Commercial Club, Civic Division of Dubuque's Women's Club, and Trades and Labor Congress, October 1, 1907.

463. Robinson, Charles M. *Report on the Improvement of Ogdensburg, New York.* July 10, 1907.

464. Robinson, Charles M. *The Report Regarding the Civic Affairs of Santa Barbara, California.* Santa Barbara: Civic League, 1909.

465. Robinson, Charles M. *Report to the Fayettesville Park Commission.* June 4, 1909.

466. Robinson, Charles M. *Report with Regard to Civic Affairs in the City of Cedar Rapids, Iowa.* Cedar Rapids: Torch, 1908.

467. Robinson, C. M., and Olmsted, F. L. *Improvement of the City of Detroit.* Detroit: Board of Commerce, 1905.

468. Rodger, Robert W. A. "Low Cost Housing for the Lower East Side." Memorandum, Avery Library, Columbia University, 1934[?].

469. Roosevelt, Franklin D. "Back to the Land." *Review of Reviews* 84 (October 1931): 63–64.

470. Rossi, Aldo. "The Blue of the Sky." *Oppositions* 5 (Summer 1976): 31–34.

471. Rowe, L. S. *Problems of City Government.* New York: Appleton, 1908.

472. Rowe, L. S. "The Social Consequences of City Growth." *Yale Review* 10 (November 1901): 298–310.

473. Rubel, Dorothy L. "Clinic: Rise of a Citizen Planning Agency." *National Conference on Planning.* 1954.

474. Ruskin, John. *The Seven Lamps of Architecture.* 1849.

475. Sabine, George H. "Pluralism: A Point of View." *American Political Science Review* 17, no. 1 (February 1923): 34–50.

476. Schmitt, Peter J. *Back to Nature: The Arcadian Myth in Urban America.* New York: Oxford University Press, 1969.

477. Schnick, Allan. "The Road to PPB." *Public Administration Review* 26 (December 1966): 243–258.

478. Schweizer, Albert C. "Popular Planning." *Journal of the American Institute of Planners* 15, no. 31 (February 1949): 14–20.

479. Scott, Mel. *American City Planning since 1890.* Berkeley: University of California Press, 1971.

480. Segoe, Ladislas. "Population and Industrial Trends." *Proceedings of the Joint Conference on City, Regional, State and National Planning.* May 1935.

481. Sert, Jose Luis. "Can Our Cities Survive?" *Science Digest* 13, no. 5 (May 1943): 25.

482. Sheldon, W. L. "The Place of the Labor Leader." *American Journal of Politics* 5, no. 2 (August 1894): 152–170.

483. Sheridan, Lawrence V. "Planning a War Cantonment." *Proceedings of the Tenth National Conference on City Planning.* May 1918.

484. Sherrill, C. O., and Hoehler, Fred. "How Cincinnati Met the Unemployment Crisis." *National Municipal Review* 19, no. 5 (May 1930): 289–293.

485. Shurtleff, Arthur. "Planning for the Metropolitan District." *New Boston* 1, no. 10 (February 1911): 432–434.

486. Shurtleff, Arthur. "Six Years of Planning in the U.S." *Proceedings of the Seventh National Conference on City Planning.* 1915.

487. "The Significance of Boston-1915." *New Boston* 1, no. 7 (November 1910): 299–301.

488. Simon, John K. "A Conversation with Foucault." *Partisan Review* 38, no. 2 (1971): 192.

489. Simpson, Herbert D. "Tax Relief for Real Estate." *National Municipal Review* 24, no. 9 (September 1935): 459.

490. Sklar, Martin J. "On the Proletarian Revolution and the End of Political-Economic Society." *Radical America* 3, no. 3 (May–June 1969): 1–41.

491. Smith, J. Allen. "Municipal vs. State Control of Public Utilities." *National Municipal Review* 3 (1914): 34–43.

492. Solon, Leon V. "The Passing of the Skyscraper: Formula for Design." *Architectural Record* 60 (January–June 1924): 135–144.

493. "Statement from Secretary Hoover to Readers of the American City." *American City* 37, no. 5 (November 1927): 575–576.

494. Stone, Donald C. "Planning as an Administrative Process." *National Conference on Planning.* 1941.

495. Stuart, David. "Rationalism: A Rationale." *Space Design* 162 (March 1978): 3–5.

496. Sumner, Charles K. "Some Principles to Guide Community Zoning." *National Municipal Review* 15, no. 12 (December 1926): 693.

497. Sussman, Carl, ed. *Planning the Fourth Migration: The Neglected Vision of the Regional Planning Association of America.* Cambridge: MIT Press, 1976.

498. Swan, Herbert S. "Does Your City Keep Its Gas Range in the Parlor and Its Piano in the Kitchen?" *American City* 12, no. 4 (April 1920): 339–344.

499. Swan, Herbert S., and Tuttle, George W. "Land Subdivisions and the City Plan." *National Municipal Review* 14, no. 7 (July 1925): 437.

500. Sweezy, Paul M. "Cars and Cities." *Monthly Review* 24, no. 11 (April 1973): 1–18.

501. Symon, William. "The Disappearing Boundaries." *National Municipal Review* 35, no. 5 (May 1946): 224–227.

502. Tafuri, Manfredo. "The Historical Project." *Oppositions* 17 (Summer 1979): 55–75.

503. Tafuri, Manfredo. *Theories and History of Architecture.* New York: Harper and Row, 1980.

504. Tappan, Robert. "Factory Production Applied to the Housing Problem." *Proceedings of the Eighth National Conference on Housing.* December 1920.

505. Taylor, Graham R. *Satellite Cities: A Study of Industrial Suburbs.* New York: Appleton, 1915.

506. Taylor, Walton R. L. "Community Participation in Planning: Getting a Plan Made." *National Conference on Planning.* 1947.

507. "Tenement House Reform in New York, 1834–1900." *American Annals of Political Science and Social Science* 15 (July 1900): 138.

508. Thernstrom, Stephan. *The Other Bostonians.* Cambridge: Harvard University Press, 1973.

509. Thompson, C. Bertrand. "The Democracy of Boston-1915." *New Boston* 1, no. 1 (May 1910): 8–10.

510. Thompson, Warren S. "The Future of the Large City." *American Mercury* 20, no. 79 (July 1930): 327–337.

511. Tishler, H. S. *Self Reliance and Social Security, 1870–1917.* New York: Kennikat, 1971.

512. Toll, Seymour. *Zoned America.* New York: Grossman, 1969.

513. Topalov, Christian. *Les Promoteurs immobiliers: Contribution à l'analyse de la production capitalists du logement en France.* Paris: Mouton, 1974.

514. Triggs, Oscar L. "The Philosophy of the Betterment Movement." *Chatauquan* 37 (August 1903): 463–466.

515. Tucci, Douglas Sand. *Built in Boston: City and Suburb.* Boston: New York Graphic Society, 1978.

516. Turner, Daniel L. "Is There a Vicious Circle of Transit Development and City Congestion?" *National Municipal Review* 15, no. 6 (June 1926): 321.

517. Untermyer, Samuel. "Who Is Responsible for the Housing Shortage?" *Proceedings of the Ninth National Conference on Housing.* December 1923.

518. Unwin, Raymond. "The Overgrown City." *Survey* 49 (October 15, 1922): 85–86.

519. Unwin, Raymond. "Urban Development." *Journal of the American Institute of Planners* 1, no. 3 (September 1935): 45.

520. Van Brunt, Henry. *Architecture and Society: Selected Essays of Henry Van Brunt.* Ed. William A. Coles. Cambridge: Belknap Press of Harvard University Press, 1969.

521. Van Cleef, Eugene. "Cities and Nationalism." *Scientific Monthly* 47 (October 1938): 5.

522. Veiller, Lawrence. "Buildings in Relation to Street and Site." *Proceedings of the Third National Conference on City Planning.* May 1911.

523. Veiller, Lawrence. "The Housing of the Mobilized Population." *Annals of the American Society of Political and Social Science* 78 (July 1918): 19–24.

524. Veiller, Lawrence. "The Housing Problem in the United States." *National Housing Association Publications* 61 (March 1930): 1.

525. Veiller, Lawrence. "Housing Progress of the Year, 1919–1970." *Proceedings of the Eighth National Conference on Housing* December 1920.

526. Veiller, Lawrence. "Housing Reform Through Legislation." *Annals of the American Academy of Political and Social Science* 51 (January 1914): 68–77.

527. Veiller, Lawrence. "Industrial Housing." *Proceedings of the Fifth National Conference on Housing.* October 1916.

528. Veiller, Lawrence. "Slum Clearance." Proceedings of the *Tenth National Conference on Housing.* January 1929.

529. Wacker, Charles C. "Gaining Public Support for a City Planning Movement." *Proceedings of the Fifth National Conference on City Planning.* May 1913.

530. Waite, Henry M. "Public Bodies and the P.W.A." *National Municipal Review* 33, no. 5 (May 1934): 246.

531. Walker, John B. "The City of the Future." *Cosmopolitan* 31 (September 1901): 473–475.

532. Walker, Robert A. *The Planning Function in Urban Government.* University of Chicago Press, 1941.

533. Walker, Robert A. "Planning Problems II." *National Conference on Planning.* 1941.

534. Wallerstein, Morton B. "Federal-Municipal Relations—Whither Bound?" *National Municipal Review* 25, no. 8 (August 1936): 453.

535. Warner, John D. "Civic Centers." *Municipal Affairs* 6 (March 1902): 1–23.

536. "Watchful Waiting." *Land Usage* 3, no. 3 (March 1936): 2.

537. Watson, Frank D. *The Charity Organization Movement in the United States.* New York: Macmillan, 1922.

538. Webber, Melvin M. "Comprehensive Planning and Social Responsibility: Toward an American Institute of Planners Consensus on the Profession's Role and Purpose." *Journal of the American Institute of Planners* 29, no. 4 (November 1963): 232–241.

539. Weber, Adna F. "Growth of Cities in the U.S." *Municipal Affairs* 5 (June 1901): 367–375.

540. Welsh, Herbert. "Civil Sevice Reform in Its Bearings upon the Interests of the Workingman." *American Magazine of Civics* 8 (1896): 631–643.

541. Wendrich, Lawrence H. "Planners Discover Diplomacy." *National Muncipal Review* 29, no. 7 (April 1940): 253–256.

542. Wentworth, Cynthia. "Housing as a National and City Problem." *National Municipal Review* 26, no. 2 (November 1937): 517–523.

543. Whitaker, Charles Harris. "Housing as a War Problem." *Proceedings of the Sixth National Conference on Housing.* October 1917.

544. Whitten, Robert H. "The Building Zone Plan of New York City." Memorandum, 1916 [?].

545. Whitten, Robert H. "The Constitution and Powers of a City Planning Authority." *Proceedings of the Seventh National Conference on City Planning.* 1915.

546. Whitten, Robert H. "Social Aspects of Zoning." *Survey*, June 15, 1922.

547. Wickwar, W. Hardy. *The Political Theory of Local Government*. Columbia: University of South Carolina Press, 1970.

548. Wiebe, Robert H. *Businessmen and Reform: A Study of the Progressive Movement*. Cambridge: Harvard University Press, 1962.

549. Wiebe, Robert H. *The Search for Order, 1877–1920*. New York: Hill and Wang, 1967.

550. Wiener, Norbert. "Short-term and Long-term Planning." *National Conference on Planning*. 1954.

551. Wilcox, Delos F. *The American City: A Problem in Democracy*. New York: Macmillan, 1906.

552. Wilcox, Delos F. *Great Cities in America: Their Problems and Their Government*. New York: Macmillan, 1910.

553. Wildavsky, Aaron. "Rescuing Policy Analysis from PPBS." *Public Administration Review* 29 (1969): 189–202.

554. Williams, William Appleman. *The Contours of American History*. Chicago: Quadrangle, 1966.

555. Williams, William Appleman. *The Tragedy of American Diplomacy*. New York: Dell, 1972.

556. Windels, Paul. "Private Enterprise Plan in Housing Faces First Test." *National Municipal Review* 32, no. 6 (June 1943): 284–288.

557. Wirth, Louis. "The Metropolitan Region as a Planning Unit." *National Conference on Planning*. 1942.

558. Wirth, Louis. "Planning Means Freedom." *National Conference on Planning*. 1947: 1–19.

559. Wood, Edith Elmer. *Slums and Blighted Areas in the United States*. College Hill, Md.: McGrath, 1936.

560. Woodbury, Coleman. "Land Assembly for Housing Developments." *Law and Contemporary Problems* 1 (1933–1934): 228.

561. Woodruff, Clinton R. "City Planning in America." *Atlantic Monthly* (June 1908): 721–726.

562. Woodruff, Clinton R. "The National Impulse for Civic Improvement." *Chautauquan* 47, no. 1 (June 1907): 24–31.

563. Woodruff, Clinton R. "The New View of Municipal Government." In *Experts in City Government*, ed. Edward A. Fitzpatrick. New York: Appleton, 1919.

564. Woodruff, Clinton R. "The Philadelphia Municipal League." *American Journal of Politics* 5 (1894: 287–294.

565. Woods, Robert A. "The Neighborhood in Social Reconstruction." *American Sociological Society* 8 (1912): 14–28.

566. Woods, Robert A. "Pittsburgh." *Charities and the Commons* 21, no. 19 (February 1909): 527–533.

567. Wright, Gwendolyn. *Moralism and the Model Home: Domestic Architecture and Cultural Conflict in Chicago 1873–1913*. University of Chicago Press, 1980.

568. Wright, Henry. "Are We Ready for an American Housing Advance?" *Architecture* 67 (June 1933): 307–316.

569. Wright, Henry. "City Planning in Relation to the Housing Problem." *Proceedings of the Twenty-Fourth National Conference on City Planning.* 1932.

570. Wright, Henry. "Housing—Where, When, and How?" *Architecture* 68 (July 1933): 1–32, 79–110.

571. Wright, Henry. "To Plan or Not to Plan." *Survey* 68 (October 1932): 468–469.

572. Wyckoff, Walter A. "Incidence of Slums." *Scribner's Magazine* 300 (October 1901): 486–492.

573. "Zoning and Platting Supervision as Fundamental to City Planning." *American City* 32, no. 3 (March 1925): 301–303.

Index

Ackerman, Frederick, 70, 191
Adams, Thomas
  on city planning, 153
  on communistic garden cities, 215
  New York Regional Plan, 184
  on regional planning, 174
  on slum clearance, 144, 215
Addams, Jane, 22
Administrative planning, 228–231,
  271–272
Advisory planning commissions, 284,
  285
  and municipal intervention, 126–130
  in 1930s, 218–219
Aesthetics
  abstraction of, 282–283
  and disciplinary order, 46, 50
  and reform movement,
    1890s–1900s, 43–55
  of zoning, 161–163
American City Planning Institute, 134
American Civic Association, 133
American Institute of Architects, 47,
  49, 191
American Municipal Association, 225
American Society of Planning
  Officials, 225
Architects
  formalists, 283
  and housing reform, 1900s,
    104–105
  licensing and control of, 47, 49
  planners, split with, 283, 285, 286,
    287
Aronovici, Carol
  on garden cities, 42
  on home ownership, 145
  on mobility of citizens, 105–106
  on Public Works Administration aid,
    239, 242

  on scientific city planning, 198
  on urban blight and obsolescence,
    214
Ascher, Charles, 196
Atlanta, zoning in, 167–168
Atterbury, Grosvenor, 42, 105
Automobiles
  post-World War I, 139–140, 179
  and regional planning, 173,
    174–175, 179–180
Aymonino, Carlos, 286, 288

Bacon, Edmund, 284
Bailey, William, 174
Baltimore
  home ownership in 1900s, 106
  neighborhood conservation,
    253–254
  Roland Park, 101
  zoning in 1900s, 94
Barr, Stringfellow, 196
Bartholomew, Harland
  on city planning, 171–172, 267
  on inner city redevelopment,
    214–215, 249
Bassett, Edward, 164
Beard, Charles, 186
Beaux-Arts design, 47, 56
Bennett, E. H., 76–77
Better Homes in America, 152–153
Bettman, Alfred, 255–256
Black, Russell, 216, 230
Bolan, Richard, 284–285
Booth, Charles, 72
Boston
  Boston 1915, 123–126
  Copley Square, 47
  home ownership in 1900s, 106

Profitability, of public improvements,
79–82
Public buildings, 53. *See also* Civic
centers
Public space, 289
Public use takings. *See* Eminent
domain
Public Works Administration, 217,
238, 239, 241
Public Works Emergency Housing
Corporation, 238
Public works projects, 216, 218–221
Puff, Charles, 101–102

Railroad station design, and aesthetics
reform, 52
Railways, *See* Transportation
Rational city planning, 61–62, 68–69,
269–270, 276–278, 282
Rauch, John H., 37–38
Reconstruction Finance Corporation,
238
Reed, Thomas, 262–263
Regional planning, 172
and automobiles, 173–175,
179–180
and citizen participation, 188–189
and disciplinary order, 181, 265
and economic growth, 180, 181
financing, 185
garden city plan, 191–197
local officials and, 186–188
master plan, 265
and monopolies, 180
National Planning Conference of
1919, 174
in 1920s, 173, 181
in 1930s, 214, 217–218
postwar, 261–267
professional planning, 189
sanitation, 178–179
and suburbs, 173–174
surveys, 181
and transportation, 173–174, 179
utopian regionalists, 190–197
water systems, 178–179
Regional Planning Association of
America, 191
Richardson, H. H., 41
River Valley authorities, 217
Roads
and congestion (*See* Congestion)
and economic growth, 85
in 1920s, 179

ownership of, 1890s–1910s, 65
and regional planning, 173–175,
179
Robinson, Charles Mulford
on city planning, 51, 53, 54
Detroit improvement plan, 79
on philanthropy, 27–28
professional ideals of, 133–134
promotional work, 132–133
on recreation, 36
Rochester, zoning in 1900s, 94
Rockefeller Brothers Fund, 266
Roosevelt, Franklin, 213
Rossi, Aldo, 286, 288–289
Rowe, L. S., 62
Rural land-use development, 1930s,
214, 217
Ruskin, John, 288
Russell Sage Foundation
Pittsburgh Survey, 73
Regional Plan of New York, 182

St. Louis
county planning and zoning, 262
neighborhood conservation, 255
parks and playgrounds in 1890s, 23
waterfront improvement,
1890s–1900s, 51–52
St. Paul, zoning in 1900s, 94
San Francisco, zoning in 1920s,
166–167
Sanitation systems
in 1870s–1880s, 19–20
in 1890s, 18–19
and housing reform, 98
ownership of, 1890s–1910s, 65
and park improvement of
1890s–1900s, 37–38
and regional planning, 178–179
Schuyler, Montgomery, 48–50
Scientific development, 3, 10, 175,
272–273
Scientific management principles, 163
Seattle, 84, 94
Segoe, Ladislas, 212
Settlement House (Jane Addams), 22
Settlement houses, 22, 25–26
Sewage systems. *See* Sanitation
systems
Simmel, Georg, 283
Social cohesion, and reform
movement of 1890s, 24–25
Social Darwinism, 20–21

neighborhood improvement districts,
    252–255
policy planning in 1930s, 222–225
redevelopment in 1930s, 243–245,
    248–252, 257–260
redevelopment in 1950s, 275–279
slum-clearance programs of 1930s,
    233–236, 238, 240–243, 255–257
and Urbanism Committee, 226–228,
    231–232
Utopian disciplinary order, 69, 70

Valuation of land, 85–87
and congestion, 87, 95–96
in 1920s, 157
and transportation improvements, 97
and zoning, 94
Van Brunt, Henry, 47–49
Vaux, Clarence, 35, 40
Veiller, Lawrence
advisory zoning committee
    membership, 164
tenement house survey, 30, 73
on workingclass neighborhood
    planning, 102
on workingman's dwellings,
    100–101

Washington, zoning in 1900s, 94
Water systems, 109, 178, 179
Waterfront areas, aesthetics reform
    movement of 1890s–1900s, 39–40,
    51–52
Webber, Melvin, 274
Whitaker, Charles, H., 144
"Wicked" problem solving, 270
Wiener, Norbert, 269
Wirth, Louis, 206–207, 271–272
Wisconsin, housing in 1920s, 151
Wood, Edith Elmer, 237–240
Wright, Gwendolyn, 105
Wright, Henry
on city planning, 198–199, 215–216
on housing, 250–251
Regional Planning Association of
    America, 191

Yosemite Valley, preservation of, 34

Zoning
aesthetics of, 161–163
and congestion, 94
constitutional issues in 1920s,
    159–161

and disciplinary order, 168–169
and economic growth, 94, 154,
    156–157, 168
and functional uses of land, 164,
    169
and housing in 1920s, 142,
    157–158
in 1900s, 91–95, 103
in 1920s, 153–170
nuisance, 168
police powers, 164, 165, 166
purposes in 1920s, 163
regional planning (*see* Regional
    planning)
setbacks, 162–163
social effects in 1920s, 166–169
state intervention, 164, 165, 166
and valuation of land, 94